CLASSICS IN CALIFORNIA ANTHROPOLOGY

FOOD IN CALIFORNIA
INDIAN CULTURE

FOOD IN CALIFORNIA INDIAN CULTURE

EDITED WITH
AN INTRODUCTION BY

Ira Jacknis

PHOEBE HEARST MUSEUM OF ANTHROPOLOGY
UNIVERSITY OF CALIFORNIA, BERKELEY

Editor: Ira Jacknis
Project Managers: Barbara Takiguchi and Nicole Mullen
Designer: Sarah Levin
Design and Production Associate: Nicole Mullen
Printer: Phoenix Color, United States of America
10 9 8 7 6 5 4 3 2 1

The paper used in this publication meets the minimum requirements
of American National Standard for Information Sciences—
Permanence of Paper for Printed Materials, ANSI Z39.48–1984.

Cover photo: Essie Parrish (Kashaya Pomo) leaching acorn meal, shore of Gualala
River, Mendocino County, California. Photograph by William Heick, 1961.

Back cover photo: Mohave bowl (1–13771) and spoon (1–1749).
Photograph by Eugene Prince, Hearst Museum.

LIBRARY OF CONGRESS CATALOGING-IN-PUBLICATION DATA:

Food in California Indian culture / edited with an introduction by Ira Jacknis.
p. cm. — (Classics in California anthropology)
"Reprints the food-related sections from many hard-to-find sources"—Cover.
Includes bibliographical references.
ISBN 0–936127–08–2
1. Indians of North America—Food--California. 2. Indians of North
America—Hunting--California. 3. Indian cookery—California—History.
4. Food habits—California—History. 5. Food preferences—California—History.
I. Jacknis, Ira. II. Phoebe Apperson Hearst Museum of Anthropology. III. Series.

E78.C15F57 2004
394.1'2'089970794—dc22   2004061720

PHOEBE APPERSON HEARST
MUSEUM OF ANTHROPOLOGY
103 Kroeber Hall
University of California
Berkeley, California 94720–3712

CONTENTS

ANIMALS

TRIBAL ACCOUNTS

ACKNOWLEDGMENTS

This publication grew out of the research for an exhibition of the same name, on display at the Phoebe Hearst Museum (September 1997–January 2000). I would first like to thank the three Native consultants who assisted me: Reba Fuller (Sierra Miwuk), Otis Parrish (Kashaya Pomo), Dugan Aguilar (Maidu/Northern Paiute/Pit River), as well as Julia Parker (Kashaya Pomo), who instructed me in the art of acorn cooking. At the Hearst Museum, I am indebted to Kathleen Hull, Rosemary Joyce, Edward Luby, M. Steven Shackley, and Barbara Takiguchi; to Virginia Knechtel, Lori Reyes, and Charles Wade for research assistance; and to Ian Whitmarsh and Vakhtang Chikovani for production assistance. I must single out Beverly R. Ortiz, who offered advice on the exhibition and read the manuscript of the introduction. Critical assistance with the illustrations came from Sherrie Smith-Ferri and William Heick. As ever, I am responsible for any errors or misinterpretations. For inspiring my interest in culinary anthropology, I am indebted to undergraduate teaching by Sidney Mintz and K. C. Chang and my participation in a graduate seminar taught by Barbara Kirshenblatt-Gimblett.

CLASSICS IN CALIFORNIA ANTHROPOLOGY:

Introduction to the Hearst Museum Reprint Series

The Phoebe Hearst Museum of Anthropology seeks to preserve its collections and improve their documentation and accessibility, sponsors research on its collections, and presents research relevant to its collections and mission in the form of publications, programs, and exhibitions. The museum recognizes a special responsibility as a repository of perhaps the largest collection in North America of the material culture produced by the Indians of California. Since the museum's inauguration in 1995 of a series of reprints on Native California, the museum has sought to fulfill its commitment to making knowledge about Native California more widely accessible.

The series initiates a new chapter in the long and distinguished history of publication of anthropological research from Berkeley. Prominent among these are the studies produced by researchers from the Anthropology Department and Museum of Anthropology, published in the series University of California Publications in American Archaeology and Ethnology (UCPAAE). Volume one, number one of the UCPAAE, *Life and Culture of the Hupa* by Pliny Goddard, marked the strong focus on California that would characterize the entire series.

The UCPAAE was initiated in 1903 with the financial support of Phoebe Apperson Hearst, and was modeled on the annual reports and bulletins of the Smithsonian Institution's Bureau of American Ethnology. Like BAE publications, the UCPAAE volumes were not for sale to the general public, but were exchanged with libraries and scholars. Studies varied in length from long articles to monographs of several hundred pages. In 1937, a second series was added, called Anthropological Records. According to a publisher's note, the UCPAAE was "restricted to papers in which the interpretative element outweighs the factual or which otherwise are of general interest." The new series was "issued in photolithography in a larger size.

It consists of monographs which are documentary, of record nature, or devoted to the presentation primarily of new data." In 1964, the series Publications in Anthropology superseded the UCPAAE. By then, fifty volumes subdivided into 237 separate numbers had been published in the UCPAAE. The vast majority of original research from Berkeley about California Indians was published in the three series. Today, almost all of these important works are out of print.

Classics in California Anthropology presents selected volumes from these series and other older sources, enhanced with new introductions by contemporary scholars and, when appropriate, additional illustrations. We intend that Classics in California Anthropology will make available to new audiences landmark works created by a pioneering generation of anthropologists.

Ira Jacknis, Research Anthropologist and Series Editor
November 2004

Tan oak acorns (1–220780).
PHOTOGRAPH BY EUGENE PRINCE, HEARST MUSEUM.

INTRODUCTION

NOTES TOWARD
A CULINARY ANTHROPOLOGY
OF NATIVE CALIFORNIA

Ira Jacknis

In the first general summary of Native Californian cultures, anthropologist Alfred Kroeber concluded that "the human food production of aboriginal California will ... not be well understood until a really thorough study has been made of all of the activities of this kind among at least one people" (1925:525). As he explained, because of the region's diverse and generalized foodways the ingredients and practices of a given group would resemble those of others. "Observers have mentioned what appealed to their sense of novelty or ingenuity, what they happened to see at a given moment, or what their native informants were interested in. But we rarely know whether such and such a device is peculiar to a locality or widespread, and if the former, why; whether it was a sporadic means or one that was seriously depended on; and what analogous ones it replaced." Only an intensive examination of culinary customs would allow us to understand what was distinctive about food in any particular culture, and by extension, in other Native cultures of California. Despite the mountain of research conducted by Kroeber, his colleagues, and his students, we still lack such a detailed description. Nevertheless, a tremendous amount of information does exist, and the present anthology offers a representation of this knowledge.

Food is now a relatively minor area of anthropological research, but at the turn of the century, when Kroeber began his research, it played a much larger role. Early anthropologists used food, which they considered under the category of "subsistence," as one of the critical criteria for the classification of peoples. American museum anthropologists such as Otis T. Mason and Clark Wissler divided the continent into regions such as the salmon area, maize area, bison area, and the like. When considering foods, Mason characterized the Pacific coast as a fish and nut region (1896:651, 658; cf. Kroeber 1939:6–7, 53–55). This comparative approach was soon superseded by the intensive study of individual cultures, but food remained at the center of investigation. Among the classics of early culinary anthropology were Frank Hamilton Cushing's 1885 study of Zuni corn and the collection of Kwakiutl recipes recorded by Franz Boas and George Hunt (1921).[1] In the British tradition, food was important in the functionalist studies of Bronislaw Malinowski in the Trobriand Islands of the South Pacific (1935) and his student Audrey Richards among the Bemba of East Africa (1939). The so-called "culture and personality" school, which followed during the 1930s and 1940s in America, focused on how attitudes toward food were developed in particular cultures and how food affected people's social and psychological relations (e.g., Du Bois 1941).

With the expansion of the discipline after the Second World War, anthropologists moved to other concerns. As Sidney Mintz has argued, in the small-scale societies they studied, food was neglected as a subject of serious study because most of the production and preparation of food was performed by women and most of the early investigators were men.

> [Food and eating] were more interesting if they offended the observer, baffled him, or were ceremonialized, than if they simply pleased those who were doing the cooking and eating. Food was an instrument for the study of other things. That it cemented loyalties, reminded people who they were in relation to others, fortified them for their tasks, and linked them to their gods, were all known aspects of eating behavior, and these features were studied. It was not the food or its preparation that was of interest, so much as what, socially speaking, the food and eating could be used for (1996:3–4).

Another reason may have been that while it is a kind of artifact—material that has been culturally shaped—food is composed of ephemeral elements that cannot be easily collected. While museums are full of objects involved in cooking and eating, the actual substance and the many behaviors and customs surrounding it were neglected.

Starting in the 1960s, the anthropological study of food underwent a substantial revival. Much of this can be attributed to Claude Lévi-Strauss's structuralist studies of American Indian mythologies (1964, 1968). In his search for universal cultural patterning, he examined culinary codes of the raw and the cooked; the roasted, boiled, and smoked; and the origin of table manners. His approach inspired Mary Douglas's analyses of pollution and taboos, and her consideration of the relationship between meal structures and social classification (1975). Partly in response, these symbolic approaches stimulated the more materialist critique of Marvin Harris (1985) and the economic studies of Jack Goody (1982) and Sidney Mintz (1996), who have emphasized social and political history. Recent years have seen the growth of the subdiscipline of nutritional anthropology.[2] Anthropology has also joined with folklore, history, and journalism in a new interdisciplinary field which may be called foodways, represented by periodic conferences at Oxford University, the journal *Gastronomica* and the magazine *Saveur*, and popular writers like Waverley Root (1958), Alan Davidson (1990), and Raymond Sokolov (1991).

The history of California Indian food studies mirrors these larger trends in the study of Native American food as well as those in general anthropology. Our first descriptions by non-Indian writers are stray comments in accounts by explorers and other travelers, followed by those of settlers. When most of these observers described Native Californians' food habits, it was to castigate them, finding a reason to marginalize Indians as uncivilized (Rawls 1984:190–95). The situation changed in 1877 when Stephen Powers, a journalist sponsored by the Smithsonian Institution, published the first systematic commentary on Native Californian cultures. A pioneer in what he called "aboriginal botany," Powers frequently supplied good, basic descriptions of culinary practices.[3] Still, the beginning of the serious study of

Native food customs in California had to await Alfred Kroeber's arrival in the state in 1900. Working for the University of California, Berkeley, Kroeber set out to systematically document and describe the region's Native cultures, research which was summarized in his comprehensive *Handbook of the Indians of California* (1925). In compiling this account, Kroeber drew upon the investigations of the first generation of his students, such as Samuel A. Barrett and Edward W. Gifford. In the mid-1920s and 1930s, he sent out a second generation, students such as Cora Du Bois, Julian Steward, and Philip Drucker, as part of the Culture Element Distribution Survey, an attempt to comprehensively map the presence or absence of cultural traits in Native societies of western North America. Kroeber also drew upon the work of independent scholars such as Philip S. Sparkman and David P. Barrows. Among the other major Californian researchers not affiliated with the University were John W. Hudson, C. Hart Merriam, and John P. Harrington. After Kroeber's retirement in 1946 the study of California Indian cultures, including their cuisines, was carried on at the University by archaeologist Robert F. Heizer and his colleague Sherburne F. Cook, a physiologist turned demographer. Both men made important contributions to ethnohistory. Berkeley's first anthropology doctorate, Samuel Barrett, returned to his alma mater in the 1950s to direct a massive film project for the Lowie (now Hearst) Museum (ca. 1957–65), which extensively recorded California food customs.[4]

In striving for comprehensive documentation, Alfred Kroeber and his students have given us our best descriptions of California Indian food, but there is much they did not consider, especially in regard to cooking and eating behavior. One of the principal reasons is that so many of them were doing salvage or memory ethnography. That is, they were interviewing people, especially elders, about customs from former times instead of observing and talking about current practices. While one does find real behavioral descriptions in some studies (e.g., Sierra Miwok acorn processing in Barrett and Gifford 1933), in general Native food systems had substantially changed since contact, and most anthropologists did not want to describe such creole or mixed customs. Another limiting factor is that many of the Berkeley students in the 1930s were in the field for only a few months over the course of one or two summers. One of the exceptions, Cora Du Bois, who was assisted by Dorothy Demetrocopoulou, spent months among the Wintu over several years. The example of Du Bois, who did some of the best culinary ethnography, also calls attention to the predominance of male ethnographers who tended to interview men (Barbour et al. 1993:164). As women did the great bulk of the collecting and processing of plant foods and most of the cooking, much information was not recorded. Scholarly concerns have shifted, and today some of these culinary issues are being addressed by researchers such as Lowell J. Bean, Craig D. Bates, and Beverly R. Ortiz, and Native writers such as David W. Peri (Bodega Miwok) and Kathleen R. Smith (Dry Creek Pomo/Bodega Miwok), but as the food customs have changed so much in the past century, there is much that we will probably never know.[5]

Because of its holistic nature, food has tremendous power as an anthropological subject. Simultaneously natural and cultural, it unites the physical/biological side of humans with the social/symbolic aspects. As most of the literature on Californian Indian food has focused on the former (e.g., Heizer and Elsasser 1980:82–113), this essay will emphasize the latter. While we have fairly good descriptions of ingredients and gathering procedures, we have a very poor understanding of what might be called "cookbook information," such as how foods were prepared, who cooked and served, and how and when meals were eaten. If most of the research may be called "nutritional" (the science of nourishment or feeding), we will focus here on the "culinary" (of the kitchen and thus of cooking) and "gastronomic" (the arrangement or laws of eating; literally, of the stomach).[6] Accordingly, this introduction will stress these culinary topics, although the other, more ecological/economic issues are represented in the reprinted selections. In the remainder of this introduction, I consider these questions according to a kind of ideal structure of the food process. Because of food's mutability, it is helpful to consider peoples' interaction with it according to a processual or narrative scheme. While the act of eating may be the central point, foods are continually transformed from gathering through storage, processing, cooking, eating, and the disposal of wastes.[7] Telling evidence from diverse groups from throughout the state has been woven together to suggest the full culinary world that must have existed for each group, ranging from gathering prayers to cooking times, from meal combinations to the disposal of leftovers. Finally, this introduction stays fairly close to a descriptive summary. Given the relative lack of scholarly attention to the subject, it is useful to first present an overview before attempting more elaborate analyses. The several comparative and explanatory frameworks offered here are only the first stage in what one hopes will be a fuller and deeper understanding of California Indian food.[8]

SELECTION OF INGREDIENTS

It has been estimated that at the time of the first Spanish settlement in 1769, the area that is now the state of California had a population of about 310,000 people, making it one of the most densely populated regions in Native America (Heizer and Elsasser 1980:25–26). It was characterized by an enormous diversity in regions and peoples, with as many as 100 distinct "cultures," each speaking a different language. These peoples, commonly called tribes, were "usually non-political ethnic nationalities" (Bean 1976:100). That is, while they might have shared common (or related) languages and basic cultural features, they were not organized into a unified society. Instead, the basic unit of social organization for most groups was the tribelet (or village-community), the largest autonomous, self-governing entity (Kroeber 1954). As ethnohistorian Randall Milliken defines them (he prefers to call them tribes), they were independent "associations of families that worked together to harvest wild plant and animal resources within fixed territories and to maintain yearly ceremonial cycles" (1995:13). Kroeber estimated that there were over 500 tribelets, with populations ranging from 50 to 500. Some groups—such as the Chumash, Pomo, Miwok, Patwin, Shasta, Gabrielino, Diegueño, and Salinan—were formed into larger confederations (Bean 1976:103). Most tribelets had a central town as their political, economic, and ritual center. Surrounded by smaller villages and led by a chief, it served as a storage place for food and other goods. Most villages had a few hundred

inhabitants, but Chumash and Sacramento River Patwin villages were inhabited by up to a thousand people.[9]

Before continuing it is important to discuss how these terms have governed the literature on Native Californian groups. Following Kroeber (1925), most scholars have composed their studies at the level of the larger language groups—the Maidu, Pomo, Yokuts, and Cahuilla—rather than the smaller social groupings in which California peoples actually conducted their lives. Acknowledging that most ethnographers and ethnohistorians have treated the language groups as "separate cultural units," Milliken argues that this creates a "misleading and overly simplistic view of the complex mosaic of cultural variation" in the region he examined, the San Francisco Bay Area. "Although some cultural traits did covary with linguistic distributions," he writes, "other traits were shared in restricted local areas by neighbors who spoke distinct languages," especially those determined by geographic and ecological factors (1995:13–14). Many of the selections reprinted in this volume, and this introduction based on them, thus disguise an enormous amount of cultural variation. We should now try to get beyond these generalizing accounts and be as specific as our sources allow, but our level of detail may not always be as precise as we might wish.

Paralleling this cultural diversity was a culinary one. In his analysis of Californian food habits, Alfred Kroeber characterized this region as "perhaps the most omnivorous group of tribes on the continent" (1925:523). He argued that while the acorn was something of a regional staple, it did not play the same role as the buffalo on the Plains or corn in the Southwest. First, there were many areas in the state where oaks did not grow, and where acorns were gathered, they were commonly combined with other forms of subsistence, such as hunting, fishing, and the gathering of other plants. Thus in the failure of an acorn crop, most Native Californian groups could switch to one of the many other foods that they typically gathered. Moreover, gathering and processing techniques are common to many foods: Acorns and buckeyes are both leached, and clams and bulbs are taken with the same kind of digging stick. In short, Kroeber found that the food process in California was not very specialized when compared to other regions of Native America.

Foods taken from the natural world will clearly vary as the environment changes—from dry southern deserts to dense northern forests. Deer, for example, are rare in the Mohave Desert and the Great Central Valley (Heizer and Elsasser 1980:103). In these areas other species filled the gap: mountain sheep in the desert, antelope and tule elk in the valley. Of the nineteen species of oak (including the related tan oak) found in California, eight were important for food purposes (McCarthy 1993:214). However, "The following groups either had no acorns or very few unless secured by trade: Desert groups, except along the eastern edge of Sierra Nevada; Coastal groups, unless they moved inland seasonally; Lake and Riverine groups of the San Joaquin Valley, except those on the east side" (Beals and Hester 1974:138).

As Kroeber suggested, Native cultures in what is now the state of California may be grouped into three regions with centers outside the state—the northwest, the Great Basin, and the southwest—leaving central California as a unique area (1925:898). These four regions also have corresponding gastronomic bases: salmon in the northwest, pine nuts in the Basin, desert and domesticated plants in the southwest, and acorns and seeds in central California. There was perhaps more overlap in matters of food than in other aspects of culture, but these regional emphases are certainly present.[10] So, much of the diversity in California comes from defining our subject according to the rather arbitrary boundary of the current state. If one were drawing borders on the basis of major food complexes, the areas would be much smaller.

In addition to these regions, which follow general environmental lines, more precise and overlapping ecological types have been defined for Native California (Heizer and Elsasser 1980:58).[11] Each of these six types is also associated with a distinct food system: coastal (tideland collectors, sea hunters and fishers); riverine fishermen; lakeshore fishermen, hunters, and gatherers; valley and plains gatherers; foothill hunters and gatherers; and desert (hunters and collectors, agriculturists). As might be imagined from glancing at a topographic or vegetation map, these zones in California run mostly in parallel, north to south. For example, the coast spans the entire length of the state on the western boundary, while the desert does likewise in the east. The territories of many tribes, such as the Pomo, Ohlone, Chumash, and Kumeyaay, extend from the coast to other zones inland. In fact, it was common for a group to occupy diverse habitats, with access to different natural resources, and thus foods (Heizer and Elsasser 1980:10, 61).

Traditionally each group followed an annual round in which some of its members traveled to different places to gather foods that became available at particular times of the year. The Sierra Miwok gathered clover in the spring, seeds in the summer, acorns in the fall, and mushrooms in the winter. Secondary "crops" were wild plums and cherries, gathered between the seed and acorn harvests, and bulbs in the spring. Their winter diet tended to have more meat than in the rest of the year, as squirrels were especially fat and nice to eat then (Barrett and Gifford 1933:137). So important was food in structuring the year that many peoples named the months after their principal food-gathering at that time. The Eastern Pomo, for example, called one month "the moon when the fish will begin to come out," and another "the moon when we will be gathering acorns" (Loeb 1926:225) [see table]. Generally, during the winter a group would stay in its "permanent" villages with relatively little gathering, subsisting on accumulated stores (e.g., Wintu, Du Bois 1935:28–29). Over the year extensive travel was often involved; the interior Pomo, inland Cahuilla, and Luiseño traveled to the coast to fish and gather seafood (Loeb 1926:192; Bean 1972:62). Where groups did not have direct access to desired resources, they commonly obtained them by trading, especially with neighboring groups who spoke the same language but lived in different ecological zones—such as coast and interior or valley and mountains—and had access to different foods.[12] Nisenan in the mountains traded black oak acorns and sugar-pine nuts with those who lived in the foothills for salt, game, fish, roots, grasses, beads, and shells (Beals 1933:365). In fact, in his study of Native Californian trade, Davis found that food (including salt) and tobacco were by far the most frequently traded items (1961:11).[13] Food was also distributed by invitations to feasts.

If one simply makes a list of everything eaten by members of a particular group, there will be a great deal of overlap from group to group, but when one examines the dominant foods and the proportions of foods, one begins to see differences and distinctive regional and local culinary styles. While both Yurok and Sierra Miwok might eat salmon and black oak acorns, salmon is actually a major part and black oaks a minor one of the Yurok diet, with the opposite for the Miwok. These focal foods are called "staples."[14] A glimpse into Native attitudes is given by T. T. Waterman's report that the literal meaning of the Yurok term for salmon is "that which is eaten" (1920:185). Following Moss, we may refer to the others as supplements, emergency provisions, delicacies, or snacks, depending on the situation

Eastern Pomo Annual Cycle

Month	Activitiy	Residence
March	Stream fishing	Main Village
April	Stream fishing by men Clover gathering by women	Main Village
May	Some clover gathering Lake fishing	Scattered; a large number camped on the lake shore
June	Root digging, tule, clams; lake fishing in early June	Scattered; camped on the lake; in hills after roots
July	Roots, tule, clams; carrying in the harvest	Main village
August	Gathering pinole seed; trips to coast and for salt	Main village
September	Pinole seeds Return from trips	Main village and camp
October	Acorns	Camp
November	Continued gathering of acorns and carrying them in; Waterfowl at end of month	Main Village
December	Waterfowl	Main Village
January	Waterfowl	Main Village
February	Waterfowl until mid-month Stream fishing at end of month	Main village

Adapted from Kniffen (1939:366).

(1993:643). Regionally, "Desert peoples used mesquite and screw-bean pods as staples. Valley groups relied heavily on acorns, deer, and hard seeds. Coastal groups harvested offshore schooling fish, seeds, and acorns. Mountain groups relied on pine nuts and venison. People of the northeastern California lake country used the wokas bulb (*Nymphaea*) as their staple. Riverine peoples relied heavily on salmon and acorns" (Chartkoff and Chartkoff 1984:147).[15] Despite these generalizations, we unfortunately have very little quantified information on the proportions of particular ingredients in the Native diet.

Native Californians are now widely regarded, by anthropologists and the general public, as acorn-eaters. For instance, Beals and Hester state: "Acorns provided the outstanding source of food for the majority of California Indian groups." Yet, capturing the ambiguous role of the nut in the region's cuisine, they continue, "This was not true of all, nor were acorns, if used, always the major food source" (1974:127). Inhabitants of the state did not live by acorns alone, but made use of an incredible diversity of plants (flowering plants, fungi, ferns, seaweeds) and a full range of plant parts (seeds, berries, nuts, leaves, stems, roots, and bulbs), from the sea as well as land. For the Kawaiisu, "Of some 250 taxa to which usage—at times multiple—was attributed, about 120 furnished food and beverage" (Zigmond 1981:4).[16] In her summary of Chumash ethnobotany, based on the research of J. P. Harrington, Timbrook found 156 plant species for which uses had been determined; of these, 55 native and another 10 introduced species were used for food (1984:144). Often several parts of a plant would be consumed. For instance, from the mesquite, the Cahuilla roasted the blossoms and squeezed them into balls, or sundried them and made them into a beverage. The pods were eaten fresh, or mashed, leached, and made into a drink. "The beans were dried and eaten directly without any preparation or ground into a flour which was stored in the form of cakes to be consumed as drinks and porridges, or eaten dry" (Bean 1972:39).

Our understanding of the relative importance of grass seeds and acorns in Native California has been skewed. By the time that anthropologists started gathering their information, around the turn of the century, grass seeds were no longer available in relatively large quantities. Radical ecological forces unleashed by early settlers—introduced grass species, widespread cattle-grazing, and the curtailment of periodic fires—all took their toll (Preston 1998:273). Ethnohistorical sources tell a different story. During Portolá's expedition from San Diego to San Francisco in 1769, "Indians occasionally gave the men acorns and pine nuts, but pinole and atole [pounded seed mixtures] made from native grasses were brought to them in large baskets at almost every village" (Ebeling 1986:169). Citing a 1786 missionary account, Milliken concluded that "the seed crops may have been the most important carbohydrate source in the Bay Area for much of the year" (1995:17). Like acorns, seeds would not have been found in every region of the state, but they were widely distributed in the great expanses of hill and valley.[17]

Among animals, California Indians ate a wide range of mammals, birds, fish, crustaceans and mollusks, reptiles, and insects. As with plants, they used most parts of the animal (muscle, internal organs, fat, blood, nerve tissue, bone, marrow). They supplemented their diet with saccharine foods (honey), salt and other minerals, and beverages (water, cider, and other herbal decoctions).[18]

Just as the position of the acorn has been overly generalized relative to other plant foods, so has the deer among the animals. While hunting for large game such as deer, elk, antelope, mountain sheep, and bear was especially dramatic, as Goddard suggests for the Hupa (1903:21), it generally took a great deal of effort to bring down these animals and hunters were not always successful. Drucker speculates that deer and elk became a more important part of the Tolowa diet after the introduction of firearms, and suggests that "the highly esteemed deer, elk, and sea lions (the 'ocean deer') were prized in proportion to the difficulty with which they were obtained" (1937:231).[19] Similarly, while deer was the most important prey for the Atsugewi, they probably obtained more animal protein from fish (Garth 1953:132). More important—or at least plentiful—prey were small mammals such as rabbits, squirrels, rats, mice, and chipmunks: "These animals probably provided the bulk of the meat protein in the Cahuilla diet because of their great numbers and the ease of capture" (Bean 1972:58). Water and land birds were also favored catches, especially among the inhabitants of the marshy Central Valley. Here, too, we find quite a variety. The Nisenan, for example, favored the quail, but they also ate ducks, geese, grouse, even blue jay and woodpecker (Beals 1933:349).

In addition to muscle, the principal animal food organ, Native Californians ate entrails and bones. Tribes such as the Hupa, Wintu, and Sierra Miwok enjoyed deer stomachs filled with innards and sometimes blood (see sections on Gathering and Cooking).[20] Bone and marrow were also relished; the Nisenan ate pounded animal and fish bones "for strength" (Beals 1933:350). Many groups dried bones, which they then pounded into a powder and made into a soup.[21] When consuming salmon bones, the Maidu ate them raw, but deer vertebrae were pounded, formed into little cakes, and baked (Dixon 1905:184). Egg consumption was less common. The Pomo ate eggs of quail, goose, duck, and turtles, but only when fresh. While the Sierra Miwok did not ordinarily eat birds' eggs, they occasionally might roast duck or quail eggs in the ashes (Barrett and Gifford 1933:138). Native Californians usually, but not always, ate the animals they killed for their furs, feathers, and bones. Pomo ate the quails that supplied plume feathers for baskets, but not the woodpeckers whose feathers were used on headdresses, belts, and baskets because the latter were said to be "the oldest bird in the world" (Loeb 1926:165). On the other hand, Nisenan captured woodpeckers for their flesh as well as their feathers (Beals 1933:350).

Fish was perhaps the main animal food where it was commonly found (Rostlund 1952); it was the primary subsistence mode in the Klamath River valley and among the Chumash and their neighbors around the Santa Barbara area. Like acorn harvests, fish spawning runs were relatively abundant and occurred at dependable places and times. Also like acorns, fish can be dried and stored easily (McLendon 1992:51). While salmon was important in all streams north of Monterey, it was the staple in the northwest. Fish were not just a maritime food; some desert-dwelling Mohave preferred their Colorado River fish to corn or wheat (Stewart 1968:29). Other important aquatic foods were shellfish (including clams, mussels, abalone, and crabs) in both fresh and salt water (Greengo 1952). Of these, the most popular seems to have been the mussel, because of its abundance, accessibility, large size, meaty texture, and sweet taste. Coastal dwellers, especially north of San Francisco Bay and around the Santa Barbara area, also hunted sea mammals such as seals, sea lions, and sea otters. Although not hunted, whales were consumed when they were found beached (Heizer and Elsasser 1980:119).

Many kinds of insects were also gathered, especially in the Great Basin area, on the eastern slopes of the Sierras. These included grasshoppers, moths, flies, ants, bees, and wasps at different life-stages (mostly larvae, as well as adults and pupae), as well as earthworms, another kind of invertebrate.[22] The advantages of insects as a food were that they were relatively high in protein, were seasonally abundant, and could be caught with relatively little effort. Maidu "highly esteemed" grasshoppers, locusts, and crickets; in their dried state they were much traded (Dixon 1905:184). Nisenan considered grasshoppers to be a healthful food, as they were believed to have acquired the medicinal benefits of the plants they had eaten (Beals 1933:347). Northfork Mono ate pandora moth chrysalises, while Eastern Mono (Owens Valley Paiute) ate the caterpillars (Gifford 1932:23). Insects also supplied sweet products like honey and the honeydew "sugar" produced by aphids.

Although relatively rare in the Native California diet, sweets—in the form of naturally sugary plants such as berries and agave, honey and other insect deposits, and plant gums—were not unknown. As the honey bee was not present in North America until the arrival of Europeans, aboriginal peoples had to make do with the relatively small amounts of honey produced by native bees (Foothill Yokuts, Gayton 1948b:223). Wintu used manzanita flour to sweeten mashed wild grapes (Du Bois 1935:21).[23] Sweets were often consumed in the form of gums.[24] The Wintu ate the gum of scrub oaks gathered in fall as candy. Sugar pine resin was an especially popular form of candy.[25] Sierra Miwok chewed the gum of pine trees; they also roasted the pithy center of green pine cones for twenty minutes in hot ashes, "yielding a brownish, pithy, sweetish food, to a slight extent syrupy"; and they sucked the nectar from flowers (Barrett and Gifford 1933:149, 150, 163). A specialty of southeastern California

(Tübatulabal, Surprise Valley Paiute, and Owens Valley Paiute) was the collection of the honeydew deposited by aphids on cane. Owens Valley Paiute gathered the dried sap of the *Phragmites* cane which had been brought to the surface by the insects. They beat this in a basket, made it into a ball, later softened it by a fire, and ate it like candy; it was "much less sweet than commercial cane sugar" (Steward 1933:245–46). Tübatulabal cut and dried the cane, beat off the crystals, and made it into a stiff dough with cold water. "When dry, lumps of sweet [were] broken off the hard brown loaf with rock and eaten dry with chia gruel" (Voegelin 1938:19). Luiseño made chewing gums from the deposits of a scale insect found on oak trees and from milkweed sap boiled in water (Sparkman 1908:196–97).

While all foods contain minerals, some minerals were consumed directly. The most important was salt, which was used in some form by almost all California groups (Heizer and Elsasser 1980:108; cf. Kroeber 1941). Salt was usually treated as a condiment—more often eaten with prepared food than added during the cooking. A lump of salt might also be chewed by itself. Some Sierran groups used it to preserve dried fish and meat, but they may have acquired this custom from white contact (Kroeber 1941:4–5). In some areas salt was considered a medicine for curing stomachaches and colds. Conversely, the eating of salt was forbidden among many central and southern groups at times of life crises, especially during childbirth, puberty, and mourning. Salt came from four sources: seaweed, grass, dry mineral deposits, and saline water (marshes, springs, lakes, and ocean). The material was typically gathered in baskets and then processed by drying and/or pounding. A kind of grass—called salt grass (*Distichlis spicata*)—was beaten to dislodge salt crystals or burned to produce saline ashes (Gayton 1948b:181). Salt was often obtained through trade by people who did not otherwise have access to it. Another important mineral ingested by Native Californians, especially in the northern and western half of the state, was red earth. An iron-bearing clay, it was added to acorn bread (Heizer and Elsasser 1980:152). The red clay neutralized the tannic acid in the acorns by bonding to it; the Pomo said it made their bread black and sweet (Barrett 1952:96). Wintu red earth, collected from gopher holes, was used only for valley-oak bread (Du Bois 1935:19).

Beverages included water, berry juices and ciders, nut drinks, and herbal teas. Except in years of drought, obtaining water was not a problem for much of Native California. People often took in water as part of prepared foods: Acorn was typically eaten in a liquid form (soup or mush); berry ciders and herbal teas were popular, especially as medicines. In addition to its use as a drink, water was employed in plant processing. Communities usually lived near a site of fresh water, but sources of water and the need to carry one's own in canteens were always more critical in the desert lands. Berry juices were welcomed; the Pomo made juices from elderberries and manzanita berries (Loeb 1926:173), and the Chukchansi Yokuts consumed fresh wild grape juice (Gayton 1948b:180). Some groups, especially those living in drier areas, made drinks based on pounded nuts. Tübatulabal mixed small seeds with cold water to make a thick, gray-colored gruel. Drunk for refreshment, "like lemonade," this gruel was often served by mothers to their children as a between-meal snack (Voegelin 1938:18). The Cahuilla mixed water with the meals of pine nuts, jojoba nuts, and mesquite beans (Kotzen 1994:12–15). Many plants were taken as "teas" or infusions. The Cahuilla used *Ephedra* (known variously as desert, Mexican, Indian, or Mormon tea) as a daily beverage as well as a medicine, a cathartic, and to relieve indigestion (Bean 1972:47–48). Owens Valley Paiute also used *Ephedra* (Steward 1933:245); they and the Luiseño made mint teas (Sparkman 1908:211). There seem to have been no fermented drinks in Native California; the Wintu, for example, regarded fermented manzanita cider as having "gone bad" (Du Bois 1935:20).[26]

Despite the vast range of plants and animals consumed, Native Californians did not passively eat whatever was at hand. They traded to obtain foods they wanted, and shunned available foods for reasons of taste or taboo. Even within a particular group there was a great amount of variation in food practices. People had definite taste preferences (see discussion under Cooking). It was a common belief that the quality of a finished object depended on the quality of its ingredients. As Lucy Smith, a Dry Creek Pomo woman, put it, "The basket is in the roots, that's where it begins" (Peri and Patterson 1976). Native Californians certainly applied this philosophy to food, now associated with Berkeley chef Alice Waters. The Sierra Miwok ranked the desirability of plants as food, from manzanita berries at the bottom through bulbs, corms, and mushrooms to certain seeds, with acorns at the top. The two favorite plant foods were black oak acorns and farewell-to-spring (*Godetia viminea*) seeds; the two most desirable animals were deer first and gray squirrel second; salmon was the most prized fish in the lower foothills, and trout in the mountains (Barrett and Gifford 1933:137). Wherever acorns and buckeyes were found together, the former was inevitably preferred because of the longer and more involved leaching process for buckeyes. Most groups had favorites among the various species of acorn available to them, for either taste or ease of preparation or both. Where it was present, the tan oak seems to have been preferred, but as it is found in only about 8 percent of the state (in the northern Coast Range), in many places it was superseded by the black oak acorn (McCarthy 1993:214). The Hupa preferred tanbark acorns, even though they could get black oak (Goddard 1903:27). On the other hand, the Wintu and many of the central groups preferred the black oak (Du Bois 1935:10). The Sierra Miwok preferred black oak; they ranked the valley oak second, even though they found it delicious, because it was difficult to shell. The blue oak was rated lowest because it made a watery soup and crumbly bread or biscuits (Barrett and Gifford 1933:142). Furthermore, the Wintu preferred green acorns because they made a "nice smooth white sticky" soup, whereas ripe acorns that had fallen to the ground made a less desirable "dark soup" (Du Bois 1935:18). In general, the Tübatulabal had a taste preference for oily vegetable varieties, such as oily or sweet acorns which needed little leaching, and they liked black piñon mush (made with parched nuts) better than the white variety (Voegelin 1938:11).

As in all cuisines, some foods were favored as delicacies. The Hupa were especially fond of roasted salmon heads because of the cartilage they contained (Goddard 1903:26). Insects were favorites among many groups: The Wintu considered salmon-flies a great treat (Du Bois 1935:15); to the Nisenan grasshoppers were a "favorite food" (Wilson 1972:36); the Pomo considered grasshoppers a great delicacy and especially liked the army worm caterpillar (Loeb 1926:163, 164).

Cahuilla found the meat of wood rat to be particularly tasty, which they "compared favorably with breast of chicken," and they also enjoyed quail and chuckwalla lizard (Bean 1972:59, 61). The Death Valley Indians also found the meat of the chuckwalla lizard to be sweet and delicate, and especially appreciated it during spring (Wallace 1978). The Cahuilla eagerly sought mushrooms, which they sliced into bits and boiled (Bean 1972:48). On the other hand, they considered some plant pods, such as cat's claw or desert willow, "less tasty than other plants," but used them when other foods were scarce, as they were high in protein (1972:43).

While Californian groups were generally omnivorous, as Kroeber maintained, in every group there were plants and animals that were not consumed. Thus the edible was defined in opposition to the inedible. Among foods that were shunned, some were categorically forbidden—that is, a given group would never eat a particular plant or animal—while other avoidances were situational—the food was forbidden to a certain person at a certain time, such as a girl at puberty (see Food as a Social Category). Almost every kind of edible plant and animal is eaten by some human group somewhere in the world; what revolts one culture is a delicacy for another (Schwabe 1979), and insect-eating in Native California is a prime example. California Indians had their own notions of repulsive foods. While each group had animals that it would not eat, in general, snakes, lizards, and carrion-eaters such as coyotes and buzzards were the most commonly avoided (Kroeber 1925:526). Prey animals such as wolves, dogs, mountain lions, wildcats, bears, eagles, and hawks were commonly avoided, but not always. These tastes were also cultural and historical. For instance, dogs, reptiles, and insects were not eaten in the northwest, but were in the central and southern areas (Barrett and Gifford 1933:271).[27]

In most cases the rationale for such taboos is uncertain, but these choices often followed a poetic logic of resemblances.[28] Atsugewi would not eat doves; if a man did "all but two of his children would die, because a dove lays only two eggs" (Garth 1953:135).Hupa would not eat small valley quail and meadow larks because they "are thought to spend the day in gambling in the underground regions which are the home of the dead. The stakes are the souls of living men" (Goddard 1903:23). Many groups would not eat bear because of its resemblance to humans. While the Wintu did eat brown bear, they did not touch the grizzly bear, which they feared. They felt that because grizzlies ate human beings, eating them would be equivalent to cannibalism (Du Bois 1935:12). They told Powers that it was because the spirits of evil people went into them (1877:240).[29] Similarly, most Chukchansi Yokuts would not eat bear because of its human posture and its occasional eating of humans (Gayton 1948b:180). Among the Pomo, some birds were not eaten; they shunned the hummingbird because its peculiar flight was thought to be under the protection of the thunder god, the owl was a bird of ill omen, jacksnipe feathers were used for poisoning, and the hawk was especially feared (Loeb 1926:167). Pomo never ate snakes or frogs, whose blood was used for poisoning; they used lizards for medicine but not for food, and did eat turtles (1926:170). Tübatulabal avoided some animals (coyote, turkey vulture) because "they smelled bad," others because their "meat is no good" (crow), because they ate pests (roadrunners eat lizards, yellowhammers eat ants), or because "people liked them, felt sorry for them" (meadowlark) (Voegelin 1938:12).

Taken together, the foods available to any given group or individual produced a generally healthy diet, in many ways healthier than what most of us eat today (Gendar et al. 2000). Distinctions between food and medicine, both of which may be ingested, are culturally defined. When ill, Native Californians consumed substances taken from their environment, especially plants that were infused in liquids and drunk. For example, Tübatulabal liked to take some salt-grass crystals dissolved in warm water every morning "for laxative purposes, to clean out [the] stomach" (Voegelin 1938:59).

The proportions among plants, fish, and other animals clearly varied throughout the state, depending greatly on local habitats, and were subject to seasonal and annual cycles. For instance, Dixon noted that among the Maidu, "Vegetable foods were perhaps a little more used in the Sacramento Valley area than in the mountains, where game was rather more abundant" (1905:181). Unfortunately, here again is a topic with little firm information, but plants probably supplied the bulk of the Native Californian diet (Heizer and Elsasser 1980:86; cf.

Baumhoff 1963). We have some figures for the Great Basin peoples living in California. The Tübatulabal regime was about 40 percent meat (including birds and fish), about 40 percent plants such as acorns and pine nuts, and another 20 percent of small seeds, stalks, raw food, etc. (Voegelin 1938:20). The diet of their neighbors, the Owens Valley Paiute, was similar: 10 percent fish, 30–40 percent game animals, 50–60 percent plants. The Panamint seem to have been more vegetarian: 60–70 percent plants and 30–40 percent animals, while the lake and riverine peoples of Pyramid Lake/Walker River in Nevada ate more animal flesh: 50–60 percent fish, 20 percent large and small game, and 20–30 percent wild plants (Fowler 1986:91–92). As these groups lived in fairly similar, dry country, the range of variation in the rest of California was probably pronounced.

It is hard to offer comprehensive and reliable proportions of the nutrients in Native Californian foods. As might be expected, plants supplied most of the carbohydrates, with meat and fish offering most of the protein. While different species of acorns do have different amounts of nutrients, even these have been reported differently in the literature. According to one estimate, Californian acorns range between 55 to 69 percent carbohydrate, 5 to 18 percent fat, 3 to 6 percent protein, and 9 percent water.[30] Domesticated crops such as wheat and barley, on the other hand, have about the same amount of carbohydrate (70 percent), less fat (2 percent), and slightly more protein (about 10 percent). For a nut, acorns are particularly high in carbohydrates; almonds have only 20 percent and pine nuts 12 (McGee 1984:265). Lean meat averages 20 to 25 percent protein, 5 to 15 percent fat, with the rest water and trace minerals. Raw, boiled, or broiled fish ranges from 15 to 25 percent protein, while the more concentrated dried fish can be from 50 to as much as 90 percent protein (Driver and Massey 1957:199, 208; Fowler 1986:92).[31] A healthy diet was made possible by the state's especially abundant food stocks. A valley oak might have an annual yield of 200 to 500 pounds of acorn; a black oak, 100 to 300 pounds. It has been estimated that "one tree can provide up to a pound of food a day for one person for an entire year" (Chartkoff and Chartkoff 1984:228). An average silver salmon weighed eight to ten pounds, a king salmon twenty to twenty-five pounds, and a steelhead trout three to four pounds; and about three-quarters of the carcass is edible. With the large river runs amounting to hundreds of thousands of fish each fall, the available food source was quite rich (ibid.).

Dependent as they were on a subsistence mode of hunting and gathering, Native Californians were subject to cyclic food shortages. For most communities the amount and variety of foods usually diminished during the winter months, and in difficult times people would often consume certain foods that were not usually eaten because of taste or nutrition. During hard winters, for example, the Wintu and the Northeastern Maidu consumed the inner bark of pine trees (Du Bois 1935:21; Dixon 1905:183). Another strategy, especially in poor years, was to raid the accumulated stores of nuts and seeds in bird and rodent nests.[32] However, over the course of years some food resources would give out. As one Nomlaki man remembered:

> They used to tell me about hard times—years when there was a scarcity. About every six or seven years there would be a time when few acorns or seeds were to be had. People who could afford to would buy from one another, but soon all would run out of food. It seems as though everything went against them, for they couldn't kill deer or meat of any kind—neither rabbits, squirrels, nor any other. They might occasionally get one, but it would never be enough. They would get so hungry that the rich people who owned hide skirts and sinew would cook these and eat them. The people would do whatever they could. Such conditions would come about in winter when there was nothing to be found, and many of the people would become too weak from hunger to move, and many, especially of the poorer people, would die before spring broke (Goldschmidt 1951:417).

While admitting that hunger and sometimes starvation were a problem, Alfred Kroeber believed that the region's general abundance obviated famines for the most part (1925:815). To cope with potential shortages, Native Californians shared and traded food and tried to store a multiyear surplus. They were served by not depending on any one food, even acorns, but their best insurance was a profound understanding of their natural environment and gathering practices that would not deplete their food resources.[33]

GATHERING

For all California Native peoples, even those who farmed, the beginning of the food process was the gathering of wild plants and animals. From centuries of experience, they knew the best time and place to gather each plant or animal. During the plant's harvesting season, entire families and villages worked together to gather an ample surplus. In fact, most foods were gathered as part of village-wide seasonal efforts. For the Cahuilla, "seed gathering was a painstaking and time-consuming operation conducted by women, sometimes aided by children. It required an entire day to collect two quarts of seed. Nonetheless, this was a valuable occupation, because the seeds were very high in protein, oil, and starch, and, after parching, were easily digested" (Bean 1972:47).

Naturally, specific implements and containers were adapted to each part of the food process. Plant-gathering implements were comparatively simple and basic; baskets for gathering and carrying were the essential object. Small seeds were dislodged from their stalks with "seed beaters" (basketry flails). The seeds fell into finely-woven burden baskets, which were then used to transport the catch for deposit in storage baskets and granaries. Baskets made with a more open mesh held larger items such as acorns or seaweed. Sharpened and fire-hardened sticks served for digging up bulbs and roots, and similar sticks were used in planting and weeding. Leaves, stalks, and small plants were hand-plucked or cut off with obsidian (later metal) knives; high-hanging nuts and buds were knocked off with long staffs. Some object types were general, others were more specialized. Most Native Californian artifacts had multiple functions; for example, soaproot brushes were used for combing hair as well as sweeping acorn meal.[34] Baskets were especially multipurpose; the Sierra Miwok, for instance, used a coarse twined triangular tray for sifting seeds, cleaning shelled acorn meats, leaching small quantities of acorn meal and manzanita cider, and draining boiled clover (Barrett and Gifford 1933:234).

*Nisenan Maidu woman gathering tarweed seeds with a seed beater
and burden basket; near Placerville, Eldorado County, ca. 1903.*
PHOTOGRAPH BY JOHN W. HUDSON (NEG. NO. 13–4159, FM 1926).

However, when needed, Native peoples created precisely focused
tools, such as a Yurok salmon-jaw breaker, made of wood (Kroeber
and Barrett 1960:pl. 19-u). In general, the objects used for plant processing were more diverse and elaborate than those used for animals.
This was a reflection of several factors: the greater processing needed
to render some plants edible, the more common preservation of
plants, and the greater dependence of California peoples on the plant
world.[35]

Native Californians did not passively gather whatever they found,
but consciously tended the environment (Blackburn and Anderson

1993). Periodic burning, pruning, digging, weeding, and irrigation, as well as the gathering itself, all encouraged the growth of plants. In the absence of fire, oak trees would be crowded out by brush and conifers. Burning also helped keep the trees healthy by reducing insect pests, ensured bigger crops by increasing the available water supply, and made it easier to gather the nuts by clearing away the underbrush (McCarthy 1993). At the same time that burning increased plant diversity, the new herbaceous growth also attracted animals. This kind of multiple husbandry was developed to a high art in the region. For instance, while Cahuilla may have captured rodents for their meat, this hunting also reduced their predation on plants (Bean 1972:60). There was a gradual road from the horticulture of wild plants to full-scale farming of domesticated crops. The Owens Valley Paiute were able to increase the yield of wild seed plots by irrigation with a system of dams and ditches (Steward 1933:247–50), and several southern Californian groups were part-time farmers. While there is some uncertainty over the aboriginality of agriculture in the state, a recent review argues that farming had diffused from the Colorado River tribes to the Cahuilla, Kamia and Southern Diegueño (Kumeyaay), Chemehuevi, certain Paiute groups, and possibly the Serrano, Paipai, and Kiliwa (Bean and Lawton 1973:35). For the Mohave and other Colorado River groups farming yielded about half of their diet, along with the gathering of wild plants and a little hunting, while the Kumeyaay of the Imperial Valley were mainly farmers (Castetter and Bell 1951). These southern farmers raised aboriginal varieties of corn, tepary beans, pumpkins, and gourds, supplemented by wheat, cowpeas, and melons after European contact. The Mohave, planting on the silt deposited by spring floods, cleared their fields, dropped seeds into holes punched out with a heavy stick, and then gave little attention to their crops until harvest (Stewart 1966).

Hunters resorted to a wide variety of methods and devices. Bows and arrows were perhaps the principal weapon, but they also used throwing sticks, clubs, spears, knives, slings, snares, nets, traps, pits, deadfalls, decoys, and the assistance of dogs. Each was adapted to catching a particular prey in a certain manner. Some animals were taken by alternate means, depending on the terrain and behavior of the creature. Most important perhaps was a keen knowledge of the habits of the intended prey. Over most of the state, hunting was usually carried out by individuals or small groups, but many societies also arranged communal expeditions. While hunting was primarily a male occupation, women and children often participated in gathering rabbits, squirrels, mice, and other small game. When families left the village for food-gathering trips, the men often hunted while the women acquired plants. Fishing was a concern not only for coastal peoples but also for interior groups who lived along rivers and lakes. Fish were captured with a wide range of devices: nets of all sorts, hooks, harpoons, traps and weirs, plant poisons, even bare hands. The most common tool for gathering shellfish was a stick resembling and in some cases identical to the digging stick (Greengo 1952:73). Once dried, fish and shellfish were often traded. Insects were typically gathered by hand, in pits, and collected in baskets.

Gathering practices varied across the state, but rarely was it a matter of simply taking plants and animals where one found them. Many groups, especially among the wealth-conscious societies of the northwest, observed family-owned hunting and gathering territories (Hupa, Goddard 1903:22, 26). Pomo families controlled the use of trees (oak, laurel, juniper, pine, manzanita), fishing spots, and fields for gathering seeds and bulbs (Loeb 1926:197–98). While Nisenan land was generally communally owned, trees such as oak and pine were privately held. "Ownership, was said by some, to be established by picking them regularly. According to others, they were marked in various ways. One way was by cracking acorns and placing them on a bare spot under the tree. Some said ownership lasted for one year only. All were agreed that unauthorized gathering from owned trees meant a fight" (Beals 1933:363–64). Owens Valley Paiute districts, composed of several villages and led by a headman, controlled pine nut territories (Steward 1933:241). On the other hand, some groups, especially the more nomadic ones, had no owned gathering territories.[36] Food distribution occurred at each stage of the food process, from the initial gathering to consumption. The Nisenan observed flexible food sharing rules in gathering: If acorns were abundant, the surplus was picked and given to the oldest man in the village, who subsequently gave them to families or other villages without supplies (Beals 1933:350).

*Eastern Pomo basket of mudballs (1–10604) and sling
(1–10605), for catching mud hens on Clear Lake.*
PHOTOGRAPH BY EUGENE PRINCE, HEARST MUSEUM.

*Karuk man fishing with an A-frame lifting net;
Klamath River, Humboldt County, ca. 1902.*
PHOTOGRAPH BY ALFRED L. KROEBER (NEG. NO. 15–1383).

Different kinds of people gathered food, but all able-bodied persons in Native California played some role. Hunting and plant-gathering could be either individual or collective. Large communal groups were common for gathering acorns and pine nuts, which ripened in large quantities during a limited harvest season. Children usually took part in gathering and often processing, too. For the Pomo and other central Californian groups, deer hunting and fishing were distinctive professions, requiring special training (Loeb 1926:170, 180–81). Among the Nisenan, quail hunting was practically a profession for some men, who traded quail and bird flesh for other meat and acorns (Beals 1933:349). For many groups chiefs had an important role in directing the local economy. Among the Atsugewi, for example, "He had to know the time of ripening of different vegetable foods, when the fish runs occurred, and had to be well versed in methods of hunting" (Garth 1953:178). In the south and east ritual leaders supervised communal rabbit hunts.

According to Nona Willoughby, who conducted the most comprehensive review of the sexual division of labor in Californian Native cultures, men were the primary gatherers of animals and women of plants. She noted, however, "the fallacy of making a rigid division of labor without an intensive study of the particular tribe in question. Actually any dichotomy which can be established represents merely the average occupation assignment and this may vary with the particular circumstances, the momentary situation, and the general personality of the individual" (1963:34). Concerning the participation of men during gathering, she found that

> Although gathering was primarily feminine, there was no rigid rule preventing men from participating. In some cases they lost prestige by assisting with women's work, but references to a good man helping his wife are surprisingly frequent. Women, however, were not as free to take part in men's work—hunting and fishing—due primarily to the negative attitudes toward sex, pregnancy, and menstruation. The greater laxity in gathering was largely due to necessity, for it would have been impossible to harvest all the acorns and pine nuts during the short season without mutual cooperation (1963:27).

Among the Wintu, for example, men gathered animals and women plants. While men took part in plant gathering and preparation and women in animal gathering and preparation, each was subsidiary to the other (Du Bois 1935:18). Among Mohave farmers, men did most of the field preparation and planting, while women did most of the harvesting, although each gender assisted the other (Stewart 1966). Moreover, in many parts of the state women actually gathered a substantial part of the animal food. Women fished in the north and the southern Sierras (Willoughby 1963:21). While shellfish-gathering was open to both genders, women tended to be the principal gatherers, if only because the technique of securing stationary food items with a pointed stick was common to plant-gathering as well. And in many areas, they and the children caught most of the rabbits, squirrels, and other small game, which often supplied more of the meat than the more prestigious deer-hunting.

This relatively gendered division of labor produced a fairly balanced mode of subsistence. According to Du Bois, among the Wintu, "the work seems to have been fairly equally distributed between the sexes"; social pressure required men to be good providers (1935:24, 23). All Modoc men were expected to hunt for their families; a poor hunter, like a woman who was a poor gatherer, penalized his own family as each family was responsible for providing for itself (Ray 1963:183). In almost every case, a young person's food-gathering abilities were a prime requisite for obtaining an attractive mate. Among the Atsugewi, "There was considerable competition among women to see who could dig the most roots or gather the most seeds, and one who outshone her neighbors was highly regarded." Consequently, "a rich man might watch girls bringing home roots and pick out the one that had the most" (1953:141, 163). Men, however, "might gamble all day while their wives dug roots, although they were said to do so only when sufficient animal food had been obtained" (1953:141).

The plants and animals gathered by Californian Indians were not inert food ingredients, but powerful substances. Traditional groups interacted with the environment according to a set of interlinked assumptions, beginning with the belief that nature is alive. According to William Benson (Eastern Pomo), "Plants are thought to be alive, the juice is their blood, and they grow. The same is true of trees. All things die, therefore all things have life" (Loeb 1926:302). Native Californians commonly believed that life remained in the food after it was killed, and that the spirits controlling it had to be propitiated by prayer and proper behavior (correct things done and negative actions avoided) (Swezey 1975). As Benson explained, "Because all things have life, gifts have to be given to all things. This is called gaXol cayoi (outwards gift)." Prayers and songs thus accompanied all stages of the food process. David Peri, a Bodega Miwok anthropologist, has explained the moral implications of taking the life of a deer. The hunter did not eat any of his kill but gave it to his relatives and friends. "By not eating the meat from his own hunt, the hunter gave back the life that he had taken. This was called 'Giving to the Deer.' That is, a man became a hunter to take the deer's life in order that someone else would live, and make possible other lives" (1988a:15). The dependence between the natural and the human world was mutual: "The acorns—and other resources as well—were put here on earth for people to use, for people's survival. The people need the plants in order to live, but the plants also need the people; they need people to gather their seeds, and leaves, and roots, and to talk and sing and pray to them" (McCarthy 1993:225). California Indians thus behaved toward animals and plants according to a kind of "land etiquette," recognizing agency and purpose in the natural world (Heizer and Elsasser 1980:210).

According to some beliefs plants and animals were controlled by higher spirits. The Hupa had gods who governed plants and deer. The vegetation god, Yinûkatsisdai ("In the south he lives"), would spend time among the people, passing unseen.

> He carries a burden basket or a large sack on his back. This is filled with acorns and other vegetable food. He throws out from his store as much as he wishes to grow the next season. If he sees the food being wasted he withholds the supply and produces a famine. The crows are then said to go to his home in the south and revile him for his stinginess. Some say they throw him out of his house. He then gives the food, which has been withheld, in such bountiful quantities that acorns are found even under the pines (Goddard 1903:77).

One must behave properly to capture a deer. The Hupa also believed in a god who tended the deer. "He watches carefully to see that the deer he does permit to be killed are properly treated. It is believed that the deer's ghost tells his master that at such a house he was well treated and that he would like to go back again. This good treatment consists in the observance of all the many laws concerning the dressing, serving, and eating of the deer and also the disposal of the bones" (1903:78).

Although all gathering had to follow proper procedure, the rules of deer hunting were particularly strict. Prayer and proper behavior were always vital to a successful hunt. Before setting out, a hunter might make offerings and abstain from food and sex for several days, often four; men were commonly enjoined against hunting during their wife's menstrual period. To become ritually cleansed and remove body odor, a hunter might bathe and rub or smoke himself with herbs. Before setting out, Atsugewi deer hunters had to make offerings of

Deer, shot by Molasses (Chilula); Redwood Creek, Humboldt County, 1907. The deer was treated ceremonially to avoid bad luck in future hunting. The eyes were dug out and the nose closed with Douglas fir so that the deer would not know who killed it.
PHOTOGRAPH BY PLINY L. GODDARD (NEG. NO. 15–4284).

food or tobacco to mountain spirits, and they were expected to not boast about killing a deer. During the hunt, a Maidu hunter prayed, and ate only the liver of the deer killed. As the deer were killed, their legs were cut off and placed on a platform in a tree. Later the meat was equally divided among the hunters, the leg bones were taken down and brought home for marrow, and the antlers and jaw bones were hung up in a bush where the animal was killed.[37]

In addition to these individual rites, most groups observed some form of collective first-food ceremony (Swezey 1975). For those following these rituals the gathering and eating of a given food was forbidden until a ceremony had been performed by a ritual specialist. This often involved prayers and the recitations of verbal formulae and a ceremonial cooking and eating of the food. Such rites were not observed for all foods, but usually for the group's most important foods, especially those that tended to have a definite harvesting season—most notably acorns and salmon. We have a good description of a Sierra Miwok acorn dance, performed in Yosemite Valley in the fall of 1931 (Ortiz and Parker 1991:37–38). It was "hosted to give thanks and dedicate the year's new acorn harvest before any was eaten." Most participants fasted for the first three days of the ceremony. On the third day, ten specially chosen women pounded and leached acorn, which they cooked on the next day. Then came a series of final dances. In his oration, the leader invited "the spirits of their ancestors to come and eat," as he threw acorn meal into the air. The dancers came out of the ceremonial house, circling around the fire where the cooking stones had been heated. "Everyone who planned to eat the acorn was invited to join this dance, which culminated with an elder woman offering acorn four times around the fire, to be carried in the four directions to the spirits." More dancing followed: "There was a fire dance for the fire that heated the cooking stones; a stone dance for the stones that cooked the meal; and a basket dance for the baskets in which it was cooked. Then there were dances to the 'First People,' who made the world, and especially to 'Coyote Man,' one of the most important of the 'First People.' "

Because the spiritual leader and/or headman often determined where and when to gather the food, these customs helped to regulate the gathering and consumption of the food.[38] Although speaking specifically of Cahuilla first-fruit rituals, Bean's analysis of the multiple economic and social functions of such rites is more generally applicable throughout Native California:

> They provided a ritual context for reaffirming or reestablishing rights of the lineage to a food-producing area; they protected the group by preventing a premature food harvest which might limit future plant productivity; they controlled potential conflict which might arise due to competition over newly available foods, because at each collecting season collecting procedures were redefined by the economic administrators of the community; they protected the individual and family rights to a specific grove by reaffirming their traditional rights to collect there; they ensured equitable food distribution at times when a valuable crop was smaller than usual (Bean 1972:144).

In both the first salmon rites in the spring and the fall acorn feast, the Hupa asked the spirits that the people be satisfied with a little food (Goddard 1903:78–80), instilling moderation, and ultimately the conservation of the resource (Anderson et al. 1998:33). While particularly elaborate in the case of first-fruit ceremonies, such moral and spiritual procedures accompanied all stages of the food process.

PROCESSING AND STORAGE

Between gathering and cooking, most foods had to undergo some kind of processing—cleaning, shelling, cutting, gutting, boning, pounding, and the like. Many of the staple California foods, such as acorns and other nuts and seeds, could be preserved relatively easily because of their tough outer coats and a relatively dry environment (Chartkoff and Chartkoff 1984:228), but most foods were treated to make them suitable for long-term storage. The preservation and storage of food for later consumption was thus a fundamental part of Native Californian cuisines, as indeed it is for all cultures. In turn, the ability to store quantities of food over long periods is believed to have encouraged the development of social complexity in Native California

(Testart 1982). Before the invention of mechanical refrigeration, which has allowed a greater consumption of fresh foods all year round, American families also had to process their fresh foods. Most agricultural households expended a great deal of effort in food preservation, first by drying, salting, smoking, souring/fermenting, and pickling, and later by canning.

Some foods were eaten only fresh. The Hupa, for instance, ate plant shoots raw; salmon heads and tails were cooked only from freshly caught fish (Goddard 1903:31, 26). Some foods did not lend themselves to preservation. The Wintu considered bear meat too greasy to be dried, so it was eaten as soon as it was caught. Spring chinook salmon, which was considered to be too oily to be dried as soon as it was caught, was baked, and what was not eaten was then dried and made into flour; salmon caught later in the year was suitable for immediate drying (Du Bois 1935:11, 15, 16). Other foods were eaten only dried, and some could be prepared either way, such as Sierra Miwok salmon roe (Barrett and Gifford 1933:190). Animal foods, unlike many plants, were more often eaten fresh, but fish, shellfish, and meat were all dried for long-term storage.

The first stages in plant preparation were cleaning and sorting. Winnowing baskets and fingers were used to separate out stones, leaves, chaff, rotten or infested items, and other inedibles. Shelling was the next stage for items like nuts and seeds. Acorns were cracked with small hammer stones on stone anvils, or even with the teeth (Atsugewi, Garth 1953:138; Wintu, Du Bois 1935:18), and their thin papery skin removed with a knife and/or by rubbing. Heat was usually used to extract the nuts from green pine cones; after a frost pine cone bracts would open naturally, releasing most of the seeds. Wintu boiled sugar pine nuts to remove pitch, while the Sierra Miwok and Chukchansi Yokuts roasted them in the fire, and the Cahuilla baked them in a pit. The seeds were extracted by tapping or beating, perhaps parched, shelled with the teeth or a stone, and winnowed before further parching and/or pounding.[39]

For large game, the initial stage was skinning, followed by butchering. Some dressing of a deer, elk, or antelope occurred as soon as it was brought down, but other processing might wait until it was carried back to camp.[40] For "convenience in carrying home," Tolowa

North Fork Mono women winnowing acorn meal;
North Fork, Madera County, 1904–5.
PHOTOGRAPH BY NELLIE MCGRAW HEDGPETH (NEG. NO. 15–20954).

North Fork Mono winnowing basket (1–21698) and acorns (1–211619).
PHOTOGRAPH BY EUGENE PRINCE, HEARST MUSEUM.

usually partially jerked the meat of an elk where it was killed (Drucker 1937:234–35). Nisenan hunters might butcher and quarter a large deer at the kill site, but they preferred to bring an undrawn deer into camp, as it was easier to butcher in the evening when the flies and yellow jackets were gone (Wilson 1972:34). The principal tool for all animal processing was the knife. The Sierra Miwok used a sharp-edged piece of deer tibia bone to skin deer (Barrett and Gifford 1933:181), but the most common materials were obsidian, chert, and quartz. "In dressing and cleaning fish," the Hupa always used "ferns and leaves … to wipe away the blood and unclean portions" (Goddard 1903:26).

Often the hunters ate some part of the deer as soon as it was killed. After skinning and quartering a deer, Modoc hunters roasted and ate the liver and rib meat (Ray 1963:185), the Hupa drank the blood at once (Goddard 1903:22), and the Hupa and Kashaya Pomo roasted the ears, considered to be a delicacy (ibid.; Oswalt 1964:303). More often the organs consumed were the viscera, because of their greater susceptibility to rapid rotting. In a distinctive style of hunter's cuisine, the stomach was used as a cooking container. Among those employing this method were the Hupa, Atsugewi (lungs, liver, or one of the ribs cooked inside), Nisenan (entrails and blood), Southeastern Pomo (cleaned intestines, often with the liver, other organs, and strips of meat), Kashaya Pomo (blood), Sierra Miwok (cleaned entrails, windpipe, lungs, longitudinal pieces of flesh near the kidneys, and some blood). Most groups baked the stomach in the ashes, but the Atsugewi and Southeastern Pomo boiled it with hot rocks and water, with the former using the skin as the container.[41]

Large mammals, especially deer, were cut up and distributed according to prescribed rules. Most body parts were used, with some reserved for special relatives of the hunter. The Sierra Miwok distributed a deer's stomach to a companion of the hunter, especially an older man; its liver (considered a delicacy, and boiled) was given to some old woman, especially one who had given the hunter acorn mush; the sirloin was for the hunter's wife and mother-in-law, and was cooked for them by the hunter, his mother, or his grandmother; the fore and hind legs went to the hunter's relatives and neighbors; and the body was for his wife's relatives and his son- and daughter-in-law (Barrett and Gifford 1933:181). A Pomo deer hunter was "particularly careful to give an ample supply to his mother-in-law. If he were recently married he had to carry home the entire deer to his mother-in-law, and the animal was quartered in the house" (Loeb 1926:171). A Kechayi Yokuts chief received the deer's ham, considered the best part (Gayton 1948b:166). Other portions were not eaten at all (the deer breast bone for the Hupa) or were forbidden to certain groups (such as menstruating women).[42] Customs differed as to who divided and distributed the meat. Among the Nisenan, the first person to reach the deer had his choice of meat (Beals 1933:348), but for the Wintu, "The man who carved the meat was usually the leader of the hunt" (Du Bois 1935:10). An Atsugewi butcher cut up the deer while a chief distributed the meat (Garth 1953:132–33). Hunters often did not eat their own catch, especially a boy's first kill. As the Wintu hunter sliced up the deer, "he tossed pieces to his companions and, in his endeavor to appear generous, often found himself with the smallest portion" (Du Bois ibid.). Similarly, by the time a Sierra Miwok hunter was finished with his distribution, there was little meat left for him. But he was compensated with seed meal from others, and of course, he received deer meat as the relative and neighbor of other hunters (Barrett and Gifford ibid.). For most groups, it was important to distribute the meat equally: Among the Nisenan, large game was generally shared with the rest of the camp regardless of the killer while small game belonged to the killer (Beals 1933:348, 350), whereas the Sierra Miwok shared deer meat equally when it had been caught on a communal hunt, even if not all had killed a deer (Barrett and Gifford 1933:181). A Modoc "man took pleasure and pride in distributing meat to his neighbors, but only in the summer time and only when the meat was fresh" (Ray 1963:183). This strong ethic for sharing large game was adopted most likely because of the prey's importance in the diet and the relative difficulty of the capture. Whereas large game seems to have been commonly distributed in a raw state, plant foods seem to have been more often shared in a cooked form (see under Cooking).

Almost all foods needed some processing before storage: drying (sun, fire, smoke); parching, parboiling, and other forms of heating (especially for seeds); and mashing, pounding, or grinding into a meal, which was sometimes formed into cakes. The removal of water in many of these methods prevented the growth of molds and bacteria.

With few exceptions, salt was not used for preservation, and intentional rotting was used only occasionally.

Drying in sunlight or smoke or both was the major form of preservation. Most groups dried acorns before storage, the shell acting as a protection against further insect and mold infestation. As soon as the gathering season was over, the Hupa shelled and split acorns and stored them until cooking (Goddard 1903:27). Many other kinds of plants were sun-dried: The Tolowa used this method for seaweed cakes; the Tübatulabal for wild grapes (making raisins), boxthorn berries, and rush roots; the Owens Valley Paiute for berries; the Luiseño for peeled fruit of the prickly pear cactus, which was stored and then eaten without being cooked; and the Mohave for their crops of corn, beans, and muskmelons, as well as for wild plants.[43]

When fish or meat was not to be eaten fresh, it was cut up into thin strips and dried, often with smoking. In the northwest, fish-drying was started outside in the sun or in a small smokehouse and then finished on racks in the family house, for a total of eight to ten days. Tolowa cut up salmon and dried the body, backbone, head, and eggs separately (Drucker 1937:234). So ingrained was this mode of preparation that the Hupa, who lived in an inland valley, refused to eat seafood that had not been dried (Greengo 1952:77). Practically everywhere that fish was taken, it was dried: The Pomo and the Sierra Miwok dried them in the sun for about a week, or sometimes in a house over a fire (Loeb 1926:172; Barrett and Gifford 1933:140). As a distinctive Northwest Coast trait, smoking was most popular in California in the Klamath River area (Kroeber and Barrett 1960:99–103). Rostlund, pointing to the overlap between drying over fire and full-scale smoking, thinks the prevalence of fish smoking in this area may have been due to the greater precipitation in the region (1952:138). The Karuk liked to use rotted woods, especially alder, which flavored the fish (Kroeber and Barrett 1960:99). Fish, especially salmon, was the principal smoked food, but northwestern groups also gave this treatment to meats such as venison and even acorns.[44] The process for drying meat was much the same, with the procedure taking one to two weeks. Most groups dried long thin strips of deer meat in the sun. Lighting a fire under the meat hastened the action, smoked it slightly,

Yurok items for processing fish (clockwise from top): bowl for catching and storing fish oil (1–1637), sturgeon egg pounder (1–1967), salmon-scaling knife (1–1538), eel slitter (1–1862).

PHOTOGRAPH BY EUGENE PRINCE, HEARST MUSEUM.

and kept the flies away.[45] Dried fowl was less common, but the Sierra Miwok split and dried quail (Barrett and Gifford 1933:140). Although salt was rarely used as a preservative, the Pomo and Tübatulabal rubbed it on fish (Loeb 1926:172; Voegelin 1938:20). Although aware of the process, Mohave did not dry meat, most likely because they obtained so little of it that they ate it all while fresh (Stewart 1968:32).[46] Details on perishability are largely unknown, but the Chukchansi Yokuts could keep their sun-dried meat and fish for two or three months (Gayton 1948b:181), and Pomo dried meat or fish reportedly lasted for four or five months (Loeb 1926:173).

Some foods were heated and thus cooked to some extent before storage. They were then either eaten as they were or cooked further. Before being ground into flour, most seeds were parched: tossed in a basket or pottery tray with hot sand, coals, or ashes to toast the exterior. These flours were usually combined with water but might also be eaten dry.[47] Bulbs and roots were also heated before drying and storage. The Atsugewi and Sierra Miwok baked Indian potatoes and other bulbs in an earth oven. The Sierra Miwok then pulverized and cooked them as mush (Barrett and Gifford 1933:141). Among the Atsugewi the bulbs were mashed, made into cakes, and dried; they were soaked when used but not made into soup (Garth 1953:138). Cahuilla baked agave heads and leaves in pits for one to two days, and then dried and cut them into smaller portions. Prepared this way, they could be "preserved for years." They also sun-dried yucca blossoms and dried the stalks after they were baked; both were then stored (Bean 1972:41–42). Sierra Miwok steamed greens in an earth oven before drying (Barrett and Gifford 1933:139). Cahuilla parboiled agave and yucca blossoms. "The parboiling leached out the bitter taste which was present in the flower and facilitated preservation of the blossom by checking enzyme action" (Bean 1972:43, cf. 41, 42). Although acorns were leached before cooking, some plants had to be heated before leaching. Because of their bitter and poisonous alkaloids, buckeyes were baked, boiled, or steamed before leaching, which might take up to eighteen hours; thereafter they might be eaten in a soup with no further cooking.[48] The Wintu had several methods: Buckeyes were baked in a pit, then mashed and leached, and made into soup; the unshelled nuts were kept over winter in seepage pits; or they were stored unshelled and leached whole (Du Bois 1935:20).

If they were not simply dried, many kinds of animals were also heated before storage; for instance, most shellfish (Greengo 1952:77). The Atsugewi baked salmon in an earth oven before they were dried and crumbled (Garth 1953:136). Parching or some other form of heating was the principal method of preparing insects, which were often killed with smoke or heat. The Wintu caught grasshoppers after burning fields, so their wings were singed off and they were partly roasted (Du Bois 1935:14). If insects needed further cooking, they were commonly parched with hot coals before storage or cooking.[49] Maidu ate grasshoppers either dry and uncooked or slightly roasted (Dixon 1905:191). After the Wintu boiled and dried grasshoppers, they were either eaten at once or mashed in a hopper and stored (Du Bois 1935:14). Similarly, after roasting, drying, and storing cricket pupae and cicadas, Cahuilla ate them "without further preparation or as a condiment with other foods like acorn mush" (Bean 1972:62). Owens

Valley Paiute sun-dried pandora moth caterpillars for storage; they were boiled or baked for eating (Steward 1933:256).

Of all the forms of processing before the actual cooking, pulverization was the most common, especially for plants, but also at times for animals. This action had several benefits: It allowed the leaching of harmful substances, such as tannic acid in acorns; reduced food into powders and flours which could then be formed into cakes; promoted the break-down of nutrients in cooking; and made food easier to chew and digest. Native Americans used two basic kinds of crushing equipment: mortars, which are operated by pounding, and milling stones, which work in a grinding or rubbing motion.[50] In California there were three kinds of mortars, made of stone or wood: portable slab or block mortars, portable hollowed mortars, and bedrock hollowed mortars. While the great diversity of pestle types was partly an expression of tribal styles, these tools were also adapted to the amount and nature of material to be pounded. They ranged from natural, unworked river cobbles to large and finely ground and polished shapes. Californian pestles were always grasped with the hands and brought down into the mortar depression. In addition to the grinding tools, associated objects were brushes, hoppers, sifting trays, and storage baskets. When using a slab mortar (and sometimes other kinds as well), a basketry hopper was placed around the central depression to catch flying food particles. North of the San Francisco area these were twined cones without peaks (which were either cut off or woven that way), forming a bottomless collar; southern varieties were coiled, smaller, and often cemented to the mortar with pitch.

Many groups used several kinds of mortars, each adapted for different foods or materials: Cahuilla pounded acorns and dried berries in stone mortars with stone or wooden pestles, mashed softer foods like piñon nuts with stone manos and metates, and pulverized soft but fibrous foods like honey mesquite with wooden pestles and mortars (Bean 1972:52). While the North Fork Mono also used their mortars for acorns, they ground seeds in their metates (Gifford 1932:24). There were notable differences in acorn pounding throughout the state: Portable mortars were commonly used in the north and south, permanent bedrock mortars in the central part of the state.[51] Although they used them for mashing small animals and medicines, the historic Sierra Miwok made no portable mortars: "All in their possession have been found by them and are said to have been made by Coyote, a supernatural being, who scratched them out or made them sexually" (Barrett and Gifford 1933:209). We may assume that they were made by their ancestors or earlier inhabitants of their homeland. There is evidence that women deliberately manufactured bedrock mortars to specified types (Jackson 1991:307; Ortiz and Parker 1991:73). Because bedrock mortars were usually on one rock, the women of a village frequently pounded their acorns together rather than at home. Wooden mortars, a hole in the side of a log, were comparatively rare. They were most common among the Yokuts and other inhabitants of the flood plains of the Central Valley where stone was scarce. The mano/metate, a smaller grinding stone (flat or cylindrical) rolled against a flat slab, was more common in the south and may be related to the Mesoamerican maize complex.

Acorn pounding and sifting were done together until all the meal was of the proper fineness. Although each tribe and person had their own techniques, the Sierra Miwok procedure is representative (Barrett and Gifford 1933:143–44). A woman sat with her legs spread out in front of her on either side of the mortar. She placed a peck (eight quarts) or two of shelled acorns in the mortar depression, lifted the pestle with both hands to about eye level and let it fall. After every fifteen or twenty blows, the meal was rolled back into the depression. Periodically the meal was scooped out of the mortar and sifted. Californian groups sifted with a variety of baskets, flat or gently curving, but also shallow and conical. Some pounded meal was placed inside the basket, which was gently bounced or tapped. Because of their inherent oiliness, the finer grains of meal adhered to the crevices of the basket-weave, leaving the rougher grains to fall back into the mortar to be reground. Fingers, tappers, and brushes swept the finished meal into a storage basket. As it was impossible in the pounding process to produce meal of consistent fineness, a cook could use this stage to separate out the meal into coarser and finer particles, which could be cooked differently. The Wintu used a finer grain, like wheat flour, when making soup; a medium grain for a thicker mush; and the

Pomo mortar stone (1–2762),
basket hopper (1–3033), and pestle (1–19).
PHOTOGRAPH BY B. F. WHITE, HEARST MUSEUM (NEG. NO. 15–4042).

coarser, cornmeal-like grains for dark bread (Du Bois 1935:19). This method of tossing in a basket was the primary Native Californian form of mechanical separation of food ingredients.

Pounding was applied to many kinds of plants. Several groups made nut butter. The Sierra Miwok version, called *lopa*, was made from roasted sugar-pine nuts. The shells and meat were pulverized in a mortar until they had the consistency of peanut butter. A special treat for feasts, lopa was eaten with the fingers along with acorn soup or manzanita cider (Barrett and Gifford 1933:151).[52] A related procedure was mashing. The Sierra Miwok, for instance, mashed Eulophus bulbs, which were then dried and stored in baskets; when needed they were pounded again and boiled (Barrett and Gifford 1933:157). Some pulverized materials yielded a gelatinous texture. The Nisenan dried and pounded one cloverlike grass into a powder. When cooked with water and cooled, it became a clear green gelatin, regarded as a "favorite" (Wilson 1972:37).

This preference for pulverization was also applied to meat and fish, resulting in either a meal or a pulpy mass, depending on the moisture content. Maidu pounded dried salmon into a coarse flour, which was stored in baskets and eaten dry (Dixon 1905:191). Although the Klamath River peoples made salmon flour, it was not as common a practice there as it was in northeastern California; it seems to have spread to California from the Plateau region to the north (Kroeber and Barrett 1960:100, 102).[53] The Wintu made salmon flour from spring-run chinook salmon. After the fresh fish was baked, it was boned and flaked, and pulverized as it dried out. The heads, guts, tails, and bones of later-run salmon were also dried and pulverized. Dried roe and pine nuts were mixed with the salmon flour, a valuable article of trade for McCloud Wintu (Du Bois 1935:15–16).[54] Wintu stored their salmon flour in maple-leaf-lined baskets. The Atsugewi preserved fish eggs by drying (Garth 1953:136), while the Nisenan dried whole mice and rats and pounded them into a meal (Wilson 1972:36). One motive for pounding up animal flesh was preservation: The Luiseño ground cooked deer and rabbit meat before storage (Sparkman 1908:197–98), while the Pomo added salt to their pounded-up quail meat (Loeb 1926:165). An even more common reason for grinding meat was to enable old people and others with bad teeth to eat these foods more easily.[55] Some groups, such as the Pomo, singed and eviscerated small mammals, then ground them to a pulp—meat, skin, and bones—before broiling them (Barrett 1952:63).

Before cooking, some foods had to undergo further preparation to change their chemical composition. Plants such as acorns and buckeyes, which contain noxious substances (tannic acid and alkaloids, respectively), were subjected to continuous leaching in water. A Sierra Miwok method for acorns is representative (Barrett and Gifford 1933:145–46). Most commonly done in a sandy spot, a shallow basin about three to four feet in diameter was scooped out, meal placed in it, and water poured over the flour until the tannins had been soaked out. To break the fall of the water and spread it evenly over the meal, the liquid was poured over green conifer branches. An even flow was sometimes encouraged by making radial furrows in the moist meal with a finger. Sierra Miwok might make an artificial basin of boughs, lined with fine grass and a layer of sand. The first several baths were cold water, but then came increasingly hotter water, for a total of about ten soakings. While hot water leaches out the tannins faster it also dissolves some of the fats and other nutrients (Alvarez and Peri 1987:12). A woman would taste the acorn flour after each water bath to determine when it had lost its bitterness.[56] Sierra Miwok also tested by observing the color of the meal; leaching was often complete when it turned from yellow or brown to whitish. After it had drained thoroughly, the leached meal was removed by spreading an outstretched hand over the meal, which adhered to the skin. If the cook had not used the sifting stage for separating out the grains, she could do it now. A Chukchansi Yokuts woman lifted off the leached acorn meal in layers, reserving the finest for the men to eat at once and the coarser meal for general use (Gayton 1948b:178–79). Leaching in a sandy depression was characteristic of the northwestern and most of the central part of the state. Baskets were used in some of the central and southern regions; the Ohlone, Sierra Miwok, Luiseño, and Cahuilla employed both methods (Gifford 1936:89). One unusual form, apparently invented independently, was restricted to the Shasta and the Chukchansi Yokuts. The acorn meal was leached in a sand basin placed over a layer of pine boughs, but this then rested on a platform of sticks raised six to thirty inches above the ground (Spier 1956).

Instead of leaching, some kinds of nuts were intentionally rotted, usually by burying in the ground. "The Hupa used to bury acorns unshelled in the damp ground and let them remain until they were well molded. They were then boiled without being ground" (Goddard 1903:29). The Wintu had at least three kinds of rotted acorn preparations. For valley-oak bread, the acorns were molded in water ("the moldier, the more tasty the bread was considered") and then pounded into flour. From rotted black oak acorns they made a relish. The acorns were allowed to mold, soaked with pine needles for a week or two until sweet, and then boiled. Live-oak acorns were "stored in water-soaked pits for six to eight months, then boiled in the shell, shelled and eaten whole; they were said 'to taste like pound cake' " (Du Bois 1935:19, 20). While acorns were perhaps the most commonly rotted food, other plants were given the same treatment. Wintu made a soup out of buckeyes that had rotted over the winter (1935:20). The Maidu buried the fruit of wild nutmeg that had been cracked and shelled. After several months in the ground, the nuts were dug up and roasted in the ashes (Dixon 1905:188). The Mohave buried screwbeans in a pit for about a month so they would became "sweet," then dried, ground, and mixed them with water for a drink (Stewart 1968:31).

Despite their understanding of the rotting process, Native Californians had no fermented beverages. Manzanita cider, their most popular beverage other than water, was always drunk fresh. The berries were picked red and dry, winnowed and cleaned, pulverized, placed on a frame or in a sieve basket, drenched (sometimes repeatedly) in water poured through into a catch basket, and were then ready for drinking.[57] This sweet drink was particularly popular in the summer. The Wintu pounded, dampened and dried the berries; this was then made into a flour that was parched and winnowed. Fine flour was mixed with water and made into a sweetish soup; the coarser flour, consisting mostly of seeds, was soaked for a cider. Sometimes the Maidu roasted the berries in order to produce a darker liquid with a slightly different flavor. Sierra Miwok cider would keep two to four days before souring (Barrett and Gifford 1933:162). After European contact, however, manzanita cider was allowed to ferment. Around 1905 the Maidu were straining and bottling it for its "mildly intoxicating" effect, while the Nisenan were making a vinegar out of it (Dixon 1905:190; Beals 1933:352).

Once pulverized or mashed, many foods were stored in the form of dried cakes or balls, which later could be moistened and heated. In addition to having a long "shelf life," cakes were a concentrated and efficient form of food preservation. They were especially common for oily seeds, which could be formed into loaves without cooking or the addition of water (Pomo, Barrett 1952:62). The Cahuilla and the Mohave made mesquite flour cakes (Bean 1972:53; Stewart 1968:31).

The Cahuilla patted the flour into cakes about a foot in diameter and several inches thick and sun-dried them. For consumption, they were rehydrated and boiled into a mush. Berries were another popular cake ingredient. Maidu berry cakes (with seeds or roots) were dried or baked, then soaked and made into soup (Dixon 1905:189). The Yokuts dried blackberries, which were then pounded, mixed with water into a paste, and then dried in the form of a cake; the cake was made into jam by pounding and boiling it with water (Latta 1949:123). Atsugewi made cakes from camas (*Camassia quamash*) roots baked in an earth oven. The roots were mashed and formed into cakes ranging from a foot in diameter to small biscuits (Garth 1953:138). Coastal peoples made cakes from seaweeds and fish roe; interior peoples such as the Sierra Miwok made cakes from salmon roe.

Acorn processing was a fairly labor-intensive operation. In the winter, during sunny weather, Nisenan women pounded acorns all day (Beals 1933:351). Chukchansi Yokuts women spent almost a day pounding half a flour sack of acorn meal (holding perhaps 50 pounds), enough to feed an "average family" for two or three days (Gayton 1948b:178). One Hupa woman observed in 1937 took three hours to pound and winnow six pounds of shelled acorns, yielding five pounds, six ounces of meal. Taking 65 percent of the original amount (three pounds, eight ounces), she leached it for two hours, thirty-four minutes, yielding five pounds, four ounces of meal (Goldschmidt 1974:311–13). In 1929 Beals observed a Nisenan woman leaching acorn over a period of three hours (1933:351); Tübatulabal leaching could take about half a day, depending on the kind of acorn (Voegelin 1938:18).

The frequency of pounding and leaching is uncertain. The Nisenan custom may have been typical: "Acorns were shelled only when needed and then only enough for a few days. Usually they were ground the same day.... The cooking was the same day, if possible, and enough soup and bread prepared to last for several days. No one minded eating it cold, and at some meals this was all that was available" (Wilson 1972:37). We know that the Atsugewi stored leached acorn meal until needed (Garth 1953:138), and that Chukchansi Yokuts kept acorn flour (in baskets) for some time, which was cooked as needed (Gayton 1948b:179). Unlike parched seeds and other foods, acorns were not stored for long periods as ground meal.[58] This may have been because of a higher degree of moisture and fat in acorns, or simply because California Indians preferred to consume their staple in a fresh state.[59] The baked breads were the form that lasted the longest.

Food storage was the foundation for all Native Californian societies. It has been estimated that a Wukchumni Yokut family consumed from 1000 to 2000 pounds of acorns a year (Latta 1949:105), and that a Nisenan family would normally need about 500 to 600 pounds of acorns (ten to twelve 50-pound sacks) to last them through a winter (Wilson 1972:36). As most oaks do not bear equally every year, many groups tried to gather enough acorns for at least two years (Heizer and Elsasser 1980:99). The Nisenan gathered as many acorns as possible; any surplus was used for trading, shared with old people, or consumed at festivals (Wilson 1972:36). Given the vagaries of climate and food supply, a surplus could also cover a shortfall in the annual harvest.

Foods, both before and after processing, were stored in large containers, either outside the home in caches or granaries or inside in baskets and pots (Kroeber 1925:828–29). Baskets were popular in the north. For instance, after hanging salmon to dry from the rafters, the Yurok stored the fish in large baskets, with laurel leaves to keep insects away and flavor the fish (Kroeber and Barrett 1960:99); the Pomo also stored dried fish in large baskets kept inside the house (Loeb 1926:172). Southern groups such as the Cahuilla stored seeds and other foods in large clay pots, up to four feet high and two feet wide, and hermetically sealed with pine pitch or beeswax (Bean 1972:54, 53). In addition to foods such as seeds, acorns, dried fish and meat, interior storage containers also held other domestic goods.[60] These large food containers were a clear sign of their owner's industry in gathering. The southern tribes stored large quantities of food in granaries loosely constructed out of interlaced twigs.[61] Somewhat similar was the central Californian type popular among the Wintu, Maidu, Pomo, Sierra Miwok, and Yokuts, and in modified form among the Western Mono. This was smaller, higher, constructed of finer and softer materials, and supported and elevated by a series of posts. One

*Sierra Miwok acorn granaries; Railroad Flat,
Calaveras County, October 1906.*
PHOTOGRAPH BY SAMUEL A. BARRETT (NEG. NO. 15–2750).

Sierra Miwok example measured twelve feet high and five feet in diameter (Barrett and Gifford 1933:207–8). Ranging in capacity from
94 to 196 cubic feet (Heizer and Elsasser 1980:99), Miwok granaries
could hold up to 500 pounds of dry acorns (Bates 1983:25). These
water-tight structures were big enough for a family's entire winter
store of acorns; a chief, who was expected to distribute food to those
in his village, had several. Large granaries stood near each Cahuilla
household and ceremonial house. "A single acorn granary, for instance, might hold several bushels of acorns; a single olla might hold
several quarts of seeds . . ." (Bean 1972:54). Sometimes food was kept
in associated store houses. The Tübatulabal kept large baskets of food
(dried meat, fish, seeds, pine nuts, acorns) in large store houses near
the family house (Voegelin 1938:20), and the Atsugewi stored shelled
acorns in baskets in the cookhouse (Garth 1953:138). In the northern
and eastern regions, pits appear to have been more popular than
raised caches (Driver and Massey 1957:247). These pits usually had a

lining such as bark (Wintu, Du Bois 1935:18) or grass (Owens Valley Paiute, Steward 1933:239). Combining methods, the Karuk preferred to store dried fish in a pit at the back of the house, where it would keep better than in large baskets on house ledges (Kroeber and Barrett 1960:100).

These food stores, normally owned by the family, were tempting targets for theft in many groups. The Modoc took great care in hiding their food pits from neighbors, retrieving the food at night and disguising it as loads of wood. "If the thief was apprehended a great altercation resulted but the object was the recovery of the food, not punishment for a wrong" (Ray 1963:183). Among the Atsugewi, "Small thefts of food might be excused on the ground that the thief was in need of it. But if a large amount was stolen, it had to be returned or paid for with beads or other valuables" (Garth 1953:179). Cahuilla also had secret caches outside the village, sometimes in buried or hidden ollas. Travelers could take some if they found it but later they had to replace what they removed (Bean 1972:54). As we shall see (in the section on Eating), while Native Californians believed strongly in food-sharing, there were limits. Substantial amounts of food should be freely offered, not taken without permission.

Distinct storage sites were only one of the places dedicated to the food process (storage, cooking, eating, and waste disposal). Although there is little detailed information on the equivalents to our pantries, kitchens, dining rooms, and garbage bins, these places were related to Native Californians' movement in space over the yearly cycle—most people had a series of seasonal dwellings; the summer ones usually being more ephemeral. Most processing seems to have been conducted near the village. Bedrock mortars, often some distance from home, were often covered with wood or brush sun shelters.[62] Many groups, the Cahuilla for example, kept mortars and pestles at acorn sites and then transferred the acorn flour back to the village (Bean 1972:37). Acorn leaching was most often carried out on a nearby river or lake bank, both because of the substantial amounts of water needed and because of the fine sand desired for a substrate. The Hupa, who usually leached acorn on sand near the river, performed it inside the house during the winter (Goddard 1903:28).

The gender of the processor often followed that of the gatherer—men for animals and women for plants. However, either men or women could prepare animal foods, depending on the society and the animal. Among the northern groups, for which we have information, the men usually butchered large game in the woods and then packed it home; women were usually forbidden this work due to menstrual taboos (Willoughby 1963:16). For example, Modoc men "did the skinning and major butchering of large game but women assisted by cutting the meat in the manner customary for drying, storage, or immediate use. Women performed all these operations for small animals" (Ray 1963:190). As in many groups, Cahuilla men did the hunting, butchering, and skinning of animals, but women cooked them. Tasks were often performed collaboratively. Many peoples made the repetitive task of shelling acorns into a social event. Among the Foothill Yokuts, "acorn-shelling was a favorite evening occupation while some old person would tell stories" (Gayton 1948b:223; cf. Wintu, Du Bois 1935:18). Among the Atsugewi, "young people had contests to see who could shell ten acorns the fastest" (Garth 1953:136). Given the lengthy processing necessary for acorns, it is not surprising that many groups adopted a method of collaborative labor. Western Mono women shared the chores of acorn pounding at the communal bedrock mortars, "with some women making the initial coarse meal (in 'starter' mortars) and others preparing the finished flour (in 'finishing' mortars)" (Jackson 1991:315). The younger women of Wintu families pounded acorns while the older women sifted (Du Bois 1935:19), probably in deference to the great degree of skill that sifting entails (Parker and Ortiz 1991:85). Other than hunters in the field (and even then not often), it was rare that anyone was alone when preparing food.

Like all phases of the food process, preparation was always more than mere mechanics:

> The Kashaya Pomo observed certain rules when the [acorn] grinder and others were at work. It was believed that grinding should be done under a brush shelter or else it would bring rain; the booming noise made by the pestle was associated with thunder,

the first sign of rain. She also never drank water while working lest the meal lose its taste. It was also believed that children standing behind her would cause her to become tired more quickly and no love songs could be sung while grinding, lest the pestle break (Alvarez and Peri 1987:12).

On the other hand, songs were a common accompaniment for acorn pounding. Like all work songs, they undoubtedly coordinated the repetitive motions and made the labor more pleasant.[63] Although it was work, for many women food preparation chores like pounding acorn could be a time of talking, teasing, and laughter (Ortiz and Parker 1991:34).

COOKING

As Claude Lévi-Strauss has argued, cooking—the preparation of food by the use of heat, as in boiling, baking, or roasting—transforms food from a natural to a cultural state. As only humans cook their food, many Indian myths emphasize the invention of the technology of fire as creating our human state of affairs.[64] In a famous essay, Lévi-Strauss analyzed cooking methods according to a "culinary triangle":

> Food presents itself to man in three main states: it may be raw, cooked or rotten. In relationship to culinary operations, the raw state constitutes the unmarked pole, whereas the other two are strongly marked, although in opposite directions: the cooked being a cultural transformation of the raw, and the rotten its natural transformation. Underlying the main triangle, there is, then, a double opposition between *processed/non-processed*, on the one hand, and *culture/nature*, on the other (1968:478).

Within the realm of the cooked, Lévi-Strauss delineates another triangle, between the roasted, boiled, and smoked: "… On two counts, the roast can be placed on the side of nature, and the boiled on the side of culture. Literally, since boiled food necessitates the use of a receptacle, which is a cultural object; and symbolically, in the sense that culture mediates between man and the world, and boiling is also a mediation, by means of water, between the food which man ingests and that other element of the physical world: fire" (1968:480). Smoking, the third term, is like roasting, as it "implies a non-mediatized operation (involving neither a receptacle nor water), but which, unlike roasting but in the manner of boiling, is a slow form of cooking, and so both thorough and steady" (1968:487). As he goes on to note, every culture will define these terms in its own way.[65] Whatever its details, the value of this structural analysis is that it focuses attention, in an informed cultural way, on the actual form and practice of cooking.

While rotting and fermentation were relatively uncommon in Native California,[66] some foods were eaten raw. Still, as Lévi-Strauss points out, there is no "pure state of the raw: only certain foodstuffs can be eaten raw, and even then only after having been washed, peeled, cut up, and frequently seasoned" (1978:478). Shellfish, particularly sea urchins, were often consumed uncooked (Greengo 1952:76–77). We know little about the doneness of cooked meats; Wintu hunters were accused by some women of undercooking deer (see below), and the Tübatulabal liked their meat "half done," never raw (Voegelin 1938:13). As in many cuisines, raw foods were mostly parts of plants such as shoots and leaves, berries and nuts, especially in the spring when many plants sent up new growth. Throughout the state, the favorite raw green was often some variety of clover.[67] Other raw leaves were miner's lettuce, wild spinach, and grasses (Wintu); wild pea (Maidu); fiddle-necks (Tübatulabal). Wintu peeled the stems of Indian rhubarb, which they ate raw, like celery; salt grass stems were also eaten by the Tübatulabal. Raw bulbs included wild onion (Pomo, Tübatulabal, Owens Valley Paiute), wild garlic (Tübatulabal), and tule roots (Tübatulabal). The Pomo ate raw mushrooms and a kind of radish. Berries needed no cooking to be appreciated. Both the Chukchansi Yokuts and Tübatulabal ate raw wild grapes, thimble and goose berries. The Luiseño prepared a mush of ground aromatic sumac and manzanita berries; it was not parched or cooked, just ground and mixed with water. Some nuts could be eaten raw: The Hupa, Chukchansi Yokuts, and Tübatulabal ate raw pine nuts, and the Hupa also ate raw hazelnuts.[68] Some plants were eaten both raw and cooked. The Owens Valley Paiute ate brodiaea bulbs (grassnut or blue dicks) raw when they were fresh, but most were dried and stored, roasted and ground into flour (Steward 1933:245). In addition to eating raw clover leaves, the Atsugewi baked the roots (Garth 1953:139), and the Nisenan dried, powdered, and baked the leaves (Wilson 1972:38).

As we have noted, dried foods might be eaten as is or further cooked. Some dried foods were soaked in water and boiled: most dried shellfish (Greengo 1952:77), small fish by the Wintu (Du Bois 1935:18), dried salmon roe by the Sierra Miwok (soaked overnight, boiled for an hour, and eaten with salt) (Barrett and Gifford 1933:190), Cahuilla meat jerky (which was also eaten plain) (Bean 1972:66). But most dried food seems to have been eaten uncooked. While the Hupa sometimes broiled dried salmon, it was "often eaten without cooking" (Goddard 1903:26); Klamath River peoples usually ate dried fish by breaking off a piece from the slab (Kroeber and Barrett 1960:100). One of the most common uncooked foods were the dry flours. Those made from seeds had usually been parched before grinding: Hupa (Goddard 1903:31), Maidu (a mixture of sweet-birch and wild oat seeds) (Dixon 1905:189), Owens Valley Paiute (Steward 1933:239). Some berry flours were also eaten uncooked: Hupa manzanita-berry flour (Goddard ibid.), Wintu skunk-bush berries (dry or with water stirred in, but not cooked) (Du Bois 1935:20). The Wintu also ate a mixture of salmon flour, dried salmon eggs, and pine nuts (Du Bois 1935:21). Finally, insects were often eaten simply dried and ground.

For our purposes, cooking methods may be classified according to the medium (air, water, or oil), the temperature and speed (fast or slow), and whether the food is enclosed in an oven or in the open. In addition to the less intense forms of drying and smoking, the various techniques of applying heat include the wet methods of simmering (85–88° C), boiling (100° C), and steaming (100+° C); and the dry techniques of broiling/grilling (150–200° C), frying (up to 205° C), roasting/baking (150–250° C), parching (550–625° C).[69] As one can see, the dry methods are also hotter than the wet, since one generally cannot get a wet food hotter than 100° C (boiling) unless one uses steam in a pressure cooker (Reid 1990:9). These methods also differ according to their closeness to the fire: over (broiling), in coals (roasting), and enclosed in a pit oven (baking). Native Californians used

Mrs. Jim Marks (Yurok) cooking dried smelt; near mouth
of Redwood Creek, Humboldt County, 1928.
PHOTOGRAPH BY THOMAS T. WATERMAN (NEG. NO. 15–11473).

most of the methods, but parching was employed more often in preliminary preparation and frying was rare in aboriginal times (probably due to the lack of suitable containers).[70] It appears that most
groups cooked with all three of the principal forms: boiling,
grilling/roasting, and baking. We have very little evidence on how
Native Californians themselves classified their foods and cooking
methods, but the Central Sierra Miwok made the following distinctions
in cooking techniques: "*tcusu*, to boil with hot stones in a basket; *yatce*,
to parch in a basket; *ulu*, to cook with steam in the earth oven, without a fire built on top; *hupu*, to cook in hot coals or ashes; *hina*, to broil
on hot coals, as a salmon" (Barrett and Gifford 1933:138).[71]

Native Californian cooking techniques were multiple and diverse.
As in most cuisines, a given food could often be cooked in different

manners. For instance, Sierra Miwok usually boiled greens in a basket, but they also steamed them in an earth oven, and ate some raw (Barrett and Gifford 1933:141, 158); the Owens Valley Paiute consumed pine nuts boiled and eaten whole, as dry flour, in a flour-water paste, or as a soup or mush (Steward 1933:242). On the other hand, certain foods were usually cooked by particular methods—deer was roasted more often than it was baked or boiled, and rabbits were broiled more often than baked. The favorite style for cooking the soft earthworm seems to have been boiling in a soup (Maidu, Pomo, Chukchansi), but Nisenan roasted them in a basketry tray (Beals 1933:346).[72] More particularly, certain parts were probably cooked in a certain way.

The Tübatulabal had an interesting approach to cooking which, while not universal in Native California, was common with many other groups:

> [The] general pattern of native cookery, which resulted in economy of effort, was to apply heat only once to any variety of food intended to be eaten in cooked state. Thus small seeds which had already been parched, and previously roasted piñons, after they were ground into meal, were merely mixed with cold water when made up into gruel (u'u·gil); neither seeds nor piñon meal recooked by stone boiling (or any other method), parched foods being regarded as "already cooked." … Same applies now to parched corn or wheat into flour … (Voegelin 1938:17–18).

The main method of cooking fish and meat was by dry heat. In broiling, which seems to have been reserved for relatively small and flat pieces, the flesh was held out on spits over an open fire. The Karuk and Yurok skewered fresh salmon on willow sticks, which were set into the ground facing the fire and periodically rotated until the fish was done. They also constructed elevated grills: Salmon heads were broiled slowly on a stick rack three feet over the coals (Kroeber and Barrett 1960:104–5, cf. Ortiz 1999:18).

However, an even more popular method of meat cooking was roasting directly in coals, ashes, and hot rocks. The degree of heat required could be moderated depending on the medium chosen, with ashes giving the coolest heat and rocks the most. Perhaps because of the fine medium, when cooking in ashes, a kind of wrapping was sometimes used. The Tübatulabal tied together four large fish, which were then wrapped in branches of odorless willow and cooked in ashes at the fishing place; they were carried home in the willow wrapping (Voegelin 1938:14), and Pomo used ashes to bake grass-wrapped eggs (Loeb 1926:165). On the other hand, the Nisenan "did not mind the charcoal that stuck to the meat and rarely brushed it off" (Wilson 1972:36). Plants were also roasted in ashes. After the Sierra Miwok roasted the bulbs of the white mariposa lily for about twenty minutes in the ashes of a fire that had died down, they were soft like boiled potatoes (Barrett and Gifford 1933:157), and the Hupa roasted peppernuts in ashes (Goddard 1903:29). Coals were the most direct method of meat-cooking. Maidu threw meat right on the coals, usually without the use of sticks (Dixon 1905:191). While many groups, such as the Hupa (Goddard 1903:23), cooked strips of deer meat in the coals, others, such as the Luiseño (Sparkman 1908:199), used this method to broil small animals (rats, mice, quail, and squirrels). Sometimes food was cooked directly on hot rocks. The Wintu placed uncleaned small fish (trout, whitefish) on hot rocks, preferably slate slabs, and covered them with more hot rocks; when cooked they were scraped loose and eaten (Du Bois 1935:17).

Often, ashes, coals, and rocks were combined. The Wintu pounded slices from a deer ham with a pestle, dampened them with water, and wrapped them around a clean hot rock. The package was laid in hot coals with the folded edges down and covered with the coals. When "dry and nice," it was removed, water sprinkled on the edges to make them unfold, and the rock removed (Du Bois 1935:10). In a kind of baking, the Sierra Miwok covered a deer stomach with damp earth, ashes, and coals, and cooked it under a slow fire for two hours (Barrett and Gifford 1933:181). In a related technique, shellfish were often baked by embedding in hot sand (Greengo 1952:81).[73] We have few reports on subtleties in cooking methods, but we know that when roasting meat swelled during cooking on coals, the Chukchansi Yokuts punctured it with sharp sticks "to let the steam out so it won't burst" (Gayton 1948b:180). Although Native Californians do not seem to have fried foods in a quantity of hot fat, frying (sautéing) did occur when cooking a slab of fatty meat on a heated stone.

Small mammals, birds, fish, and reptiles were often roasted whole in the coals, sometimes with hot coals placed in the belly to make the cooking more rapid and even.[74] When cooking a small animal something was often done to moderate the heat, either leaving the skin on or sewing up the belly with a stick or both.[75] Some groups practiced a special form of roasting—a kind of clay pot cooking resembling the Chinese "beggar's chicken." The Nisenan gutted a rabbit or waterfowl and sewed the body cavity shut with sticks. The animal, often with its skin still on, was then coated with mud. After cooking, the mud was cracked and the skin or feathers pulled away, resulting in a very white meat (Wilson 1972:36). The Cahuilla molded thick, soft clay around whole small animals, such as quail and rabbits, and cooked the package in coals. "After roasting in the fire, the clay container was broken open and the meat neatly removed" (Bean 1972:65).

A related form of container cooking was heating in a gut or paunch (see also under Processing). Making a kind of "sausage," the Atsugewi stuffed wildcat intestines with its blood and fat and cooked it in hot ashes (Garth 1953:133–34). Both they and the Wintu used the same approach in cooking with a deer paunch. After cleaning the paunch and filling it with blood and chunks of fat, the Wintu roasted it, very slowly after it began to shrivel, in hot ashes. Believing that to point at it would make it burst, they sent the children away during the roasting. After it was cooked through, it was cut into pieces and eaten. The guts were straightened and untangled while still warm, cleaned, and eaten first; the meat was eaten off the sinews (Du Bois 1935:10).

Small mammals might frequently be pounded, before and/or after cooking. The Wintu singed off the hair of rabbits and other small game and removed the entrails. For rabbits, they removed the larger bones, pounded the carcass with a flat rock, and roasted it on coals.[76] The meat was then put in a hopper mortar and pounded into a "doughy mass" which was rolled into balls and distributed (Du Bois 1935:13). For other small mammals they cut off the paws and tail before roasting the carcass. With the hide left on or removed, the head was cut off and the ribs and large bones taken out. The body was then pounded, bones and all, until it was fine and crumbly; sometimes the pounding was done before the roasting (1935:14). The Mohave also broiled rabbits, which they then pounded and roasted. They found this to be "good eating. Some people liked the bones better than the meat" (Stewart 1968:36).

When longer and more intense heat was necessary, Native Californians employed a pit or earth oven.[77] This method, the most elaborate for cooking animals, has not been given the study it deserves partly because it is ephemeral and the artifact cannot be collected. There are a great number of variables in earth oven or pit cooking. The pits could be relatively shallow or deep, open or covered, dry or wet (thus roasting/baking or steaming), rock-lined or not, with a fire on the bottom only or on top and bottom. The length of time the pit was sealed and the food cooked would probably vary according to the amount and density of the ingredients. As cooking often took about twelve hours, the sealed oven was commonly left overnight. Once the pit was closed, the cook could not make any adjustments, but he or she could regulate a secondary fire on the top, if that method was being used. The food was usually wrapped in leaves, which served many functions; they kept the food intact and clean, insulated it against heat loss, and imparted flavors.[78]

We can take the Sierra Miwok pit oven as an example (Barrett and Gifford 1933:200). The pit, twelve to eighteen inches deep and a foot or more across, was excavated and lined with hot rocks. Next came a layer of green leaves, a thin layer of food, another layer of leaves, then stones, leaves, food, and so on until the pit was filled. Finally a layer of soil was placed on top and often a fire lit on top. The sealed oven was left overnight, sometimes for twenty-four hours. "This oven, with the heated stones interspersed so as to evenly distribute the heat, would remain at a reasonable temperature for many hours, and the food would be hot and delicious almost any time during the following day" (1933:139). The Sierra Miwok used a similar method for cooking grasshoppers, but the food was baked for less than half a day, and several families cooked together, their portions being segregated by tule partitions (1933:191). Still, each group had its own approach to pit cooking.[79] The Atsugewi made a careful use of rocks when cooking small animals in pit ovens. After lining the pit with pine needles, a relatively large heated rock was placed inside the animal with smaller rocks around the limbs. The package was bound in a bunch and a flat heated rock set on top (Garth 1935:134). The Wintu used pits for baking salmon, but not for venison (Du Bois 1935:15), while the Tübatulabal used them for baking deer heads (Voegelin 1938:13).

The pit oven was also used to cook plants, especially roots, bulbs, and other dense ingredients. Among northern groups, the pit oven was used to bake soaproot bulbs (Hupa), brodiaea bulbs (Atsugewi), Indian potatoes and buckeyes (Pomo), bulbs and greens (Sierra Miwok), as well as acorn bread (see below). In the south, pit ovens were used for agave (Tübatulabal, Cahuilla), yucca (Cahuilla, Luiseño), opuntia buds (Tübatulabal), and tule potatoes (Cahuilla). While the Sierra Miwok method for cooking brodiaea bulbs resembles other uses of the earth oven, the distinctive feature was the water that was poured around the edges, allowing the bulbs to steam for about an hour (Barrett and Gifford 1933:156).[80]

Ortiz has given us a good description of a contemporary Kashaya Pomo practice (1989). The cook, the late Wayne Marufo, dug a pit, preferably in clay which will bake hard and retain the heat. He burned wood into coals, which were covered with a layer of soil to keep the meat from burning. Wrapped successively in aluminum foil, butcher paper, and soaked burlap (in place of leaves), the food was placed in the pit and covered with a layer of soil. Another fire was built over it and left for more than eleven hours. While Mr. Marufo had two fires, he did not use any rocks in the pit. Ortiz also describes an innovative Sierra Miwok method which employs a brick lining, metal mesh, and a single fire.

Boiling was perhaps the most common method of cooking plants, particularly the signature Californian dish—acorn mush. Native Californians practiced both forms of American Indian boiling: direct, in clay or stone pots placed over a fire, and stone boiling, by placing hot rocks in water-tight baskets (Driver and Massey 1957:229–33). Stone boiling was the principal method used along the Pacific Coast and adjacent region. Both methods require a container, and for this reason Lévi-Strauss maintained that boiling was closer to culture than roasting (1978:480).[81] Generally Californian cooking did not call for an elaborate set of pots, pans, and utensils—a *batterie de cuisine*—but boiling was, without doubt, the cooking method that involved the greatest use of objects. While Californian baskets tended to be generalized in form and multi-purpose, those for boiling may be recognized by their characteristic shape: a wide mouth and straight or slightly tapering sides to allow easy access for stirring. The size varied depending on the quantity to be cooked, but the average cooking basket measured about twelve to eighteen inches across.[82] As with all basketry, techniques varied regionally; twined baskets in the north and central area overlapped with coiled baskets that ranged from the south, where they were most common, into the north. Boiling baskets of the Klamath River region usually contained an extra reinforcing rod around the middle; the bottom often took the shape of an inverted cone which helped the stirred rocks to roll to the sides. The fibers of cooking baskets, twined as well as coiled, were closely woven and swelled up when soaked, thus closing any gaps between the strands. In addition, just as cooks will season an iron skillet before cooking, so, too, boiling baskets (especially when new) were often coated with some thin acorn gruel to help make them water-tight.[83]

Although at first glance clay pots may seem superior to baskets, each has its own advantages. While pots are easier to use, baskets are less breakable, lighter, and more transportable. Stone boiling is actually a faster cooking method if enough stones are used, as more of the hot surface area is in contact with the food. Native Californians are not usually known for their pottery, but ceramics were present, distributed in two separate complexes: one in the east-central part of the state (Yokuts, Western Mono, Tübatulabal, Owens Valley Paiute) and a more elaborate tradition in the south (Cahuilla, some Chemehuevi, Luiseño, Juaneno, Cupeño, Mohave, Kumeyaay) (Rogers 1936; cf. Mack 1990). Pottery has been associated with farming societies, as most of the southern group were, but it is not limited to them. Compared to other pottery-using peoples the Mohave had an especially wide range of pots (for water jars, cooking pots, cups, bowls, dippers), taking the place of basketry forms in other cultures (Kroeber and Harner 1955). Californians also used several other less widely-distributed container forms. Several groups cooked in stone bowls: The Chumash peoples used large hollowed-out soapstone pots, while the Yokuts and North Fork Mono had smaller steatite bowls.[84] Many groups also used a deer stomach as a container, although it was usually restricted to hunting trips and was obviously not reusable (see Processing).

In addition to the container, boiling required just a few other implements. Most critical were the rocks, but only certain varieties were suitable for boiling. The Wintu, for example, chose smooth round rocks, about the size of tennis balls. Women were always on the lookout for suitable rocks, which they saved from one occasion to another. Four or five were placed in a basket and stirred with a paddle; after cooking, the rocks were removed and wiped off with the index finger (Du Bois 1935:19). As it was critical that these rocks not explode when subjected to heat, varieties such as soapstone or basalt were preferred (Ortiz and Parker 1991:110). The rocks were usually picked up with a set of tongs—two long, straight, and tapered sticks. Once in the basket the rocks were stirred with a wooden paddle or looped stick. The mush paddle was among the most distinctive of Californian cooking implements, yet as Kroeber points out, it was common only in the northern part of the state: "It has been found among all the northwestern tribes, the Achomawi, Atsugewi, Shasta, Pomo, Wappo, southern Maidu, northern Miwok, Washo, and Diegueño. The Yokuts and southern Miwok, at times also the Washo, use instead a looped stick, which is also convenient for handling hot cooking stones. The Colorado River tribes, who stew ... corn, beans, or fish in pots, tie three rods together for a stirrer" (Kroeber 1925:829). One somewhat specialized utensil was the bent willow or hazel ladle that the Wintu used to retrieve boiled salmon from a basket (Du Bois 1935:134).

Certainly the most characteristic Native Californian food was a soup or mush made of seed or nut meal and water. Acorns, of course, were the most common ingredient, but a wide variety of seeds were also cooked in the same manner. In some areas, the mixture of parched seeds was known as pinole.[85] The water and meal were mixed together in varying proportions and then boiled to produce a wide

Mohave stew pot (1–13789) and fish-mush stirrers (1–13860).
PHOTOGRAPH BY EUGENE PRINCE, HEARST MUSEUM.

Pomo mush paddle (1–1411), fire tongs (1–1412a,b),
cooking basket (1–444), boiling stones (1–198237).
PHOTOGRAPH BY EUGENE PRINCE, HEARST MUSEUM.

diversity of finished dishes. The thinner soup was drunk as a liquid or eaten with a spoon, while the thicker mush was usually eaten with the fingers. Barrett and Gifford have given us a particularly good historic description of a Sierra Miwok method of cooking acorn mush (1933:147–48), which is amplified in Ortiz and Parker's thorough discussion of contemporary styles (1991). About a dozen stones were heated in a fire, lifted one by one with wooden tongs, and the ashes briefly rinsed off in a basket of water. The stones were placed in a large basket of water and stirred gently and slowly with a paddle or looped stirrer. While this may have kept the basket from burning, as is often supposed, its main reason was to distribute the heat evenly and keep the mush from burning (Ortiz and Parker 1991:114). About six or seven quarts of this warm water was mixed by hand in a small basket with about two quarts of newly leached acorn meal. Most of this thin mush was poured into another large basket and heated with hot rocks until it was boiling and cooked through. More water or more mush was added during the cooking to achieve the desired consistency. As the stones were lifted out of the cooking basket the mush was scraped off with the fingers and the stones dropped into a small basket of cold water. The congealed mush was later peeled off and eaten or added to the cooking basket. From the original two quarts of acorn meal, this boiling procedure yielded ten to twelve quarts of cooked soup, or slightly less of the thicker mush. The Maidu proportions were about the same, two quarts of dough to three gallons of water for soup, and less water for mush (Dixon 1905:187).[86] A special by-product of rock boiling was the mush dried onto the rock; children especially liked to peel off and eat this toasted acorn meal (Nisenan, Wilson 1972:37). This preparation, also called "acorn chips," would work only with thick mush, and then, of course, the rocks were not rinsed off (Ortiz and Parker 1991:116–17).

While boiling was secondary to roasting and baking as a method of cooking meat, it was not unusual. For example, the Tolowa boiled dried fish, meat, and fish eggs; fresh meat was boiled in a wooden trough by men, especially for feasts (Drucker 1937:235).[87] Atsugewi boiled birds' eggs, which could then keep for a week or more, and prepared pounded fish eggs as a mush (Garth 1953:135, 136). The Wintu

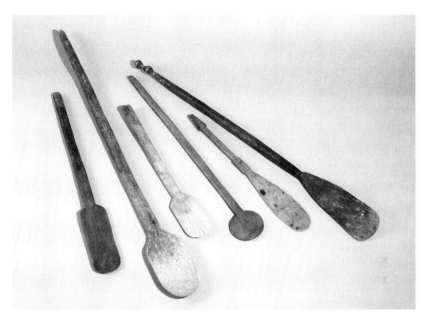

Mush paddles (left-right): Kumeyaay (1–14470), Northern Sierra Miwok (1-9905), Maidu (1–64124), Northern Pomo (1–1411), Hupa (1–922), Tolowa (1–2506).

PHOTOGRAPH BY EUGENE PRINCE, HEARST MUSEUM.

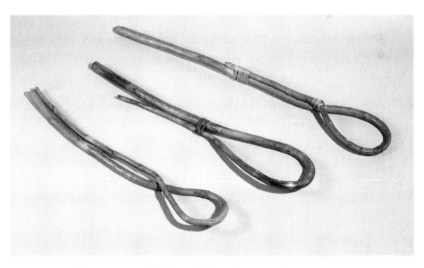

Mush stirrers/rock lifters (left-right): Washoe (1–236795), Kawaiisu (1–20995), Sierra Miwok (1–71242b).

PHOTOGRAPH BY EUGENE PRINCE, HEARST MUSEUM.

boiled (or roasted) clams and mussels to open their shells; the meat was either consumed at once or dried if there was a lot (Du Bois 1935:18). Like the Hupa, who used flat pieces or strings of venison (Goddard 1903:23), meat for boiling was usually cut up into small pieces to help it cook faster. In fact, one reason why Native Californians did not commonly boil meat may have been the longer cooking times necessary when using the hot-rock method. It does appear that meat and fish were more commonly boiled where stone or clay pots were used, both in California and elsewhere in Native America (Driver and Massey 1957:233). A method related to boiling was the preparation of meat or fish soups, in which one drank a flavored broth. Many northwestern groups made soup from salmon bones, sometimes with the gills and eggs (Kroeber and Barrett 1960:105; Shepherd 1997:217).

There were several other methods of moist cooking. Compared to boiling, steaming was relatively rare and often combined with other methods. The Wintu steamed clover shoots by laying hot rocks in a basket, placing the shoots over them, and sprinkling them with water. They also partly steamed deer meat by placing a little bit of water and hot rocks in a basket, laying meat strips on the rocks, and covering with a basketry lid (Du Bois 1935:20, 10). Sometimes water was poured into an earth oven to partly steam the food, such as Sierra Miwok brodiaea bulbs (Barrett and Gifford 1933:139). One unique method combining boiling and jelling in cold water was a preparation of acorn biscuits, common in central California.[88] One Sierra Miwok method started by cooking acorn mush longer; it was thickened and made more gelatinous by dropping some mush from a height of about two feet back into the basket; then placed into a small basket which was set for a minute or two in cold water, preferably in a pool of running water. As the biscuit cooled it became easy to slide out when it was turned out into the water, where it cooled further until it had the consistency of gelatin. "It was an excellent daily food and found much use at feasts" (Barrett and Gifford 1933:146–47). Mashing, which was also a preparation method prior to cooking, was sometimes used after heating. The most significant example was the several varieties of "Indian potatoes," which were mashed after they were boiled.[89]

In addition to the ubiquitous soups, nut and seed meals were commonly prepared as breads and cakes. In fact, most groups that boiled these as mushes also cooked them as breads. Although the meals were commonly mixed with water, the forming of the loaf was aided by the natural oils in the pounded seeds. (The Pomo, for example, made balls from ground peppernuts that had been roasted but were otherwise uncooked.) The cooking method is commonly called baking, and while breads seem to have been most often baked in an underground pit oven, they were also cooked on a hot stone griddle. The Wintu, for example, made several varieties of acorn bread. When using black oak acorns, a rock-lined pit was heated for almost a day, the rocks covered with maple leaves, and the damp flour patted into the pit. This was covered with leaves, soil, and rocks and a fire was built over the pit. After cooking all night, the loaf was removed in the morning. The bread, of a "rich, greasy consistency, would keep for months." For valley-oak bread, the acorns were first rotted. The flour was combined with red earth that had been soaked in water to make a stiff batter; there was no leaching (the rotting and red earth neutralized the tannins). Again, the loaf was cooked all night in a pit. This yielded a black bread, "its darkness a measure of its palatability" (Du Bois 1935:19). While the Maidu used a pit oven, they also baked their bread in the ashes. They formed the leached acorn meal into a loaf about fifteen centimeters in diameter. The dough was flattened and wrapped around a hot rock that had been rolled in oak leaves. After the dough was pressed down, the whole mass was wrapped in oak leaves and baked. Their method produced a very heavy, solid bread (Dixon 1905:187). The Miwok, who also had both cooking methods, made one kind of bread with "leavening," blue oak ashes, which made it sweeter but did not make it rise, as well as an unleavened variety (Barrett and Gifford 1933:148). Maggie Howard, a Paiute woman, cooked acorn meal patties on top of a heated stone (Ortiz and Parker 1991:116); and the agricultural Mohave used hot ashes to bake breads of corn and, later, wheat (Stewart 1968:36–37). In addition to nuts, cakes were made from roots and berries. The Maidu combined them; dried roots were pounded fine and mixed with berries, then baked in small flat cakes (Dixon 1905:189).

Ingredients transformed by these cooking methods created distinct dishes. Unfortunately, we have little information on the range of Native Californian recipes.[90] Generally, Californian foods were prepared directly and not in combination with other ingredients, although they might be eaten together. Mixtures of plant and animal ingredients seem to have been rare. One interesting exception was the acorn-mush batter that Sierra Miwok smeared over dried fish before they were broiled on sticks over a fire (Barrett and Gifford 1933:139). The Owens Valley Paiute, a Basin group, made a stew with rabbit meat and acorn soup (Steward 1933:246). More common, perhaps, was the addition of plant materials at the end of cooking as a thickener; for example, acorn meal in Bodega Miwok beef stew (Peri 1987b:23), and a little cornmeal in Mohave fish stew (Stewart 1968:36).[91] Boiled milkweed was a Sierra Miwok thickener for manzanita cider (Barrett and Gifford 1933:159). They also used the green leaves of Spanish clover to absorb excess oils, and sometimes added the pulverized root of Indian rhubarb (*Peltiphyllum peltatum*) to whiten acorn meal; neither affected the flavor (1933:144). Cakes were another opportunity for mixing ingredients: The Tolowa combined pulverized fern roots with salmon eggs or dried fish (Drucker 1937:235), while the Maidu mixed berries with roots or seeds (Dixon 1905:189).

Native Californian foods tended to be prepared simply, but additional flavorings were not absent. As a general principle, it seems that these flavorings were eaten along with foods rather than cooked with them. Thus any distinction between condiments and side dishes is somewhat arbitrary, depending on quantities rather than cooking methods. In a sense almost all the region's flavorings were side dishes. In their mild approach to spicing, Native Californians were like most cultures living in temperate climates. As with the use of spices in other parts of the world, such flavorings that were present undoubtedly encouraged the ingestion of relatively large quantities of the staple— acorn mush, in this case—which was relatively high in carbohydrates and fats, and often bland tasting. As indicated above, salt in several forms was a major flavoring. Essie Parrish (Kashaya Pomo) said Indian potatoes tasted good with salty foods (Oswalt 1964:307).

Wintu used the mineral on raw clover and grasshoppers, occasionally in acorn mush and manzanita cider (Du Bois 1935:21). Somewhat unusually, they sprinkled salt over small fish (trout, whitefish) when they were cooked between hot rocks (1935:17). Yurok ingested salt in the form of dried seaweed cakes, which they broke off into pieces and chewed between spoonfuls of acorn mush (Kroeber 1960:134). The salt that Yokuts obtained from salt grass had "a sour, salty taste much like that of a dill pickle" (Latta 1949:118). Groups that had access to both rock salt and salt grass often used them differently. Chukchansi Yokuts ate rock salt with meat, nuts, or seeds (but burned it first when consuming it with acorn mush); salt from grass was eaten with clover and sour berries (Gayton 1948b:181). Tübatulabal used salt from salt grass for seasoning raw chopped clover, or sprigs of salt grass and clover were rolled between the hands and eaten; rock salt was used sparingly with cooked meat and for drying meat and fish, but never with plant foods such as acorns or pine nuts (Voegelin 1938:19–20).

In addition to salt, a range of plants were used for flavoring. The Maidu, as well as other groups, added flavor during acorn leaching with cedar-boughs used as water-breakers (Dixon 1905:187).[92] Most pit-cooked foods were wrapped with aromatic leaves, which also served to separate layers of food. The Tolowa covered their meat with thimbleberry leaves, fir twigs, and other aromatic leaves; the Hupa wrapped bulbs with wild grape and wood sorrel leaves; the Pomo used black oak, madrone, and other leaves, but especially esteemed the wild grape; and the Sierra Miwok preferred mule-ears, sometimes wild grape or green tule.[93] On the other hand, the Tübatulabal specifically preferred to wrap up fish for roasting in special varieties of willow "as these willows did not impart any odor to food" (Voegelin 1938:11). Sometimes plants were added directly to acorn soups: Maidu might add a leaf or two of bay or mint (Dixon ibid.), and Nisenan used dried mushrooms (Beals 1933:351).

Nuts and other kinds of seeds were often used as condiments, especially when eating acorn. Sparkman suggested that some Luiseño seeds were used as seasonings because they were so small and difficult to gather (1908:196), but the widespread use of nut and seed condiments more likely indicates that their distinctive flavor and textures were appreciated. Many groups added small amounts of seeds to their soups: Pomo added spicy anise seeds to other pinoles "to give them added zest"; Northfork Mono added pinches of dry meal (and recently home-grown wheat) to thick, cold chia soup; Chukchansi Yokuts flavored acorn mush with pulverized seeds; and Cahuilla mixed ground seeds as a condiment with other foods.[94] Other groups used larger quantities: Owens Valley Paiute made a mush mixture of ground seeds in a pine-nut base (Steward 1933:240). In a similar fashion Tübatulabal were able to adjust the flavor of acorn soup by mixing the bitter maul oak acorn flour with a sweeter variety (Voegelin 1938:18).

As in many cuisines, some foods were served only hot, some only cold, and others either way. Nisenan, who considered hot foods to be unhealthy, usually ate their acorn mush cold (Beals 1933:351–52). Acorn mush was also eaten cold by the Chukchansi Yokuts (as a between meal snack, see Eating section) and the Northfork Mono (with strips of venison cooked on coals). Seed mushes and soups were also eaten cold: a thick, cold soup of chia seeds (which had been parched before grinding) by the Mono (Gifford 1932:21, 23) and a seed mush by the Luiseño (Sparkman 1908:193).

Cooking and eating generally took place in a multipurpose living space, most often outdoors when the weather was good. Among groups where men and older boys slept in a sweat house (including Klamath River groups, Wintu, Pomo, Owens Valley Paiute, but not Sierra Miwok), the family house, where the women and children slept, was always used for cooking and eating. Thus, while males might share a certain sociability, eating was associated with women and the family. Several families often shared a cooking space, especially during the winter. In order to conserve heat in the winter, Atsugewi cooked in a larger version of the sweat house, owned by a chief or rich man. "Each family in a house cooked for itself and had its own utensils, although occasionally two families did their cooking together. If there were four families, there might be four baskets of acorn mush beside the fire. Stores of food, however, were used communally, at least within one house. Each family in turn obtained food from its store and divided it among the other families"; cooking utensils were stored in a rough bark cookhouse (Garth 1953:140). The several families living in a Pomo communal house shared its interior earth oven; an outdoor oven was used in good weather (Barrett 1952:61). In most of the state, weather was a factor—processing or cooking that might be done outside in the summer was conducted inside during the winter or rainy weather. The desert-dwelling Mohave usually did their cooking outside the house, often in a windbreak (Stewart 1968:33). Not all cooking took place around the home; Tübatulabal often cooked acorn mush at the spot where they leached the meal (Voegelin 1938:29).

We do not know as much as we would like about the gender and social roles of Californian cooks, but as Willoughby concludes, "the preparation and cooking of food by roasting and boiling was generally a feminine occupation,... particularly the preparing of plant products," while "the preparation of meat appears to have been primarily masculine" (1963:34). Yet she cites numerous exceptions to these generalizations. For instance, among the Chukchansi Yokuts, "If the women were on a gathering trip, the men prepared the meal which was ready when their spouses returned, while if the men were away the reverse occurred. If both sexes were home, the women generally cooked, but the men might fix the meat while the women prepared the acorn dish" (cf. Gayton 1948b:177).

Most cooking seems to have been carried out alone by the wife in the family, but groups also cooked together. Like all food processes in Native California, cooking was inevitably a social occasion, with older people and children around, if not actually participating. As with almost all aspects of Native Californian life, one became a cook by observing the process and by gradually helping out with the simpler tasks until one could execute the procedure by oneself. Upon marriage, a Chukchansi Yokuts woman went to live in her husband's house, with her mother-in-law. She was the housekeeper, deciding when and how acorns would be gathered and prepared; her mother-in-law might help out with some acorn pounding. If there were several daughters-in-law in one family, they shared the work; the woman who had priority in marrying into the family directed the others (Gayton 1948b:195). While Nisenan acorn gathering and leaching was often a communal affair, cooking was usually done in a familial context

(Wilson 1972:37). Collaborative cooking of acorn mush has been reported for the Owens Valley Paiute; one person handled the hot rocks while another stirred them in the mush and removed the cold rocks (Steward 1933:246). Cooking in earth ovens was often communal. Several Sierra Miwok families might cook simultaneously in an earth oven, separating their portions with layers of leaves (Barrett and Gifford 1933:139). Similarly, two or three Wintu families might join in preparing a pit for baking salmon. When baking valley-oak acorn bread one woman was appointed to open the pit in the morning. "All gathered then with much merrymaking and hilarity except on [the] part of [the] baker" (Du Bois 1935:15, 19). Cooking in an intergroup situation was likely to involve related families, but there is no definite evidence on this point.

As in many cuisines, experienced cooks did without precise measurements. Basic proportions were well-known—such as the relative amounts of acorn flour to water needed to produce a soup or a mush—and these could be measured in baskets or by handfuls. Yet these quantities were determined in most cases by tasting, as well as by appearance, feel, and sound (when pounding, for instance), and, of course, by taste. For instance, when preparing manzanita cider, a Sierra Miwok woman kept tasting the liquid until all the sweet flavor had leached out of the meal (Barrett and Gifford 1933:162). A Sierra Miwok cook would judge the doneness of acorn mush by its viscosity: "When it dropped from the [cooking] stones of itself, leaving them bare and clean, it was properly cooked" (Grinnell 1958:44). There is also some suggestive evidence for what might be called cooking etiquette. Wintu people were taught not to be in a hurry to talk to visitors: "If a woman is cooking when somebody comes, she doesn't talk to him until she tells him to eat" (Du Bois 1935:49).

While most adult women cooked for their families, as in all societies some were known for their special culinary skills, which they presented to guests at household or village feasts. Among the Wintu, expert bakers of valley-oak bread were "requested to bake at dances or meets, a mark of distinction in which women took pride" (Du Bois 1935:19); and a Cahuilla woman had to be an efficient cook in order to be judged a "proper" woman (Bean 1972:52). The diners appreciated what was being served: "People were very critical of each acorn maker's product. Properly made acorn was a source of great pride; if made improperly, it was bound to bring comments" (Ortiz 1990b:17). However, as Otis Parrish (Kashaya Pomo) points out, this criticism was never offered at the feast, as it would be impolite (pers. comm. 1997). Culinary distinctions and variations were noted. When Wintu men were hunting in the hills, they sometimes roasted a whole side or quarter of deer over a fire, only partly cooking the meat. One of Du Bois's female consultants described this style "with considerable disdain for [the] lack of culinary nicety as 'hunter's way of cooking' " (1935:10). All stages of cooking were the subject of Native culinary criticism. To some extent, the quality of a finished meal rested directly on the quality of the ingredients. Some Nisenan groups were noted for the excellence of their acorns, "and the soup they made at big times was a favorite" (Wilson 1972:37).

We have only a few indications of what Native diners and critics were looking for. A good Cahuilla cook ground her materials "very fine in quality and free of foreign substances"; her acorn meal should be "sweet, bland, and smooth" (Bean 1972:52). When Ishi, "the last Yahi," came to live in San Francisco, he expressed definite tastes in food. For instance, he liked all vegetables and fruit and preferred his potatoes, rice, or bread served plain. "There was a discernible pattern of dislikes for the cloudy, the too smooth, and the too soft, despite Ishi's fondness for his staple food, acorn mush, a dish of indubitably glutinous texture; and for a mixture of flavors and textures of foods which he preferred cooked separately, in clear broth or water" (T. Kroeber 1961:167–68).[95] Ishi also thought that food boiled on a stove was cooked too fast and too long. Stone boiling would ensure "meat firm, broth clear, vegetables good, not soft and coming apart" (1961:168). Despite the keen attention paid to cooking and food, Native Californians lacked what has been called "a gustatory approach to food" (Appadurai 1988:5). Food was not a specialized aspect of life, prepared and criticized by professionals, but a part of everyday experience. In this sense, it was, like their basketry, a "folk art."

Despite the state's regional complexity, it may be useful to try to formulate a set of unifying stylistic themes, what Elisabeth Rozin calls "flavor principles" (1973), for Native Californian cuisines. A cuisine will be defined by its characteristic selection of a set of basic foods, accompanied by a common set of flavorings. These will be subjected to distinctive styles of processing (e.g., chopping or heating). Finally, these materials will be combined and eaten in patterned ways on both a daily basis and special occasions. Before the substantial culinary acculturation of the nineteenth century, the region had a cuisine that emphasized a wide range of seasonal foods, the use of dried foods (especially in winter), a preference for nuts and seeds instead of domesticated grains, simple preparations, pounding for both plants and animals, parching, the roasting of meats in coals and the boiling of plants in baskets; with a relative absence of stews and other combinations, strong spices (such as garlic or chili peppers), and dairy products. While such a cuisine might seem so plain as to be unappealing to some, in many ways it resembled that of Japan and clearly left room for tasty and stimulating meals for its cooks and eaters. For within such general principles, there was still a substantial amount of complexity and variability, allowing culinary pleasure and criticism (Rozin 1982:201).

EATING

Once cooked, food is never presented randomly, but always forms a part of some sort of system of meals, "the food served and eaten at one time." Invoking a language analogy, we can speak of culinary vocabularies and grammars, that is, of ingredients and their possible combinations. Meal systems are based on principles of alternation, items that can replace each other, filling the same function, such as different kinds of meats or vegetables; and principles of combination, such as the necessity for a meal to have both a meat and a starch (Lévi-Strauss 1958:85). As explained by anthropologist Mary Douglas, a proper dinner meal for a working-class family in England must consist of some animal protein, cereal, and vegetable (1975). Anything else counts as a snack. At the lowest level of analysis, food ingredients will be combined into distinctive recipes; in turn, these dishes will make up a given menu or meal. Considering the meal structure, though, begins to move us beyond composition to temporal patterning, that is, how the food is presented and eaten in sequence. For instance, in India the dishes are normally served all at once, but in Europe sequentially. Moving beyond a single event, meals will form cycles, operating over a day, week, year, or life span. A proper analysis must take all these levels into account. Even within a given society there are variations, depending on the degree of the meal's formality and elaboration, with more separate dishes and courses for a feast than for a simple daily meal. Like language and other social behavior, with food there is a range of contexts—formal and casual, sacred and secular (cf. Goode, Theophano, Curtis 1984:71–72).

The evidence we have for Native California suggests that in most of the state the mild acorn mush was the staple, playing a role similar to that of rice in Chinese or Japanese cuisines, and was often balanced with smaller side dishes of meat or fish and greens or seeds. That is, one had not eaten a proper meal unless one had eaten acorn mush. At the same time, though, it was probably never consumed alone. In fact, probably reflecting a regional focus, the Yurok linking of salmon and food (Waterman 1920:185) indicates that other ingredients could take the central place of acorn. If meat or fish was not available, acorn was probably eaten with some nut meal or leafy plant. While this would insure a balance of protein and carbohydrate/fat, it would often also combine contrasting textures, dry and moist, as in Japanese culinary practice.[96] This ideal schema would vary throughout the year, depending on the availability and proportions of particular fresh and preserved foods. As far as we can tell, with a few minor exceptions, these societies consumed their foods all at the same time rather than in separate courses.

We have some indications of what counts as a Native Californian meal. The Yurok insisted on serving what they considered balancing foods together. A typical meal would be a bowl of acorn mush combined with a piece of dried fish on an open-work platter laid across the top, with perhaps some seaweed; one ate a little bit of one and then the other (Kroeber 1960:139). The Sierra Miwok ate broiled fish with acorn biscuits (Barrett and Gifford 1933:139), and the Chukchansi Yokuts had dried and pounded creek fish with acorn mush (Gayton 1948b:185). Among the meats eaten with acorn mush were roasted venison (Wintu, Du Bois 1935:10), strips of venison, also trout and salmon (Northfork Mono, Gifford 1932:21), baked deer liver or baked abalone (Kashaya Pomo, Oswalt 1964:303). If they did not have any meat at hand, Chukchansi men would go out and catch a rabbit or the like, to eat with their acorn soup (Gayton 1948b:177). Insects were another popular side dish for acorn soup: Wintu boiled and mashed grasshoppers with salt (Du Bois 1935:14), and Sierra Miwok ate chrysalises (which had been dried and soaked in hot water) (Barrett and Gifford 1933:191–92). Preparing them as a flavoring instead, Nisenan mixed the soup with grasshoppers that had been dried and finely pounded (Beals 1933:347).

As vegetable accompaniments for acorn soup or mush, the Sierra Miwok ate boiled or steamed greens and boiled white mushrooms; they had slightly sour cooked toyon berries with seed meal (Barrett and Gifford 1933:158, 164, 163). The Chukchansi Yokuts ate greens such as clover with acorn mush or manzanita cider (Gayton 1948b:180). Atsugewi had baked wild parsley leaves "as a meat substitute when acorns were eaten" (Garth 1953:139). The Sierra Miwok consumed some greens because of their sour or vinegary flavor (sheep sorrel, cow clover), while others were enjoyed for their sweet taste (mule-ears) (Barrett and Gifford 1933:160–61). As indicated, seed and nut meals were esteemed, but rather than being added during the cooking, they were consumed with the meal. The Sierra Miwok regarded seed meal as "particularly fine eating.... Visitors were given it to eat along with their acorn mush, which was regarded as insipid without such accompaniment" (1933:141). Wintu ate ripe gray pine nuts with acorn soup (Du Bois 1935:21). One popular form was the cake of ground nuts. The Pomo roasted and ground peppernuts (laurel), and the oily meal was kneaded into balls or logs. These cakes were consumed along with acorn bread or clover; one popular custom was to wrap the ball inside a bunch of sweet clover.[97] Similarly, Chukchansi Yokuts ate balls of ground pine nuts with acorn mush (Gayton 1948b:180).

Several foods were considered appropriate with drinks. Chumash consumed chia meal or drink "a little at a time, between bites of other foods, to vary the taste and cleanse the palate" (Timbrook 1986:50). Sierra Miwok drank manzanita cider as an "appetizer" (Barrett and Gifford 1933:162).[98] Conversely, they served dried and rehydrated lupine leaves "as a relish with manzanita cider" (1933:160). For the Chukchansi Yokuts, wild oat biscuits were a favorite accompaniment to manzanita cider (Gayton 1948b:179). California Natives did have sweets but they were probably eaten as a snack instead of a dessert.

Some food combinations were actively prohibited. A Nisenan woman, for instance, "would not put cut deer meat on a winnowing basket that was used for acorn preparation, as the acorn meal would taint the meat," although it is not clear in what way (Wilson 1972:36).[99] The Maidu, as well as other groups, singled out bear meat; it was cooked separately from deer meat, "and the two were not eaten together. In the Sacramento Valley a wholly different word is used to denote eating bear meat, from that indicating the eating of all other kinds of meat" (Dixon 1905:191). Northwestern peoples appear to have adopted a sea/land distinction. Tolowa could not cook or eat any seafood, such as clams or mussels, with the flesh or grease of any land animal, especially bear, nor with mud hens (which once were bears) (Drucker 1937:262), and Yurok forbid the combination of whale with deer; and fish with bear, grouse eggs, or mud-blackened acorns (Kroeber 1960:139, 146). Still, in many cases we are simply not aware of the cultural logic behind these customs.

Meals serve to punctuate the daily cycle. Throughout the state, the most common pattern was to eat twice a day, near the beginning and end of the day. The Hupa and Yurok ate a light breakfast, with their principal meal in the evening, while the Pomo, Tübatulabal, and Owens Valley Paiute all ate in the early morning and again in the late afternoon.[100] Eating often alternates between regularly scheduled meals, when people are expected to eat together, and snacks, more casual eating determined by personal hunger. The Yurok strongly disapproved of any who ate between meals (Kroeber 1960:137), but most groups expected casual snacking throughout the day. Pomo ate "at almost any time of day whenever hunger dictated, but as a rule only two regular meals were taken" (Barrett 1952:63). Some people had only one scheduled meal. The Sierra Miwok single meal was breakfast eaten at sunrise; eating during the rest of the day was unstructured, people eating when they were hungry (Barrett and Gifford 1933:138). The Choinimni Yokuts had a similar pattern, but their regular meal was in the late afternoon (Gayton 1948b:146). Some groups added a regular afternoon meal. Foothill Yokuts groups ate just after sunrise, about noon, and just before sunset (1948b:224). The midday meal was informal eating in camp of prepared food. The Chukchansi Yokuts always had some cold acorn mush available in the house for those who wanted to eat between meals (1948b:177); similarly for the Foothill Yokuts, midday meals were odd bits as one wanted them, such as honey, pine nuts, leftover cooked food (1948b:224). Mohaves' scheduled meal was at sunrise or earlier; "After that, the Mohaves ate whenever they felt like it during the day, if they had food handy.... Another meal was customarily eaten in the evening" (Stewart 1968:37). Chukchansi Yokuts men would eat a meal after returning from a long hunt around midafternoon, and before the evening meal (Gayton 1948b:177). These patterns followed daily work rhythms; people tended to leave their homes early to gather food and were often away from the village during the midday, returning in the evening, which became the prime familial social occasion. The Yurok would not eat their breakfast until late in the morning, after several hours of hard work (Kroeber 1960:137). Most likely certain foods were appropriate for particular meals, but there is no hard evidence for this. It seems that acorn soup might have been more suitable for breakfast and snacks, with meat reserved for the main family meal, especially in the evening.

Certain foods were favored for journeys but many people went without eating when traveling short distances. Foothill Yokuts, who could usually return home in the late afternoon, would not take food unless they would be gone for more than twenty-four hours (Gayton 1948b:224). The Nisenan might skip meals if they were out of the village where food could not be prepared, or they consumed old acorns found in the leaf litter, which had been leached by the rain (Wilson 1972:34, 37). Tübatulabal women out for a day of seed-gathering would take a lunch with them, which they ate in the late morning (Voegelin 1938:19). For journeys, the Hupa carried dried salmon eggs, which they also used for lunch, as well as acorn bread, which might also be soaked and eaten as mush (Goddard 1903:26, 29). Because of its dryness, acorn bread lasted longer than mush, and because of its relative lightness was easier to carry on journeys (Driver and Massey 1957:235); Atsugewi acorn bread, which might keep a week, was often taken by hunters (Garth 1953:138). When Northfork Mono made extended trips over the Sierras they carried whole acorns, "which the women pounded at the stopping places. The men hunted game for the meat supply" (Gifford 1932:19). As part of ritual observance, hunters often fasted until they captured their prey, and then would consume particular portions such as the liver.

Compared with some of the world's foodways, restaurant cuisines in which one often eats outside of the home, Native California followed a domestic mode—in which one ate with one's family or as an invited guest in someone else's home. While hunters and travelers certainly ate alone, most meals seem to have been consumed in family groups (e.g., Chukchansi Yokuts, Gayton 1948b:177). As a general rule, the chef in Native California ate with the diner, with the principal exception of gender distinctions. At meals, deference was frequently shown to elders and guests, and, somewhat less commonly, to men. Elders habitually ate first, or at least were served first (Ortiz 1989:27); Atsugewi "children, especially if visitors were present, remained outside until the adults were through eating before they could eat" (Garth 1953:170). Children were rarely singled out, but among the Chukchansi Yokuts acorn dough breads, baked on stones, were usually cooked and given to children before the mush-cooking (Gayton 1948b:179). In the north, at least, men commonly ate apart from or before the women and children. When a Yurok family dined, "men, women, and children ate together, although the men were served first. If there were guests, the women waited until the men finished" (Kroeber 1960:139). Similarly, Tübatulabal men and children ate before the women (Voegelin 1938:19). "The [Hupa] women sat in silence with uncovered heads and hidden feet that they might show great respect to the men" (Goddard 1903:57). Wintu men ate rabbit apart from the women, and when they held a feast for snare-caught deer, the men were invited to the feast, and the leftovers brought back to their families (Du Bois 1935:13, 9). Such deference to male diners is not uncommon in the world, for example, in traditional Japan, but in California it tended to be found in the more hierarchical societies. Communal eating in the form of village feasts was rather common, and from time to time people from other villages and tribes ate together. The Northfork Mono practiced an especially formal style. In their moiety system of social organization, the entire community was divided into two groups, turkey vultures and golden eagles. "At a ceremony or feast the members of each moiety prepared the food for the opposite moiety. The moieties ate separately. Rarely, a woman might eat with her husband's moiety, if she belonged to the opposite moiety. Children ate with their father. After the feast the nitdenap [assistant chief] returned the children to their mother, if they had been separated from her" (Gifford 1932:36).

Most Californian groups adhered to a strong ethic of sharing food. Within a Chukchansi Yokuts village, any available meat was shared with all present, so that each person received a piece (Gayton 1948b:177). A successful Wintu hunter or fisherman was expected to share with others in the village, as was a woman who had cooked acorns. When a woman had finished cooking something, her husband invited the local men to eat, and the wife took an equal share of the leftovers to all her neighbors, "however small the portions might be." The invitation was reciprocated if the guest found cooked food on his return home. "It was considered ill-mannered to refuse. Repletion was no excuse" (Du Bois 1935:28, 49–50).[101] Similarly, when a Nisenan woman offered food to a guest, it could not be refused, otherwise that person would never be invited again. Presenting her best basket to the guest, a good woman washed her hands and mixed the acorn mush with a hand which, after scraping it off on the basket's edge, she licked clean (Beals 1933:375). Foothill Yokuts always offered food to a visitor, first at the chief's house and then at others' in the village (Gayton 1948b:224), and visitors to a Sierra Miwok community were served as soon as they arrived (Barrett and Gifford 1933:138). Atsugewi visitors were given a place at the family mush bowl, "and if there was no room, members of the household waited" (Garth 1953:170). Atsugewi visitors from distant villages commonly brought gifts, ranging from a basket of roots or acorn mush to a bow; the gift was reciprocated by the host (1953:183).

Yet, as in many societies, hospitality in meals was a delicate matter of etiquette. Wintu guests were "welcome to food and lodging for as long as they wish it," but this privilege should not be abused (Du Bois 1935:49). Some Modoc individuals asked for food, "despite the fact that such requests were considered improper and were seldom granted. The only persons privileged to ask for food from another family during the late months of winter were the ill. In these circumstances the food was generally provided, if possible. However, a well person might properly buy food if he could find a seller. The courtesy of providing food to bona fide visitors was continued through the winter by most families but some simply stopped serving meals when others were temporarily present" (Ray 1963:183). In many other groups food could be sold. In times of scarcity, Tübatulabal bought food; a person with food stores was not expected to give it away (Voegelin 1938:57). Among the Tolowa, a more stratified society, "all food was distributed with the clear expectation of immediate repayment, either in labor (as with canoe-building) or in prestige goods (as when an improvident family ran short of food). In those rare cases when a family short of food could not pay for it, it was given grudgingly as a form of charity" (Gould 1975:76).

Once the diners were assembled, serving and eating were relatively simple affairs. Often diners helped themselves from the cooking basket; sometimes they used dippers to transfer a smaller amount to a serving dish. Klamath River peoples were noted for their relatively elaborate place settings. Each Hupa man had his own open-twined plate for salmon, placed over a serving basket for acorn mush; women often ate from the large pot in which the acorn mush was cooked (Goddard 1903:29). Sitting around the cooking basket, the entire Northfork Mono family scooped out acorn mush with their fingers (Gifford 1932:21). On the other hand, Foothill Yokuts never ate directly from the cooking basket. Food was apportioned into smaller, individual baskets, although two or three small children would often share a bowl (Gayton 1948b:224). Atsugewi also had individual serving baskets (Garth 1953:138), and Mohave diners each had an individual bowl (Stewart 1968:37). Most drinking seems to have been directly out of a small basket or dipper, but the Wintu used Indian rhubarb leaves as impromptu drinking cups (Du Bois 1935:20). Several groups used special objects for drinking manzanita cider: The Atsugewi and Wintu dipped a deer tail tied to a stick into a container, sucking the cider off the tail (Garth 1953:138; Du Bois 1935:20), while the Sierra Miwok used a dipper of several short hawk feathers tied to a stick, as well as a grass-fiber brush (Barrett and Gifford 1933:162).

Serving objects included mats and trays, baskets, pots, ladles, and spoons. Many of these objects came in related sets. When cooking and eating containers were not the same, they were often larger and smaller versions of the same type. Especially large baskets were used for serving at feasts; food was cooked in smaller baskets and poured into the feast basket (Bibby 1996:61–62). For the Chumash, we have a good ethnohistorical review of serving dishes and implements. Among the wide range of items reported are bowls of plain and tarred basketry, wood, and stone; dishes of basketry, wood, stone, gourd, and shell; trays of basketry, wood, and bark; cups of basketry, wood, stone, gourd, shell, sea crab, and horn; ladles of wood and gourd; spoons of wood, shell, and horn; as well as a reed straw and a wooden toothpick (Hudson and Blackburn 1983:221–320). While some of these forms were rare and/or poorly documented, and some, such as the gourd and horn cups, were probably post-contact developments (1983:305, 309), other groups may have had similarly diverse sets. Meat and fish were often served on a mat or tray; the Klamath River peoples set aside special wooden trays for deer meat. Hupa set the basketry fish plate down on a mat of leaves (Goddard 1903:26). The Pomo served roasted fish on tule instead of wood trays because the coals would not adhere to fish as they did for meat, and fish was not as juicy as meat; ducks and dry meats were often served on tule trays (Loeb 1926:186). Sierra Miwok spread meals on tule mats and used a mat of very fine grass as a "tablecloth" (Barrett and Gifford 1933:246).

Eating utensils played a minor role in Native California: Spoons were relatively rare, knives were restricted to food preparation, and forks were unknown.[102] The most common kind of spoon in the region

Mohave serving bowl (1–13771) and spoon (1–1749),
Karuk basket (1–1790) and Yurok spoon (1–2069).
PHOTOGRAPH BY EUGENE PRINCE, HEARST MUSEUM.

was a large mussel shell. As California ocean mussel shells could reach six or seven inches in length, they could hold quite a bit. Most mussel spoons were left plain, but Pomo polished the back of the shell; beyond improving the appearance of the object, this smoothing made eating more comfortable (Loeb 1926:186). Tübatulabal used antelope horn and wood for their spoons (Voegelin 1938:19), and the Mohave created a range of spoons and ladles from clay (Stewart 1968:37). However, the most elaborate forms were the elk antler spoons of the Klamath River region. Wealthy families kept sets of these spoons for serving male guests; women ate with simpler shell or bone spoons (Jacknis 1995:16). The handles were richly carved in geometric patterns, but hosts made no attempt to serve their guests with a matched set. As the bowl of the average elk antler spoon measured 3 by 2½ inches and held two tablespoonfuls, it was not taken into the mouth but held up to the lips and sipped from (Kroeber 1960:135).

When they were not drinking acorn soup directly from small baskets, people usually ate with their hands. The thicker acorn mush was most often eaten by dipping the index and middle fingers into the bowl and licking or sucking off the gruel.[103] There were variations

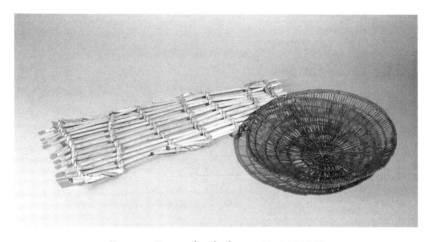

Eastern Pomo food platter (1–143103)
and Yurok salmon plate (1–9552).
PHOTOGRAPH BY EUGENE PRINCE, HEARST MUSEUM.

from group to group. The Foothill Yokuts used the three middle fingers (Gayton 1948b:224), and the Chukchansi Yokuts dipped in the whole hand within one inch of the wrist; it was just hot enough not to burn (1948b:179). The Mohave also used the whole hand when eating beans, but for stew ate with the first two fingers of the right hand (Stewart 1968:37). The Northfork Mono inserted the fingers "in the mouth palms down, the lower incisors serving as scrapers to remove the mush as the fingers were withdrawn" (Gifford 1932:21). Large pieces of dry food—fish, meat, or solid vegetables—were also eaten with the fingers (Yurok, Kroeber 1960:138). Foothill Yokuts tore apart meat and fish with their fingers, "as the cook had already hacked it up with an obsidian blade before putting it on to stew" (Gayton ibid.). Similarly, Mohave used their fingers to break off bite-sized pieces of grilled fish (Stewart 1968:36). Little is known about eating postures, but the Yurok rule "not to eat—or for that matter, to smoke—standing up" was probably common (Kroeber 1960:137).

While it was certainly polite to eat with one's fingers, there were other table manners that had to be followed. We have several good accounts of mealtime decorum among northern groups. At a Hupa evening meal, "The men ate very slowly, looking about and talking

Spoons: clay (Mohave, 1–1749), mussel shell (Eastern Pomo, 1–26551), skull (Yurok, 1–1850), elk antler (Yurok, 1–2069), wood (Hupa, 1–790).
PHOTOGRAPH BY EUGENE PRINCE, HEARST MUSEUM.

after each spoonful of soup.... A basket of water was passed after the meal that the men might wash their hands" (Goddard 1903:57). The Yurok were also encouraged to eat slowly (Kroeber 1960:137). Similarly a proper Tolowa gentleman "doesn't grab his acorn-soup basket and begin to eat, he waits until other people have something to eat too; he doesn't keep looking at his dish, eating fast without speaking; he eats slowly, looks around and talks so people don't think he's hungry and thinking about his belly all the time" (Drucker 1937:254). The Hupa, too, discouraged gluttony: "It was thought right and wise to be temperate in eating, for the time of scarcity was sure to come. Then the pangs of hunger would not be so great for the one who had practiced depriving himself in time of plenty" (Goddard 1903:88). On the other hand, for the Atsugewi (Garth 1953:170) and Wintu, "When food is offered, a guest smacks his lips in appreciation, or indicates his hunger by licking his lips (Du Bois 1935:49).[104] Respect was also shown for the food itself. Like many groups, the Wintu treated the bear with reverence. If a piece of bear meat was dropped, "the people were required to dodge as though avoiding a blow from the bear" (Du Bois 1935:11). Some offerings were more general: Among the Wintu old people prayed before eating in the morning (1935:73),

and Nisenan elders always put something in the fire before eating
(Beals 1933:354).

At the end of the meal there will often be leftovers and wastes, yet
another topic for which we need more information. Cooked food was
at times intentionally preserved between meals. Even without refrigeration, acorn mush could keep a long time. The Chukchansi Yokuts ate
cooled acorn mush over several days (Gayton 1948b:179), and
Nisenan diluted it to make soup (Beals 1933:351). Tübatulabal acorn
biscuits lasted two to three days (Voegelin 1938:18). The Sierra
Miwok stored cooked meat by covering it with earth (Barrett and
Gifford 1933:140).[105] Sometimes, however, it was bad form to have
leftovers. While the Tolowa might give away raw meat "in baskets
(which must not be returned empty), cooked meat had to be eaten
where cooked." All food had to be eaten for a naming feast, and any
leftovers had to be burned (Drucker 1937:262, 253).

In addition to the parts of foods that are discarded in preparation,
some become wastes that need to be disposed of after the meal. Every
community had its dedicated garbage area, usually separate but not
too far from the houses. In some Yokuts camps "there were rules that
the kitchen refuse and the offal from freshly killed game must be disposed of in [the] family fire-pit" (Latta 1949:101). Many coastal prehistoric sites, especially around large estuaries such as the San
Francisco Bay, are composed of huge mounds of discarded shells
(Moratto 1984:219). The fact that so many of these contain burials
has led Luby and Gruber to suggest that they also served as sites for
feasts held to honor the ancestors (1999). Thus the consumption and
disposal of food would have spiritually united the living and the dead.

Just as there were procedures for gathering so were there proper
ways to handle and remove the remains. Of all the foods, etiquette
seems to have been strictest for eating venison, especially among the
Tolowa, Yurok, and Hupa. After eating deer meat, the Yurok and
Hupa diner washed his or her hands in a special wooden bowl, and
the water was carried away from the house to be thrown out. By en-
suring that no particles of meat would be left inside respect was shown
to the prey spirits, and they would return to give their bodies to
humans (Kroeber 1960:138; Goddard 1903:23). A similar belief mo-

tivated the Tolowa to throw salmon bones back into the water so the bones would regenerate as salmon (Drucker 1937:262). In a Maidu village no deer bones could be thrown away or burned or eaten by a dog (Dixon 1905:193). The Wintu covered the remains of deer with rocks; all who ate the head meat washed their hands in a container and the water was poured over the rocks. The lower jaw was cleaned and hung in a tree to attract more deer (Du Bois 1935:9). The Sierra Miwok, on the other hand, had no such deer restrictions (Barrett and Gifford 1933:180).[106] It is hard to generalize about hand-washing. It was not only a matter of eating deer. All Tolowa diners had to wash their hands after eating or they would get cramps (Drucker 1937:262), but Atsugewi washed their hands and faces before eating, and not after (Garth 1953:170).

Some meals were more elaborate than others, and Native Californians looked forward to feasts, when they might have a chance to partake of special foods and good cooking (cf. Dietler and Hayden 2001). Often called a "big time" in English, these were opportunities

Yurok water bowl, for deer meat and for washing
hands after eating deer meat (1–11801).
PHOTOGRAPH BY M. LEE FATHERREE, HEARST MUSEUM.

for neighboring groups to meet and socialize, filled with speeches, trading, games, ritual sweating, and dances. Many occasions called for a feast. As in almost all societies, weddings were celebrated with feasts, but in much of central California a more important feast was part of the ceremony to mark the end of a mourning period (Sierra Miwok, Gifford 1917:263–64). Some feasts had more specifically social pretexts. The appearance of visitors from neighboring villages usually demanded a Pomo feast (Barrett 1952:64). Tolowa hosted them upon completing a house or a canoe. Using a brush of herbs, a priest "painted" the wall boards or canoe with acorn soup. The men who helped build it ate, and the leftovers were thrown on the fire (Drucker 1937:267). In addition to the major banquets given by chiefs and rich men, Pomo individuals might host smaller feasts, upon fulfilling a vow or naming a child, for example (Barrett ibid.).

Throughout Native California, many feasts were explicit food ceremonials, celebrating seasonal events such as the arrival of the first salmon or the acorn harvest. On the last night of a successful communal rabbit drive, the Owens Valley Paiute celebrated in the sweat house. The men put their rabbits in one pile and the women put seeds in another; the men took seeds that they wanted, and women whose seeds were taken took some rabbits. This was followed by a feast and songs (Steward 1933:255). At times, these celebrations had an ulterior agenda. The Wintu, as well as many other peoples, often gave feasts when large groups collected food—pine nut and clover gathering, salmon runs, rabbit and quail snaring, deer and bear hunts, burnings for grasshoppers. They held three or four communal rabbit drives a season. Accompanied by dancing and gambling, these were also times for matchmaking and philandering. "In fact, one informant suggested that these were the chief purposes of the drives" (Du Bois 1935:40, 13). Similarly, among groups of Cahuilla men, "Although harvesting the agave was an arduous task, it was a very festive time accompanied by hunting of small game and mountain sheep. It is recalled vividly as a time when the men played games, told stories, sang songs, and generally enjoyed themselves while waiting for the agave heads to bake" (Bean 1972:42).

In anticipation of the feast, both men and women made a special effort at gathering seasonal items which could supplement their stored (and thus usually dried) foods. Although the gathering was often communal, the chief or headman usually sponsored the feast and distributed the food.[107] "If a [Nisenan] captain asked for acorns for a big time, families were obliged to contribute even if this left them short. The captain, however, would often return the acorns if he knew it would cause hardship" (Wilson 1972:36). When invited to a feast, Kashaya Pomo were encouraged to be as generous as possible in bringing food (Otis Parrish pers. comm. 1997). The amount of food prepared at any given time varied, of course, depending on how many people were to be served. C. Hart Merriam estimated the quantity of acorn served at a Sierra Miwok mourning feast that he witnessed at Bald Rock, Tuolumne County, in 1907. He counted about fifty huge cooking baskets, each holding from one to two bushels of acorn mush, plus at least fifty loaves of acorn bread, making more than a ton of cooked acorn (1918:131–32). To produce this quantity, two cooking places and five leaching areas had been in active operation for several days. Customs varied, of course; during Nisenan feasts there was no regular meal time, people eating when they wished (Beals 1933:397).

Feasts naturally served as an occasion for exchange—of food as well as other items. At one of these gatherings, the Nisenan chief would distribute the assembled baskets of acorn mush to visiting chiefs who in turn would give them to the families of their village (Beals 1933:397). Among many groups, "surplus food was divided among the guests before they departed" (Atsugewi, Garth 1953:171). In fact, the production of such leftovers was intentional. The end of a Nisenan big time was marked by the distribution to each family of uncooked rabbits and small baskets of acorn soup in the foothills, and deer in the mountains (Beals 1933:397). At Kashaya Pomo feasts, whatever was left over was equally distributed to all; one should not take back the food that one had brought (Otis Parrish pers. comm. 1997).

As Marcel Mauss maintained in his study of the gift in archaic societies (1925), the exchange of food can be a means of establishing a social alliance, both within and between groups. Nowhere is this better demonstrated than in marriage transactions. For instance,

Cahuilla marriages set up enduring economic relationships between families; the frequent rites of passage were celebrated by feeding guests, who, in turn, often brought gifts of food (Bean 1972:92). In many cases, gifts of food tended to be gender-related; that is, the men of the groom's family supplied meat, while the women of the bride's family gave cooked acorns, seeds, and other plant foods (Gayton 1948b:195). Yet such associations were common at other times as well, such as the feast celebrating the birth of a Chukchansi Yokuts child (1948b:193). Beyond forging and strengthening social ties, however, such offerings played a critical role in redistributing food, particularly within villages, to those who lacked it for some reason: A Hupa village headman gave food to the poorer people of his village in times of scarcity (Goddard 1903:58), and a Nisenan captain would "ask the group to help a family if they were in need, but only 'if they were a good family and had really tried to help themselves' " (Wilson 1972:36). Food was often exchanged at events organized for other reasons, such as Nisenan gambling sessions (Wilson 1972:33), but many Californian groups sponsored feasts with the explicit purpose of trading food. The Wintu practice is typical: A feast was given "when a village found itself with a large supply of food on hand.... Each sub-area brought its food specialties and after the feasting the surplus was divided among the departing guests" (Du Bois 1935:40, 24).[108] Such trading could operate at the level of nations as well as tribelets. For example, the Owens Valley Paiute, inhabiting the eastern slopes of the Sierras, exchanged salt, pine nuts, and other seeds for acorns and manzanita berries brought by the Western Mono, who lived on the other side (Steward 1933:257).

As in all matters of cultural symbolism, the absences and negativities of food help create reality as much as substantive practices. In addition to the unmarked mode of daily eating and the positive pole of feasting, there are the negative states of hunger, fasting, and poison. As we have already seen, while hunger due to food shortages was not unknown, it was usually not a serious problem in Native California. Yet some individuals in the region voluntarily chose to go without eating. There is no record of avoiding food for reasons of bodily appearance, a symptom of our modern culture of abundance. In fact, the few clues we have suggest that at least some of these societies preferred a larger body image. Among both the Wintu and their neighbors, the Atsugewi, the ideal male was heavy set, his female partner should be shorter and "plump." The Atsugewi wanted a woman to be "solidly built so that she could do much work. A slim woman was considered too weak ..." (Garth 1953:170; cf. Du Bois 1935:50). Instead, conscious fasting was a matter of achieving a state of ritual "grace." Fasting was common for hunters and others embarking on a quest. Yurok, for example, believed that fasting during ritual activities made one purer and more successful. "If the occasion was both serious and prolonged—for five or 10 days—acorn gruel was the only food or drink taken, and then only at sunset of each day" (Kroeber 1960:137, 138). At puberty an Atsugewi boy went on a power quest, during which he fasted for two or three days, and a doctor in training went through an elaborate process of fasting and singing (Garth 1953:162, 188). Among the Tübatulabal, those taking jimsonweed refrained from food and water for three days before ingesting the drug, as well as for the day following. Only after six days did they take a thin acorn gruel, and for the next two months they refrained from eating meat or grease (Voegelin 1938:67).

Just as one defines a community by sharing food, so one defines strangers by not eating with them. The converse of food as hospitality is food as poison, a belief commonly held in Native California. Among the Nisenan, for example, "When visiting another group, one was suspicious if given soup in a very old basket, as it might be poisoned. Usually when a family ate in a neighboring village, the members cooked and ate their food separately from the villagers because of the danger of poisoning" (Wilson 1972:37; cf. Beals 1933:375). The Tübatulabal rarely ate after dark because they feared that ghosts "might throw something in the food that would make a person sick." Furthermore, because strangers were potential enemies who might put poison in food, people avoided eating with them (Voegelin 1938:19, 63). In some societies poison was more of a spiritual weapon than some noxious element to be ingested. The Yurok, like the Pomo and other groups, believed in both; feeling that poisons could work both naturally and supernaturally at the same time (Kroeber 1960:147–48;

cf. Loeb 1926:329–34). A Yurok person might add to someone's food scrapings from decayed grave planks, perhaps mixed with dried rattlesnake meat or starfish. The poison, which might take up to a year to work, could only be cured by a doctor sucking out the pain object. Even supernatural poison was conceived of according to a nutritional metaphor. Atsugewi shamans, like others in Native California, were equally capable of curing or poisoning people. They cured with the aid of supernatural spirits, which could also attack a person. By feeding on the individual, these spirits would gain strength. The shaman could then employ this power for extortion: "If a shaman demanded some of a man's property or food, the man had to give it up under the threat of being poisoned if he did not" (Garth 1953:189). Food customs and beliefs were thus directly implicated in the web of social life.

FOOD AS A SOCIAL CATEGORY

To a great extent, the identity of a Native Californian was defined by what, how, and with whom she or he ate. Beyond the social act of consuming a meal lies a broader arena of food as an emblem of social status and relations: gender (men or women), age (newborns or the elderly), life crises (birth, puberty, marriage, death), rank and wealth, social role (hunters, doctors, or chiefs), and ethnicity. People of differing categories may have to follow certain rules of consumption, eating differently, at least some of the time. Situational food taboos of various sorts were common in Native California. These were most often invoked during liminal moments, passage between one social state and another, when a person was thought to be especially powerful and especially at risk to themselves and others. These rules were observed especially by woman, whose most critical liminal time was puberty, but similar moments were giving birth and becoming a widow. According to Mary Douglas, states of pollution arise when there are anomalies in classification, that is, when some entity crosses conceptual categories (1975). Many of these food taboos were sympathetic magic, a kind of poetic parallelism in which it is believed that like causes like. Most of the extensive Atsugewi deer taboos obey this logic. Some were positive—if men ate deer's eyes they would have sharp vision—but most were phrased negatively: A pregnant women should not eat the ears of a deer or her baby's ears would be large; boys could not eat a deer's nose or the deer would smell them when they hunted; if a person ate the tail of a deer, he would travel too much, like a deer's tail (Garth 1953:133).

A pregnant woman often had to follow certain food regimens for her health and that of her child. As Du Bois points out, many of these beliefs were founded on two principles: sympathetic magic and prenatal influences (1935:45). The Atsugewi, who believed that the behavior of the expectant parents greatly affected the development of the child, followed a number of rules, among them not eating double fruit or nuts, which could cause the birth of twins (Garth 1953:157). An expectant Pomo mother could have no hot food, meat or fish: "The fish would drink up all of the liquid inside of her and cause her death" (Loeb 1926:249). Among Foothill Yokuts, however, there were no definite observances during pregnancy. "Some women ate only soft food as a matter of personal preferences. Some avoided doing heavy work, such as pounding acorns, during the last months," and it would be performed by a female relative (Gayton 1948b:233). The proper foods also encouraged a successful delivery. An Atsugewi mother should not eat too much "or the child would become large in her stomach and refuse to be born quickly" (Garth ibid.); similarly, a pregnant Owens Valley Paiute woman "avoided much meat lest the child become too large for an easy delivery" (Steward 1933:289). Young Wintu women could not eat deer flank meat, as it would stretch their abdomens when pregnant; nor should they consume the uppermost ribs of the deer or its entrails as it would prevent proper childbirth (Du Bois 1935:10). A Northern Pomo "mother was given a piece of raw meat, just touched to the coals, the day on which the child was to be born. This made the child come quickly" (Loeb 1926:150). In matters of sexuality such as birth and menstruation, married couples often had to obey the same or similar rules. Like his wife, a future Pomo father could not eat meat, and a Wintu man had to refrain from deer ribs. Such customs were often linked to men's hunting: During the last month of pregnancy, if a Tübatulabal woman ate meat her husband would be unsuccessful in deer-hunting (Voegelin 1938:45).

Following the birth, both mother and child commonly had to eat certain foods. The rationale of these beliefs has not always been elucidated, but it often had to do with the production of milk. In fact, sometimes a baby took no milk right after its birth: A Tolowa child was fed only drops of water mixed with scrapings of abalone shell for its first five days (Drucker 1937:252), and a Tübatulabal baby was fed only acorn or piñon gruel for its first three days (Voegelin 1938:45). For the first month, the Tübatulabal mother drank only warm water, so her blood would not get thick; she ate no meat, salt, or grease "as these foods would get into her milk and make [the] baby sick" (Voegelin 1938:45).[109] A number of substances would stimulate an abundant flow of milk: The Wintu used wild grapevine sap (Du Bois 1935:46), the Central Coast Pomo mother ate plenty of salty things (Loeb 1926:254), and the Chukchansi Yokuts mother ate acorn gruel for the first two weeks (Gayton 1948b:194). Acorn soup was also given to the Chukchansi Yokuts child if it could not nurse for some reason; the mother did not resume her normal diet until two months after the birth (ibid.). Conversely, Central Coast Pomo used California poppy to dry up the milk (Loeb 1926:254).

In rituals resembling puberty customs, some post-partum mothers (and fathers) were secluded. A Foothill Yokuts woman who had just given birth was steamed on a bed of stones and ashes for six days. She drank large amounts of hot water and her only food was acorn gruel. After not eating meat for three months, she had a cleansing ritual. A woman who ate meat would either grow very fat or become emaciated; eating meat made her sick, "her insides weren't clean." With each successive child the meat taboos were gradually lessened (Gayton 1948b:233–34). A Hupa mother ate alone for a period of forty days (for a boy) or fifty days (for a girl), consuming no meat or fresh fish (Goddard 1903:51). A Wintu mother and father were secluded for a month and could not eat flesh, salt, and cold water (Du Bois 1935:45). Among the Central Coast Pomo, the father stayed at home for eight days, avoiding meat, fish, and grease (Loeb 1926:253).

In many societies, the mother and the father had to both obey similar food taboos. The mother's typically lasted longer, no doubt because she was the one who had just given birth. A Tolowa mother could not eat meat, fresh fish, or cold water for ten days, but it was five days for the father. Tolowa parents underwent an even lengthier food purification procedure after a miscarriage or stillbirth (Drucker 1937:253). Similarly, an Owens Valley Paiute mother avoided meat, grease, and cold water for a month to recover, while the father avoided them for five days (Steward 1933:290). Eastern Pomo parents could not eat hard-mouth pike for the first month or the child's legs would become sore. Sucker and dried blackfish and several kinds of vegetables would give the child loose bowels, and squirrel meat would give the child an itch—all if consumed by the parent, not the child (Loeb 1926:254). According to Loeb, "All food restrictions which the father and mother underwent were for the sake of the child. It was feared, and not without a certain foundation of fact, that the wrong kind of food would injure the mother's milk." He added that "the peculiarity of the custom lay in the fact that the same restrictions were imposed upon both parents. Since the baby was fed on its mother's milk until it could walk, the restrictions must have proved very irksome to the father, if they were fully maintained" (ibid.).

The completion of food observances, construed as a period of purification, was often marked by a ceremony. At the end of the Tolowa period a formula was recited over the foods to purify the person and end the taboo (Drucker 1937:253). The Nisenan mother and father could not eat salt, meat, and grease until the child's navel had healed; at the end of the taboo period both washed and were given good food. If the new parents did not give a feast, it was felt that they would have bad luck, and the woman was likely to die in her next childbirth (Beals 1933:368–69). After a ceremonial dance, Atsugewi parents could eat meat, prepared by the mother of the new mother. For good luck, the couple chewed the meat and spit out the first bite so that the dog could eat it; it was thought this would also prevent consumption (Garth 1953:158). Food and feasts could also be celebratory. Among the Eastern Pomo, a day or two after the birth, the mother's relatives gave a present of pinole balls in a basket decorated with red woodpecker feathers (Loeb 1926:151). To insure a child's success, a rich Tolowa man would give a feast six months to a year after the birth, with a priest conducting a food purification (Drucker 1937:253).

Nursing patterns are undocumented, but for the Owens Valley Paiute we know that "infants were nursed normally at about 6 a.m., again at 9 or 10 a.m., and at equal intervals throughout the day, and when they cried" (Steward 1933:291). Weaning in most Californian societies was a gradual process, and the age of weaning thus varied, generally ranging from two to four years.[110] A Chukchansi Yokuts child nursed for several years. After the age of three to five years, this was supplemental to the basic diet, but he or she could take the breast until about ten. From the age of one month on, children were given gradually increasing amounts of acorn soup. To start a child on solid food, a Chukchansi mother would give her child some meat that she had chewed. After the meat, the mother would hold up to the child's mouth a small basket of acorn soup. A child could hold its own basket of soup by the age of five. From the age of two years, children could eat any food they wanted and could manage (Gayton 1948b:194). Certain foods were recommended for weaning. A Pomo child began to eat mush, pinole, and certain kinds of fish (Loeb 1926:255–56); in the 1930s Owens Valley Paiute children were given bean, potato, or mulligan soup (Steward 1933:291). As with expectant mothers, some foods were thought to be more or less appropriate for young children. Chukchansi Yokuts gave quail soup to infants to hasten their growth; as the quail is quick, the child would walk early. Conversely, ground rabbit meat was sometimes avoided as it was thought to make them lazy (Gayton 1948b:194). A Pomo child could not eat hard-mouth fish, blackfish, squirrels, blue jays, clover, and honeysuckle. (At certain times these forbidden foods were given if the child was constipated.) "At different ages the child was allowed more liberty in his diet, and when he became two or three years old all restrictions were removed" (Loeb 1926:255).

As the child got older, he or she began to learn how to obtain food. Nisenan children "were taught at an early age to find food as they worked and played" (Wilson 1972:33). From an early age, Atsugewi children were encouraged to be industrious; at about the age of eight they were taken food-gathering by the parent of their respective gender; girls would play "house," "going out with sticks and pretending to dig roots or pounding dirt as though it were acorns" (Garth

1953:160). From about the age of ten or eleven, Chukchansi Yokuts boys and girls would learn from the parent of the same sex how to acquire food: a boy, hunting with his father; a girl, gathering and preparing acorns, seeds, berries, and roots. "A girl did not learn to sift [acorn] meal, a more skillful task, or to cook until she was about fourteen." These children were forced to acquire these skills whether they wanted to or not, with the constant admonition that if they failed to learn them they would go hungry later in life (Gayton 1948b:194).

For most California Indians, a girl's puberty was marked by elaborate food practices and restrictions, whereas among most northern groups, at least, a boy's puberty was usually not noted in any clear way, except perhaps for a modest feast. Neither the Eastern Pomo nor the Wintu had any male puberty ceremony, but in both the parents would give a feast: when the boy was about eight or ten among the former (Loeb 1926:270), and when he had killed his first deer or caught his first salmon among the latter (a small feast for near neighbors) (Du Bois 1935:48). In many societies, a boy could not eat his first kill.[111] If an Owens Valley Paiute boy did, hunting would become difficult for him (Steward 1933:293). At his first kill, the father of a Tübatulabal boy put a piece of meat on an ant hill three times for the ants to eat, thereby making him a good hunter (Voegelin 1938:66). In the north and south boys were initiated into the Kuksu dance societies and toloache cult, respectively (Kroeber 1925:866). Among these southern groups, the boy undergoing his puberty initiation was not allowed to have salt (Kroeber 1941:6). Fasting was a common form of abstinence: During his two- to three-day power quest, a pubescent Atsugewi boy could not eat (Garth 1953:162), nor could a young Cahuilla boy during his puberty ceremony (Bean 1972:142–43). During their puberty fasting, both boys and girls of the Pass Cahuilla wore a "hunger belt" of twisted grass around their waists (Strong 1929:117–18). Following his esoteric trials and instruction, the family of a Cahuilla boy sponsored a three-day ceremony, and in order to amass the large amounts of food distributed at the feast, the lineage had to devote months of effort.

In most groups pubescent girls were secluded in a small house for a period of days, during which time they were allowed to eat only certain foods. On this occasion they were often required to show that they could accomplish the tasks of adult women. On the last day of her puberty rites, and as she emerged from her confinement, a Pomo girl was given a large but shallow basket one-half or two-thirds full of acorns, hulled but not yet ground up, and an acorn pestle. It was the girl's duty to grind these acorns into meal. This was her first attempt at making acorn meal. After the meal was prepared the girl went down to the leaching place on the sands. Here her mother instructed her in the domestic art of acorn meal leaching. Finally she took the prepared meal home, heated rocks, and made the mush. The mush was served to her family and a few friends. As the dinner was partaken of, everybody complimented the girl on her cooking, "This is what you will do when you are a woman and get married," they said. The party was a small affair; there was no great feast given (Loeb 1926:272–73).

This was called the "food milling appearance." "The girl's grandmother taught her a food incantation song at this time, and the girl used it throughout her life" (Parkman 1994:27).[112] Among the Atsugewi, a girl's behavior during her puberty ceremony was thought to be a sign of her industry later in life; therefore she would work hard digging roots (Garth 1953:161–62). These ritual practices paralleled the observances of a boy's first kill—a recognition of adult food-gathering. The Atsugewi had an elaborate ceremony, including public dances; the Wintu public ceremony, with a feast and dance, was optional. A girl's puberty feast was given only if the father was "a man of importance," and the village could help him sponsor it; otherwise it was a private affair, the girl following her restrictions (Du Bois 1935:40).

The most common of the food taboos for a pubescent girl were not to eat meat and/or fish, grease, and salt. Often she must not cook and had to eat alone. A Wintu girl's seclusion was one of the longer ones, lasting one to several months. During this time she could not cook, could eat only acorn soup, and ate from her own baskets, which were not used for anything else (Du Bois 1935:52). Like their Wintu neighbors, an Atsugewi girl also had her own special cooking utensils and her mother and female relatives cooked for her; she was not allowed to eat meat and plugged her nose with leaves so she would not smell things cooking, especially grease (Garth 1953:162). At her first menstruation, a Nisenan girl fasted for sixteen days and was forbidden to eat meat, fat, and salt (the same taboos for a new mother) (Beals 1933:369). For ten days, a Tolowa girl ate a meal of dried fish, acorn soup, and warm water; she was not permitted to eat if the sun had risen, as "she would be eating the sun, wouldn't live long." All the leftovers from her meals were saved and thrown away in the water when she bathed; "if they were thrown on land, bird or dog might eat them, making her ill" (Drucker 1937:254). At puberty a Hupa girl could eat only one meal a day, at midday, and was not allowed to drink water for ten days, and like all her subsequent menstrual periods, she had to be alone for ten days, cook her own food, and avoid meat or fish (Goddard 1903:53, 56). Although these are northern examples, these customs were fairly uniform throughout the state. In the south, the Tübatulabal pubescent girl drank only warm water for six days and avoided meat, grease, and salt for a month (Voegelin 1938:46).

In most cases, we do not have access to the cultural logic behind these (as well as most other) food taboos, but a few have been recorded. A Pomo girl, secluded in a small hut for her first menstruation, could not eat meat or fish, only mush and pinole. For the Pomo, "Meat was forbidden because it contained blood. Blood would have poisoned the girl as it was the very thing that she was trying to get rid of" (Loeb 1926:272). At puberty, an Owens Valley Paiute girl was secluded for five days, during which time she avoided meat "lest its richness 'stop her blood,' killing her children, and lest she should make hunters lazy and poor shots" (Steward 1933:293). A Foothill Yokuts girl stopped eating meat when her breasts grew large enough for some milk to be exuded, and this abstinence lasted until after her first menstruation; "otherwise she would have large breasts" (Gayton 1948b:234). Although a rule of lesser significance, an Atsugewi girl could eat most plant foods except wild plums which would give her bad teeth (Garth 1953:162). While the linkage between meat and menstrual blood seems persuasive and perhaps broadly applicable, the common food avoidances, for many rites of passage, from grease, salt, and hot foods remains obscure.

Similar behavior was enforced on subsequent menstruations but the observances were not as strict. Upon marriage, many husbands had to curtail hunting during their wife's periods, and they themselves might have to follow the same dietary restrictions. An Atsugewi girl went through the same menstrual behaviors for about five or six months, but the duration was shortened from a four- to six-day period to three. Later she continued to avoid meat, as did her husband; when she got older she could eat with her family but had to follow the same prohibitions (Garth 1953:162). For subsequent periods, a Tolowa woman was not secluded but did have to remain at home. During her ten-day observance she ate only dried fish and acorn soup, eating apart from her family and from separate plates. For her first four periods she could eat only in her own home, even between periods (Drucker 1937:254). During her later periods, a Nisenan woman abstained from meat, salt, and fat for four days; she prepared and cooked food for herself. While her husband followed no food restrictions himself, if he went hunting, anything he shot could run off and die in an inaccessible place. If they had a male visitor, the husband informed him that there was a menstruating woman in the household so he would not enter or eat food there (Beals 1933:369). Similarly, during her period a Wintu woman was forbidden meat, fish, and grease, but she could cook her own food. A menstruant could not eat with men, especially hunters, gamblers, and shamans, as it would destroy their "powers" (Du Bois 1935:53, 54). After the ceremony or seclusion, a Wintu woman was free to follow her usual habits, although meat, fish, and grease was still forbidden during each period. "Some women, however, abstained from meat for much longer periods. For example, Ellen Silverthorne ate no deer meat for ten years. She still feels apprehensive when she eats mountain squirrel" (1935:53).

Native Californian groups varied on the social recognition they gave to marriages, but food was commonly part of the nuptial negotiations. When exchanging foods, the respective families typically followed gender roles. For a formal Wintu betrothal a suitor might bring game to the girl's family for several months, or a girl might go to the boy's family and help grind acorns or gather seeds. If the food was accepted, then the wedding could take place; if the girl rejected him, her family would make a return gift (Du Bois 1935:54). In many other groups, as well, the groom and his family gave meat and fish, which was reciprocated by acorn meal and other vegetable foods from the bride and her family.[113] In the Owens Valley Paiute situation, gifts, including food, were exchanged after a marriage (Steward 1933:295). Perhaps because weddings were celebratory and called for feasting, food proscriptions were relatively muted. In one more unusual custom, a Tolowa bride did not eat at her wedding feast, as "she would be eating all her children." Instead her parents-in-law gave a feast to the escort who had accompanied her to the feast; the escort "ate for her," in her honor (Drucker 1937:255).

Death and burial often included the sacrifice of food and the necessity for purifying oneself from the pollution of death. Although food was not generally interred with the corpse, the Wintu sometimes buried acorn and manzanita flour with a woman's body and venison with a man's (Du Bois 1935:65). More common was a liquid offering for the soul's journey to the other world: The Atsugewi set down a basket of water (Garth 1953:166), and the Wintu placed a basket of acorn-meal water at the right side of the body in the grave (Du Bois 1935:65). Meal offerings were common, especially in southern California (Kroeber 1925:253). Pomoan women would "feed the spirits of the dead" for one year. The women walked over the paths where the dead used to walk, singing mourning songs and scattering pinole or acorn meal (Loeb 1926:289). At an Owens Valley Paiute funeral, relatives sprinkled pine nuts and seeds (and later wheat) on the ground for the ghost (Steward 1933:297). A Wintu person would offer acorn meal when she or he saw a whirlwind of dust, which was taken to be the spirit of a deceased person (Du Bois 1935:77). All such acts affirmed the ties between the deceased and the living community.

Polluted states necessitating food taboos lasted a period of days following the funeral, with other observances for a longer period, often a year, after the death. An especially widespread custom was refraining from the consumption of fish, meat, and/or grease during a period of ritual impurity, often four or five days.[114] Most often these taboos applied to the relatives and ritual specialists, but everyone in an Atsugewi village avoided meat on the day of the funeral (Garth 1953:166). The Tübatulabal forbade certain relatives from eating meat, grease, or fish for three weeks to six months after the death. This period was broken with the face-washing ceremony, which included a feast with meat. A failure to observe the meat taboo showed disrespect for the dead, "as it meant one was eating corpse"; violators were subject to witchcraft from relatives of the deceased (Voegelin 1938:47, 68). The Owens Valley Paiute followed a similar custom, with the mourning period lasting a year (Steward 1933:298). After a Tolowa funeral, mourners needed a purification rite before they could eat; during a five-day mourning period, no villagers were allowed to search for food, nor could the mother of a deceased child cook for its father (Drucker 1937:255–56). Just as during menstruation and pregnancy, the eating habits of Atsugewi husband and wife were linked. Accordingly, the surviving spouse would not eat meat for several days after the burial, as it was believed that a gopher might smell the meat in the corpse and dig it up (Garth 1953:167). In some death rituals food played a symbolic role: After a Nisenan burial relatives covered their faces with a mixture of ash from burned acorns and pine pitch, which they could not remove until a public mourning ceremony a few weeks or months later (Beals 1933:377).

Beyond the biological states of gender and age, social status was rarely correlated with food in Native California, partly because of the prevailing egalitarianism throughout the region. While wealthy men in the Northwest owned particular food resources, they ate much as their poorer neighbors did. In fact, among the Yurok, as in most groups, wealthy men or those in a position of leadership were expected to generously distribute food to others (Kroeber 1960:143). In most societies, however, food proscriptions applied to those with special skills or specific occupations, particularly shamans and other seekers of spiritual power. Some taboos were absolute. Members of Pomo secret societies could never eat the flesh of gray squirrels, woodpeckers, orioles, quails, or wild pigeons; they were forbidden the birds because they imitated their sounds during ceremonies. Pomo doctors and members of the secret society could never eat any kind of caterpillar, nor could the latter eat eggs (Loeb 1926:175, 164). Among the

Cahuilla, flesh of large carnivores such as bears and mountain lions was avoided by all but old people and shamans: "Only they could dare to eat the flesh, because they had access to supernatural power ..." (Bean 1972:63). All these individuals, especially initiated and prospective doctors, had to follow situational food taboos. When preparing for a ceremony or training to be a doctor, a Hupa individual could eat only acorn mush. One doctor, refraining from water during his "medicine hunting," ate seaweed to intensify his thirst, thereby attempting "to influence the divinities by self-torture" (Goddard 1903:29, 65, 31, 88). During the five-day period of Wintu shamanistic instruction, the candidates were supposed to observe a complete fast. Although they may not have done it, at least they abstained from meat and salt (Du Bois 1935:89). Wintu shamanistic observances included numerous food-related customs. A shaman had to follow any food taboos imposed by his particular spirits, not eat hot foods (which destroyed his sucking powers), not drink intoxicating liquors, and not eat with menstruating women. When the shaman was in a trance the odor of cooking food was distasteful to spirits (1935:115).

In an important essay on Yurok menstruation, Buckley noted the "direct parallels in conception, ritualization, and goal orientation between male training and female menstrual practice" (1988:197). While Native Californians clearly differed in their beliefs, the Yurok practice may be an indication of more general beliefs. The resemblance of shamans' food taboos to those of menstruating women suggests that in much of the region food was directly implicated in states of power, pollution, and purification, linking all the transitional periods of birth, puberty, marriage, and death (including hunting and warfare), as well as times of illness. Certainly women often encountered the same food taboos throughout their life cycle. For instance, among both the Atsugewi and Central Coast Pomo, mothers who had just given birth went through the same restrictions as a girl at puberty (Garth 1953:158; Loeb 1926:253). While in many groups seekers of spiritual power were male, this was not always the case. Pomo women, for example, could be sucking doctors (Patterson 1995:110), and most Yurok and Hupa doctors were female (Kroeber 1925:137). Atsugewi women rarely went on power quests to acquire guardian spirits, but they did obtain spiritual power. "Usually their power came to them during the puberty dances, when they bore a child, or when they were in mourning" (Garth 1953:188). Notably, these gifts involved food: "Common powers for women were those that aided in root digging or seed gathering" (ibid.), paralleling the spiritual cultivation (and isolation) practiced by hunters. Among the Foothill Yokuts, those seeking spiritual power induced dreams by avoiding meat or grease in any form. "Acorn mush and gruel is the regular diet during such quest periods" (Gayton 1948b:239), the same diet as a pubescent girl's.

In understanding these customs, it is important, whenever possible, to bear in mind the distinction between a taboo (supernaturally sanctioned law) and pollution (symbolic contamination) (Buckley and Gottlieb 1988:4). Reportedly, fresh meat and fish were taboo to those Tolowa who were "unclean"—menstruants and men and women who had recently had sexual intercourse; these foods made them ill and gave hunters bad luck (Drucker 1937:262). While the Tolowa may indeed have conceived of these states as impure, such beliefs may have been much more complex. In the scholarly literature, these customs have been seen as only negative and contaminating, and from a male perspective; both the Native consultants and the anthropologists were commonly male (although it is true that Native women also held such views). Viewed from another perspective, however, the customs may have been ambiguous or even beneficial. The resemblances among these taboos may indicate that women at these times might themselves have been spiritually powerful. Buckley indicates that Yurok women at menstruation were at the peak of their spiritual powers and needed to be kept separate so that they could concentrate and focus their minds. These restrictions on female behavior—forbidding women to eat with men—may have been for the protection of the women as much as the men.

Young women were also related to food on a more metaphorical level. In some groups, a girl's puberty ceremony was considered a kind of "ripening" or "cooking." The Kechayi Yokuts term for the first fruits ceremony for acorns, seeds, and salmon was the same as the word for a girl's first menses ceremony (nahala'oša) (Gayton

1948b:165). As part of a girl's puberty rite, some southern groups (Tübatulabal, Cahuilla, Luiseño, Diegueño, Mohave) included "baking" the girl in a pit of hot sand (Kroeber 1925:862).[115] Kroeber argues that this was to keep the girl warm, as she also drinks and bathes in warm water. The same reason, preventing her from catching a cold, was given for the Eastern Pomo. During her four-day seclusion, a pubescent girl was required to lay on a tule bed built over a smoldering fire (Loeb 1926:271–72). The custom is similar to a woman's seclusion after childbirth among the Eastern Pomo. For the birth of an important family's child, the head of the secret society placed herbs and medicines in a pit of coals, and the mother was put over it on a bed of grass: "It was warm and comfortable and supposed to have healing qualities" (1926:251). While suggestive, the implications of these customs are obscure. Parkman notes that the Pomo invoked taboos for a woman at the moments when she was most distinctly female—birth and puberty—and citing Lévi-Strauss, argues that Pomo men remained associated with a state of nature while women began in it and were transformed into a cultured state (1994:26). We lack enough information to clarify these arguments, but women were definitely associated with the cultural practice of cooking throughout the region.

Finally, these menstrual customs had serious implications for Native subsistence practices (Yurok, Buckley 1988:205; Pomo, Patterson 1995:140–41). During the period of observance—ten days (a third of the month) among the Yurok—the food quest for the entire family would have been curtailed. As neither the wife nor the husband could gather food, the family had to live off stores, unless aided by older and younger men and women. Both Buckley and Patterson cite the literature on synchronized menstruation, in which women living in close proximity may cycle at the same time. If so, this would have an even stronger effect on the community's subsistence practices. In any case, these practices would tend to limit exploitation of available food resources, serving perhaps as a conservation mechanism. And just as the husband-wife observances strengthened and publicly affirmed the conjugal bond, so would such beliefs deepen kinship ties within and without the nuclear family.

In Native California, as almost everywhere, food was a marker of ethnicity and subcultures (Brown and Mussell 1984). These cultures were above all local. Individuals generally lived their lives within a ten- to fifteen-mile radius of their birthplace, and people noted that those who spoke different languages often ate different foods. One widespread myth, dealing with the theft of fire, accounted for diversity in both food and languages. In one Sierra Miwok version, Flute-player was distributing fire to the people in the assembly lodge when Coyote interrupted him.

> The middle people talked correctly, for they were around the fire. The people who were around the fire cooked their food. The people in the middle obtained the acorns and the manzanita. The others had nothing to eat. That which they ate was always raw. It was Coyote's fault that the others talked incorrectly. If Coyote had said nothing, all would have received fire. He spoiled the scheme, when he shouted at Flute-player, for Flute-player stopped. He stopped before he had played the fourth flute and before he had distributed all of the fire (Gifford 1917:286).

As noted in the first section, cuisines in California fell into geographic patterns, both within and without the region.[116] Roughly, there was a northwestern, central, southern, and eastern (Great Basin) style of cooking, defined more on the basis of focal ingredients than on modes of processing or preparation. Even here, though, there were regional distinctions, such as the preference for smoking in the northwest and the prevalence of direct boiling with clay pots in the south. Native Californians recognized these culinary distinctions. Some groups, especially among the Shoshonean peoples of the Great Basin, referred to others by the food they ate; one Atsugewi group was named "fish eaters" (Garth 1953:130). Often, the foods of exotic groups were disparaged. The Wintu, a group that inhabited diverse territories with differentiated access to foods, were keen critics of their neighbors' cuisines.

> The Upper Sacramento Wintu were called derisively "mussel-eaters" and ridiculed by the McCloud Wintu for grinding deer bones into flour, to which the Upper Sacramento people responded that the McCloud people ate salmon-bone flour and "besides they stank of salmon and bear." Tildy Brock (McCloud) was asked by

Jake Cornish (Upper Sacramento) to live with him after the death of his Shastan wife. The old lady of eighty-five years spiritedly replied that she didn't want to live up north there and eat old stale clams. Disdaining the food supply of another subarea was a frequent way of refusing an undesirable offer of marriage from an outsider (Du Bois 1935:6).[117]

The Gabrielino and Mohave tended to reject food from other groups, such as the Spanish, in the belief that "every nation had its own peculiar food and that for one to partake of the characteristic nourishment of the other or to mingle with its women, or in fact associate in any prolonged contact, was bound in the very nature of things to bring sickness" (Kroeber 1925:631).

Given these local and regional differences, can one speak of a Native Californian cuisine? It depends on one's definition. A cuisine implies a technical and cultural elaboration of food preparation and consumption (Appadurai 1988:3). According to Mintz:

> What makes a cuisine is not a set of recipes aggregated in a book, or a series of particular foods associated with a particular setting, but something more. I think a cuisine requires a population that eats that cuisine with sufficient frequency to consider themselves experts on it. They all believe, and *care* that they believe, that they know what it consists of, how it is made, and how it should taste. In short a genuine cuisine has common social roots; it is the food of a community—albeit often a very large community (1996:96).

Although the evidence is not definitive, it appears that many Californian groups did think of food in this way. However, as the preceding discussion implied, they defined their culinary communities in local or perhaps regional terms rather than those applying to the entire state. In this regard they were actually similar to most historic cuisines. Whether speaking of large regions of culinary diversity such as China and India, or smaller areas such as France or Italy, until quite recent times peoples' foods and food customs were localized.

What Native Californians did not have is what has been called a high (*haute*) cuisine (Goody 1982). With the rise of class hierarchies and specialization, food is elaborated. In such cultures, as in France, there has been a tendency to differentiate between high and low cuisines, court and peasant foods, foods of the city and of the countryside. Using the example of India, Appadurai has commented on "a gustatory approach to food" (1988:5). As in nineteenth-century France, for example, such a cuisine is "a partly autonomous enterprise, freed of its moral and medical constraints." Only recently, he finds, did this approach emerge in India. The Native Californian situation was similar. First, even the wealthy elite ate the same as their poorer companions (although the well-off may have had more to eat). More importantly, for most of its history, the cultures of the region embedded their food customs in a fundamentally moral and religious context, leaving this stage (though not entirely) only in recent years, with the radical change in their foodways.

HISTORICAL PERSPECTIVES

Records of food traditions are relatively meager, as the "artifact" produced is consumed.[118] Yet change and intercultural exchange have been especially important in food customs. Italians did not always eat pasta and tomatoes; Indians and Chinese did not always have chili peppers.[119] Until recently, only elite Japanese ate white rice. Thinking of Native California in a timeless and static "ethnographic present" (represented by many of the selections here) can give us only a partial understanding at best.

People have been living in what is now the state of California for over 13,000 years, and during that time they have been constantly changing (Fagan 2003).[120] Acorn-eating may now be commonly associated with the region, but this was not always the case. While Native Californians have been able to exploit a fairly stable range of plants and animals, the specific technologies and customs they used for the hunting of animals and gathering of plants evolved. The first settlers moved into the region at least by the end of the last Ice Age, about 11,000 to 12,000 years ago. Like other nomadic groups throughout the continent, these Paleo-Indians subsisted largely on big game, supplemented by small game and plants. As newcomers, they needed time to learn their way around their environment and develop methods to exploit its resources. Starting about 11,000 years ago, inhabitants of the state began to settle in larger, more permanent villages. By moving around during the year into differing habitats, these Archaic peoples were able to choose from a much more diversified selection of foods. It was during this period that many characteristic Californian culinary object-types were introduced to the state: mortars and pestles, boiling stones, and basketry. Along with these tools came the complete processing sequence of leaching the tannic acid in acorns. While acorns and salmon were consumed during the Archaic period, they did not become staples in much of the state until 4000 to 1000 years ago, depending on the area (Basgall 1987:35). An important plant resource of the Archaic was seeds, which were ground with milling slabs and handstones, a sort of mano/metate. During this so-called "Pacific Period," which lasted until Euro-American contact in the late seventeenth century, people again developed a focal economy. They consumed many kinds of plants and animals, but concentrated on a few, key items for most of their diet. The fish catch, for example, was increased by the systematic use of nets, traps, and dams. In hunting, the more efficient bow and arrow replaced spears and darts. Methods of long-term food storage, such as granaries and drying, allowed a greater population density and social complexity. It has also been suggested that it was during this period that strongly gendered subsistence activities (female acorn processing and male big-game hunting) replaced an earlier regime in which men, women, and children more often cooperated in gathering food (McGuire and Hildebrandt 1994).

This ancient subsistence style was shattered and transformed upon European contact. The first encounter with what is now California came in 1542, when Juan Cabrillo entered San Diego Bay, claiming the lands for Spain. Effective Spanish control, however, did not come until 1769, when the system of missions was initiated throughout southern and central California. As Sidney Mintz (1996) maintains, food is always implicated in questions of power. Just as it was woven into the fabric of slavery, so did food become a central part of the Euro-American attempt to eradicate and suppress Native Californian cultures. During the colonial period (primarily Hispanic, but also Russian in Mendocino County), the missions exposed Natives to new foods as well as new beliefs; the converts were expected to supply much of their own diet, ingredients such as barley, peas, beans, and beef (Heizer and Elsasser 1980:227). At the same time, however, that they worked in the mission kitchens, Indian laborers continued to gather aboriginal foods (Hackel 1998:124–25). We have a few reports of the early Native attitudes toward these strange goods. The Kashaya Pomo initially threw out the new foods they were given by white men, thinking they were poison, and they boiled whole coffee beans as if they were acorns (Oswalt 1964:251). When some Cahuilla first saw bacon they thought it was wood and used it to fuel their fire; they threw out the fresh figs they were given because they took the seeds for worms (Dozier 1998:77). Acculturation in food customs continued during the Mexican period (1821–1846); while the secularization of the missions in 1834 led to a system of large land-grant ranches (ranchos). Some of the foods and implements introduced during the Spanish/Mexican period have become thoroughly integrated into Native cultures. The Chumash, for example, used a soapstone frying pan (*comal*) to cook flat wheat breads, and they incorporated introduced ingredients such as beans and garlic into their folktales (Hudson and Blackburn 1983:196; Blackburn 1975:315).[121]

The upheaval following the discovery of gold in 1848 brought a massive influx of Anglo settlers. With it came a severe loss of aboriginal population due to disease, murder, and slavery, as well as a dispossession from their land and traditional gathering practices. Food, a basic cultural expression, was naturally at the heart of American settlers' views of Native Californians. As a mode of subsistence, farming was commonly believed to be inherently superior to hunting and gathering, and Natives were derogatorily referred to as "Diggers," for their customs of digging for roots and bulbs. For instance, T. Butler King, in his official report on conditions in California in 1850, described the state's Indians as "the lowest grade of human beings. They live chiefly on acorns, roots, insects, and the kernel of the pine burr; occasionally they catch fish and game. They use the bow and arrow, but are said to be too lazy and effeminate to make successful hunters. They do not appear to have the slightest inclination to cultivate the soil, nor do they attempt it" (in Rawls 1984:190). To many settlers, Native Californians were little more than animals, obtaining whatever was available. According to the *San Francisco Bulletin* of 1857, they fed "on roots, snakes and insects, and on the grasses of the fields like beasts." The animal comparison was underlined by accounts of hunters eating blood and innards; when whites sampled such staples as acorn mush or bread, they found them uniformly unpalatable. As we have seen, Native peoples were skilled hunters and gatherers who carefully cultivated wild plants and animal resources, and some, in the south, were indeed farmers. Still, compared to Anglo-Americans, they did consume a wider variety of foods and ate foods that the new settlers did not. Attitudes toward foods thus became part of the ammunition used to suppress and exterminate the Native populations of the state.

These radical environmental and demographic changes could not help but have a substantial effect on Native food customs. Our best understanding of this process of acculturation comes from ethnohistorian Sherburne Cook (1941), and those who have followed in his path (Milliken 1995; Preston 1998). During the century following the discovery of gold, Native peoples gradually lost control of their food supply. It became harder to obtain traditional foods as private property and game laws restricted access to gathering territories, the diversity and quantity of animal and plant populations declined drastically, food-gathering in a cash economy came at a high cost in time and effort, and traditional subsistence knowledge and skills diminished. At the same time, Native Californians had greater access to new foods. As part of the forced acculturation in missions and reservations, they were given new foods and raised their own, and they purchased commercial or processed foods as they became part of the cash economy (Keller 2002). Because of these forces, many Native people came to prefer the taste of new foods. These changes were gradual, however, varying from region to region and across the generations— with rural and older people maintaining the old ways.

Native Californians made creative adaptations to these new foods, in many cases accommodating them to old categories and customs. Among the Wintu, for example, "Food names and words concerned with the preparation and consumption of food... show a preponderance of old words with new meanings" (Lee 1943:435). The Wintu word for pine sugar was used to refer to store sugar, which had replaced it. Similarity in appearance was another basis for terms; the

"Indians [probably Sierra Miwok] making Chemuck"
[food, e.g., acorn meal], ca. 1870.
BY J. D. SMILLIE, REPRODUCED FROM WILLIAM CULLEN BRYANT, ED.,
PICTURESQUE AMERICA, VOL. 1 (NEW YORK, 1874).

same words being used for thick gravy and thick acorn soup, melted butter and thin acorn soup. The word for cracking open buckeyes was used for shelling peas. However, recently introduced foods (such as apples, tomatoes, and peaches) retained their white names. Similarly, among the Indians of the southern part of the state, new foods were often processed with old technologies. Cahuilla women in the late nineteenth century treated wheat grains like grass seeds—parching the grains with hot coals in a basket or pot, winnowing them with a basket, and grinding the meal in a mortar (Griset 1990:188).[122]

Contemporary Native food habits are a continuation and adaptation of traditional foodways. Writing at the outbreak of World War II, Cook predicted that traditional Californian foods would be gone within a generation or two (1941:59), but like similar predictions for the oblivion of their culture in general, this has not come to pass. A wonderful sense of continuity and change is evident in Kathleen Smith's accounts of the food traditions of her Dry Creek Pomo/Bodega Miwok family in the 1940s and 1950s (1990a, 1991b). Smith—like Kashaya Pomo Essie Parrish (Oswalt 1964:295, 297) and Cahuilla Katherine Saubel (Dozier 1998:76–77)—remembers always having food during hard times. Like many rural families, the Smiths planted a vegetable garden, raised hogs, chickens, and cows, made sausages, canned fruits and vegetables, and took foods from the wild—hunting and fishing, gathering abalone and seaweed. It is true that few, if any, Native people today eat a wholly traditional diet; they have added new items such as wheat (in the form of bread or tortillas), beef, chicken, and processed foods. Yet old foods are prepared in new ways (such as acorn pulverized in an electric grinder, leached in a sink, and cooked in metal pots on a stove), and new foods are cooked in old ways (large pieces of beef substituted for deer in pit earth ovens).[123] Many meals combine old and new foods.[124] And intertribal influences have continued; in the past few decades, Southwestern Indian cre- olized foods such as fry bread and tacos have become popular both at home and at community events (Peri 1987a; cf. Cox and Jacobs 1991:160). Many foods, such as pit-roasted deer and boiled acorn mush, are still prepared and eaten in a more or less traditional man- ner, especially during feasts and ceremonies.

Cuisines, like all cultural traditions, are actively selected and con- structed for personal and social ends, not passively received and repli- cated. As in many cultures, for Native Californians food has become a self-conscious affirmation of ethnicity, "a performance of group identity" (Brown and Mussell 1984). Distinctive foods and styles of eating distinguish peoples, a fact recognized even in Native myths.[125] The importance of traditional Native Californian foods and food- related objects can be readily seen from their frequent occurrence in aesthetic versions. Baskets and acorns are common in paintings and drawings, and objects used for cooking and eating are a prime subject for miniaturization. In contemporary society, the acorn has become the Native food *par excellence*.[126] Although important, acorns were only part of the vast array of the traditional Native larder of seeds, leaves, and roots, not to mention insects, mollusks, and other kinds of animals. Acorns have become so prominent due partly to the difficulty of obtaining these other foods, partly because of their greater palata- bility to western tastes, and only partly to their place in the traditional diet. And as with many ethnic symbols, this adoption is partly in re- sponse to non-Native understandings, so widely reported in anthro- pological accounts. However, unlike interethnic foods such as the Italian pizza or the Jewish bagel (Gabaccia 1998), acorns and other

Californian Indian foods have not been taken over by many non-Natives. Unlike the foods of other ethnic, immigrant groups, Native Californian foods were wild and are now greatly diminished and restricted. This is true even for the salmon, one food that has been adopted by non-Natives (McCovey 2003).

As we know from Marcel Proust's famous memory of the madeleine tea cakes of his childhood, food can be a powerful agent of nostalgia (Sutton 2001). Essie Parrish and Kathleen Smith recall the foods of their youth with fondness. Smith writes of roasted abalone on the beach, soda made from oranges and mineral spring water, and her sister's Crab Louis. Intertwined with these feelings of family and nature is also sorrow for those who have passed on. Acorn soup is offered as a "healing and soothing food to elders or others who are ill" (McCarthy 1993:213). Food is an especially vulnerable symbol for living cultures. As food journalist Dorothy Kalins writes, "Hunting antique food is not like hunting antiques. Furniture survives as long as someone has the sense to bring it in out of the rain; cooking dies without the cook" (1995). As with other performative traditions such as language, Native Californians now struggle to maintain their culinary repertoire. The memory of those who came before motivates Kashaya Pomo Julia Parker to demonstrate and teach the art of stone pounding and boiling acorn (Ortiz and Parker 1991). In addition to the many food-related dances and ceremonies, some Native people are maintaining traditional food customs during puberty and menstruation.[127] It is because of such efforts that Native Californians will honor their ancestral foods as long as they think of themselves as distinct peoples.

Yet foods of the past can be more than nostalgic. A recent movement advocates returning to traditional foods in a wide-spread, sustainable way. In this enterprise, culinary ethnography—like ethnography in general (Marcus and Fischer 1986)—can serve as cultural critique, using descriptions of one culture to challenge the premises of another. Since the Romantic era, Western culture has included a strong element of anti-modernism. Notions of conservation and preservation were exemplified in the Progressive era by the Arts and Crafts movment, the creation of the National Park system, and even the beginnings of American anthropology. Until the mid-twentieth century,

Rae Navarro (Chumash) with an ear of roasted corn,
Fall pow-wow, Santa Ynez, Santa Barbara County, 1996.
PHOTOGRAPH BY DUGAN AGUILAR. COURTESY OF THE PHOTOGRAPHER.

however, self-conscious preservation had not been applied to food. Stimulated by James Beard, the "American Cuisine movement" of the 1950s and 1960s called attention to vanishing and now-prized foods and customs (Brenner 1999:190–91).

This was followed, in the 1970s, by what has been called the New American Cuisine. Associated with chef Alice Waters and her Berkeley restaurant, Chez Panisse, it insists on simple preparations of fresh, local, and organic ingredients. Waters looks for her inspiration to France, with a Mediterranean climate comparable to northern California. Regarding Chez Panisse's culture as the "foraging" of a "hunter-gatherer," she writes, "I have always believed that a restaurant can be no better than the ingredients it has to work with. As much as any other factor, Chez Panisse has been defined by the search for ingredients" (1990:113, cf. 114).[128] This is the same philosophy announced by Lucy Smith, a Dry Creek Pomo woman: "The basket is in the roots, that's where it begins." Ethnobotanist Gary Paul Nabhan has taken this to its logical extreme, recently trying to eat food only from his local "foodshed," items gathered or produced within 200 miles of his home (2002). Moving beyond nostalgia, the movement for sustainable food and agriculture is attempting to change the basic supply system, an effort best seen in the many farmers' markets. Among its many efforts, the international Slow Foods association is methodically identifying and preserving endangered foods and culinary practices (Petrini 2001).

The foods and culinary techniques of Native Americans can be an inspiration to those who now live on their lands. Although the local cuisines of the Southwest have inspired chefs such as Mark Miller, Native California has been ignored as a model. Such an exemplar would call for a diverse range of organic foods, with a greater reliance on a vegetarian diet, freshness for taste and nutrition, naturally preserved foods, and an effective, sustainable agriculture, all consumed in a setting of family and friends. The preservation of traditional Californian food systems helps support our common environment, both natural and cultural. There is, then, much that we all can learn from Native Californian cuisine.

A NOTE ON THE SELECTIONS

Several criteria have guided the selection of essays in this anthology. The core of this volume of reprints is the food-related sections from classic ethnographies (most published by the University of California). These present food in one integrated discussion, from gathering through storage, processing, cooking, and eating. Most of this literature and the analytic work that has followed it has stressed basic food resources and ecological adaptation (well-covered in two recent anthologies, Bean and Blackburn 1976; Blackburn and Anderson 1993). Because of this, where possible, the selections here focus on the relatively neglected aspects of cooking and eating. An attempt has been made to include representative selections from all major regions of the present-day state, including groups from the Great Basin culture area living in eastern California. In terms of subdiscipline and time perspective, this volume focuses on ethnographic and ethnohistoric studies (mostly from the nineteenth and twentieth centuries), rather than those by archaeologists (see Raab and Jones 2004). With the exception of the section on contemporary perspectives, selections have been generally chosen from before 1960 (and which may thus be referred to as "classic"). This anthology is therefore not a full, comprehensive ethnography of contemporary California Indian food practices. (The closest to this are the writings of Beverly R. Ortiz; see also the continuing coverage of the topic in *News from Native California*, especially Dubin and Tolley 2004.) As desirable as such an investigation would be, it would not replace the usefulness of a collection such as this, devoted to the description of customs which are no longer fully practiced. In making choices, the quality of the fieldwork was a factor, greater emphasis being given to studies based on more numerous consultants over a longer period of time. The stress here is on the descriptive rather than analytic and on older rather than more recent studies. The necessary contemporary and Native perspective is placed at the end.

In terms of publication format, I have chosen published material rather than archival or manuscript sources. (The only exceptions are the two field-note extracts that accompany the Enos and Hudson photographic portfolios.) At the same time, preference has been given to material that is out of print and not included in other recent anthologies (although exceptions have been made for critical essays, such as Gifford's "California Indian Balanophagy"). Readers should consult perhaps the two best published overviews of Native food customs in what is now California: the chapter on "The Food Quest" in Heizer and Elsasser (1980:82–113) and Fowler's summary of "Subsistence" in the Great Basin volume of the *Handbook of North American Indians* (1986). Generally, the selections included here are of moderate length; fewer, longer selections have been chosen over many, shorter selections, while at the same time omitting important works (e.g., the long section on food in the Miwok volume by Barrett and Gifford 1933) that were too long and difficult to excerpt. While an attempt was made to present complete discussions, in some cases (e.g., Greengo, Barrows, and Swezey) cuts needed to be made for reasons of space. Finally, when given a choice, more readable selections were chosen over raw field notes.

Editorial changes to the reprints have been minimal; the major change being the placement of all references and notes in one listing at the end. For practical reasons, most original illustrations were omitted, but this has been compensated by the addition of photographic portfolios of similar material. Similarly, in some cases (especially in Steward and Parrish), special linguistic symbols have been rendered in a simpler spelling. While a few obvious misspellings and factual errors were corrected, the reprinted text reproduces the author's original. This also means that matters of style vary somewhat throughout the volume.

Given the great number and extent of potential selections and the necessarily limited size of this volume—despite its length—the current selections can only be representative and not comprehensive. In my introductions to the selections, I have included basic biographical information on the authors, something about the circumstances of their fieldwork, and just a few points of relevant ethnography. For further information on the tribal cultures, readers should consult the basic ethnographies cited and the two Handbooks devoted to California Indians (Kroeber 1925; Heizer 1978). For authors with several selections, readers might want to consult all the introductions for further biographical data. The bibliography is a guide to some of the many good sources that could not be included here. *Food in California Indian Culture* must be an appetizer, not a meal.

OVERVIEW

THE FOOD PROBLEM IN CALIFORNIA

Alfred L. Kroeber

With the *Handbook of the Indians of California*, Alfred Kroeber essentially created the field of California Indian studies. Alfred Louis Kroeber (1876–1960)
grew up in New York City, the son of a German-born importer, and attended
Columbia University (B.A. in 1896, M.A. in 1897, both in English). After studying with Franz Boas, in 1901 Kroeber became the first to earn an anthropology doctorate at Columbia, one of the first such degrees in the nation. That
September he was hired for the new anthropology program at the University
of California, where he remained for the rest of his life, serving in the
department (instructor in 1901, assistant professor in 1906, associate professor in 1912, professor in 1919, emeritus in 1946) and museum (curator in 1908,
director in 1925, emeritus in 1946). In the course of his long teaching career,
Kroeber was responsible for training almost all the scholars of Native
Californian cultures during the first half of the twentieth century. In addition
to California, Kroeber conducted fieldwork in the Plains (1899–1901), New
Mexico (1915–20), Mexico (1924, 1930), and Peru (1925, 1926, 1942).

   Kroeber began the research for what would become the *Handbook* upon
his arrival in the state in 1900, and by 1903 he was planning a comprehensive
review of Californian ethnology. He based the lengthy compendium on his many
research trips throughout the state, especially among the Yurok and to a lesser
extent the Mohave, and on the work of his colleagues and students. Although
he finished the manuscript in 1918, the volume was not published until 1925
because of war-time reductions at its publisher, the Smithsonian's Bureau of
American Ethnology. Kroeber structured the book by geography and ethnic
group, concluding with several summary chapters. He also scattered general
summaries throughout the tribal entries. For example, "The Food Problem in
California" was part of the Yokuts chapter. Although clearly somewhat
simplified, the passages included here were the first to systematically review
the food customs of the state's Native peoples.[1]

Handbook of the Indians of California (1925). Bureau of American Ethnology
Bulletin 78. Pp. 523–26, 814–17, 828–29.

THE FOOD PROBLEM IN CALIFORNIA

The California Indians are perhaps the most omnivorous group of tribes on the continent. The corn, salmon, buffalo, reindeer, or seal which formed the predominant staple in other regions, did indeed have a parallel in the acorn of California; but the parallel is striking rather than intrinsic.

To begin with, the oak is absent from many tracts. It does not grow in the higher mountains, in the desert, on most of the immediate coast; and it is at best rare in districts like the baked plains inhabited by the southern Yokuts valley tribes, a fact that may help to explain the permanent association and commingling of the majority of these tribes with their foothill neighbors. It is true that at worst it is rarely a far journey to an abundant growth of bearing acorns anywhere in California; but the availability of such supplies was greatly diminished by the habits of intense adherence to their limited soil followed by the great majority of divisions.

Then, where the acorn abounded, the practices both of collecting and of treating it led directly to the utilization also of other sources of nourishment. The farmer may and does hunt, or fish, or gather wild growths; but these activities, being of a different order, are a distraction from his regular pursuits, and an adjustment is necessary. Either the pursuit of wild foods becomes a subsidiary activity, indulged in intermittently as leisure affords, and from the motive of variety rather than need, or a sexual or seasonal division becomes established, which makes the same people in part, or for part of the year, farmers and in part hunters. An inclination of this sort is not wanting in many districts of California. The dry and hot summer makes an outdoor life in the hills, near the heads of the vanishing streams, a convenience and a pleasure which coincide almost exactly with the opportunity to hunt and to gather the various natural crops as they become available from month to month. The wet winter renders house life in the permanent settlement in a valley or on a river correspondingly attractive, and combines residence there with the easiest chance to fish the now enlarged streams on an extensive scale, or to pursue the swarms of arrived water fowl.

But this division was not momentous. The distances ranged over were minute. Fishing was not excluded among the hills. Deer, rabbits, and gophers could be hunted in the mild winter as well as in summer. And while acorns and other plant foods might be garnered each only over a brief season, it was an essential part of their use that much of their preparation as well as consumption should be spread through the cycle of the calendar.

Further, the food resources of California were bountiful in their variety rather than in their overwhelming abundance along special lines. If one supply failed, there were a hundred others to fall back upon. If a drought withered the corn shoots, if the buffalo unaccountably shifted, or the salmon failed to run, the very existence of peoples in other regions was shaken to its foundations. But the manifold distribution of available foods in California and the working out of corresponding means of reclaiming them prevented a failure of the acorn crop from producing similar effects. It might produce short rations and racking hunger, but scarcely starvation. It may be that it is chiefly our astounding ignorance of all the more intimate and basal phases of their lives that makes it seem as if downright mortal famine had been less often the portion of the Californian tribes than of those in most other regions of the continent. Yet, with all allowance for this potential factor of ignorance in our understanding, it does appear that such catastrophes were less deep and less regularly recurring. Both formulated and experiential tradition are nearly silent on actual famines, or refer to them with rationalizing abstraction. The only definite cases that have come to cognizance, other than for a few truly desert hordes whose slender subsistence permanently hung by a thread, are among the Mohave, an agricultural community in an oasis, and among the Indians of the lower Klamath, whose habits, in their primal dependence on the salmon, approximated those of the tribes of the coasts north of California.

The gathering of the acorn is like that of the pine nut; its leaching has led to the recognition of the serviceability of the buckeye once its poison is dissolved out; the grinding has stimulated the use of small hard seeds, which become edible only in pulverized form. The securing of plant foods in general is not separated by any gap of distinctive process from that of obtaining grasshoppers, caterpillars, maggots, snails, mollusks, crawfish, or turtles, which can be got in masses or are practically immobile: a woman's digging stick will procure worms as readily as bulbs. Again, it is only a step to the taking of minnows in brooks, or gophers, or lizards, or small birds: the simplest of snares, a long stick, a thrown stone even, suffice with patience, and a boy can help out his grandmother. The fish pot is not very different from the acorn receptacle, and weirs, traps, stiff nets, and other devices for capturing fish are made in the same technique of basketry as the beaters, carriers, and winnows for seeds. Even hunting was but occasionally the open, outright affair we are likely to think. Ducks were snared and netted, rabbits driven into nets, even deer caught in nooses and with similar devices. There is nothing in all this like the difference between riding down buffalo and gathering wild rice, like the break from whale hunting to berry picking, from farming to stalking deer.

The California Indian, then, secured his variety of foods by techniques that were closely interrelated, or, where diverse, connected by innumerable transitions. Few of the processes involved high skill or long experience for their successful application; none entailed serious danger, material exposure, or even strenuous effort. A little modification, and each process was capable of successful employment on some other class of food objects. Thus the activities called upon were distinguished by patience, simplicity, and crude adaptability rather than by intense endeavor and accurate specialization; and their outcome tended to manifold distribution and approximate balance in place of high yields of concentration along particular but detached lines.

The human food production of aboriginal California will accordingly not be well understood until a really thorough study has been made of all the activities of this kind among at least one people. The substances and the means are both so numerous that a recapitulation of such data as are available is always only a random, scattering selection.

Observers have mentioned what appealed to their sense of novelty or ingenuity, what they happened to see at a given moment, or what their native informants were interested in. But we rarely know whether such and such a device is peculiar to a locality or widespread, and if the former, why; whether it was a sporadic means or one that was seriously depended on; and what analogous ones it replaced. Statements that this tribe used a salmon harpoon, another a scoop net, a third a seine, a fourth poison, and that another built weirs, give us in their totality some approximation to a picture of the set of activities that underlie fishing in California as a whole: but for each individual group the statement is of little significance, for it is likely that those who used the nets used the spear and poison also, but under distinctive conditions; and when they did not, the question is whether the lack of one device is due to a more productive specialization of another, or to natural circumstances which made the employment of this or that method from the common stock of knowledge impracticable for certain localities.

There is, however, one point where neither experience not environment is a factor, and in which pure custom reigns supreme: the animals chosen for the list of those not eaten. Myth, magic, totemism, or other beliefs may be at the bottom; but every tribe has such an index, which is totally unconnected with its abilities, cultural or physical, to take food.

Among the Yokuts, one animal stands out as edible that everywhere in northern California is absolute taboo and deadly poison: the dog. The Yurok give as their formal reason for not drinking river water that a large stream might contain human foetuses or a dead dog. The Yokuts did not shrink from eating dogs.

Coyote flesh was generally avoided, whether from religious reverence or magical fear is not clear. Grizzly bear meat was also viewed askance. The bear might have devoured human flesh, which would be near to making its eater a cannibal. Besides, in all probability, there was a lurking suspicion that a grizzly might not be a real one, but a transformed bear doctor. The disposition of the animal showed itself in the muscular fibers bristling erect when the flesh was cut, the Yokuts say. Brown bears had fewer plays of the imagination directed upon them, but even their meat was sometimes avoided. Birds of prey and carrion from the eagle down to the crow were not eaten. Their flesh, of course, is far from palatable; but it is these very birds that are central in Yokuts totemism. And the rigid abstinence may have this religious motivation. All reptiles were unclean to the southern Yokuts, as to the Tübatulabal; but the northern tribes exercised a peculiar discrimination. The gopher snake, water snakes, and frogs were rejected, but lizards, turtles, and, what is strangest of all, the rattlesnake, were fit food to the Chukchansi. There is a likely alien influence in this, for the neighboring Miwok probably, and the Salinans to the west certainly, ate snakes, lizards, and even frogs. On the other hand, the southern Yokuts relished the skunk, which when smoked to death in its hole was without offensive odor; while to the Miwok and Salinans it was abomination.

FOOD

Plants appear to have furnished a larger part of the diet than animals in almost all parts of California. Fish and mollusks were probably consumed in larger quantities than flesh in regions stocked with them, especially the salmon-carrying rivers of northern California, the Santa Barbara Archipelago, Clear and Klamath Lakes, the larger bays like that of San Francisco, and in a measure the immediate coast everywhere. Of game, the rodents, from jack rabbits to gophers, together with birds, evidently furnished more food the seasons through than deer and other ruminants. Foods rejected varied locally, of course, but in general northern California looked upon dog and reptile flesh as poisonous, but did not scruple to eat earthworms, grasshoppers, hymenopterous larvae, certain species of caterpillars, and similar invertebrates when they could be gathered in sufficient masses to make their consumption worth while. In south central California, the taboos against dogs and reptiles were less universal, and south of Tehachapi and east of the Sierra snakes and lizards were eaten by a good many groups. In much of the greater part of the State acorns constituted a larger part of the diet than any other food, and a lengthy though simple technique of gathering, hulling, drying, grinding, sifting, leaching, and cooking had been devised. Many other seeds and fruits were treated similarly; buckeyes (*Aesculus*), for instance, and the seeds of various grasses, sages, compositae, and the like. These were whipped into receptacles with seed beaters, which varied only in detail from one end of the State to the other; collected in close-woven or glue-smeared conical baskets; parched with coals in trays; winnowed by tossing in trays; ground; and then eaten either dry, or, like acorn meal, as lumps of unleavened bread baked by the open fire or as boiled gruel. Leaching was on sand which drained off the hot water. In the north, the meal was spread directly on the sand; in central California fir leaves were often interposed; in the south, also an openwork basket. Pulverization was either by pounding in a mortar or rubbing on the undressed metate or oval grinding slab. The history and interrelations of the various types of these implements is somewhat intricate and has been discussed in the chapters on the Maidu, Chumash, Luiseño, and Cahuilla. The grinding process had become a well-established cultural pattern. Besides seeds, dried salmon, vertebrae, whole small rodents, berries, and fruits were often pulverized, especially for storage. In analogous manner, other processes of the acorn and seed preparation complex were extended to various foods: leaching to wild plums, parching to grasshoppers and caterpillars. This complex clearly dominates the food habits of California.

Where the acorn fails, other foods are treated similarly, though sometimes with considerable specialization of process; the mesquite bean in the southern desert, the piñon nut east of the Sierra, the water lily in the Klamath-Modoc Lakes.

Agriculture had only touched one periphery of the State, the Colorado River bottom, although the seed-using and fairly sedentary habits of virtually all the other tribes would have made possible the taking over of the art with relatively little change of mode of life. Evidently planting is a more fundamental innovation to people used to depending on nature than it seems to those who have once acquired the practice. Moreover, in most of California the food supply, largely through its variety, was reasonably adequate, in spite of a rather heavy population—probably not far from one person to the square mile on the average. In most parts of the State there is little mention of famines....

FISHING

In fresh-water and still bays fish are more successfully taken by rude people with nets or weirs or poison than by line. Fishhooks are therefore employed only occasionally. This is the case in California. There was probably no group that was ignorant of the fishhook, but one hears little of its use. The one exception was on the southern coast, where deep water appears to have restricted the use of nets. The prevalent hook in this region was an unbarbed or sometimes barbed piece of haliotis cut almost into a circle. Elsewhere the hook was in use chiefly for fishing in the larger lakes, and in the higher mountains where trout were taken. It consisted most commonly of a wooden shank with a pointed bone lashed backward on it at an angle of 45° or less. Sometimes two such bones projected on opposite sides. The gorget, a straight bone sharpened on both ends and suspended from a string in its middle, is reported from the Modoc, but is likely to have had a wider distribution.

The harpoon was probably known to every group in California whose territory contained sufficient bodies of water. The Colorado River tribes provide the only known exception. The type of harpoon is everywhere substantially identical. The shaft, being intended for thrusting and not throwing, is long and slender. The foreshaft is usu- ally double, one prong being slightly longer than the other, presum- ably because the stroke was most commonly delivered at an angle to the bottom. The toggle heads are small, of bone and wood tightly wrapped with string and pitched. The socket is most frequently in or near the end. The string leaving the head at or near the middle, the socket end serves as a barb. This rather rude device is sufficient be- cause the harpoon is rarely employed for game larger than a salmon. The lines are short and fastened to the shaft.

A heavier harpoon which was perhaps hurled was used by the northwestern coast tribes for taking sea lions. Only the heads have been preserved. These are of bone or antler and possess a true barb as well as socket. A preserved Chumash harpoon has a detachable wooden foreshaft tipped with a flint blade and lashed-on bone barb. The foreshaft itself serves as toggle.

There is one record of the spear thrower; also a specimen from the Chumash. This is of wood and is remarkable for its excessively short, broad, and unwieldy shape. It is probably authentic, but its entire uniqueness renders caution necessary in drawing inferences from this solitary example.

The seine for surrounding fish, the stretched gill net, and the dip net were known to all the Californians, although many groups had occasion to use only certain varieties. The form and size of the dip net, of course, differed according as it was used in large or small streams, in the surf, or in standing waters. The two commonest forms of frame were a semicircular hoop bisected by the handle, and two long diverging poles crossed and braced in the angle. A kite-shaped frame was sometimes employed for scooping. Nets without poles had floats of wood or tule stems. The sinkers were grooved or nicked stones, the commonest type of all being a flat beach pebble notched on opposite edges to prevent the string slipping. Perforated stones are known to have been used as net sinkers only in northwestern California, and even there they occur by the side of the grooved variety. They are usually distinguishable without difficulty from the perforated stone of southern and central California which served as a digging stick weight, by the fact that their perforation is normally not in the middle. The northwesterners also availed themselves of naturally perforated stones.

Fish weirs were used chiefly in northern California, where the streams carry salmon. In the northwest such "dams" sometimes became the occasion of important rituals.

Fish poison was fed into small streams and pools by a number of tribes: the Pomo, Yana, Yokuts, and Luiseño are mentioned, and indicate that the practice was widely spread. Buckeyes, the squirting cucumber, and soaproot (*Chlorogalum*) as well as probably other plants were employed.

HUNTING

Among hunting devices, the bow was the most important. Deer were frequently approached by the hunter covering himself with a deer hide and putting on his own head a stuffed deer head. This method seems not to have been reported from the south. This area also used snares little if at all; whereas in the northwest deer were perhaps snared more often than shot. Dogs seem to have been used in hunting chiefly in northern California. Driving large game into a brush fence or over a cliff was a rather unusual practice, though specifically reported from the Mountain Maidu. The surrounding of game—rabbits, antelope, occasionally deer or elk—was most practicable in relatively open country and is therefore reported chiefly from the southern two-thirds of the State. Rabbits were frequently driven into long, low, loose nets. Through southern California a curved throwing stick of southwestern type, of boomerang shape but unwarped, was used to kill rabbits, other small game, and perhaps birds. Traps, other than snares for deer, quail, and pigeons, were little developed. Deadfalls are occasionally reported for rodents. The Achomawi caught large game in concealed pits.

ACORN STORAGE, STIRRERS, AND FIRE

The storage of acorns or corresponding food supplies is provided for in three ways in California. All the southern tribes construct a large receptacle of twigs irregularly interlaced like a bird's nest. This is sometimes made with a bottom, sometimes set on a bed of twigs and covered in the same way. The more arid the climate, the less does construction matter. Mountain tribes make the receptacle with bottom and lid and small mouth. In the open desert the chief function of the granary is to hold the food together, and it becomes little else than a short section of hollow cylinder. Nowhere is there a worked-out technique. The diameter is from 2 to 6 feet. The setting is always outdoors, sometimes on a platform, often on bare rocks, and occasionally on the ground. The Chumash seem not to have used this type of receptacle.

In central California a cache or granary is used which can also not be described as a true basket. It differs from the southern form in usually being smaller in diameter but higher, in being constructed of finer and softer materials, and in depending more or less directly in its structure on a series of posts which at the same time elevate it from the ground. This is the granary of the tribes in the Sierra Nevada, used by the Wintun, Maidu, Miwok, and Yokuts, and in somewhat modified form—a mat of sticks covered with thatch—by the western or mountain Mono. It has penetrated also to those of the Pomo of Lake County who are in direct communication with the Wintun.

In the remainder of California large baskets—their type, of course, determined by the prevailing style of basketry—are set indoors or perhaps occasionally in caves or rock recesses. In the desert south there was some storage in jars hidden in cliff crevices.

The flat spoon or paddle for stirring gruel is widely spread in California, but far from universal. It has been found among all the northwestern tribes, the Achomawi, Atsugewi, Shasta, Pomo, Wappo, southern Maidu, northern Miwok, Washo, and Diegueño. The Yokuts and southern Miwok, at times also the Washo, use instead a looped stick, which is also convenient for handling hot cooking stones. The Colorado River tribes, who stew more civilized messes of corn, beans, or fish in pots, tie three rods together for a stirrer....

Fire was made only by the drill, except that the Pomo are said sometimes to have scraped together two rough pieces of quartz. The materials of the fire drill varied considerably according to locality; borer and hearth were sometimes of the same wood. The drill, whether for fire or for perforation, was always twirled by hand rubbing. The Pomo pump-drill is taken over from the Spaniards.

PLANTS

MAKING ACORN BREAD IN YOSEMITE
Elizabeth Grinnell

Several sympathetic observers in the nineteenth century have left us with our earliest detailed accounts of Californian acorn processing (Powers 1877:421; Hudson 1900; Merriam 1918). "Making Acorn Bread" is one of the best, despite its often ethnocentric language. Its author, Sarah Elizabeth Pratt Grinnell (1851–1935), was a prolific children's book writer, who wrote under the name Elizabeth Grinnell. (The original source of this article, The Youth's Companion, was a periodical for young readers.) The wife of Fordyce Grinnell, a physician in the Indian service, Elizabeth and her husband were both the children of Quaker ministers from New England. Elizabeth Grinnell was quite familiar with Native peoples, as she had lived on the Kiowa, Comanche, and Wichita Indian Agencies in Indian Territory (now Oklahoma). After moving around the country, including three years at the Indian school in Carlisle, Pennsylvania, the family settled in Pasadena, California, in 1891. Grinnell later co-authored several books with her son, UC Berkeley zoologist Joseph Grinnell. From her base in southern California, Elizabeth Grinnell explored Yosemite Valley, where she encountered the Southern Sierra Miwok. As Ortiz and Parker note (1991:130–33), Grinnell's account is puzzling because it mentions the women cracking acorns with their teeth, omits the winnowing stage and includes a roasting stage, and describes cooking rocks that seem much too large. Nevertheless, it is a useful and informative early account of California Native cooking.

The Youth's Companion (1893), 66–67:559. Reprinted (1958), *Reports of University of California Archaeological Survey*, no. 41:42–45.

WHILE VISITING THE YOSEMITE VALLEY of California not long ago we camped a hundred feet from the Merced River, with an Indian village between us and Sentinel Rock. The village huts were of boughs and brush, constructed much like the huts of the Penobscot Indians as I saw them many years ago. The villagers are a band of the Digger Indians, whose right in the valley no one questions. They are indeed a feature of the valley itself, and are protected, like the game.

In customs they are much as they always have been, but their wardrobe is replenished from time to time by the discarded garments of tourists so that in this particular they are quite civilized, or would be if they wore more clothing. In summer they are willing to part with the greater portion, and so escape the burdens of fashion.

They subsist on the abundant trout of the Merced, manzanita berries, and the never-failing acorn. The acorns are stored in great baskets or bins, built around strong poles about fifteen feet in length.

The pole is firmly planted in the ground; then armfuls of cured rushes are brought, and the bin begun three feet from the earth. This space between the ground and the bin is for safety against rats and squirrels. From the point of beginning the basket rounds outward until it becomes five feet in diameter, and is then carried to a height of ten feet or more, where it is left unfinished, with the rushes projecting some distance above the last web.

When acorns ripen, they are spread in the sun to cure for a few days, and then poured into the granaries. When a bin is full, the projecting reeds are brought together over the whole and fastened. More reeds are adjusted to form a complete watershed, as well as shelter, and the harvest is garnered.

About a week after we had pitched our camp we were disturbed early in the morning by an unusual stir. Women were bustling about. The men went away to the brush, and after a while returned with loads of wood, dried leaves and twigs, which they deposited on the river-bank, and then disappeared for the day, probably trouting down the stream.

The women opened one of the acorn bins, which would hold perhaps fifty bushels, took out several baskets full, and carefully covered the bin. They then squatted on the grounds and the day's work of bread-making began.

Every little acorn was shelled by the teeth of these patient folk. Each nut received two turns, or a bite and a twist, and the meat came out intact. The strong, white teeth of these women might well be the envy of our own peoples who dare not even crack a filbert or a peanut between their brittle grinders.

When the kernels were all out they were roasted on hot stones, removed one at a time with a little stick, and gathered, thus partially cooked, into baskets. This roasting took several hours, and was the most tedious part of the day's labor.

There was no lounging or gossiping, as one might expect who happened to know something about "sewing circles" among civilized women. Every one was diligent, and there was no visible shirking or selfish preference.

When the roasting was done the acorns were carried to the mills to be made into meal. These mills are mortars chiseled true and even in the solid granite rocks. The acorns were thrown into the mill and reduced to fineness by the motion of round stones.

As the grinding went on, the coarser meal came to the top. This was scooped off into fine basket sieves, and sifted, the bran to be again pounded into the mortar. When the whole was of uniform consistency, it was poured into a great basket and carried down to the river. Enough water was added to it to make a thin batter which was stirred with wooden paddles.

On the beach was silvery sand in abundance, clean and pure. Some of the women knelt down, and scooped small basins in the sand, heaping up regular sides for strength, and smoothing out the inside. When the basins were finished, tufts of pine-needles were spread over the bottom to prevent the sand from being disturbed. Then the batter was poured in. Immediately the pine tufts rose to the surface and were skimmed off.

The mixture then began to "settle." When the water had all

filtered into the sand more pine needles were laid in, and more water poured on until the process had been repeated three times. The purpose of this process was to rid the batter of the poisonous bitter principle of the acorns, leaving only the nutritious amber-colored flour.

While this was going on, other women had kindled a fire and heated upon it several stones the size of a child's head, to a white heat.

Then began the separating of the inferior from the superior flour. There were three grades—the coarser, which was on the surface of the reservoir; the bottom or leavings which was next to the sand filter; and between these two, the clean, fine sort.

With the edges of the two hands, the top of the meal was scraped off into a basket, into which hot water was poured and rapidly stirred. The agitation caused the meal to separate from the sand, and it was turned off, leaving the residue of debris in the bottom. This operation, repeated three times, left a clean coarse material for "mush."

Instead of setting the mush into the stove, the stove was put into the mush. When the big basket was half-full of the acorn flour, several hot stones were thrown in. The mixture began to boil. Then dexterity, strength and skill were essential, for the stones must be constantly moved about with two strong sticks, in the hands of the alert attendant.

How she perspired, leaning low over the hissing, thickening mass! The "kneading" of light bread by our American housewives on the cool, floured "cake board" would seem like child's play in comparison. Occasionally a stone, exhausted of its heat, was lifted out by the two sticks and replaced by a hotter one.

At the woman's side was a basket of cold water, into which she dipped her hand while she poised a stone against the edge of the mush pot, and deftly, with two strokes, divested it of the batter. She determined the exact moment when the mush was "done" by its adhesiveness. When it dropped from the stones of itself, leaving them bare and clean, it was properly cooked.

The bushel basket of boiling porridge was then lifted to the back of a woman in waiting, where it was secured by a cloth which encircled its brim and passed around the forehead of the carrier. She bore it to camp ready for succeeding breakfasts.

It is eaten without salt or sugar, and washed down with cold water; these Indians drink neither beer nor coffee.

Now the first layer of meal in the filtering reservoir has been disposed of and we hasten to the next or middle portion. This was scooped out by the hooked fingers placed in a basket and set to one side.

There was now nothing left in the basin but the lining coat of flour. This was peeled off with its adhering sand, and treated to several generous washings and drainings, similar to the first batch. When it was ready for the porridge pot, there was supposed to be no trace of grit in the whole basket. This was cooked by hot stones as was the first, and sent to camp as second quality.

All this has been but incidental to the making of the real bread. That best, middle meal, which had been set to one side in a basket, was then made into a thicker batter than for mush, and was consequently harder to stir. It was cooked for a long time, and with great labor in agitating the hot stones.

When the bread was ready to be made into loaves, the women took off a portion of their clothes and waded a little way into the river, where was an eddy, but no current. Here, with the same paddles which had stirred the mush, they scooped a hole in the bottom sand under water, and banked up the sides just high enough to allow the play of the eddy over the brim.

Small baskets were then filled with the boiling dough and taken to the pool, where they were plunged again and again into the cold water. A little shaking from side to side, as the baskets came dripping to the surface, together with the rapid cooling, caused the bread to loosen from the baskets in free, ball-like masses.

At the right minute the baskets were inverted, and the "loaves" slipped out into the pool, where they could bob about without the least danger of floating down stream.

There were a great many of these loaves each resembling in appearance and texture a rubber ball, and they had about the same taste to my palate. They were of the size of a baker's ten-cent loaf, hard and heavy, of a light amber color. After they had remained in the river two or three hours they were perfectly cold, and ready to "keep."

By this time the sun was setting and the men could be seen coming home to supper. The loaves were fished out of the water and carried to the camps in baskets where they were deposited on the summer scaffoldings about the huts to be drawn upon as needed, until the next baking-day should come around in about three weeks.

The Indians of this coast seem to gain from their acorn bread something of the strength and longevity of the oak, for they are said to attain the greatest age of any known people. It is said that many live beyond the term of one hundred years, while some attain the great age of one hundred and forty years, falling at last to the ground like an oak leaf, withered and dry.

THE ACORN, A POSSIBLY
NEGLECTED SOURCE OF FOOD

C. Hart Merriam

One of the most influential scientists of the nineteenth century, C. Hart Merriam began his career as a biologist and ended it as an ethnologist. Clinton Hart Merriam (1855–1942) studied natural history as a boy. After a private school education, he attended Yale (1874–77), graduated from Columbia University with a medical degree in 1879, and practiced for six years. Merriam began his career as a biologist in 1885, with a survey of bird distribution for the Department of Agriculture, were he served as head of the Division of Biological Survey until 1910. During his extensive collecting expeditions, his innovative methods included a stress on detailed documentation, which he carried over into his ethnological work. His interest in geographic distribution led to his development of the concept of life zones, relating elevation to latitude. With his friends Theodore Roosevelt and George Bird Grinnell, Merriam was a leader in the conservation movement. In 1910, Merriam's life was transformed when the wife of railroad financier Edward H. Harriman established a trust for him, administered through the Smithsonian Institution. He resigned from the Survey and began to study California Indians, whom he had first encountered on his biological field trips. A founder and active member of many scientific societies, Merriam retired from his Smithsonian post in 1939.

Essentially self-taught as an ethnologist, Merriam was particularly noted for his work among Sierran peoples, especially the Miwok. Naming and distribution, his earlier concerns in biology, also characterized his ethnographic research. For several decades (most actively between 1911–30), he would spend five to six months a year traveling throughout the state, interviewing Indian elders and recording their knowledge. Unfortunately, he published very little of this research during his lifetime, and most of his ethnological writings were edited posthumously by Robert F. Heizer (e.g., Merriam 1955).

National Geographic Magazine (1918), 34(2):129–37.

This essay reveals Merriam's interest in biology. His recommendation of the acorn as a nutritional source was stimulated by food shortages during World War I.

IN VIEW OF THE PRESENT PRESSURE on the food supply of the United States, and with special reference to the universal effort to reduce the consumption of wheat by the substitution of corn meal, bran, and other cereal products, it may be worth while to call attention to the high nutritive value of a wholly neglected food of wide distribution. I refer to the acorn.

There are in the United States more than 50 species of oaks, of which 30 occur in the Eastern States and about 15 in the single State of California.

To the native Indians of that State the acorn is, and always has been, the staff of life, furnishing the material for their daily mush and bread. And when it is remembered that the Indian population of California at the time of its discovery numbered probably not less than 300,000 persons, and that from the Oregon boundary to the Mexican line, except in the desert region, where oaks do not grow, acorns were universally eaten, and in most cases were the principal article of diet, some idea may be had of the vast quantity and high food value of those annually consumed.

In the fall, when the acorns are ripe, the Indians gather them and spread them out to dry in the sun, and when thoroughly dried store them in large baskets and wickerwork caches, sometimes in trees, but usually on rocks or poles.

These receptacles are built to shed the rain and to keep out rats and mice, but are sufficiently open to permit the circulation of air, thus avoiding the danger of molding.

Another and very different way of preserving acorns, practiced by the Wintoon Indians of western Tehama County, in California, was described to me by F. B. Washington, of Oakland. The acorns were buried in boggy places near cold springs, where they became swollen and softened and turned nearly black in color, but remained fresh for years.

When needed they were dug out and roasted, never dried or pounded for flour, the mush and bread being always made of dried acorns.

White men in plowing have opened up caches of acorns that had lain in these cold, boggy places for fully 30 years, and found the acorns black, but still good.

When preserved dry in the usual way, the acorns are shucked as needed, and the dry meats, each splitting naturally in two parts, are pounded in stone mortars until reduced to a fine meal or flour. This at first is disagreeably bitter, but the bitter element is removed by leaching with warm water, which in seeping through acquires the color of coffee and the bitterness of quinine. The meal is then dried and stored to be used as required, for mush or bread.

According to V. K. Chesnut, the Indians of Round Valley, California, sometimes practice another method of getting rid of the bitter element, namely, by burying the acorns with grass, ashes, and charcoal in a sandy place and afterward soaking them in water from time to time until they become sweet.

BOILED IN BASKETS BY USE OF HOT STONES

The ordinary method of cooking is by boiling in baskets by means of hot stones, the result being a thick jelly-like mush or porridge. Acorn flour makes a rich, glutinous food and contains a surprisingly large quantity (18 to 25 percent) of nut oil of obvious nutritious value.

Mrs. Merriam tells me that it is easy to work, being what cooks call a "good binder," which means that it holds together well even when mixed with several times its bulk of corn meal or other coarse or granular materials.

Mush and bread made wholly of acorn flour are not pleasing to our taste, but leached acorn meal mixed with corn meal in the proportion of one part acorn to four parts corn makes excellent corn bread and pones, and mixed with white flour or whole-wheat flour in the same proportion makes palatable bread and muffins, adding to the cereal value the value of a fat nut product.

I have often eaten the pure acorn mush and bread as made by the Indians, but prefer the mixed product above mentioned. John Muir, during his arduous tramps in the mountains of California, often carried the hard, dry acorn bread of the Indians and deemed it the most compact and strength-giving food he had ever used.

Another kind of bread was made by the Indians of the Sacramento Valley. The eminent geologist, James D. Dana, who traversed the valley with the Wilkes Expedition in 1841, said: "Throughout the Sacramento plains the Indians live mostly on a kind of bread or cake made of acorns ... kneaded into a loaf about two inches thick, and baked. It has a black color, and a consistency like that of cheese, but a little softer; the taste, though not very pleasing, is not positively disagreeable."

Chesnut tells us that this kind of bread usually contains a red clay which is mixed with the dough before baking, in the proportion of one part clay to 20 of acorn dough. It is then embedded in leaves and baked overnight on hot stones, either in the cooking hole in the ground or covered with earth and hot stones.

"When removed the next morning the bread, if previously mixed with clay, is as black as jet, and while still fresh has the consistency of rather soft cheese. In the course of a few days it becomes hard.... It is remarkable for being sweet, for the original meal, and even the soup, are rather insipid. The sweet taste is very evident, and is due in great measure to the prolonged and gentle cooking, which, favored by the moisture of the dough, gradually converts some constituent of the meal into sugar."

Chesnut adds that the clay really serves a useful purpose, converting any tannin still remaining in the dough into an insoluble form, thus removing the indigestible element. He states further that bread made in the same way, but without the clay, is likewise sweet, differing only in color, the color varying from light tan to dark reddish brown.

The quantity of acorn meal cooked and eaten by Indians is almost beyond belief. At a ceremony for the dead, held near Bald Rock, Tuolumne County, California, in early October, 1907, the preparation of the acorn food for the mourners and guests was begun several days in advance. Two cooking places and five leaches, each about 4 feet in diameter, were in active operation for several days.

On the opening day I counted at the cooking places about 50 huge baskets, each holding from one to two bushels, full of freshly cooked acorn mush (*nup'pah*). The mush is so heavy that the services of two strong women were required to lift each basket and place it in the large conical burden basket on the back of a third woman, who slowly carried it to the roundhouse where the ceremony was held.

In addition to the mush, there were at least 50 turtle-shapes loaves of acorn bread (*oo-laẏ*), made by dipping out the hot mush in a special basket and plunging it (turning it out of the basket) into a cold, running stream.

The action of the cold water, curiously enough, causes the loaves to contract and harden. They are then placed on rocks to drain, and in the course of a few days become dry and hard and may be carried for weeks, until consumed.

The total quantity of acorn mush and bread made for this ceremony must have exceeded a ton in weight.

In some parts of California the Indians husk the acorns as soon as ripe, without waiting for them to dry. The shells, being at that time somewhat flexible, cannot be easily cracked with the cracking stone, but are torn open with the teeth.

INDIANS ESTABLISH ACORN CAMPS IN AUTUMN

A very intelligent full-blood woman named Che-ne-wah Weitch-ah-wah [Lucy Thompson], belonging to the *Po-lik-lah* or lower Klamath tribe [Yurok], writes that in her country when the acorns ripen, in late October and in November, the families establish acorn camps in favorite localities, gathering and bringing in the nuts in the large burden baskets. In the evening, when the evening meal is finished, all the family—men, women, and children—engage in removing the hulls with their teeth, an occupation at which they are very expert. The hulled green acorns are put into large, flattish circular receptacles of basket work, which are placed on top of a high frame over the fire in the house, so that the heat in rising dries them.

All acorns are not equally desirable from the food standpoint. Of the edible qualities of the numerous eastern species I have no personal knowledge, though it is well known that acorns of several species were eaten by various eastern tribes from Canada to the Gulf of Mexico.

It is known that the Algonkin tribes of our Eastern States used acorns for bread and for oil, and mixed boiled acorns with their fish and meat.

The Iroquois of the State of New York, according to F. W. Waugh, commonly made use of acorns for food, apparently favoring the sweet kinds, as those of the white and chestnut oaks, but in times of necessity resorted to the bitter acorns of the black and red species.

Waugh states further that nut meats (presumably including acorns) were pounded, boiled slowly in water, and the oil skimmed off into a bowl; the oil was boiled again and seasoned with salt, to be used with bread, potatoes, pumpkins, squashes, and other foods, and nut oil was often added to mush. The meats left after skimming off the oil were seasoned and mixed with mashed potatoes, and nut meats were crushed and added to hominy and corn soup to make it rich.

And the Hurons of eastern Canada, according to the Jesuit Relations, prepared the acorns by "first boiling them in a lye made from ashes, in order to take from them their excessive bitterness." Another way was by boiling them in several waters.

During the famine winter of 1649–1650, after the Hurons, defeated by the Iroquois, had taken refuge on the Island of Saint Joseph, at the north end of Lake Huron, the Jesuits of the Mission at that place "were compelled to behold dying skeletons ekeing out a miserable life; ... the acorn was to them for the most part what the choicest viands are in France."

The Jesuits, before the snow had covered the ground, had bought 500 or 600 bushels of acorns, and had dispatched several canoes to procure a supply of fish from the Algonkin tribes 60 to 100 leagues away. But the quantity of food obtained provided insufficient, and early in March the famished Hurons were compelled "to go on search of acorns on the summits of mountains which were divesting themselves of their snow." These poor Indians were drowned by the sudden breaking up of the ice on the lake (*Jesuit Relations*).

USE OF ACORNS IN SOUTHERN STATES

The Choctaw, of Louisiana, according to David Bushnell, used to make flour by pounding the acorns of the water oak in a wooden mortar, when the meal was leached, by putting it into an openwork basket and pouring water through several times. It was then boiled or used as corn meal.

In the Southern States, where more than 20 species of oaks occur, and in parts of Mexico, acorns are sometimes eaten by the people, and they are relied upon to supply the principal food of the countless thousands of hogs that roam at will through the glades and forests, thus contributing materially, albeit indirectly, to the support of the population.

And there is every reason to believe that a fair proportion of the species might be utilized with advantage to vary or supplement the daily diet of the people. This would be especially desirable in the case of the ill-nourished poorer classes—those subject to the inroads of hook-worm and pellagra.

In California the relative merits of the different kinds are well known. At middle elevations in the interior of the State the fruit of the black oaks is the favorite while in the humid coast belt that of the tan-bark oak is most prized. Besides these, the fat acorns of the blue oak of the dry foothills and the elongate ones of the valley oak of the bottomlands and adjacent slopes are gathered and consumed in large quantities; and in years when the nut crop of the favorite species fails, most, if not all, of the others are turned to account.

Even at the present times hundreds of bushels of acorns are annually gathered and eaten by California Indians; but the quantity consumed by the white population is negligible, the main part of the crop (amounting to thousands of bushels) being devoured by hogs, bear, deer, squirrels, and other animals or allowed to go to waste on the ground.

ACORNS AS A BREAD SUBSTITUTE IN EUROPE

In the old world the utilization of acorn food for man and beast dates from very ancient times, and notwithstanding the importance of the wood for timber and fuel, and of the bark for tanning, acorn mast was long considered the most valuable product of the oak forests.

In England, France, and Italy, during periods of food scarcity, boiled acorns were used as a substitute for bread; and in most of the

Mediterranean countries the sweet fruit of *Quercus esculenta* (mind the name) is still prized by the inhabitants. In Algeria and Morocco the large acorns of an evergreen oak are eaten both raw and roasted, while in Spain those of the Gramont oak are regarded as even superior to chestnuts.

V. K. Chesnut quotes Giovanni Memmo to the effect that in Spain and Italy sometimes as much as 20 percent of the total food of the poorer people consists of sweet acorns. But as the indigestible tannin is not removed, it has been found that 10 percent of the acorns pass away undigested. The superiority of the methods employed by our Indians is obvious.

That a food of such genuine worth should be disregarded by our people is one of many illustrations of the reluctance of the white man to avail himself of sources of subsistence long utilized by the aborigines.

We seem to prefer crops that require laborious preparation of the soil, followed by costly planting and cultivation, rather than those provided without price by bountiful nature.

While on the subject of Indian foods, it may be mentioned that the nutritious nuts of the sugar pine and digger pine and the berries of certain species of manzanita are much used by California Indians; that the seeds, roots, and fruits of numerous other plants form valued additions to our diet, and that in times of scarcity the nut of the California laurel and buckeye, of which hundreds of bushels may be had, are so treated as to be edible.

In the arid mountains of the desert region east of the Sierra the rich oily nut of the pinyon or nut pine takes the place of the acorn as the dominant element of the food supply; and in certain canyons bordering the Colorado desert the same may be said of the native date, while in the open deserts the mesquite bean is the staple commodity.

PHOTOGRAPHIC PORTFOLIO
SIERRAN ACORNS, ca.1902–8
C. Hart Merriam

Like many scientists of his day, C. Hart Merriam (1855–1942) was a dedicated photographer. He took most of his Indian pictures while documenting the languages of California Indian tribes. His images, like all his collections, are generally well-documented. Although Merriam's principal period of ethnographic research came after 1910, some of his most important observations and photographs come from the previous decade.

Merriam's article on acorns in *The National Geographic* was illustrated with eight photographs, three of them from Smithsonian ethnologist Henry W. Henshaw, with the rest by Merriam himself (reproduced here are the acorn caches, mortar holes, Mono and Miwok leaching basins). These illustrations focus on the principal region of Merriam's ethnography: the Maidu, Sierra Miwok, Yokuts, and Western Mono of the Sierra Nevadas. Most of the stages in acorn cooking are represented in Merriam's photos. His images of acorn shelling are particularly valuable as this subject seemed to interest fewer photographers.

After Merriam's death, his collection of over 4,000 photographs—consisting mostly of prints—was given by his heirs to Robert F. Heizer of the UC Berkeley anthropology department. These were transferred to The Bancroft Library in 1977. All the images in this portfolio are reproduced from the C. Hart Merriam Collection of Native American Photographs, BANC PIC 1978.008, The Bancroft Library, UC Berkeley. Merriam's original captions are given in quotation marks, where available.

Southern Sierra Miwok acorn caches;
Yosemite Valley, Tuolumne County.
"The outer covering is of branches of fir, cedar, and pine, closely
appressed, with the tips directed downward to keep out the rain and
the native rats, mice, and squirrels. The interior lining is mainly
of the long slender branches of *Hosakia* or *Lotus*."

(NEG. NO. V/21d/P5, NO. 3).

Nisenan Maidu couple shucking acorns;
Yankee Jim, Placer County; September 8, 1902.
(NEG. NO. U/20m/P8, NO. 1).

Western Mono (Monache) woman shucking acorns;
Waksachi, Eshom Valley, Tulare County; probably October 1903.
(NEG. NO. X/23n/P2, NO. 1).

Southern Sierra Miwok acorn mortar holes and pestles
in solid granite; near Kaweah River, Tulare County.
"These ancient grinding mills in hard granite rock are common
on the middle and lower slopes of the Sierra Nevada of California and
some of them have as many as 20 or 30 mortar holes. The pestles
are large and heavy with smoothly rounded striking ends and are held
in both hands.... When pounding the acorns, several women usually
work together, sitting at neighboring holes and singing
in rhythm with the strokes of the pestles."

(NEG. NO. V/21d/P22, NO. 3).

Western Mono (Monache) platform leaching basin;
Waksachi Indians, Eshom Valley, Tulare County; October 1903.
"This type of leach consists largely of sand placed on a bed of dry, dead
leaves and twigs supported on a square framework of poles. The looped
stick resting against the leach is used for stirring the hot stones in the
basket while the cooking is going on." *This technique is described*
in Spier (1956). A seed beater is on top of the platform.
(NEG. NO. W/22a-hh/P2, NO. 2).

Opposite top: Northern Sierra Miwok preparation of acorn mush;
Ha-cha-nah (Railroad Flat), Calaveras County; October 1908.
"Open-air kitchen, where the acorn meal is leached and cooked. Beyond
the leach is the fire, covered with stones which are being heated to cook
the mush in the baskets on the left. The leach is a low, concave mound
of dry debris gathered under the manzanita and lilac bushes, consisting
mainly of dead and broken leaves and bark, which together form
a porous bedding through which the water easily finds its way.
The leach is lined with a fiber mat, or cloth, and the branch
of an evergreen tree is laid on the meal to catch and spread
the water so that it will not dig into the meal."
(NEG. NO. V/21a/P3, NO. 5).

*Northern Sierra Miwok preparation of acorn mush; Ha-cha-nah
(Railroad Flat), Calaveras County; October 1908.*[1] *The woman
is lifting the hot cooking rocks with a pair of tongs.*

(NEG. NO. V/21a/P3, NO. 11).

CALIFORNIA INDIAN BALANOPHAGY
Edward W. Gifford

Edward Winslow Gifford (1887–1959) accomplished much for a man whose highest degree was a high school diploma. Born in Oakland, California, Gifford was associated with the California Academy of Sciences from 1904 to 1912 (assistant, assistant curator of ornithology), making expeditions to Mexico and the Galapagos Islands. Upon meeting Alfred Kroeber, his life was transformed, and he soon began work at the University anthropology museum. Gifford gradually assumed more responsibility, serving as assistant (1912–15), associate (1915–25), and full curator (1925–47), and finally as director (1947–55). He also took on teaching duties, as lecturer (1920–38), associate professor (1938–45), and professor (1945–55). Gifford's extensive research in California gave him a wide and detailed knowledge. Unlike the work of his mentor, Gifford's was noted for his attention to the individual. In addition to ethnology, he made important contributions to the archaeology and physical anthropology of the state, and while he did no work in linguistics he did investigate folklore. Gifford was also known for his important ethnographic and archaeological research in the Pacific (Tonga, Fiji, New Caledonia, Yap), as well as Mexico.

This essay is a good comparative review of acorn use in California (balanophagy literally means "acorn-eating"). Particularly interesting is how much of Gifford's argument is based on conjectural history. In a style of anthropology popular at the time, cultural history was reconstructed on the basis of logic and distribution, in the absence of archaeological evidence. In place of the earlier view, popularized by Gifford, that acorn-eating was such an obvious food source that it would have developed early, contemporary archaeologists such as Basgall argue that acorn use involved a high cost in labor and thus developed relatively late in Native Californian history. In this view, such resource intensification is due to increased population density (1987:42–44). Other good reviews of acorn use in Native California include Mayer (1976), Jackson (1991), Ortiz and Parker (1991), and Pavlik et al. (1991:95–102).

Essays in Anthropology Presented to Alfred L. Kroeber (1936), ed. Robert H. Lowie. Berkeley: University of California Press. Pp.87–98. Pp. 87–91 reprinted.

This reprint includes only the California portion of Gifford's essay, omitting his review of acorn use in the rest of Native America and in the Old World, an issue touched on by Merriam's article.

BALANOPHAGY, OR ACORN EATING, was probably the most characteristic feature of the domestic economy of the Californian Indians. In fact, the habit extended from Lower California northward through the Pacific states practically whenever oaks grew. The northern limit of abundant oaks was the Umpqua divide in Oregon.[1] Beyond that they were relatively rare and played a correspondingly small part in the native dietary. A few grew in the Williamette valley and in the Puget Sound region.

Wherever hard seeds or grains are eaten, some sort of pulverizing or grinding device is employed, in order to render the food assimilable. Acorns do not belong in this class of foods. The nuts can be masticated as readily as walnuts or almonds. The universal use of grinding or pulverizing implements on the one hand and the limited distribution of acorn pulverizing on the other hand, point to the likelihood that the former is exceedingly ancient and the latter far less so, and that the acorn industry has here and there taken over the grinding process, not because of the hardness of the food, but for the sake of reducing it to meal, or to aid in leaching it. In California this is further apparent when it is noted that the same species of acorns which were pulverized were sometimes treated by immersion or burial and eaten without pulverizing.

The crux of the Californian acorn industry is the removal of the objectionable tannic acid from the nuts. The discovery of the relatively rapid process of leaching pulverized acorns made available a vast new food supply of high nutritive value. It is likely that once this discovery was made it spread rapidly and resulted in a greatly increased consumption of acorns. It is probable that the cruder method of rendering acorns edible by immersing them in water or mud, without pulverizing, was the antecedent of leaching the pulverized nuts in a sand basin or basket. The immersion or burial method, sometimes accompanied by boiling or roasting of the nuts, was employed to some extent among the Yurok (Kroeber 1925:88), Hupa (Goddard 1903:29), Shasta (Dixon 1907:426), Pomo and Yuki (Chesnut 1902:334), the last-named burying the acorns in a sandy place with grass, charcoal, and ashes, and then soaking them in water from time to time until they became sweet. Gunther mentions burial or immersion for the Klallam, Nisqually, and Snohomish (Gunther 1927:216), and Spier and Sapir describe burial in mud by the Wishram (1930:184). It should be emphasized that the immersion method dispenses entirely with the mortar and pestle.

Certain species of acorns apparently have less tannic acid than others. Among the Shasta, *Quercus chrysolepis* acorns were sometimes roasted in ashes and eaten without any preliminary burying or boiling (Dixon 1907:426). However, burial whole in mud for several weeks was the customary treatment for these acorns.

The striking thing about the acorn eating of the American Pacific coast is the well-nigh universal knowledge of leaching, attributable no doubt to diffusion rather than separate inventions. Leaching of pulverized meal had the advantage of rendering edible at once the acorns which otherwise had to undergo months of immersion in mud and water. The time necessary for the spread of the leaching process throughout the oak districts of California was probably brief. Judged by the rapidity of the spread of maize and tobacco cultivation among primitive people in the Old World in post-Columbian times, it seems likely that two or three centuries would be ample for the spread of so important a discovery as the leaching of acorn meal over so small an area as California. However, as to when it spread—whether 1000 years ago or 10,000 years ago—there is as yet no clue.

The uniformity of the Californian acorn-meal leaching process, either in a sand basin or in a basket, contrasts with the multiplicity of pulverizing devices and seems to indicate that leaching carried with it no special pulverizing device, but rather superimposed itself on the local varieties of pulverizing devices which had already developed. Possibly some methods of pulverizing developed after leaching was introduced, but no method is wholly limited to acorns.

Cabrillo's expedition was the first to record (Ferrel 1879:309, 312) the use of acorns in California, but the account, which refers to the Santa Barbara region in 1542, makes no mention of leaching.

Removal of tannic acid by immersion or burial of the nuts is obviously a simple process which might be arrived at through testing the qualities of accidentally immersed acorns. Pulverizing and leaching are more complicated and involved processes, and appear as inventions to improve and hasten the tannic acid removal. The overlapping distribution of the two methods seems to indicate their genetic relationship. Reason dictates that immersion was the earlier process.

However, if leaching is a process which formed part of the original stock of culture of the ancestors of the American Indians, and not an independent Californian invention, we may look upon manioc leaching in South America and acorn and buckeye leaching in California as based upon this early knowledge. But, that leaching is such an ancient invention is by no means assured. The absence of leaching for acorns in the Southeastern area of the United States makes the case dubious. However, there the interest in extracting oils and the development of agriculture may have obliterated an earlier leaching complex. With the development of agricultural products a people would hardly resort to leaching acorns, except in time of famine.

If there was no widespread fundamental concept of leaching, then California would appear to be a region in which the leaching process was independently invented. The only clue, and that uncertain, as to the part of California in which the invention might have been made, is offered by the number of plants treated by leaching. Nevertheless, this criterion is dubious, as a people learning to leach acorns may have been enterprising enough to test the method for other likely foods. However, the opposite case is offered by the Yavapai of Arizona, who leach ironwood seeds by boiling (Gifford 1932b:208), but have not applied the method to acorns.

In regard to the acorn industry on the Pacific coast, California seems central, Washington marginal. At least, this view is dictated by the methods of tannin removal. For Oregon it is to be noted that the Takelma leached (Sapir 1907:257).

Leaching in a sandy shallow depression or basin seems characteristic of the northwestern Californian culture area and most of the central Californian culture area. The Luiseño and Cahuilla (Barrows

1900:52) were the only southerners reported to employ this method, but they also employed the southern method of leaching in a basket (Sparkman 1908:194). The Costanoan (Kroeber 1925:467) and Sierra Miwok (Barrett and Gifford 1933:146) of central California also employed both methods. People reported using the sand basin only were the Yokuts (Kroeber 1925:527), Western Mono (Gifford 1932a:22), Eastern Mono (Steward 1933:246), Patwin (Kroeber 1932:275), Southern Maidu (Powers 1877:421), Northern Maidu (Dixon 1905:186), Pomo (Holmes 1902:175; Powers 1877:188), Chimariko (Dixon 1910:299), Hupa (Goddard 1903:28), and Yurok (Powers 1877:49; Kroeber 1925:88). Beals (1933:531) reports leaching on bare hard ground for the Southern Maidu, which may be a degeneration from the sand basin reported by Powers. Reported to employ only the basket leacher were the Salinan (Mason 1912:119), Gabrielino (Reid 1926:11), and Southern Diegueño (Spier 1923:335). The Shasta employed a device which seems to have been sort of a compromise between the sand-basin leacher and the basket leacher (Dixon 1907:425). The Kamia (Gifford 1931:23) used a sand basin covered with a layer of foliage. Some Eastern Mono (Steward 1933:246) lined the leaching basin with bark.

Coniferous twigs used to break the fall of the water in leaching acorn meal are recorded for the Miwok (Barrett and Gifford 1933:145), Nisenan (Beals 1933:351), Northern Maidu (Dixon 1905:186, 187), Pomo, and Yuki (Chesnut 1902:306, 337), but probably are used by other tribes, too.

None of the Californian people extracted the oil of acorns, as was done in the Southeastern area (Swanton 1928:692), where it was used in preparing food and to anoint the body. Chesnut states that the oil was extracted by boiling the nuts in water containing the ash of maple wood (Chesnut 1902:340).

As might be expected among pottery-using peoples, acorn meal was boiled in pots among some Eastern Mono (Steward 1933:246), the Southern Diegueño (Spier 1923:335), the Luiseño (Sparkman 1908:194), and the Kamia (Gifford 1931:27), and in steatite vessels among the Gabrielino (Reid 1926:11, 26). Probably other pottery-using peoples did likewise, but there is no record. Stone boiling of the meal in baskets was the customary central and northwestern practice. However, so far as the published record goes it has been mentioned specifically only for the Pomo of Ukiah and Yuki (Chesnut 1902:337), the Southwestern Pomo (Powers 1877:188), Patwin (Kroeber 1932:276), Southern Maidu (Powers 1877:421), Northern Maidu (Dixon 1905:187), Salinan (Mason 1912:119), Hupa (Goddard 1903:29), Yurok (Kroeber 1925:87), Chimariko (Dixon 1910:299), Shasta (Dixon 1907:426), Miwok (Barrett and Gifford 1933:147), Western Mono (Gifford 1932a:22), and some Eastern Mono (Steward 1933:246).

According to Powers, the Yurok slightly parched their acorns before grinding. He also records that they cooked the meal in the leaching basin (Powers 1877:49), which seems a most unlikely procedure.

Of additional methods of cooking we find the Shasta roasting the moistened meal (Dixon 1907:426), and the Pomo (Holmes 1902:175), Lake Miwok, Patwin (Kroeber 1932:276, 295), Central Wintun, Plains and Northern Miwok (Barrett and Gifford 1933:148), and Salinan (Mason 1912:120) baking it in the earth oven. The Pomo (Laufer 1930:173), Lake Miwok, and Central Wintun mixed red (presumably ferruginous) earth with the meal, a custom also followed in Sardinia. The Plains and Northern Miwok sometimes mixed ashes of *Quercus douglasii* bark with the dough.

Whenever tan oak acorns (*Pasania* [formerly *Quercus*] *densiflora*) were obtainable they seem to have been preferred. This is essentially a northern coast species. Among the other species, the preference varied: *Quercus kelloggii* (*californica*) with the Southern Maidu or Nisenan (Beals 1933:351), Miwok (Barrett and Gifford 1933:142), Shasta (Dixon 1907:423), Luiseño (Sparkman 1908:193, 233); *Quercus dumosa* with the Cahuilla (Barrows 1900:62); *Quercus gambeli* with the Southern Maidu (Powers 1877:421), (although Beals [p. 351] mentions black oak, presumably *Quericus kelloggii*); *Quercus kelloggi*, *Quercus chrysolepis*, and *Quercus wislezenii* with the Northern Maidu (Dixon 1905:181); and *Quercus agrifolia* with the Pomo (Holmes 1902:175). The distribution of the various species of oaks was largely the determining factor as to the species most highly regarded by each tribe and as to the number of species used by each tribe. After *Pasania densiflora, Quercus kelloggii* seems to have been the favorite. The Klamath of southern Oregon did not eat the acorns which grow near Klamath Falls in their territory (Spier 1930:165). This lack of interest may be due to scarcity of oaks and to specialization in other foods, notably water-lily seeds.

The leaching out of the tannic acid after the nut meats had been reduced to meal seems to have been limited to the Pacific coast. In central Arizona only sweet acorns were eaten by the Yavapai, and the bitter ones neglected (Gifford 1932b:193). The acorns of *Quercus oblongifolia* were obtained by the Pima from the Papago by trade. After the hulls had been removed they were parched and ground into meal (Russell 1908:78). Consequently, in Arizona a vast supply of bitter acorns was neglected as food. In southern California, the Diegueño, close linguistic relatives of the Yavapai, were thoroughly familiar with leaching (Spier 1923:335). It would seem that the separation of these two groups took place before leaching of acorns was invented, or at least before it had become known to them. It is entirely possible, of course, that the Diegueño, moving into California, came in touch with people already familiar with leaching. Between the Yavapai and Diegueño lies a 200–300 mile stretch of oakless desert country.

Thus, a more or less concentric distribution appears for the methods of acorn utilization in the western United States—a highly specialized leaching process bordered by an area in which only sweet acorns, unleached, were utilized. To the southward, in the highlands of Mexico, lies the peripheral area of complete neglect of acorns. This concentric distribution in western America seems to indicate complete separation from the acorn-boiling area of the Eastern Woodlands.

ANIMALS

PHOTOGRAPHIC PORTFOLIO

ISHI (YAHI) HUNTING DEER AND RABBIT, 1914

Alfred L. Kroeber and Saxton T. Pope

Ishi (ca. 1860–1916), widely known as "the last Yahi," seems to have been the last survivor of his people. The Yahi were the southernmost of the Yana-speaking peoples, living in the valley and foothills east of the upper Sacramento River. The man known as Ishi appeared alone and starving in Oroville in August 1911; he spent the remainder of his years at the UC Museum of Anthropology, which was then in San Francisco. Here he collaborated with Alfred Kroeber and other anthropologists to document Yahi culture (T. Kroeber 1961).

One of this group was Dr. Saxton T. Pope (1875–1926). In 1912 Pope was appointed instructor in surgery at the University Medical School, located next to the anthropology museum. Pope served as Ishi's physician, but he soon developed a passionate interest in archery from his friend, a knowledge documented in his *Yahi Archery* (1918, cf. 1974).

One of the major topics of their conversations was Ishi's knowledge of hunting, the main food-gathering occupation of a traditional Yahi man. In fact, most of the objects that Ishi made for the museum relate to hunting in some way: arrow-points, arrows, bows, quivers, as well as fishing nets and hooks.

These customs were also documented in a striking series of photographs. The images included here were part of 121 taken by Kroeber and another 29 taken by Pope during a trip back to Ishi's last home along Deer Creek, Tehama County between May 14 and June 2, 1914.

Stimulated by Pope's interest in archery, the team focused on Ishi using his bow and arrow. These photos, however, were posed. According to Pope (1918:128), on this trip Ishi was not able to bring down a deer with his bow and arrow, so the carcass being treated must have been shot with a rifle. Nevertheless, this series is especially valuable. For obvious reasons, scenes of traditional Native California hunting are virtually non-existent, and there are almost none showing butchering.

Ishi calling rabbits.
PHOTOGRAPH BY SAXTON T. POPE (NEG. NO. 15–5814).

Ishi shooting his bow.
PHOTOGRAPH BY ALFRED L. KROEBER (NEG. NO. 15–5696).

Ishi pulling arrow from deer.
PHOTOGRAPH BY ALFRED L. KROEBER (NEG. NO. 15–5706).

Ishi skinning deer.
PHOTOGRAPH BY ALFRED L. KROEBER (NEG. NO. 15–5709A,B).

Ishi cutting sinews from back of deer.

PHOTOGRAPH BY ALFRED L. KROEBER (NEG. NO. 15–5716).

Ishi preparing skin of head of deer.

PHOTOGRAPH BY ALFRED L. KROEBER (NEG. NO. 15–5725).

Ishi with deer skin.
PHOTOGRAPH BY ALFRED L. KROEBER (NEG. NO. 15–5724).

Ishi walking with a bow.
PHOTOGRAPH BY ALFRED L. KROEBER (NEG. NO. 15–5702).

FISH AND THE MIWOK
Craig D. Bates

Among animal foods of the Native Californians, fish have by far been the sub-ject of the most comprehensive research and publication (e.g., Rostlund 1952; Kroeber and Barrett 1960). The reasons for this are moot. While it may have been due to the specialization of the methods, it was more likely because such practices continued relatively unchanged into recent times, unlike aboriginal hunting of large and small game, which rapidly succumbed to legal restrictions and habitat change.

This essay is a fine description of the several methods that one Calif-ornian people use to fish and of the role that the food plays in their culture. Craig Bates (b. 1952) has spent years studying the Sierra Miwok of Yosemite National Park, where he has been employed since 1973. A fifth-gen-eration Californian, Bates developed an interest in Native American cultures as a small child. He acquired most of his knowledge from tribal elders, espe-cially Maidu Henry Azbill, but he has also studied museum and archival col-lections. He practices many traditional arts, including basketry and featherwork. Since 1980, Bates has been curator of ethnography at the National Park Service Museum at Yosemite National Park. He is also active as a consultant, guest curator, teacher, and author.

Masterkey (1984), 58(1):18–23.

FISH FOUND WITHIN THE STREAMS of the Sierra Nevada have always been an important aspect of Miwok livelihood. The Sierra Miwok were a major group of California Indians who occupied the western slope of the central portion of the Sierra Nevadas. This area has always had a considerable aquatic habitat and has produced abundant quantities of fish resources. Archaeological evidence suggests that people living in this California region have subsisted on fish for over 2000 years. Fish not only served as an important source of food, but were utilized for a variety of purposes.

The Sierra Miwok are divided linguistically into Northern, Central, and Southern groups, and many still live in California's central Sierra Nevada region. Today their only self-governed land base is the Tuolumne Mewuk Rancheria, located not far from the town of Sonora and the Dodge Ridge Ski area. Yet from Mariposa in the south and throughout the Mother Lode-gold belt north to Placerville, one may find hundreds of Miwok people. However, few currently speak the native language (whose dialects differ greatly as French, Spanish, and Italian), practice traditional skills such as basketry, or participate in ceremonial dancing. Fishing is one activity many Miwok people continue to partake in and that harkens back to the time before the *Alini*, the white man, arrived.

Fish played an intricate role in the Miwok symbolic system. For example, a salmon's head was said to contain four or five small, white stones. Shamanistic healers would carefully clean and save these stones. The shaman or "Sucking Doctor" would heal ailing people by making an incision with a salmon stone, then sucking out the pain caused by the illness.

The Miwok do not consider fish, as well as other animals, to be direct ancestors, but rather they are descendants from beings who inhabited the world before the Miwok people were created. It is in this ancient time of quasi-human beings that most legends take place. The Miwok people practice a clan or "moiety" system, where people always marry outside of their group. Their names often reflect those animals that "belong" to their moiety. There are two such moieties, land and water. Fish belong to the water moiety, and thus the fish-oriented names are given to those people born into this clan. The names in and of themselves are peculiar. In a simple, concise manner the name denotes an activity associated with fish that would otherwise take many more words to express in conversational Miwok. Names are often related to the salmon, reflecting perhaps a time when that fish was very important to the Miwok economy. Certain names are given only to men and others only to women. Appellations for men include: *Tcumutuya*, a bear catching with its paws salmon in a riffle; *Tunaa*, salmon intestines pulling out like string; *Hotckern*, spearing salmon; or *Kosumi*, going fishing with a spear. Female names include: *Liptcu*, the dropping of eggs when a female salmon is lifted up; *Pootci*, cutting open a salmon; *Putbana*, catching small fish with a basket; *Hutamsi*, salmon getting together in a bunch; and *Tcipuyu*, tying up salmon in willow branches before cooking.

According to the Miwok, salmon fishing was a dangerous undertaking. One story tells of a man who was spearing salmon when a huge supernatural serpent suddenly reared out of the water and grabbed his spear. The man struggled with the serpent, trying to wrench away his spear and stab the beast, but to no avail. The serpent jerked him into the river, bit him, and held him deep under the water. While searching for the man, the village people saw in the middle of the river the water boiling and full of blood. A shaman with great supernatural powers painted himself, dove into the water, and brought the injured man back to shore. With the help of the villagers, the shaman carried the salmon spearer back to camp where he was restored to life. Following this harrowing experience the man became a shaman and always returned from salmon fishing with many, many fish.

In pre-Anglo times only a few varieties of fish lived in the streams and rivers of the Sierra Nevada. The whitefish was found in great abundance at lower elevations such as today's Knight's Ferry on the Stanislaus, where the Miwok would catch them in large amounts. A different species with the same name was secured in the higher regions. The rainbow trout was the only trout originally found west of the Sierra crest, although some six trout species are found there today.

Chinook salmon, twenty-four to sixty inches long and weighing sixteen to seventy pounds, were commonly found in the Sierra's streams and tributaries during their annual fall spawning migration.

When the streams' water level was low in late summer or early fall, the Miwok often caught the fish in the simplest fashion of using their bare hands. They also used a large dip net with a circular opening, which was attached to a very long pole. This was used to catch fish by sweeping the deep holes of major rivers. Seines, called *yo'ho* (Northern Miwok), were six to eight feet in width and reached a length of forty feet. Several men drove the fish into their net stretched across a river or lagoon. As the net was drawn ashore the gills of fish would catch in the net's mesh or the fish would become trapped with other flailing and writhing fish.

The *yu'gu* (Northern Miwok) or the *lu'sume* or *lassa* (Central Miwok) was like the seine but smaller. Its lower edge was fastened to a bow made of a bent sapling weighted with stones. Set within a riffle, it formed a deep pocket. Across the opening were several vertical trigger strings that were attached to a cord then secured to a cocoon rattle, or to a string wrapped around the neck of a man waiting on shore. The man would be alerted to fish passing through the net by a tug of the string or the sound of the rattle. He would then pull up the net, remove the fish, and reset the net. Sometimes assistants splashed in the water upstream to frighten the fish into the net.

Basketry fish traps or *kes-a-pah* (Southern Miwok) were also constructed by twining whole willow shoots together. This cone-shaped trap was about two feet wide and six feet long. Sometimes these were set in a stream with a dam-like structure that diverted fish into the trap.

The Miwok were quick to modify their fishing equipment with materials made available by the Anglo's presence. Early in this century, nets and basket traps were replaced by traps made from discarded barley or gunny sacks. These Anglo materials, available for nothing, replaced many traditional items requiring many hours to produce. Used in smaller streams when the water was low, these traps were usually set by older Miwok with the help of their grandchildren. A willow shoot or piece of heavy wire was used to keep the sack open. The sack was then placed across the stream and fitted close to the bottom. The children used sticks to flail the water and chase fish downstream into the improvised trap.

Spearing was the favorite fishing method when salmon spawned upstream. The salmon deposited their eggs in nests made in the sand with their tails. This stationary behavior made them a particularly good target. A two-pronged harpoon, called *si'laa* (Northern Miwok) and *gula'a* or *tco'llo* (Central Miwok), was preferred. The pole was some 10 or 15 feet long and was made of ash in the lower watercourses or of the strong mountain mahogany in the higher elevations. Detachable points made of deer leg bone were attached to the pole by a short, strong leader of native string—fibers of hemp or milkweed. The Miwok made a toggle by securing the points at their middle. This allowed the points to release as they thrust through the body of the fish and not pull out as the fish was pulled in.

A second type of fish spear, the *lul-ne*, with only one prong was made by the Southern Miwok of Yosemite. It too was shaped from deer bone and had a leader of native cordage. The bindings of this and other Miwok harpoons were coated with melted pine pitch, a waterproof and long-lasting adhesive.

The Central Miwok of the higher mountain lakes used a different sort of fish spear to impale whitefish. Not unlike other Miwok spears, it was simply comprised of a finely worked obsidian point attached to a six to seven foot shaft of scraped and seasoned mahogany. Before spearing the six to eight inch long fish, a young fisherman sometimes would cry *Yenene, Yenene*, a call resembling the noise the captured fish makes after it is removed from the water.

Fishing with hook and line was also an ancient practice. The Miwok utilized two types of fish hooks. The *hunemmah* (Southern Miwok) was a bi-pointed piece of deer bone approximately one inch long with milkweed fiber string secured to its center. A worm was threaded onto this "hook." After the fish swallowed the worm, the fisherman jerked the line, causing the bone hook to turn crosswise in the stomach and hold fast. The other style of hook consisted of two pieces of ground deer bone. One piece, approximately one-half inch in length, was sharpened on one end. The other end was bound to the bottom of the second piece which was about three inches in length.

This produced a check-mark like design. A line of native fiber was then attached with sinew. Once dry, the sinew wrappings were water-proofed with pine pitch.

The Southern Miwok of Yosemite carried their bait in a specially constructed "worm box" or *huki* made of native grasses—variously identified as blue grass, cyperus, or straw. Whichever grass was used, it was gathered in the summer when it grew nearly three feet high, formed into a bundle four to five inches in diameter and finally cut near the base with a knife. After the loose, short, and dead leaves were shaken out, it was secured at the butt end by tying with cord, the butts being cut close to this binding. This was held upright, the long blades separated and bent back over the tie, so a cavity was left in the center of the bundle. It was again tied securely six to eight inches from the bend in the grass, and once more the bundle was separated, bent back on itself, and tied over the first bend, thus creating a cigar shaped bundle. Those loose ends were trimmed, and the final tie was often furnished with a loop, so it could apparently be attached to a belt at the waist. The sides of the carrier were easily separated, and worms were easily placed inside with or without damp soil and subsequently removed. Many of the Indian curios collected in the Yosemite region at the turn of the century contained examples of these worm carriers.

Another technique was used in the summer when streams were low and trout hid in quiet shallow pools. It was at this time that the Miwok of Yosemite Valley would resort to using *buyapna* (Southern Miwok) or fish poison. Many plants produced the poison; however, the most popular source was perhaps the soaproot bulb. Approximately fifty bulbs were taken to a place in the stream where the water rolls above a quiet pool and then beaten on rocks causing a soap-like, foaming action to occur. After a half hour the fish would rise to the surface where they were scooped up in openwork, twined basketry winnowing trays. It appears the fish were actually killed and not merely stupefied by this operation. The soaproot's saponin would enter the trout's gills and absorb into the bloodstream, causing respiratory failure. Other plants used in the same manner include vinegar weed, manroot, and California Laurel.

Fresh fish were broiled whole over the coals of a fire. They were then skinned and eaten, usually with acorn mush. Fish were occasionally stored for later consumption by drying over a small, smoky fire where they were imparted with a delicious smoked flavor. After drying, they were stored in the household in large, twined storage baskets. At a later date dried fish were sometimes smeared with thick acorn dough, skewered on sticks, and roasted over the fire.

Salmon eggs, called *pu'le* (Southern Miwok), were a delicacy just as caviar is today. When fresh they were boiled in a watertight cooking basket just prior to the meal. The eggs were also dried for use in the winter months. To prepare the dried eggs, the natives soaked them overnight in water, then boiled for an hour prior to eating. Frequently a little salt was added for extra flavor.

Most of these traditional fishing practices continued long after intensive contact with Anglos. Accounts by the first non-Indians entering the Yosemite Valley in 1851 mention how local Miwok people used fish dams and single-tined spears to catch salmon. Samuel Kneeland, a member of a tourist party visiting Yosemite in 1871, recalled the use of the grass worm carriers at that time. During the later 19th and early 20th Centuries, when trout were still plentiful, elderly Miwok men fished early in the morning in Yosemite Valley's Merced River, so they could sell their catch to local hotels. Guests dined on trout for breakfast and dinner, causing the hotels to buy all the fish that the Miwok could supply. Bone fish hooks required a great deal of work to produce. So it is not surprising to find the sale of commercial steel fish hooks to Miwok men documented in extant ledgers from Yosemite stores as early as 1884.

By the 1930s very few of the aboriginal fishing techniques were still practiced among the Sierra Miwok. The National Park Service employed Chris "Chief Lemee" Brown of the Yosemite Miwok to demonstrate ceremonial dances and various traditional skills to the public. Brown remembered the traditional fishing methods of his people, and constructed worm carriers for museums such as the Museum of the American Indian and the National Park Service's Yosemite Museum. He also demonstrated the use of soaproot bulbs in Yosemite Creek, and the series of photographs taken at that time ... provide us with a carefully documented record of this activity. Chris enjoyed fishing in his free time. Former members of the National Park Service naturalist staff would accompany him on occasion. He even made worm carriers for their use. After work they would carry to a nearby stream the *huki* full of worms and a simple rod with attached hook and line. The rangers recall how Chris would "creep like a cat" upon his favorite fishing holes and carefully drop his hook into the placid waters. They respected Chris' knowledge of traditional Miwok life and watched with awe as he pulled fish after fish out of the water.

The fishing techniques of the Sierra Miwok were varied and well suited to the rugged Sierra Nevada that they still call home. While many of their methods—such as spearing and trapping—were common among other Californian groups, other aspects of fishing—such as the worm carrier and the two-piece bone hook—appear to be unique to the Miwok. Today, salmon no longer migrate high up into the Sierra streams; flood control projects and dams interfere with their journey. In addition, the introduction of nonnative species, such as the German Brown trout, have caused competition with native fish, and new species of fish, not found in ancient times, now occur in high Sierra lakes.

Today Miwok people often resort to obtaining salmon from Department of Fish and Wildlife officials, who collect the salmon eggs from those migrating upstream. More than one hundred and thirty years after the first non-Indians described the Miwok fishing practices, Miwok people continue to enjoy fishing, and visitors to the Sierra Nevada can still find descendants of these people fishing the streams and rivers in their native homeland.[1]

SHELLFISH FOODS OF
THE CALIFORNIA INDIANS

Robert E. Greengo

After several decades of field research among Native communities, anthropology students at UC Berkeley began to compile very useful reviews of the scholarly literature, particularly for their masters papers. This comprehensive essay is an example of such a study. Like Hewes's research on fishing (1947), it is very systematic. The original version, "Aboriginal Use of Shellfish as Food in California," earned a masters in anthropology for Robert Eugene Greengo (b. 1923) in 1951. His fieldwork was supported by the UC Archaeological Survey. Greengo went on to obtain a Ph.D. from Harvard in 1957, and taught for many years at the University of Washington, where he is now an emeritus professor of anthropology and an emeritus curator in the Burke Museum. An archaeologist, Greengo's areas of specialty are the Northwest Coast and Mexico.

With California's 1,100 miles of coastline, as well as abundant rivers and lakes, it was natural that the region's aboriginal population would make shellfish a prime component of their diet. In his essay, Greengo includes mussels, clams, abalone, oysters, snails, limpets, chitons, barnacles, crabs, and sea urchins. Shellfish of various sorts were also sources of ornament and currency.

Because of the essay's length, we have omitted several sections. After a brief introduction, the first section considers the "Kinds and Distribution of Shellfish." Here, Greengo reviews the major food species found in the ecological zones of the coast, the open coast, bays and estuaries, and inland waters. In the section on "Dietetic Factors," he discusses the contribution of shellfish to human nutrient requirements. From the long discussion of "Shellfish Poison," we offer the concluding summary, before ending with his general conclusion.

Kroeber Anthropological Society Papers (1952), 7:63–114. Pp. 69–82, 90–92 reprinted.

THE SEASONAL ROUND

Before entering into a discussion of shellfish gathering in California, it might be well to consider briefly the seasonal round as exemplified by a number of well known groups. We may first consider the seasonal gathering activities engaged in by a coastal group; for this purpose we will discuss the Coast Yuki, who have been excellently described by Gifford (1939:329–30). This group, which consumed a large number of marine shellfish, may be taken as an example of an exposed, outer coast, kitchen-midden population (as differentiated from those who left remains on protected inner bays such as Humboldt, Bodega, or San Francisco Bays). These people lived in more or less temporary camps in the hills in the winter, and occupied the beach from about April to October. The period between the latter part of January and the first of March was the worst time of the year, for the food supply was then low, the stored food was largely used up, and the streams were too swollen by rains to permit salmon fishing. By March, however, excursions were being made to the coast for the mussels and other shellfish. In April some people constructed dwellings at the beach, although the food quest still had an inland orientation, for in May clover leaves were ready to eat, and by June clover flowers and seeds, grass seeds, bulbs and corms were plentiful. More time was spent at the beach in July, and such things as mussels, abalone, and surf fish were dried. Seafood drying activities continued through August; the diet being augmented by such food as berries and hazel nuts, and perhaps an occasional deer. By September short trips were made into the hills for acorns and other seeds. In October, winter houses were erected in the hills; those were occupied in November. Salmon were largely caught and dried in December, but toward the end of this month the rains intensified and salmon fishing terminated.

Thus, it appears that among this group the main protein supply in the diet was shellfish, especially mussels, for salmon could not have been very important if the greatest quantity of them was caught in December, and if the food supply was running low by the end of January (Gifford 1939:326).

A brief sketch is available of the annual food cycle of the Tolowa. Shellfish here figure prominently in the diet, though not to the extent that they did among the Coast Yuki (Drucker 1937:232). The most important food resources were salmon and acorns; those were followed by smelt, shellfish, and sea mammals (Drucker 1937:231; Greengo ms.:20). Unlike the Coast Yuki and very much in the pattern of the Yurok, who also relied on salmon to a great extent, the Tolowa congregated along the Smith River for the spring salmon run. During this time the roots and berries began to ripen and could be gathered. From the river the people moved to the beach in order to gather, hunt, and dry seafood. In the late summer when the salmon were again running they returned to the river, and from there moved to the hills to gather acorns. The Tolowa spent the winter in their villages along the river, around Lake Earl, and on the coast.

The general pattern along the coast must have been similar to the two cases described above, though groups living on the coast probably gathered a goodly quantity of shellfish in the winter as well as during the rest of the year.[1]

Inland peoples apparently made frequent excursions to the coast to gather shellfish—probably mostly during the summer. The Coast Yuki and their inland neighbors developed this practice to a formal pattern (Gifford 1939:304–06).[2] Freshwater shellfish were evidently more sought for in the summer by the Eastern Pomo (Kniffen 1939:365). In the south, the Yokuts, and probably other valley groups, are also known to have made excursions to the coast to procure shellfish. An instance recorded in historic times took place in May (Pilling 1950:438).

The most important reason, apparently, for the decrease in shellfish gathering during the winter is to be found in the climate. The northern California coast can be very unpleasant at times during the summer, and even more so in the winter when gales whip down out of the northwest. Indians whose territory adjoined the open coast, such as the Coast Yuki, retreated before the storms to more pleasant climates. Those living on relatively protected bays such as Humboldt, Bodega, and San Francisco most probably occupied sites the year around, however.

GATHERING TECHNIQUES

As one specialized aspect of the hunting and gathering types of subsistence, the procuring of shellfish is one of the simplest means of obtaining food known to man. There are, however, certain facets to the problem of collecting these unobtrusive animals that require skill and ingenuity. The simplest and most direct method of gathering shellfish is to pick them up by hand. This is possible with only certain species, and even with these it is often necessary to resort to some kind of implement. The more important factors governing the methods of gathering are the physical characteristics of the animals, their numbers, and their ecological relationships.

An animal fulfilling the requirements of ease of handling, occurrence in substantial numbers, and exposed habitat at low tide is the sea urchin. This species was probably usually gathered by hand, though this practice is not mentioned specifically in the literature. One might conclude that they were not gathered with the aid of an implement since the use of implements usually attracts the attention of the observer, and no such connection is cited for sea urchins along the California coast.[3] This point can be illustrated by referring to the Kwakiutl who used a multi-pronged spear for sea urchins (sea eggs). It was constructed of a hemlock shaft three and one-half fingers thick, with yew wood prongs two spans and four fingers widths long, and bound to the squared end of the spear by split spruce roots (Boas 1921:154, 488). This invention was similar to the one used in gathering *Dentalium*, a mollusk which had a direct and powerful influence on California Indians through its use in trade (Drucker 1950:204).

It is possible through a slow and painful process to take mussels by hand. The only specific mention that the writer has found of such a practice is of the Wappo picking mussels off rocks by hand (Driver 1936:184). The authority does not specify whether these are sea or bay mussels. The latter might be easier to deal with in some cases.

Since most of the clams live below the surface they usually have to by dug out with the aid of some sort of implement. There are a few instances on record of the Indians having dug for various species of clams with their hands. According to Nomland, not only clams, crabs, and river crawfish were taken by hand by the Sinkyone, but also the abalone—although she indicates that the latter was also pried off the rocks with a stick sharpened at one end (Nomland 1935:154). A Tolowa man said that the razor clam (*Siliqua patula*) was seized by hand in the mornings at low tide (Greengo ms.:18). The Lower Chinook at the mouth of the Columbia River sometimes used their hand to remove the sand from around clams. This group also used implements—in this case of a rather specialized kind.

Evidence as to how the native west coast oyster (*Ostrea lurida*) was gathered is meager. The Coast Miwok dug a few with digging sticks at the mouth of Valley Ford Creek (Kelly ms.:T-2, 15h). For San Francisco Bay, where this species is most in evidence archaeologically, there is no ethnographic material to indicate how it might have been procured. Very likely they were dealt with in a manner analogous to the Seri practice. This group would gather oysters "with the hand, aided perhaps by a stone or stick for dislodging the shells either from the extended off-shore beds at extreme low water, or from the roots of a mangrove-like shrub at a medium stage" (McGee 1898:195).

The main types of crustaceans represented in aboriginal menus were crabs and barnacles. Both of these were perhaps more often taken with the aid of tools of greater or lesser complexity, but in some instances they were taken by hand. Crabs were caught in such a manner by the Coast Yuki (Gifford 1939:325). One of the most ingenious methods of procuring any shellfish was practiced by the Pomo, who, according to Loeb, would at low tide build a fire over a bed of barnacles living on the rocks (Loeb 1926:164; Stewart 1943:60). This was kept going, cooking the barnacles, until the incoming tide extinguished the fire and cooled the meal which was eaten the next day. This practice would very probably give rise to an underestimate of the amount of barnacles eaten by the Pomo groups in question if that estimate were based upon an analysis of their refuse sites alone. However, Loeb notes that barnacles were also gathered and cooked in hot ashes at their camps, while the writer has seen barnacle shells on Pomo sites as far as four miles in from the coast (Loeb 1926:164).

The trait of cooking barnacles before they were removed from the rocks or gravel is also recorded for the Kwakiutl. Boas writes that barnacles (probably *Balanus cariosus* or *glandula*) were roasted by building a fire over a large bed of barnacles which were then peeled off in sheets (Boas 1921:505). These people would also gather stones with many barnacles on them, and cook the animals by steaming (Boas 1921:500).

In the interior where river and lake mussels were eaten, gathering was apparently most often accomplished without the aid of a tool. However, an American explorer who ascended the Sacramento River as far as the territory of the Northern Wintun observed that "these Indians had small fishing-nets, somewhat resembling the size and shape of a lady's reticule. These they made use of when diving for mussels, and in a short time procured half a bushel of them" (Wilkes 1845:188–90). Repeated references have been made to the practice of diving for mussels by the Wintun (Powers 1877:233; Kroeber 1932:278–79; Du Bois 1935:18). Powers says of the Wintun on the Sacramento River, "They would dive many feet for clams—and rise to the surface with one or more in each hand and one in the mouth" (1877:233).

Land snails were probably most often merely picked up by hand, although references to their use by Californian Indians do not usually include the method of taking them. One ethnographer specifically states that the Pomo women picked up snails from the ground and water (Loeb 1926:164).

SPECIALIZED TECHNIQUES

The type of artifact employed to the greatest extent by the Indians of the state for the purpose of obtaining shellfish was most likely some sort of wooden implement resembling, and in many cases identical with, the digging stick (Driver 1936:184; Barnett 1939:234).

A stick was sometimes used to locate the shell of clams living in sand or mud flats. The sand or mud would then be loosened and scooped away by hand until the clam could be seized. Kelly's notes contain a good description of digging for a long neck clam (probably

Schizothaerus nuttallii) by the Coast Miwok at Bodega Bay: "Dug at low tide on flats-with stick,[4] or with stick for this particular animal. Sharp on end, but not very sharp. Thrust stick in to locate shells. Then go with fingers. Gathered by both men and women. Found above elbow depth. Gathered in conical burden basket" (Kelly ms.:sec. 2:31). The employment of a special instrument in collecting this clam may have a long history at Bodega Bay, for the popularity of the species at site Son-299 (with Middle Horizon affiliations) is shown by the relatively large proportions of *Schizothaerus* shells among those of other species (Greengo 1951:table I:24). Driver gives a similar description for the digging of clams by the Wappo (Driver 1936:184).

The famous money shell clam (*Saxidomus nuttallii*) was also dug with a stick by the Bodega Bay Indians. " 'Rock clams' (*Lupu-guta*) are the ones from which thick beads are made, have to have a hard wood stick for these clams. They are in the rocks. Pretty good eating too. Just like the Washington clams" (Kelly ms.:sec. 2:30).

Apparently these people distinguished between specimens of *Saxidomus* on the basis of thickness of shell, for there is fair range of variation in this particular (from two to three millimeters), as observed by the writer. In several places in her manuscript, Kelly gives the native name of the Washington clam (*Saxidomus nuttallii*) as, *Ku.ta*, *guta*, or *Kuta* (Kelly ms.:sec. 2:30, 2:31, 5:42), while the so-called "rock clam" is repeatedly referred to as *lupa-guta* or *Lupa-Kuta* (Kelly ms.:sec. 5:42). The form *Ku.ta* or *guta* is apparently the root word referring to the species, and the prefix *lu.pu* (*lupu*) qualifies the thickness of shell and its concomitant utilization for disc beads.

The name "rock clam" is misleading, however. *Saxidomus* thrives in mud flats, as well as in fairly coarse gravel. The latter is probably what is meant by the ethnographer.

The most important single component of site Son-299 at Bodega Bay was the sea mussel (*Mytilus californianus*). As with *Schzothaerus* the mussel was important enough in late times also, to merit a special name for an implement used in its procurement. Kelly tells how these people gathered mussels: "Found only in salt water. Principally on island at mouth of bay and on Bodega Head (ocean side). Get mussels at low tide off rocks. Hammer off with hardwood stick (*hoiyo'n*).

Only men got mussels. Got to watch the water all the time. Carry basket to put them in" (Kelly ms.:T-2, 15b).

The manufacture of this tool (also used in taking abalone) is described thus; "Use a pretty sharp stick (*hoiyo'n*). Sharpen it good and put it in the fire to dry. Don't burn it too much. Make it sharp by rubbing on a rock" (Kelly ms.:T-2, 15b). Other instances of the employment of a sharp stick have been recorded for the Wiyot who used it to get abalones as well as sea anemones (Greengo ms.:11, 13).

Abalones (*Haliotis rufescens*) were sparsely represented in Son-299 but may have been more important during the later period.

To this day the type of implement used in procuring the abalone has retained the form employed by coastal dwellers at the time of contact. It consists of a rod-like instrument with a fair degree of fractural strength, sharpened, and often flattened at the working end. The present day "tire-iron" made of a section of automobile leaf spring serves the purpose well, whereas the Indian used a hardwood stick as described above or one with a spatulate end.[5] The function of the instrument is to insert the end under the edge of the shell of the animal and quickly flip it off the rock to which it adheres by its strong muscular foot. Failure to perform the act in one quick motion gives the abalone time to draw its shell down tight against the rock with such strength that it is sometimes very difficult to remove the tool, much less loosen the animal. It has been suggested that the strength with which an abalone adheres is due in part to the secretion of mucus on which this sea snail slides. The mucus would aid in creating a vacuum (Ricketts and Calvin 1948:60).

The difficulties presented to the Indians by the characteristics of abalones and the nature of their habitat is vividly described in the following excerpts: "Bodega Head is a bad place to get abalone. Got to climb up rocks with a big load. Got to go through tunnel to get abalone there." "Get on ocean side. Hand down under rocks. You got to feel for them. Dangerous. Catch your finger and you got to stay there.—Use a pretty sharp stick (*hoiyo'n*). Hit them quick not slow" (Kelly ms.:sec 2:32).

The Coast Yuki also used a specialized tool for abalones and mussels. It was made of a hard wood, rhododendron or *Garrya elliptica* (a species of dogwood) one yard in length with a flat chisel-like end. When broken off in use the end was resharpened with a musselshell knife. After the stick became very short it was driven under the abalone shell with a stone. The instrument was made to last longer by hardening in the fire. It was also used to remove abalone meat from the shell (Gifford 1939:337–38).

On the Northwest Coast the Kwakiutl, who specialized in wood-working, had at least two different types of spatulate prying implements to aid in gathering shellfish. A mussel stick which was probably used as a blade to scrape mollusks off rocks is described as being made of a broken yew-wood paddle, four spans long with a round handle, the flat end being four fingers wide (Boas 1921:480). What must have been a similar looking instrument was employed to peel chitons off rocks.[6] This was made of a hemlock branch three spans long and had a flattened point (Boas 1921:480). A sharpened, flattened instrument of ironwood, three to four feet long and seasoned over the cooking fire for several months was used by the Coast Yurok to pry loose mussels, abalones, and chitons (Greengo ms.:15, 16), while a similar form is described for the Tolowa who used it for mussels, horse-neck clams, and sea anemones (Greengo ms.:19). This type of instrument probably had a continuous distribution along the Northwest Coast as far south as the Lower Chinook, who employed an even more specialized tool. This was from two to four feet long including a handle and a blade which was cupped and tapered to a point (Ray 1938:112, figs. 13a,b).

Among the Wappo who lived somewhat more distant from the abalone habitat than the above mentioned groups, abalones were pried off rocks with sticks, or, "shell crushed and meat taken out without removing the shell from the rock" (Driver 1936:184).

In extreme southern California the Diegueño took abalones with hardwood bars (Drucker 1941:171).

Except for the above citation our information as to gathering techniques refers to groups north of San Francisco Bay. For most of the species discussed thus far, the gathering techniques were probably similar on the south central and southern Californian coasts. Certainly more data are necessary, on the Chumash especially, before the picture can be completed. There is, for example, little or no information as to how the famous Pismo clam was located and gathered aboriginally. Today a rather specialized clam fork is often used to locate these clams. It is sometimes possible to find this species by looking for its siphons which protrude slightly out of the sand. Once the siphon is located it is a relatively simple matter to dig the animal out by hand. Quite possibly the Indians probed for the Pismo with sticks, as the Coast Miwok did for another species. Another manner of locating and gathering these clams was that employed by the Seri in the Gulf of California. McGee designated the Pacific Coast clam (probably *Tivola stultorum*) as the most important species in the shellfish class of the Seri diet (McGee 1898:195).[7] The method of procuring them was as follows: "The clams are usually taken at low tide without specialized apparatus. They are located by feeling with the feet in shallow water, and caught either with toes or with fingers, to be tossed into any convenient receptacle. When the water is entirely withdrawn from the flats, they are located by means of their holes, and are extricated either with a shellcup or with some other improvised implement" (McGee 1898:195).[8]

Of the many species of crabs along the California littoral only two were eaten to a substantial extent by the aborigines. Many of the shore species are too small to provide enough gastronomic reward for the effort of capturing them. Two species answer the criteria necessary to insure their use as an important food source, viz: *Cancer antennarius* and *Cancer productus*. These two species are to be found among rocks at low tides on the protected outer coast (Ricketts and Calvin 1948:80ff). To collect crabs a number of methods have been used by Californian Indians.

The Sinkyone caught crabs and crawfish by hand (Nomland 1935:154), as did the Coast Yuki (Gifford 1939:325), while the Wappo are said to have swum after them as well as picked them off the beach (Driver 1936:185). Another simple method was to poke a stick or pole through the carapace of the animal. This practice is described for the Indians along southern Oregon Coast (Barnett 1937:165), the Yurok,[9] and for the Wiyot (Greengo ms.:11). The Tolowa would merely thrust a stick down into a tide pool. The stick, which was seized by the crab, was then drawn back together with the animal. Octopi are said to have been caught in this manner also (Greengo ms.:19).

Together with the simple techniques for catching these crustaceans, more elaborate ones were used on the northern Californian coasts. The Pomo used an intricate combination to catch crabs as illustrated by the following excerpt: "Crabs were caught on the coast with a piece of string, using meat as bait. The fisherman summoned the crabs with the cry of '*Po po po po.*' Then the crab came out from his place of concealment. A hand net was used for the purpose of removing the crab from the water. Lobsters (*K'i*, Central Pomo) needed no enticing, but were netted out of the water at low tide" (Loeb 1926:165).

Stewart mentions that the Central Pomo caught crabs with dip nets at low tide (Stewart 1943:60), but says nothing about catching them on baited strings.[10] Also he gives the Central Pomo name for crabs as "*Ki*" (Driver 1939:379). This is almost identical with the word Loeb gives (above) for lobsters. Since the only lobster on the West Coast is the "spiny lobster" (*Panulirus interruptus*), which does not range north of Point Conception (Ricketts and Calvin 1948:107), Loeb was in error in referring to the crustacean as a lobster. What was probably meant was another species of crab.

On the northwestern coast of California at least two types of crab pots were used. One was a circular frame netted across, used by the Karok (Driver 1939:313, 379), Yurok, Wiyot, and Mattole. The latter group made the mesh of the inner bark of willow, and baited the pot with mussels; the Karok, on the other hand, used salmon viscera for bait (for crayfish). In addition, the Karok and Yurok employed an openwork twined form of pot for crabs and their freshwater relatives. The Bear River Athabascans probably used a contrivance similar to that first described above, for, although it is called a dip net, it functioned as a crab pot.[11]

METHODS OF PREPARATION

The modes of preparation and consumption of shellfish by the California Indians were—like their technique of gathering—direct and unspecialized. The entrees were often, perhaps more so than actually recorded, eaten raw. This seems to have been especially true in the case of the sea urchin, *Strongylocontrotus purpuratus*, whose only edible portions, the eggs or gonads, were eaten raw by the Tolowa (Greengo ms.:20), Wiyot (Greengo ms.:13), and Central Pomo (Greengo ms.:10; Stewart 1943:60). This species was also exploited by the peoples of the Mediterranean area, and even today Californians of Italian descent can be seen during low tide at Pacific Grove collecting this *Frutta de Mare*, washing eggs in the sea water, and placing them in two-quart jars (Ricketts and Calvin 1948:240).

According to Jochelson (1925:106),[12] the gonads of a closely related species are fully developed only from April to June and from September to October. During the rest of the year the eggs are absent or very rare.

The Wiyot also ate limpets (*Aemaea* sp.) raw upon occasion (Greengo ms.:12). The writer's Wiyot informant declared that he has seen a descendant of the Mattole people eating limpets raw near Petrolia.

Undoubtedly clams were sometimes devoured with [no] more preparation than removing them from the shell, as with the Wappo (Driver 1936:184). This practice was also observed among the Seri (McGee 1898:195).

Perhaps the main problem with shellfish that had been gathered was that of preparing for storage those that had been caught and were not to be eaten immediately. As far as is known this was always done by drying them in the sun or smoking them in a fire.

Non-coastal groups would sometimes travel half the width of the state in order to enjoy the benefits and delights of fresh sea food as well as to preserve some for transportation to their homes (Pilling 1950:438–39; Greengo ms.:19; Gifford 1939:304–6). On these trips trade was carried on for shells and other articles between the coastal and inland groups. The impracticality of transporting fresh sea food over long distances is reflected in the taboo by the Hupa against bringing any fresh sea foods into the valley, all such products had to be dried (Driver 1939:375; Greengo ms.:18).[13]

In many cases the food was cooked before drying, as with the Tolowa who, when they had a large quantity of mussels, clams, or barnacles to be dried, would build a large fire on the beach, scoop out the hot coals and bury the shellfish in the hot sand which was re-covered with the coals. When a portion of the dried product was to be eaten, it was soaked over night in fresh water, then boiled a bit and consumed along with acorn mush (Greengo ms.:19).[14] The Yurok are known to have used this "pre-cooking" method for the pig's foot barnacle (Greengo ms.:15).

The Yurok cooked mussels before drying them by placing the live animal directly on the fire or on hot rocks in the fire, where they sim-mered in their own juices.[15] They were done when the shell opened. Some were eaten freshly cooked; others were dried in the sun, the small children brushing away the flies with branches. When the mus-sels were dry they were stored in baskets between layers of fine grass. These were stone boiled in baskets after being soaked over night in fresh water (Greengo ms.:13, 15).

Further light on mussel drying may be derived from data on the Wiyot—who not only broiled fresh mussels on an open fire but also boiled them fresh. The meat was dried and smoked in the twined, open-work basketry tray set on a frame over a fire of myrtle or alder wood. This process lasted for three days. In historic times the smoked and dried mussels were stored in a sack, though aboriginally a storage basket was undoubtedly used as with the Yurok. Again the dried mussels are said to have been soaked over night in fresh water and re-cooked by boiling (Greengo ms.:12). Preservation of shellfish, especially mussels, by drying or smoking occurred among all the northwestern Californian coastal peoples—the elements forming a complex of traits: cooking, drying, storing, soaking in fresh water and re-cooking by boiling the dried product before eating.

Nomland mentions this process for the Bear River Athabascans in the vicinity of Cape Mendocino (Nomland 1938:113). The Sinkyone practice in this regard was not recorded,[16] while the Coast Yuki varied the mussel drying complex only slightly. They regarded mussels quite highly but went about preparing them somewhat differently. The first part of the Coast Yuki process corresponds rather closely to that of the more northerly groups; the stored mussels, however, were eaten dry without further cooking (Gifford 1939:315). The Coast Yuki method is described thus by Gifford: "Mussels for drying were placed among hot coals to open shells. Then the meats were spitted on young hazel twigs to dry. These twigs with their loads of mussels were tied together so that they radiated like the spokes of a wheel. Usually the mussels were dried in the sun, though sometimes smoked too. If not thoroughly dried they spoiled. When ready for transport inland, the sticks of mussels were packed in the man's burden basket (*olo*). They were eaten dry without further cooking. People were never poisoned by dried mussels, as they were sometimes by fresh mussels" (Gifford 1939:315).

Farther south, the Pomo followed the practice of the northwestern groups—boiling or roasting the mussels on hot coals to open them, sun-drying them, transporting them home, and sometimes stringing them on grass fiber.[17] The dried mussels were made ready for eating by being soaked in fresh water until they were swollen, after which they were boiled (Greengo ms.:10).

South of San Francisco Bay our knowledge of mussel drying must be largely inferred. The Costanoans dried food by both sun and smoke, while the Chumash admitted sun drying but denied the smoking process. The Serrano and Gabrielino also said they dried food in the sun (Harrington 1942:9). Mussels were definitely eaten by the Costanoans (Kroeber 1925:467),[18] Salinans and Chumash (Harrington 1942:8).

In general the emphasis in coastal activities was laid upon the ubiquitous mussel. At various times and in certain localities, however, other forms of shellfish and sea food were the foci of attention. Among the shellfish, the abalone, in Monterey Bay and to the south, was almost equally important (though specific citations as to drying of them for future use are lacking). Woodward stipulates that the most plentiful and most useful species on the coast of Southern California was the black abalone (*Haliotis cracherodii*), and that this species was one of the most prevalent at the important Chumash village site of Muwu (Woodward 1930:106). Another very important mollusk at this site was the present day market variety of cockle, *Protethaca staminea*, of which the author says that there were, "solid layers of cockle shells, unmixed with earth or other debris, evidently the remains of ancient feasts or a heavy catch prepared for future use" (Woodward 1930:106).

Though abalones were less frequent to the north, they were at least occasionally dried along with mussels and clams. The same method used for mussels was evidently extended to other kinds of shellfish— and to fish as well. At the seashore the Yurok took—besides shellfish—various types of sea mammals (including stranded whales),[19] surf fish, and seaweed (Spott and Kroeber 1942; Kroeber 1925:84; Greengo ms.:13–17). All of these were dried in greater or lesser quantities. Indeed, dried smelt were apparently a staple among the Tolowa, for one informant declared that they were eaten at almost every meal along with acorn mush (Greengo ms.:20).[20] The taking of smelt in fair sized quantities extended at least as far south as the Coast Yuki, for Gifford includes them along with mussels, abalones, chitons, bullheads, kelp fish, and rock cod as foods dried at the seashore and taken inland to winter sites in the fall (Gifford 1939:315). Not much abalone was dried and taken inland, however, because the small supply was usually eaten immediately. In the process of preparation, "an abalone [which was] to be dried was cooked in coals, removed from the shell, and the meat cut into three broad horizontal slices with a flint knife. In cutting into small pieces for eating, a mussel shell was used" (Gifford 1939:315).

Sea mammals were generally less important south of northwestern California until the Chumash area was reached. Here, another seagoing people took them as evidenced by remains in archaeological sites.[21] The coastal Gabrielino, too, are said to have subsisted principally on fish, whales, seals, sea otters, and shellfish (Reid 1852:no. 5).

Two species of smelt—*Spirinchus starksi* and *Allosmorus attenuatus*—comprise the bulk of present day surf fish catch, and probably did so in aboriginal times also. The former species is the most abundant and ranges as far south as Monterey Bay; the latter ranges only to San Francisco Bay. For both species, however, the largest recent landings were made at Eureka (Roedel 1948:41). This fact reflects the aboriginal distribution of this food.

Of shellfish other than mussels and abalone that were dried or smoked for later use, specific mention may be made of chitons (*Crypochiton stelleri* and *Katherina tunicata*) for the Wiyot. These were cooked in hot ashes, the plates and viscera then being removed, and the foot only eaten. The drying process was similar to that used for mussels (Greengo ms.:11). The initial cooking process was essentially the same for the Coast Yuki. However, "the white and blue 'intestinal parts' were dried for use later, when they were parched, or soaked in water and eaten. The meat was washed and eaten at once" (Gifford 1939:327). What appears to be a survival of an ancient Pomo practice in treating the "gumboot" was recorded recently at the Ukiah Rancheria. The informant was drying a couple of dozen chitons (*Cryptochiton stelleri*) on a table covered with newspapers in the yard. She said that "they are collected on the coast. They are boiled and then the shells are removed, then they are dried in the sun for about a week. When they are desired for a meal, they are again boiled and then sliced and served, ... not many of the Indians eat these any more."[22]

The northern Pomo formerly made trips to the coast lasting at least four to five days in order to gather and dry mussels, abalone, sea fish, kelp, and seaweed. They gave abalone feasts, and also dried them in the sun to be stored in baskets for relatively great lengths of time (Loeb 1926:192).

The process of stone boiling in baskets was widely distributed in aboriginal California—and where shellfish were eaten this was one of the means of preparing them. It has been pointed out above that boiling was the usual method of preparing dried shellfish, and probably other dried products also, for eating, being done with stones in most of California. In northwestern California all groups, except the Nongatl, Kato, and Coast Yuki, boiled meat, nevertheless, all are said to have dried meat and fish (Driver 1939:315, 381; Drucker 1937:234). In this area the most common method of preparing fresh meat or fish (and shellfish) was that of roasting or broiling the animal on hot coals. However, river mussels were boiled, for a species of "Unio" found along the Klamath River[23] in Karok country moved an early traveler to record the following: "These form a favorite article of food with the Indians, who boil them in baskets by means of hot stones" (Gibbs 1860:158). From these and the few other statements that can be found relating to the utilization of freshwater mussels, it might be concluded that the manner of preparing them differed little from that employed by the coastal peoples for salt water species. Both boiling and roasting were resorted to by the River Wintu. If a surplus was accumulated over what could be consumed immediately, they would be dried on flat basketry trays for winter use (Du Bois 1935:18), and for trade with the mountain people (Powers 1877:235). Powers also states that the Washo boiled a bivalve—which he calls "*Onondonta*," but which may now be called generically *Anodenta* or *Gonidea*—found in the Owens River and in many other parts of California (Powers 1877:430).

Freshwater lake mussels (probably *Anodenta* sp.) are reported roasted in a strikingly similar manner in both north central California among the Lake Pomo and by Yokuts around Buena Vista Lake in the southern Central Valley. Kniffen says of the Pomo: "Freshwater clams (*xala*) were well distributed about the lake. In summer they were taken in some numbers and cooked near the shore. They were placed on the ground in a flat spiral, hinge upward. Over the top a light fire was built with small sticks so that when cooked the shells were easily opened" (Kniffen 1939:365). Latta records that the Chunut and Wowol Yokuts prepared large quantities of lake clams in the following way: "First they put on the ground a layer of tules four or five inches thick. They put the clams on top, with the open edges down as thick as they could, so they would not roll over. They piled tules on top of the clams. Then they set fire to them. When the tules burned, the water ran out of the clams and steamed them so they cooked nice. My people ate lots of them that ways. They were good with salt from salt grass. Sometimes they baked lots of fires of them" (Latta 1949:253).

The quite simple and efficient method of cooking food in hot sand was employed to some extent by the Tolowa. Hot sand was also employed to loosen the tough hides of such animals as chitons and octopi. The loosened hides were then scraped off—the meat of the former being broiled on live coals, the arms of the latter being chopped into six inch pieces and stone boiled in baskets (Greengo ms.:18, 19).

Crabs are said to have been boiled by the Wiyot and Hupa; the latter also baked them in hot sand (Greengo ms.:11, 18). Further up the coast the Yurok either baked them in hot sand or broiled them on the open fire (Greengo ms.:13, 17). The Tolowa, again, cooked them in sand. Other shellfish said to have been prepared by this method include Washington clams (*Saxidomus nuttallii*) by the Hupa, and pig's foot barnacles (*Mitella polymerus*) by the Yurok (Greengo ms.:18).

Although the information is incomplete, it seems that the technique of baking food in hot sand seems to have occurred only on the northwest coast of California. Here, its use was confined to the preparation of shellfish. Broiling or roasting on the open fire or in hot ashes appears to have had a general distribution along the entire coast, however. In fact, this latter method is the only one reported for the Coast Yuki, who applied it even to the sea urchin (Gifford 1939:315, 325–28). Elsewhere, sea urchins were raw, with the possible exception of the Bear River people, who sometimes placed them on hot stones. They did not, apparently, place sea food in direct contact with a fire (Nomland 1938:113).[24] Their closely related neighbors to the south, the Mattole, broiled all meats and fish on the fire (Driver 1939:315). Pomo practice was apparently equally divided between preparing seafood by boiling and cooking it in hot ashes or live coals. The Northern Pomo prepared even the seaweed for their feasts by cooking in hot ashes, as well as their abalone (Loeb 1926:192; Chesnut 1902:299).

Another food which was gathered along with shellfish, and which has not been previously mentioned, was a sea anemone (*Cribrina xanthogrammica*). The fact that this animal was utilized was first pointed out by Loeb in 1926 (1926:164). Stewart's description of its utilization by the Northern Pomo bears quoting:

> Although extremely soft when removed from the water, they were found to keep several days without spoiling and were wrapped in leaves and tied with grass and transported fresh into the interior valleys. When cooked and dried they became very hard, but soften when soaked and warmed again. As prepared by my informant they had a texture like calves' brains and, except for the usual "sea flavor" and the sand which could not be removed, might have been mistaken for them. Loeb noted their use by the Pomo, but they have not been reported for other California Indians and I find no reference to their use in other part of the world (Stewart 1943:60).

Although this description is excellent, Stewart is in error on the last point, for the Coast Yuki usage had also been noted by Gifford in 1939. This latter author describes these people as removing sea anemones from the rocks with a wedge-like abalone spatula, cleaning the mussels, barnacles, and other hard objects from their exteriors and interiors,[25] and cooking them in hot ashes (Gifford 1939:328). Further up the coast, the modern Wiyot slice and fry sea anemones. At least one informant doubted, however, if his people used them in the old days (Greengo ms.:13). The Tolowa seem to have eaten sea anemones since before the coming of the white man. At present they have to remove them from rocks with mussel bars, after which they wash them in fresh water, scrap them clean, and broil them on beds of live coals.

Still another cooking device which was used extensively in California was the so-called earth oven. This device consisted of a pit in the ground measuring between one or two feet in depth and one or two feet in diameter, which was filled with alternate layers of hot stones, leaves, and live stones. The food was protected from the heated stones by leaves, which also served to prevent the heat from escaping. Water was often poured over the stones before the live coals were put on; this served to steam the food as well as to prevent the leaves from burning.[26]

In northwestern California the Yurok,[27] Nongatl, Mattole, Kato, Coast Yuki, and Sinkyone used the earth oven for preparing meat or fish, and, presumably, shellfish (Driver 1939:315). The Tolowa cooked only shellfish in the earth oven, never mammals or fish. This was largely true for the Wiyot also, while the Karok used the earth oven especially for bear meat (Driver 1939:382).

Other specific references to the use of the earth oven for shellfish are rare or entirely lacking. One clue for the Pomo is given in an account which states that shell food was baked covered with leaves, coals and hot rocks (Kniffen 1939:387). That other tribes along the coast possessed the earth oven and probably used it for shellfish seems to be a reasonable assumption. Harrington (1942:9) lists the earth oven as present for seventeen Costanoan, Salinan, Chumash, Serrano, Fernandeno and Gabrielino groups, but in only four instances are the food cooked in the device recorded.[28]

SHELLFISH POISON

The relationship of shellfish poisoning to the food habits of the Californian Indians can be summarized as follows: The seasonal gathering pattern of most of the inhabitants of the coast and hinterland brought them to the shore largely during the months of April through October. It was within this period that toxic shellfish were a serious threat, especially during the mid-summer and early fall. Apparently some groups rightly correlated presence of the fatal toxin with luminescence of the water and refrained from eating shellfish at such times. However, it is equally apparent that, although they may have recognized the presence of the poison, a large number of Indians falsely believed that mussels gathered from below the low water mark were safe. This belief was bolstered by the fact that shellfish were safe most of the year. *Gonyaulax* multiplies to dangerous proportions only once each summer and then only for a short period in quite localized areas. During such occurrences, those Indians who did not refrain from eating shellfish must have succumbed from the effects of the toxin.

SUMMARY AND CONCLUSIONS

Ethnological and archaeological evidence indicate that all coastal Indians partook freely of shellfish, an abundant and easily gathered food. There were, however, differences in emphasis on shellfish by various groups up and down the coast. For some, such as the Coast Yuki, Bokeya Pomo (of Point Arena), Coast Miwok, and probably most of the Costanoans, this resource was a staple. Others, among whom were the Tolowa, Yurok, Wiyot, Mattole and the Chumash, ate large amounts of shellfish but did not depend on them to the extent that the above mentioned tribes did. These differing emphases have both cultural and ecological explanations. All of the latter groups had larger food resources open to them because they possessed sea-going canoes which enabled them to hunt sea mammals as well as to visit outlying rocks for mussels. In addition the Chumash in the south practiced marine fishing from their plank canoes.

On the northwestern coast the bulk of the population was concentrated along the excellent salmon streams including the Smith, Klamath, Mad, Eel, Bear and Mattole rivers. There were a few permanent villages scattered along the coast between the mouths of these rivers, and their inhabitants probably ate as much shellfish as other meat for their protein requirements. The Pomo speaking groups considered as a whole shared as wide a variety of ecological conditions as any other Californian people. Probably those along the Gualala and Russian rivers concentrated mostly on salmon. We have evidence that at the mouth of the Garcia River (near Point Arena), the Bokeya Pomo depended mostly upon shellfish, although salmon were taken when available.

Molluscan fauna in inland bodies of water was utilized to its fullest extent, but nowhere did this supply occur in the abundance nor assume the importance that it did on the coast.

Techniques utilized in gathering shellfish were not very involved. The tool most employed in gathering clams, mussels and abalones was essentially the digging stick, sometimes modified by flattening the end. Crabs and crayfish were, at some places, captured in basketry traps very similar to modern crab pots. Often many of the species of shellfish were taken by hand without the aid of implements.

Methods of preparation too were very simple. Much of the shellfish gathered was preserved for future use by drying, either precooked or raw. Dried shellfish meat was usually soaked in fresh water and boiled before being consumed. Raw shellfish were mostly broiled on an open fire. Stone boiling and baking in hot sand were also often resorted to. The earth oven was employed for preparing these animals to a significant extent in northwestern California.

Shellfish are so high in nutrient value that as few as fifty medium sized sea mussels would fill the daily protein requirements of a moderately active man. Somewhat larger quantities of clams or crabs would fill these needs.

Paralytic shellfish poisoning was most likely fatal to a good number of Indians who ate shellfish at the places and during the times that the toxin was present.

THE ARMY WORM:
A FOOD OF THE POMO INDIANS
Samuel A. Barrett

Although he had a wide and extensive field experience, Samuel Alfred Barrett (1879–1965) is best-known for his work among the Pomo. Growing up in Ukiah, he worked in his father's general store, where he soon began to collect baskets from the local Pomo Indians. Barrett entered the University of California as an undergraduate in 1900, and graduated with a B.S. in 1905 and an M.A. in 1906. During this time he had already begun to work for the Museum of Anthropology as a curatorial assistant and field collector. Between 1903 and 1907, he carried out substantial fieldwork among the Pomo, Sierra Miwok, Maidu, Yokuts, Yuki, and Wintun. In 1908 Barrett earned the first anthropology doctorate from UC Berkeley, with a dissertation on Pomo basketry. Following a research expedition to Ecuador (1908–9), Barrett spent most of his later career at the Milwaukee Public Museum, as curator of anthropology (1909–20) and director (1920–40). During his years as a curator, Barrett made collecting expeditions to the Menomonee and Chippewa, Hopi, Kwakiutl, Paiute and Washoe, and Blackfoot, in addition to archaeological fieldwork and a trip to East Africa. Barrett had a real flair for museum work, and his ethnographic approach stressed collecting and factual recording over theoretical analysis.

Perhaps because it is so different from Euro-American food habits, Californian Indian insect-eating has attracted a good bit of scholarly attention (cf. Sutton 1988). Samuel Barrett's essay on the army worm caterpillar is one of the more important contributions. Like the Gifford essay on acorn-eating, this little study was produced to honor Kroeber's sixtieth birthday. Readers of this essay will note that Barrett does not specify exactly which species the army worm is, a mystery that was clarified when Sean Swezey (1978) identified it as a kind of moth caterpillar (*Homoncocnemis fortis*), which derives its common name from its habit of attacking crops in large "armies."

Essays in Anthropology Presented to Alfred L. Kroeber (1936), ed. Robert H. Lowie. Berkeley: University of California Press. Pp. 1–5.

The Yokaia (Yokayo) rancheria that Barrett visited was home to a self-owned community of Central Pomo, located just south of the city of Ukiah. The woman illustrated in his photos is Joseppa Dick (early 1860s–1905), one of the most famous Pomo basket-weavers of her time and a prime consultant for Dr. John Hudson as well as for Barrett (Smith-Ferri 1993).

AMONG THE POMO, as among most Californian tribes, practically everything in nature was called upon to furnish its quota of foods. Insects were not omitted from the dietary of this tribe, grasshoppers, angleworms, yellow-jacket grubs, and various others being esteemed.

Perhaps the most interesting insect used as food by the Pomo is the so-called army worm [1i'].[1] Like certain other insects this worm has a cycle which causes it to appear in vast numbers once every several years. The exact periodicity is not known and could not be determined by questioning the Indians.

It happened to be the writer's good fortune to drop in at the Yokaia rancheria on the morning of May 15, 1904, only to find that the entire village was deserted except for two of the very aged. From these he learned that the entire population had moved down to a certain grove on the eastern bank of Russian river, where the army worms had suddenly appeared in hordes, the first time since 1898. Taking one of these old men along in the buggy, for he was too feeble to walk the several miles, the author immediately joined in the "hunt" and spent the entire day observing the gathering of this, the rarest, of all Pomo foods. The following statements are not, therefore, mere hearsay but direct personal observations confirmed by photographs, four of which are reproduced here.

The army worm is a caterpillar which is almost hairless, having not to exceed half a dozen hairs on its entire body. It is about 2½ inches in length and is a general brownish color with Indian red stripes along the sides. The male [li'baiya] is distinguished, according to the Indians, from the female [li'mata] by the fact that it has a pinkish white belly, while the belly of the latter is always yellow in color.

According to the Indians' statements this worm comes only for at most a few days, in the early summer and only in years when there is a great deal of fog. It is said to belong to Thunder and to travel on the fog from the west. It feeds exclusively on the leaves of the ash [kala'm], and when an army of these worms finishes with a grove of this species there is not a vestige of green to be seen. Figure 1, shows some very small ash saplings at the edge of an opening and immediately adjacent to the larger ash trees of a grove. These had been completely stripped by the army worms so that they looked like the naked branches of deciduous bushes in the winter time.

It is an interesting fact that these worms move from tree to tree or from grove to grove chiefly in the afternoon. From observations made, this fact may be explained as due to the sun's heat. Eating during the night and early part of the day, the worms divest the trees of their leaves and the sun's rays pour in upon them, causing them to drop to the earth and seek the shelter of the leafy canopy of another ash which has not been disturbed. There is of course more or less movement of the worms all day long for, regardless of the hour, if a tree has been stripped of its leaves the worms descend to earth in search of a new food supply. However, by far the greatest number move in the afternoon. Their descent from the tree is as a rule most precipitate. They simply let go and drop, and this apparently without harm to themselves, regardless of the height. Almost never is one seen to descend the trunk of a tree. During the day the author spent in this ash grove, he was subjected to a continuous hail of falling army worms and a shower of leaf fragments dropped by the worms from their lofty dinner table.

The Indians know very well the route the worms will take when they do drop to the ground and move on to the next ash tree or grove. They prepare for this advance by digging large numbers of pits and trenches across the line of march of the worms and by encircling the bases of the ash trees toward which they are moving. These pits are of various sizes and shapes, circular, square, or rectangular. Each is about 6 inches in width and rarely more than 2½ feet in length. They are always from 4 to 6 inches in depth, and are vertical-walled little moats dug in the solid damp sand. As the worms race over the ground, with incredible rapidity, they fall into these little moats in large numbers. Yet seeing that they can ascend the vertical trunk of a tree, surely a vertical wall of solid damp sand proves no obstacle and they will climb out of this prison with the utmost ease. And so they would if it were not for the clever device employed to prevent just that kind of escape. When the little moats are dug the Indians bring over a quantity of fine, dry sand, with which they line the edges of the tops of these pits. The captive caterpillar finds no difficulty whatever in ascending the vertical wall of his prison, but when he reaches the edge of the pit his feet encounter the line of shifting, dry sand so that he loses his balance and topples over backward to the bottom of the pit again. Try as he may, he never can get out so long as the line of dry sand lasts at the edge of the pit. For this reason fresh dry sand is added from time to time. Also this line of dry sand serves another purpose. While it is true that these worms race along at great speed they are cautious to a certain extent. When they reach the edge of such a pit they could easily turn aside. They, however, are on the dry sand which shifts and rolls them headlong to the bottom of the pit.

There is one means of escape, however, which must be carefully watched. When a pit is fairly well filled with worms, the topmost ones can make their escape fairly easily. Therefore pits must be emptied quite frequently to prevent this.

In figure 2, we have a very characteristic set of these sand-lined pits completely surrounding the base of a tree. In this particular instance, there were fourteen circular pits each about 6 inches in diameter and together making about 120 degrees of the circle. There were also six rectangular pits varying from 9 to 30 inches in length. These finished the line which completely encircled the base of this tree, and which formed a circle about 5½ feet in diameter. The spaces between successive pits is not to exceed an inch in each case, a space too small to allow a worm much chance to slip by on the dry rolling sand.

Another tree had a circle about 25 feet in diameter encircling its base and made by only eighteen pits varying in length from 1 to 3½ feet. Each had a width of about 6 inches and was 6 inches in depth.

Other such pits are arranged in straight or curved lines many feet in length across the general line of march of the army worms.

Fig. 1. Ash saplings stripped by army worms.

PHOTOGRAPH BY SAMUEL A. BARRETT, 1904 (NEG. NO. 15–2637).

Fig. 2. Sand-lined pits for catching army worms,
surrounding the base of a tree.

PHOTOGRAPH BY SAMUEL A. BARRETT, 1904 (NEG. NO. 15–2635).

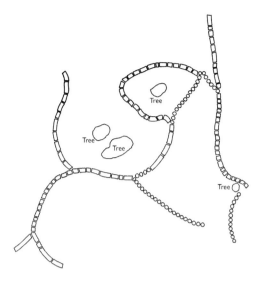

Fig. 3. A system of sand-lined pits for catching army worms.

One such set of pits numbered forty-two. They were rectangular and varied from 6 to 15 inches in length. Another line of thirty-seven pits measured nearly 50 feet in length. Another rather intricate pit system is shown in figure 3.

With all these deadly pitfalls we might think that no worms could possibly escape. However, some do, and to insure the fullest possible harvest, the Indians place girdles or collars [li hubeu] of ash leaves about the bases of the trees, 3 or 4 feet from the ground, as shown in figure 2. The worms that do run the gauntlet and escape the pits start to ascend the tree, are arrested by the fresh ash leaves, and are easily collected by hand.

Other workers also obtain quite a harvest by hand-picking worms from the low young ash saplings.

When the worms are obtained, whether it be from the pits, from the collars, or from the saplings, they are immediately placed in a vessel of ordinary cold water, where they quickly drown.

They are then roasted in hot ashes or are boiled and are devoured in large quantities on the spot. When everyone has satisfied his appetite, the cooked worms are spread out in the sun to dry for winter use.

Fig. 4. Live army worms crawling on the inner surface of a basket.
PHOTOGRAPH BY SAMUEL A. BARRETT, 1904 (NEG. NO. 15–2632).

*Fig. 5. Pomo woman [Joseppa Dick] sifting worms in an openwork
basket to separate them from ashes after roasting.*
PHOTOGRAPH BY SAMUEL A. BARRETT, 1904 (NEG. NO. 15–2634).

Figure 4, shows some of the live worms crawling about on the inner surface of a basket before being placed in the water. Figure 5 shows a Pomo woman sifting out some of the army worms. They are first placed, with live coals and hot ashes, in a tightly woven basket to roast, after which they are placed in an openwork sifting basket, to separate them from the ashes. This method of cooking turns the worms a reddish color and is said to produce a very excellent sweet flavor.

Custom requires that conversation shall be carried on in low tones and that no undue noise shall be made by those gathering the army worms, because it is said that the worms become alarmed and leave. If any noise is made the army worms in the immediate vicinity will stop eating, raise the forward half of their bodies at an angle of about 30 degrees and sway the elevated part of the body rapidly back and forth in agitation for some time.

No one may speak crossly to another under penalty of being bitten by a rattlesnake.

Loeb (1926:164), in speaking of the army worm, states that they are gathered with much ceremony and great solemnity. His information comes from the Northern Pomo and is undoubtedly merely a statement made by an informant. It does not correspond with the above direct observations among the Central Pomo. In our work we found no solemnity; on the contrary we found much joy, though not boisterous, for reasons already stated. There was no singing of ceremonial songs and no idea that this food must be kept and treated with special respect. It was eaten on the spot and handled in every way just as any other food might be.

Just as the army worm appears, so suddenly and mysteriously does he disappear. Without warning of any kind he is gone and does not reappear again for several years.

It was really a red-letter day in any Pomo community when this little caterpillar made his appearance, and the Indians made this the occasion not only of an immediate feast but they stored for winter use as large quantities as possible of the dried caterpillars. No opportunity presented itself to check the amount dried upon this particular occasion, but certainly several hundred pounds of the dried product were garnered by the inhabitants of this relatively small village.

TRIBAL
ACCOUNTS

LIFE AND CULTURE OF THE HUPA
Pliny E. Goddard

An appropriate place to begin a section of tribal accounts is with the first in the University of California anthropological publications, a series that contains so much of what we know about Native Californian food customs. This engagingly-written study is devoted to the Hupa people of the Trinity River valley in the northwestern part of the state. Like their neighbors, the Yurok, Karuk, and Tolowa, they represent the southernmost extension of the Northwest Coast culture pattern—with salmon-subsistence, dugout canoes and plank houses, and economic stratification.

Of Quaker parentage, Pliny Earle Goddard (1869–1928) attended Earlham College in Richmond, Indiana, where he studied classical languages (B.A., 1892; M.A., 1896) before teaching secondary school in Indiana and Kansas between 1892 and 1896. In March of 1897, Goddard went as an inter-denominational missionary to Hoopa, California. This experience stimulated him to enroll in the fall of 1900 at UC Berkeley, where he obtained his Ph.D. in linguistics in 1904. Goddard taught anthropology at his alma mater (instructor, 1901–6; assistant professor, 1906–9) until 1909, when he joined the anthropology department of the American Museum of Natural History (assistant curator, 1909–10, associate curator, 1910–14, curator, 1914–28); after 1915, he was also lecturer at Columbia University. Most of his California Indian language research came in the years before going to New York. In addition to his study of Hupa and related languages of northern California and southern Oregon, Goddard investigated the languages of the Navajo and Apache of Arizona and New Mexico, as well as those of other Athapaskan-speakers in Canada.

Goddard gathered the information that went into *Life and Culture of the Hupa* mostly during his time as a missionary on the Hoopa Reservation, supplemented with several subsequent trips for the University. The monograph was essentially completed during his first year in Berkeley. Although Goddard's ethnography was always incidental to his linguistic work, the work is quite substantial. Despite its gaps and limitations, it remains the best single volume on Hupa culture.

Food. *Life and Culture of the Hupa.* University of California Publications in American Archaeology and Ethnology (1903), 1(1). Pp. 21–32.

FLESH AND HUNTING

Nowhere in the temperate zone, perhaps, has Nature been more bountiful in providing a variety and abundance of food. The procuring of the animal food was the work of the men.

Elk and deer were killed with the bow and arrow by still hunting or taken in set snares into which they were sometimes driven with the help of dogs. In still hunting the man went either from his home or from a temporary camp to the feeding ground of the animals, reaching the chosen spot early in the morning or late in the evening. Before starting out the bodily odor was minimized by bathing and smoking with green fir boughs. Some of the hunting medicines employed were fragrant and no doubt were of practical value, although they were used from a religious motive rather than for any well understood, direct effect.

The hunter, masked with the head and antlers of the game and covered with its skin, simulated the movements of the animal. This he did so well that not only did the game often approach him, but the ever watchful panther sometimes mistook him for a deer and attacked him. To guard against such an attack the Hupa were accustomed to do up their long hair in a bunch on the back of the neck and to thrust through it long pins sharp at both ends. When the man had worked his way as close as possible, he discharged a well directed arrow which brought down the game. Animals wounded with a barbed arrow are not so likely to survive as those hit in non-vital spots by a leaden ball. The successful hunting of large game without firearms required a splendid physique, senses nearly as keen as those of the animals, and an intimate knowledge of the habits of the game. Few men under such conditions were successful hunters.

Snares were set for elk and deer in some trail which they were likely to use. Sometimes in the surrounding mountains, ridges and cañons are found where there is but one road to the feeding ground, saltlick,or watering place. These places naturally good for the purpose were often improved by placing obstructions and by making lanes of brush and vines. In this trail at the proper place was hung a noose so arranged that the passing animal could not escape it. The rope needed to be very strong and the man who possessed a supply of it was rich. It was made by patient twisting together of twine made of fiber obtained from the leaf of the Iris. The deer and elk were driven to these snares by men provided with sticks which they beat upon their hands as a supplement to their shouting. The native dogs are said to have been employed in these drives. Late in summer the grass on Bald Hill and perhaps in other places was fired and the fleeing deer taken in snares or killed with weapons while frantic from fear.

All the region near the valley was held by heads of families as hunting rights. Many men had no holdings of their own but assisted some more fortunate man as dependent friends or as actual slaves.

Deer are now often seen swimming down the river. They are then pursued in canoes and killed with clubs. In primitive times deer were driven into the river by the help of dogs and afterward secured by some one waiting below.

The man who succeeded in securing an elk had a large quantity of welcome food, a skin which, when properly tanned, would defend him in battle from the arrows of the enemy, and antlers which furnished him with material for spoons and wedges.

The deer-skins were also very valuable. They were in constant demand for clothing and bedding. The hides were retained by the master of the hunt. They were carefully removed with flint knives about three and one-half inches long and two inches wide and quite thin. These blades were hafted to short wooden handles. The carcass was cut in accordance with prescribed rules. Some portions were not eaten at all, among them the flesh on the floating ribs and the breast-bone. Other parts were forbidden to women. None of the animal was wasted save from religious scruples. The blood was drunk at once. The stomach in which other parts were put was buried in the ashes until cooked and then eaten. The ears were a delicacy to be roasted in the campfire and eaten after the hunt. The bone of the leg was saved with its marrow, which was of service in mixing paint. The sinews were saved for bowstrings. The brain was removed and dried that it might be used in dressing the hide. The meat which was not needed for immediate consumption was cut into strips by the women and cured over a fire.

Meat was roasted on the coals or large pieces were placed before the fire and turned until cooked. The basket pot was used for boiling, the heat being applied by dropping in hot stones. The meat was cut in flat pieces called kiniltats, or in strings, LoLkyuwiltowen, before it was put in to boil. The basket was kept only for this purpose. The meat was served in wooden trays called kisintokiwat. For religious reasons these were never washed. After the meal a wooden bowl was passed for each to wash his hands. The water was carried away from the house and thrown out. This was done to prevent the least particle of the animal remaining in the house.

Squirrels, woodrats, and other small animals were killed with arrows and eaten. The ruffed grouse, pheasant, and mountain quail were killed for food. The small valley quail, the meadow lark, and the mourning doves, birds esteemed by white people, were not eaten by the Hupa. The first two mentioned are thought to spend the day in gambling in the underground regions which are the home of the dead. The stakes are the souls of living men. The snow in winter drives large flocks of the varied robin into the valley. These were taken in snares made of twine, baited with acorns. The Hupa did not eat earth-worms and yellow-jacket grubs as do the Indians of many parts of California.

FISH AND FISHING

The spring salmon begin to run in April. They are caught with a net which is stretched on three poles, arranged in the form of a triangle. The main shaft is held upright. It is about ten feet long. The lower end rests on the bottom while fishing. About six inches from the lower end a pole six feet long is placed at right angles. From the outer end of this the third pole runs to the upper end of the upright shaft.

A crib of logs and rocks is built out into the stream in the backwater just below a riffle. On this crib is placed a board and on the end of the board is usually seen a block of wood on which the fisherman sits. Hanging close at hand is a club used to dispatch the fish before it is removed from the net. Usually the fisherman has a billet of wood or a flat piece of elk-horn in his hand from which a string passes to the body of the net. Any slight motion in the net is easily perceived in this way.

The fall salmon begin to run after the first rains in September or October. During the summer preparation is made for catching them. A dam or weir is built across the river at Medildiñ and TakimiLdiñ in alternate years. Stout peeled stakes are driven in the river bottom in pairs, crossing near the top and firmly withed together. Heavy logs are laid into the crotches thus made, end to end, forming a continuous stringer across the river. Stakes about four inches in diameter are driven on the upper side, about four feet apart, at an angle of forty-five degrees. These are bound to the stringer by withes. A lattice work is then made on the upper side of the dam, consisting of small saplings bound together by chains of withes. This is made close enough to stop the upward migration of the salmon while impeding the flow of the water but little. Small platforms, to stand on while fishing, are made by driving a stake a little below the dam and running poles from the dam to the top of the stake.

The fishing is done at night or when the sun's rays are not too vertical. Tons of salmon are taken if the run happens to be good. The men have a rude shelter on the shore at one end of the dam where they sleep between times of fishing. The dam constructed with so much labor is swept away by the first high water.

Long seine-like nets are set in still water. One of these nets is sixty feet long and three and a half feet wide. It is provided with sinkers of stone, discs three and a half inches in diameter with holes chipped in the centers. Twelve of these are attached to this net. Floats of wood are provided to buoy up the top edge. When the net had been set, several canoe loads of men went out and drove the fish into the net.

V-shaped obstructions used to be constructed in the river; the opening of the V was up-stream, one wing resting on the shore and the other projecting well into the stream. At the point of the V was built a boat-shaped trap of round poles somewhat higher than the surrounding water. The fish passed up around the end of the obstruction. They were frightened back by men in canoes and in trying to escape entered the trap, through the bottom of which the water passed freely leaving them helpless.

Salmon were sometimes speared before the Trinity was made foul by mining. A long pole was provided with two diverging prongs of wood at one end. On these prongs were placed spear points of bone about four inches long, provided with two barbs of bone or horn. The point and barbs were united by wrappings of twine covered with pitch. A socket was formed between the barbs to receive the end of the wooden prong of the shaft. A line of doubled and twisted, two-ply twine was attached to the spear point. This line, which was about thirty inches long, was made fast to the pole. The spear points on entering the salmon were pulled free from the prongs of the shaft but were still attached to it by the line.

Sturgeon are sometimes taken in the salmon net, or in a stronger one made for the purpose. The sturgeon is valued not only for its mass of edible flesh, but for the glue obtained from its head.

Trout and other small fish are caught in dip nets fastened to three poles arranged in the form of an isosceles triangle. The short third side, bowing out slightly, is at the bottom. The apex of the equal sides is held against the head of the fisherman and the sides are grasped by the hands. The net thus held is drawn to and fro in quick water.

Trout and other small fish were caught in the river and creeks by means of primitive hooks. These were made by placing a small sharp-pointed bone between two small sticks at an angle of thirty-five degrees. These were bound together and to the line of primitive twine by careful wrapping with fine thread. These hooks were usually placed on a set line in sets of ten or more.

Lamprey eels are caught in great numbers during the warm nights of spring. They are taken in nets similar to those used for salmon. The Hupa are equally fond of them in their fresh state or when dried. Suckers used to be caught and eaten by the Hupa.

No poisons, such as the buckeye and soap-root, were used to stupefy the fish in shallow pools. The buckeye is not found in the valley;

and the streams are fairly constant throughout the year. These and other means of killing fish by wholesale are resorted to by the Pomo of Mendocino county.

Varying lengths of river shore were held as private fishing rights by the heads of families. These included one or more riffles suitable for the construction of a fishing crib. These rights passed from father to son and were always respected.

The women attend to the dressing and curing of the fish. For cutting fish the stone knife is still used. The salmon eggs are saved and dried. They are used to lunch upon. Probably the Indian knew no form of food more concentrated and at the same time so easily portable for a journey. The heads and the tails of the salmon are used while fresh for immediate consumption. The heads when roasted are considered very fine. The Indians are fond of the cartilaginous substances which are abundant in them. The body of the fish is cut into three or more layers. If the flesh is not held together by the backbone or the skin, round sticks are thrust through to keep the flesh from falling to pieces while it is curing over the fire of the xonta [family house].

Eels are drawn and slit many times to the skin with a sharp bone. They are then hung over the fire to dry.

In dressing and cleaning fish, ferns and leaves are always used to wipe away the blood and unclean portions. Salmon and eels are broiled before the fire when eaten fresh. In the dried state they are sometimes broiled but are often eaten without cooking. They are served on disk-shaped baskets set upon a mat of leaves.

The Hupa used a dish of stone about eight inches long, six inches wide and three inches deep to catch the dripping oil of the cooking eels.[1]

VEGETABLE FOOD

The gathering of vegetable food is the duty of the women. Acorns constitute the staff of life for the Hupa. Those of tanbark oak, *Quercus densiflora*, are the most esteemed, but in case of a short crop those of the Pacific post oak, *Q. Garryana*, black oak, *Q. Californica*, and the maul oak, *Q. chrysolepis*, are used as well.

The acorns are gathered in a conical basket called kaitemi, about sixteen inches deep and twenty-one inches in diameter at the top and six inches at the bottom. The basket is carried on the back, the apex resting in the small of the back and the top reaching well to the neck. A carrying strap (formerly of elk-hide) passes around the middle of the back part of the basket, over the woman's shoulders and around her head halfway between the crown and the forehead.

If the weather is good, the acorns are placed in the sun to dry. The roof of the house is often used as a place for drying, a ladder similar to the one used in the house being leaned against the eaves to enable the women to tend them with ease. The acorns are stored in large hampers called djelo. One of the largest is thirty-two inches deep and thirty-nine inches in diameter at the base and narrowed at the top to twenty inches. These are made after the close-twined style of Hupa basketry.

As soon as the gathering season is over the shelling begins. This is done by resting the acorn, held between the thumb and fingers, on a rock and tapping it with a stone. The men sometimes assist in this work. The acorns when shelled and split are called djoaslai. They are thoroughly dried and stored again in hampers.

When needed for food the women grind them into flour. A buckskin or cloth is spread down on a hard flat stone which is set in the earthen floor of the xonta. On this is placed a funnel-shaped basket, kaiist, about four and a half inches deep, sixteen inches in diameter at the top and five inches at the bottom. The top of this basket is made firm by a heavy rim turned in so as to be horizontal. The basket is stiffened by withes placed around on the outside covered by the material used in twining the basket. A split withe is also placed inside under the rim for the same purpose. The woman sits with the basket under her legs just below the knees. With the stone pestle, meïst, she pounds the acorns to a fine powder. She has a brush at hand to sweep up scattered meal and to brush it from the mill when she has finished. This brush is made of fibers taken from the sheath of the bulb of soaproot, *Chlorogalum pomeridianum*, bound with buckskin.[2] From time to time she takes out the fine flour and sifts it in a shallow basket called miLdakidiL, by giving it a gentle motion up and down as it is held at an angle over a large basket-pan, kiwat. The flour is constantly drawn toward the sifter with the hand. During this process the fine flour runs over the lower edge of the basket, the coarser pieces being retained for a second grinding. At this stage the material is called witwat.

The woman now goes to a place on the river shore where there is washed sand (fig. 1).[3] She scoops out the sand, at the same time building up the edges, until she has a hole large enough to hold her flour. The flour is then placed in this saucer-shaped hole. She builds a fire near by and heats the hard, flat stones kept for the purpose. When they are hot, by means of two sticks she drops them into a basket-pot called miltoi. The water is heated until it is nearly scalding hot. It is then dipped from the large basket with a basket-cup and poured on the flour. As fast as it soaks away more water is added until the material loses its bitter taste. The wet uncooked meal is called kitast.

Before removing the flour the woman roughens the surface with her hand. She then puts her hand on it palm down and removes it, taking up the underlying material with a coating of the sand. She holds this over the basket-cup and washes off the sand (fig. 2). In this way it is all taken up and washed. A little is usually cooked on the spot and eaten. The remainder is taken to the xonta and cooked. It is placed in a basket about ten inches in diameter and six inches deep twined with material taken from the root of a pine. This is water-tight. A little water is added and the hot stones are dropped in. After a few minutes a quantity of water is added with more hot stones. It is vigorously stirred with a wooden paddle called miLteunakyokût. The cooked mush is called saxauw. The mush is placed in smaller similar baskets called xaitsa. These are passed to the men, each having his own. They eat the mush with spoons of elk-horn called kitekin or of wood. The bowl of the spoon is rather large (two and seven-eighths by two and three-eighth inches) with the handle sometimes nearly at right angles to the bowl. The handle is four or more inches long and carved and cut to form geometric designs. These are kept in a basket hanging on the wall of the xonta.

The women use a valve of *Mytilus Californianus* [California mussel], in its natural state, for a spoon and often eat from the large pot in which the mush is cooked. The Hupa are very fond of this acorn mush.

Fig. 1. Woman [Mrs. Freddie] soaking meal on the river shore.

PHOTOGRAPH BY PLINY E. GODDARD (NEG. NO. 15–3329).

Fig. 2. Woman washing the sand from the under surface
of the acorn meal after the leaching is completed.

PHOTOGRAPH BY PLINY E. GODDARD (NEG. NO. 15–4544).

Those who have plenty of food such as white people use still make the acorn mush occasionally. When a little salt is added it is quite agreeable to a white man's taste. No other food is allowed to one who is preparing for a ceremony. The Hupa used to bury acorns unshelled in the damp ground and let them remain until they were well molded. They were then boiled without being ground. Bread was sometimes made of the acorns by putting the mush on a hot flat rock. This was taken on a journey or to the hunting camp. It was sometimes soaked and eaten as mush.

The hazel-nut, *Corylus rostrata* var. *Californica*, kilatconde, is excellent food. The nuts are ripe in June and July, and are gathered as soon as ripe, for the bears are very fond of them. They are dried and eaten raw from the shell. A few chinquapin, *Castanea chrysophylla*, grow near the valley. The nuts are eaten when found. The nuts of the pepperwood, *Umbellularia Californica*, are roasted in the ashes and eaten. The seeds of the sugar pine, *Pinus Lambertiana*, are much valued by the Hupa. They go in large companies, men and women together, to the tops of the ridges, where the trees are found, and camp for some time. The seeds are in proper condition for gathering in October. In olden times the men used to compete with one another in tree climbing to secure the cones. Now-a-days the trees are felled and stripped of their cones. The cones are pounded until the seeds loosen and drop or are easily plucked out. These nuts are eaten raw, either shelled or shells and all.

The seeds of the digger pine, *P. Sabiniana*, are also used, but are not so highly esteemed as those of the sugar pine. The cones of the digger pine are eaten in June when they are green. They are rolled in the dust to render the pitch less troublesome, and then trimmed with a knife. The cone is split and the central portion with the soft unripe seeds is eaten raw. It is not an article of food that would tempt a white man.

The Hupa use the bulbs of many plants, mostly the members of the lily family. These have the generic name yinetau. The women dug the bulbs in former times with pointed sticks, the men sometimes accompanying them with their stone knives to renew the points when necessary. The soap-root, *Chlorogalum pomeridianum*, is the largest and most plentiful of these bulbs. They are cooked for about two days in the following manner. A large pit is dug and lined with rocks. A hot fire is maintained until the rocks and surrounding earth are well heated. The fire is then drawn, the pit is lined with leaves and a quantity of the bulbs thrown in. Leaves are placed on top and the whole covered with earth. A big fire is then built on top. The leaves of the wild grape, *Vitis Californica*, and wood sorrel, *Oxalis Oregana*, are used to line the pit, and are also mixed with the bulbs. They are said to improve the flavor. When cooked in this manner they are agreeable and nourishing food. The Indians of Mendocino county seem never to use the bulb of this plant for food, but employ it for stupefying fish (Chesnut 1902:320), while the Hupa are ignorant of its value for that purpose. The Hupa use the bulbs of *Calochortus Maweanus, Hookera laxa, H. congesta, Brodiæa multiflora*, and probably other species of this genus. The bulbs are roasted in the ashes or boiled in baskets.

The fresh shoots of many plants are eaten raw. Food of this kind is called salu*w*. Among the plants so used are *Wyethia angustifolia*, tcalatdûñ, *Leptotaenia Californica*, mûxatcexolen, *Heracleum lanatum*, selkyo, *Angelica tomentosa*, xonsiLsalu*w* "summer salu*w*."

A seaweed, *Porphyra perforata*, called la, was brought from the coast at the mouth of the Klamath by boats or from Trinidad by parties making the journey overland. This furnished the salt required for good health. One doctor is said to eat this seaweed to make his thirst still more intense when he refrains from water in medicine hunting.

The seeds of grasses, certain *Compositae*, and other plants were beaten into a basket with a wicker beater. They were carefully cleaned by winnowing and hand picking. The seeds were cooked by placing live coals of tan-bark oak among them in a basket-pan. The basket was constantly shaken and tossed to prevent the burning of the seeds and the basket. When the seeds were sufficiently cooked they were pounded in the same manner that acorns are reduced to flour, but with a pestle of lighter weight. The flour was served without further preparation on small saucer-shaped pieces of basket-work. The weeds introduced since the coming of white people have so crowded out and mingled with the native plants used for this purpose that the Hupa do not now attempt to gather the seeds. One woman was found who had a small quantity of seeds gathered many years ago. She prepared these in the manner described.

The valley and surrounding hills furnish an abundant variety and quantity of berries. Many acres are covered with manzanita, *Aretostaphylos Manzanita*, dinu*w*. The fresh fruit is eaten when ripe in midsummer and even later when it has become dry and powdery. The fruit used to be gathered in large quantities and dried on the sand by the river. When required for food these berries were pounded in the basket-mortar and the flour was separated from the seeds.

The flour was eaten dry without cooking. The seeds were soaked in water and the liquid was drunk without fermentation. The fruit of the madroña, *Arbutus Menziesii*, isdeau, are shaken in a basket with hot rocks and then eaten. The berries of *Heteromeles arbutifolia*, called by the Hupa isdewitc, "little madroña berries," are also eaten. Huckleberries, *Vaccinium ovatum*, tcwiltc, are very plentiful. They remain on the bushes until Christmas. The berries of the elder, *Sambucus glauca*, tcuhwu*w*, are eaten. Thimble berries, *Rubus parvi-florus*, wûndau*w*, raspberries, *R. leucodermis*, blackberries, *R. viti-folius*, and several species of *Ribes* (gooseberries and currants), are in fruit during the spring and summer months.

THE NORTHERN MAIDU
Roland B. Dixon

As Alfred Kroeber wrote in Roland Dixon's obituary, *The Northern Maidu* was "the first modern and intensive ethnographic monograph on any Californian people" (Tozzer and Kroeber 1936:295). This is the principal ethnography of the Maidu, similar to Goddard's Hupa monograph (1903), which actually pre-dates it. Upon his graduation from Harvard in 1897, Roland Burrage Dixon (1875–1934) was appointed assistant in Anthropology at the university's Peabody Museum. The following year he worked with Franz Boas on the Jesup Expedition in British Columbia. In 1899 Dixon began seven years of Californian research with the Maidu, Shasta, and other groups of northeastern California. Sponsored by the Huntington Expedition of the American Museum of Natural History, Dixon worked with the Maidu all of the first season and parts of the summers of 1900, 1902, and 1903. In this research he was aided by Dorius Leon Spencer, a local non-Native married to a Maidu woman.

After earning a Ph.D. in anthropology in 1900, Dixon became an instructor in anthropology at Harvard in 1901. He remained associated with Harvard until his death, as assistant (1906–15) and full professor (1915–34) of anthropology, also serving as librarian and curator of ethnology. In addition to his Californian fieldwork, Dixon worked in Australia and other areas in South and East Asia. Much of his later research was addressed to establishing universal patterns of cultural diffusion.

While Dixon did some artifact collecting among the Maidu, he principally spent his time gathering folktales and linguistic data. Consequently, his understanding of material culture is sometimes faulty. For instance, in the selection included here, he wrote that "The Maidu had no mush-paddles for stirring their acorn-soup, making use, for this purpose any common stick" (1905:180). But as Bernstein points out, "Charles Wilcomb collected three mush paddles ca. 1910" (1993:25). Maidu paddles are in the collections of the Hearst Museum,

Food and its Preparation. *The Northern Maidu.* American Museum of Natural History Bulletin (1905), 17(3). Pp. 181–91.

though they are credited to the southern Maidu in Kroeber's *Handbook* (1925:829).

The people that Dixon wrote about here have been called the Northern, Northeastern, or Mountain Maidu. Together with the Konkow and the Nisenan, Maiduan-speaking groups who live to their south, they have been collectively referred to as the "Maidu." Ecologically, they resemble other Sierran groups such as the Sierra Miwok to the south.

THE FOOD-SUPPLY OF THE MAIDU was large, and included practically everything edible to be found in the region. Vegetable foods were perhaps a little more used in the Sacramento Valley area than in the mountains, where game was rather more abundant.

The chief dependence of the Maidu, in common with most of the Indians of the central part of the State, was upon the acorn. The Maidu recognize about a dozen different varieties of these. In the creation myth it is declared that the Creator's first act, after forming the dry land, was to cause a great oak-tree to spring up, on which grew all the twelve varieties of acorns. Later these different varieties came to grow on different trees. The miraculous tree, however, created by Ko'doyanpe, was still standing, according to old men, at Durham (Ta'doikö) at the time when, in the early 1840s, the first settler arrived. The tree was cut down by him in spite of strong protest by the Indians; and it is declared that the stump bled profusely at the first stroke of the axe, and that in the heart of the tree was found a peculiar substance "like a roll of thin, strong paper," from which the blood flowed. The exact spot at which the tree stood is still pointed out.

Although the acorns of all species of oaks growing in the region are eaten, some varieties are distinctly preferred to others. In general, *Quercus Kelloggii* Newberry, *Quercus chrysolepis* Liebmann, and *Quercus Wislizeni* A. D. C., were the favorite species.

Besides the acorn, a great number of other nuts, fruits, and berries were eaten. The fruit of the buckeye (*Aesculus californica* Nutt.) and the wild nutmeg (*Tumion californicum* Greene) were eaten, but required more preparation than the acorn. The nuts of the digger-pine (*Pinus Sabiniana* Dougl.), the sugar-pine (*Pinus Lambertiana* Dougl.), and the yellow pine (*Pinus ponderosa* Dougl.), were very largely used. The nuts of the digger-pine were most used in the foot-hill region, where alone the species grows in quantity, but the nuts were sent in trade to considerable distances. Other nuts, such as the hazel (*Corylus rostrata* Ait., var. *californica* A. D. C.), were collected also.

Of berries and fruits there were many sorts, particularly in the higher Sierra occupied by the Northeastern Maidu. Throughout the area the manzanita (*Arctostaphylos Pungens* H. B. K.) grows in immense quantities, and the berries were collected in abundance for use in making the so-called "manzanita-cider." The berries of the snow-brush, sweet-brush, or buck-brush (*Ceanothus integerrimus* Hook. and Arn., and probably also *Ceanothus cordulatus* Kellogg.? and *Ceanothus velutinus* Dougl.?) were used to some extent; and there were also the strawberry (*Fragaria* sp.), the thimbleberry (*Rubus glaucifolius* Greene), the service-berry (*Amelanchier pallida* Greene), the elderberry (*Sambucus glauca* Nutt. and *racemosa* L.), the chokecherry (*Prunus demissa* Walpers), the wild plum (*Prunus sub-cordata* Benth.), the gooseberry (*Ribes occidentale* Hook. and Arn.), the black currant (*Ribes sanguineum* Pursh., var. *variegatum* Wats.), and several others of less importance. Rose-hips of *Rosa Pisocarpa* Gray were also eaten.

Roots and bulbs of many sorts were eaten, and, while never a predominant portion of the food-supply, their use gave to the Maidu their early name of "diggers." The following is a partial list of those most used by the Northeastern Maidu, although many were common also to the other portions of the stock: *Allium parvum* Kellogg., *Allium platycaule* Wats., *Brodicea Douglasii* Wats., *Brodicea lactea* Wats., *Camassia esculenta* Lindl., *Hastingsia alba* Wats., *Lewisia nevadensis* Rob., *Lilium washingtonianum* Kellogg., *Polygonum blistortoides* Pursh.

Grass-seed, other seeds, and clover were also appreciable factors in the food-supply of the Maidu, the seeds being stored in considerable quantities for winter use. The following are a few of the plants so used: *Aquilegia formosa* Fisch., *Madia glomerata* Hook. (tar-weed), *Madia* sp., *Wyethia angustifolia* Nutt.

Early travelers and explorers speak frequently of the fondness of the Maidu and neighboring tribes for fresh clover and a variety of wild pea, and describe them in the Sacramento Valley as getting down on hands and knees in the fields, and browsing like so many cattle. The Northeastern Maidu, in times of want or in early spring, occasionally ate the inner bark and sap of the tamarack pine (*Pinus contorta* Dougl., var. *Murrayana* Wats.). It was, however, more in use as a medicine, because of its marked cathartic properties. The leaves of the fir and cedar were used occasionally to make teas of, but, like the pine-bark, their uses were mainly medicinal. Horse-mint (*Mentha* sp.) and other aromatic plants were used in a similar manner. The "sugar" of the sugar-pine (*Plinus Lambertiana* Dougl.) was eaten in small quantities.

The mistletoe (*Phorodendron juniperinum* Engelm.) was used now and then as a medicine. The tobacco formerly grown and gathered by the Maidu of the Sierra region was *Nicotiana attenuata* Torr.

A large number of other foods of vegetable origin were collected, but, owing to the fact that most of them were gathered by Indians for the writer, they were impossible to identify, as the specimens often consisted, unfortunately, of merely the seeds, roots, or a few leaves, which were insufficient for purposes of identification.

Of animal food there was an abundance. In the mountains, deer, elk, mountain-sheep, and bear were plenty; while in the Sacramento Valley there were great herds of antelope. Of smaller game, rabbits, raccoons, and squirrels were numerous. In addition to the animals mentioned, nearly all others known in the region, such as the badger, skunk, wildcat, and mountain-lion, were eaten. Only the wolf, coyote, and dog were not used for food, and in the southern section the grizzly bear was also exempt. All birds practically, except the buzzard, were eaten, ducks and geese in particular being caught in hundreds at the proper seasons. Lizards, snakes, and frogs were not eaten. Yellow-jacket larvae were, however, eagerly sought, as were also angle-worms. Grasshoppers, locusts, and crickets were highly esteemed, and in their dried condition were much used in trade. Fish of many kinds were to be had, salmon being caught in considerable quantities in the early days. Eels were a favorite food, and, dried, formed an indispensable part of the winter's food-supply for the foot-hill and valley people. Shell-fish, such as mussels, were to be had in some abundance, particularly in the Sacramento River. Salmon-bones and deer-vertebrae were pounded up and used for food; the salmon-bones being eaten raw, whereas the deer-vertebrae, after pounding, were made into little cakes and baked.

The collection and preparation of acorns for food were among the most important industries of the Maidu, in common with most of the Central Californian tribes. At the time in the autumn when the acorns are ripe, every one is busy. The men and larger boys climb the trees, and, by the aid of long poles, beat the branches, knocking off the acorns. The women and smaller children gather these in burden-baskets, and carry them to the village, storing them in the granaries or in the large storage-baskets in the houses.

The first step in the preparation of the gathered nuts is to remove the shell and dry the meat. This, as well as all other labor in connection with the preparation of the acorn, is done by women only. The acorns are usually cracked by means of two stones, the acorn being placed point down on one, and the butt-end being struck several sharp blows with the other. The acorn is thus cracked in halves, and the shell is then separated from each half by the aid of the teeth. The split meats are then spread in the sun, where they rapidly become dry.

The preparation of acorn-meal from the dried nuts is carried on with or without a mortar or milling basket. Perhaps most commonly this mortar-basket is dispensed with. Selecting a flat rock or boulder, or using a flat stone sunk in the floor of the house, the woman sits cross-legged, or with legs extended, on the ground, and, in the absence of a mortar-basket, spreads out a couple of quarts of dried acorns in a circle. Holding the pestle in the one hand, she strikes regularly in the center of this circle, and with the other hand constantly gathers, and sweeps back under the descending pestle, the acorns that scatter with each blow. The pestle is changed from one hand to the other now and then, thus insuring an even pounding of the acorns, and resting the hands and arms. When a considerable quantity of acorns has thus been reduced to meal, the finer flour must be separated from the coarser particles. In this process, several handfuls of the meal are placed on one of the flat winnowing baskets or trays, and are tossed and caught several times. Then, holding the tray on the palm of the left hand, and tilting it at an angle of about 40°, the edge of the tray is tapped with a deer-bone or wooden tapper (fig. 1–a), the tray being slowly revolved meanwhile by the aid of the fingers underneath. In this manner the coarser particles are separated, and roll off over the edge of the tray, leaving the fine flour behind. Sometimes the same result is accomplished without a beater, by holding the tray by the edge, in both hands, and tilting and shaking it dexterously.

In whatever manner the coarser grains are separated, the basket with the fine flour on it is brushed with a brush of soap-root fiber (fig. 1–b), and all the flour brushed off into a soup-basket near at hand. The coarser particles are then thrown back into the center of the ring of acorn-meats, and pounded again until they are reduced to the requisite fineness, more acorns being added from time to time to keep the mass that is being pounded about the same. The winnowing is likewise repeated from time to time until a sufficient quantity of the fine flour has been prepared.

In case the mortar-basket is used, there is not the necessity of constantly throwing the meal and acorns under the pestle, as these are kept from scattering by the sloping sides of the basket. Otherwise the process is identical.

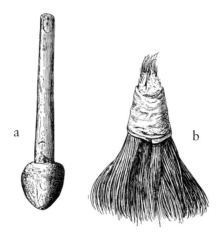

a   b

fig. 1. Tapper and brush used in sifting acorn-meal.
AMERICAN MUSEUM OF NATURAL HISTORY: A–50/1616, B–50/1612.
LENGTH, 17 CM., 14 CM.

The flour must next be sweetened by removing the bitter element present. For this purpose a spot is selected where the soil is sandy and soft. Here a circular depression is scraped out to a depth of five or seven centimeters, and the earth heaped up in a little wall round about the excavation. The diameter of these bowl-like hollows may vary from one third of a meter to a meter. The acorn-flour, being first dampened, is carefully plastered over the whole interior of the hollow, the layer of dampened meal being about five centimeters thick. Over this layer of meal a few small cedar sprigs or boughs are laid, so that in pouring on the water the meal shall not be disturbed. Warm water, heated in baskets by hot stones, is now poured gently on the cedar-boughs, and allowed to trickle through until the hollow is filled to the brim. Slowly the water soaks through the layer of meal, and is absorbed by the sandy soil. As soon as the first water has soaked away, a second lot is poured in, this time somewhat hotter; and so on, until finally water at boiling-heat is used. From time to time the woman tastes the flour, until she finds that every trace of the bitter principle has been dissolved out. The sweetening-process is then completed, and the flour is ready for its final cooking.

Taking the dough from the hollow in pieces, the sand adhering to the under side is carefully removed, and the mass placed in a cooking-basket, with the addition of water. For the usual soup the proportion is about two quarts of dough to three gallons of water. The mass is stirred, and then hot stones, taken from the fire with the aid of two sticks, are placed in the basket, till the whole contents is brought to a boil. The soup is then ready to eat, and is taken either hot or cold. A thicker soup, or mush, was made in the same way, only less water was used in mixing. If it is desired to make bread of the flour instead of soup or mush, the dough, after its sweetening as above described, is made into a lump or loaf perhaps fifteen centimeters in diameter. This loaf is then flattened, a hot rock rolled in oak-leaves placed in the center, and the dough folded over and pressed down all around it. The whole mass is then wrapped in oak-leaves, and placed in the ashes or under a pile of hot stones to bake. The resulting bread is very solid and heavy, resembling almost a lump of putty, and is, like the soup and mush, almost tasteless.

In both soup and bread there is a frequent mixture of sand and ashes, which makes the bread, in particular, rather gritty. The use of the cedar-sprigs in the process of sweetening imparts usually a slight flavor to the flour, which is not disagreeable. In some cases a leaf or two of bay or mint is added to the soup in its final cooking, to give it an added flavor.

The fruit of the buckeye (*Aesculus californica* Nutt.), like the acorn, has to have the bitter principle extracted before it can be eaten. The buckeye fruit, however, requires more thorough and protracted leaching. The "balls" are usually steamed for some time first, then boiled and washed in running water for ten or fifteen hours. The fruit of the wild nutmeg (*Tumion californicum* Greene) requires even more thorough treatment than the buckeye. The nuts are first cracked, and the shell removed. They are then buried in the ground for several months. At the end of that time they are dug up, and roasted in the ashes.

Grass and other small seeds were formerly eaten in considerable amount. The seeds were gathered by the women with the aid of a beater. One of these (fig. 2–a) is the type used by the Northwestern Maidu; the other (fig. 2–b), that used by the Northeastern. Holding one of these in the hand, the grass or plant heads were struck by it, thus knocking out the seeds, which were caught in a tray-basket held underneath. From the latter the seeds were transferred to the burden-

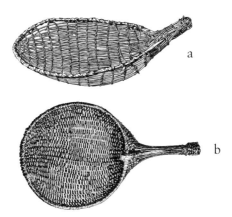

fig. 2. Seed-beaters.

AMERICAN MUSEUM OF NATURAL HISTORY: A–50/1608, B–50/5239.

LENGTH, 51 CM., 38 CM.

basket on the back. In the region occupied by the Northeastern Maidu the seeds seem to have been frequently ground with water on the rude metates, and either made into a dough and baked in little cakes, or made into a soup in a manner similar to that followed in the case of the acorn-flour.

The seeds of the sweet-birch were thrashed from the hulls when dry, mixed with wild oats, and parched in a tray-basket with hot sand, coals, and ashes, the mixture being stirred to keep the basket from burning. When cold, the sand and ashes were winnowed or blown away, the seeds pounded fine and eaten dry, with no further preparation.

Roots were gathered by means of a digging-stick, usually one meter or more in length, straight, and with the end hardened in the fire. The roots were eaten in a variety of ways—raw, roasted, or boiled, or sometimes dried, pounded fine, mixed with berries, and baked in small flat cakes.

Pine-nuts were collected in the fall in large quantities, the mountain people trading the sugar-pine nuts to the Sacramento Valley people for digger-pine nuts. The cones of the latter are very large and solid. To extract the nuts, the cones or "burrs" were generally piled in heaps of ten or twelve, and set afire. The pitch burned off in this manner, and the heat partially opened the "burr," which was then crushed by means of heavy stones.

Berries of various sorts were gathered, and dried for winter use; or mashed, made into little cakes with seeds and pounded roots, and either dried, or wrapped in leaves and baked (fig. 3). To prepare these cakes for use, they were soaked, and then made into a sort of soup. Manzanita-berries are still stored in considerable quantities, and largely used to prepare the so-called "manzanita-cider." The berries consist, when ripe, of a mass of sweet, dry meal, surrounding two or more hard seeds. To prepare the "cider," the berries are first crushed, and then mixed with water to form a stiff dough. A rough frame of willow, large enough to cover the top of a soup-basket, is then made, and cross-strands of bark twined about it so as to form a rude, flat, open-work tray. On this a few large leaves are laid, and the mass of dough placed on these in the shape of a truncated cone from fifteen to twenty centimeters in diameter and from ten to fifteen centimeters

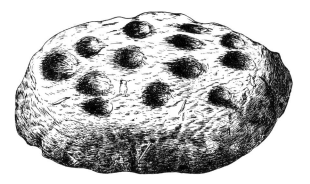

fig. 3. Cakes made of seeds, roots, and berries.
AMERICAN MUSEUM OF NATURAL HISTORY: 50/5234.
DIAMETER, 15 CM.

high. A small depression is made in the top of the cone, and then the whole affair placed over a soup-basket. Water is poured into the depression in the top of the conical heap of manzanita-dough, and, as it slowly soaks through and drips into the basket below, more is poured in, and the process continued until all the flavor has been dissolved out of the berries. The resulting liquid is of a clear amber color, and has a strong, sweet taste not unlike that of cider. Occasionally the berries are first roasted, with the result that the liquid is darker in color, and has a slightly different flavor. This so-called "cider" has always been the favorite drink of the Maidu; and is still made in large quantities, particularly in summer, when it proves a cooling and refreshing beverage. At the present time it is sometimes strained and bottled, when it ferments and becomes mildly intoxicating. It is also used to make an excellent vinegar. Both of these products are entirely modern, and were unknown before the coming of Europeans.

Grasshoppers and locusts were eaten eagerly when they were to be had. The usual method of gathering them was to dig a large, shallow pit in some meadow or flat, and then, by setting fire to the grass on all sides, to drive the insects into the pit. Their wings being burned off by the flames, they were helpless, and were thus collected by the bushel. They were then dried as they were. Thus prepared, they were kept for winter food, and were eaten either dry and uncooked or slightly roasted.

Angle-worms were much relished. They were collected in considerable quantities by planting a pole in the ground in a favorable spot, and then working this pole round and round, running around it at the same time, and stamping hard upon the ground. The worms quickly came to the surface, and, when gathered, were generally cooked into a thick soup.

Eels were speared, split, and dried. In preparing them for food, they were usually cut into small pieces, and stewed. Salmon were split, and dried by hanging them over a pole. When thoroughly dry, the fish was usually pounded up till it was reduced to a coarse flour, and kept in baskets. It was eaten dry, as a rule.

Deer and other meat was cut into strips and dried. Usually this was done in the sun; but occasionally a fire was lighted under the drying meat to hasten the process, and to smoke the product slightly.

Salt was used sparingly, but was highly prized. It seems to have been obtained largely from local salt deposits and springs, but considerable is declared to have been brought from deposits of some size near the Marysville Buttes.

The usual methods of cooking meat were boiling, baking, and roasting. Boiling was not much used for meat. In baking, a hole was dug, rocks thrown in, and a fire started in it. When the earth and rocks were thoroughly heated, the fire was raked out; the meat, wrapped in leaves, was placed in the hole, and the hot rocks piled over it. Earth and leaves were then heaped over the whole, and after an hour or two the meat was nicely baked. In roasting, the meat was generally thrown directly on the coals, rarely put on a stick. When bear-meat was eaten, it was the custom to cook it separate from deer-meat, and the two were not eaten together. In the Sacramento Valley a wholly different word is used to denote eating bear-meat, from that indicating the eating of all other kinds of meat.

WINTU ETHNOGRAPHY
Cora A. Du Bois

Especially detailed and well-written, this is the major Wintu ethnography. The Wintu are the northernmost of the Wintun-speakers (who also include the Nomlaki and Patwin). Du Bois felt that their territory at the conjunction of three major river drainages (Pit-McCloud, upper Sacramento, and upper Trinity) explained their mixing of cultural elements, and their position as culturally intermediate between Northwestern and Central California. She also characterized the Wintu as a hill rather than valley people.

Cora Alice Du Bois (1903–91) graduated from Barnard College in 1927, earning a M.A. from Columbia in history in 1928. She came to Berkeley in 1929, and obtained her anthropology Ph.D. in 1932. She spent the next two years researching the history and spread of the Californian Ghost Dance of 1870. After her university-sponsored fieldwork in northern California, coastal Oregon, and lower Columbia River, Du Bois went on to extensive fieldwork on the Indonesian island of Alor (1937–39), and later in India. After teaching at Hunter College (1936–37) and Sarah Lawrence (1939–42), and subsequent work with the Office of Strategic Services and the State Department, Du Bois was appointed in 1954 as Harvard University's first female tenured professor of anthropology. Upon her retirement from Harvard in 1969, she taught at Cornell University (1970–75). Her specialties were psychological anthropology, cultural change in complex societies, and multi-disciplinary approaches.

Because Du Bois did not report the circumstances of the fieldwork in her monograph and because her fieldnotes have not been located, the exact details of her Wintu research remain vague. She seems to have begun her Wintu fieldwork as a graduate student in 1929, when she entered the university, and continued, periodically, for the next several years. On her first trip she probably joined fellow student Dorothy Demetracopoulou, a linguist who was already studying the language and folklore of the area (see Demetracopoulou and Du Bois 1932). Most of this report is devoted to the McCloud area,

University of California Publications in American Archaeology and Ethnology (1935), 36(1). Pp. 9–21.

site of the largest tribal population. While outlining the cultural norms, in the manner of her mentor Alfred Kroeber, Du Bois frequently offered specific, individual opinions and practices. In part because of this, *Wintu Ethnography* is one of the best of the UC Berkeley tribal accounts.

HUNTING

Deer hunting. This was pursued either individually or communally. Deer (nop) were either snared or stalked by a single hunter. If a few men were engaged in the enterprise the one whose arrow first grazed the deer was felt to be the owner of the carcass, whether or not he had actually made the kill. In the Upper Sacramento region the deer-head decoy was used, a recognized borrowing from the Shasta to the north. Farther south the antlers alone were used occasionally as a method of decoying, but fear was expressed that they served simply to attract bears. Deer pits were also reported; but if they were used, it was only rarely. Deer caught in snares were handled with particular magico-religious precautions. The men carried the carcass to the dwelling, outside of which the animal was skinned and quartered. The meat was brought into the dwelling through a rear entrance made by removing a part of the bark covering, because women might have contaminated the ordinary entrance with menstrual fluid. This is an interesting commentary on the fact that the ideological isolation of women during menstruation may have lapsed in actual practice. The floor of the house was covered with evergreen boughs to receive the meat. The men then carefully washed off any blood stains and entered the house to finish cutting up the animal. The meat was passed to the women, who stood outside and distributed it to the women of other households. If the family which had procured the deer wished to give a feast, little or no meat was distributed in this fashion. Instead it was cooked and the men of the local group were invited to the feast. After they had finished, the remnants were given to their families. A special fir poker called klapum was used to stir the fire over which deer meat was cooked.

Regulations concerning the consumption of deer meat were as follows:

Heads roasted separately. Forbidden to young women. Old might eat of the head meat but not in conjunction with salt, water, or hot mush; only with cold mush. Remains were covered with rocks. All who ate head meat washed their hands in a container and the water was poured over the rocks. Lower jaw of skull was cleaned and hung in tree to attract more deer.

Sinews forbidden to young men. If they ate sinew it would shine at night and the grizzly bears would see them. Each boy also forbidden to eat any part of first deer he killed.

Uppermost ribs forbidden to young people. In women this meat would interfere with parturition. In men it might affect their wives at childbirth.

Young women forbidden meat from the flank; it might stretch their abdomens when they were pregnant.

Young women forbidden entrails; they might prevent proper parturition.

Paunch might give young women premature wrinkles; forbidden to them.

The foetus and uterus forbidden to all but old women, who ate them raw.

Ovaries (tcatetcate) eaten only by old people.

Various procedures for cooking deer were employed:

Paunch cleaned and filled with blood and chunks of fat. Roasted in hot ashes. To point at it while it cooked would make it burst. Children usually sent away during the roasting. After paunch began to shrivel it was roasted very slowly. When cooked through, it was cut into pieces and eaten.

Guts straightened and untangled while still warm. Emptied and eaten first.

Sinews cut out lengthwise; adhering meat stripped off with teeth.

Meat roasted in strips on hot coals. Slices from hams pounded with a small pestle (satak), dampened with water, and wrapped around a clean hot rock. Resulting bundle laid in hot coals with folded edges of meat underneath; then covered with coals. Meat, when "dry and nice," taken from coals, a little water sprinkled on edges to make them unfold, and rock removed. Roasted meat usually eaten with acorn soup. Men hunting in hills might simply roast whole side or a quarter over fire. Meat often only partly cooked. This described by feminine informant with considerable disdain for lack of culinary nicety as "hunter's way of cooking." Such a feast was not attended by women; called malibas. Meat sometimes steamed by placing a little water and hot rocks in cooking-basket. Meat strips laid on rocks. Basketry tray used to cover cooking-basket and retain steam.

Deer hides stretched out taut with rocks as weights; fleshed and used for bedding or clothing. Hair retained if good.

Invitations for a communal deer hunt could be issued by any enterprising individual. Its duration was specified, and is said to have been usually about three days. All the people gathered in a place where the deer were observed to have been numerous. In the center of the camping place a brush shelter was erected for the leader and the young men. Brush houses for families were put up around it. Snares might be set on the game trails. Powers (1877:241–42) reports that deer were directed into the snares by passageways of bark tied from one tree to another. The scent of human beings on the bark drove the deer forward and, by frightening them, kept them from breaking out of the prearranged path-way. On the morning of the hunt the men were aroused by a cry from the leader, and all rushed to a creek to bathe. The women began at once to prepare acorn meal. The snares were visited and any animals which had been trapped were shot. The deer were then skinned and quartered, and each man was given a load to carry back to camp. There the meat was divided in the manner previously described. The man who carved the meat was usually the leader of the hunt. As he sliced it up he tossed pieces to his companions and, in his endeavor to appear generous, often found himself with the smallest portion.

A communal hunt might also take the form of a deer drive.

The less skilled persons, including women and children, moved from the mouth of a canyon toward its head, beating the brush and shouting. Dogs[1] were trained to assist in the chase. At the head of the canyon the best marksmen were posted to shoot the animals as they were driven toward them.

Bear hunting. Brown bears (tcil) were usually hunted in the fall when they were fat and sluggish. Nosono village on the upper McCloud was a favorite spot for such hunts. The one who called the hunt used a circumlocution, such as "Let us visit our friends." Similarly, if bear tracks were seen the comment was made, "Here is one of my people," or "I see that my friend has been here." To get a bear three or four men went at night with a torch to a den. Into it the bravest man crawled and, if he were fortunate, killed the bear with a short spear or bow and arrow before it emerged. If the bear were only aroused by the torch, the man's companions slew it as it left the den. Sometimes a single hunter smoked a bear to death in its den. Bear pits were used also by individual hunters. If trees were cut down in the vicinity of a den, bears were thought to avoid that lair for two or three years. After the animal was slain, it was quartered and taken to camp where the men feasted on it. The man who initiated the hunt, and not the actual slayer, was host on this occasion. Bear meat was considered too greasy to be dried, so it was usually consumed without delay. If a piece of meat were dropped, the people were required to dodge as though avoiding a blow from the bear. Stillwater people refused to eat any kind of bear meat.

After the feast the young men made a square frame on which the hide was stretched. The frame was propped in an upright position against a tree to facilitate the scraping, which was done by women with stone flakes. They stood in front of the hide, jumping up and down and grunting like bears as they scraped. Everyone gathered about them and special bear songs were sung. Those who did not sing accompanied the dancers with a "Hu, hu!" The women danced and sang more than the men. The festivity was hilarious and lasted all night. Toward morning, one or two young men donned the bear hide, which was now thoroughly fleshed, and danced about in it imitating the bear. Their antics provoked merriment. This was also the occasion for making requests of the bear. If the animal were a female, a woman might seize its right paw and say, "Give me your skill in basketmaking"; or, grasping an ear, she might wish for its earrings. If the bear were a male, a young man might say, "I want the belt that you wear"; or, "I want to handle things as you did in your young days, have strength and plenty of bows and arrows." Children also were given the opportunity to ask for any skill or good fortune for which they might wish. Both brown and grizzly bear hides were greatly prized as burial shrouds.

Brown bears were hunted communally like deer. Young people beat the brush and shouted "No uni!" to drive the bear up to the canyon's head, where marksmen were posted. These were the older and more experienced hunters. A watchman was posted high at the canyon's head to observe the movements of the bear and warn the marksmen. Dogs were employed to assist in such drives. Since the undertaking entailed a certain amount of danger, the shaman's prophecies on the night preceding the hunt were listened to with particular respect. His statements might take the following form: "So-and-so (giving a proper name), who is standing on a certain rock in the stream, has dropped his pipe." This was interpreted as meaning that the person named would lose his life. Or he might say, "This woman has broken her root" (i.e., in the basket which she was making), which meant that a female bear would be killed; or, "This woman's children are crying," which signified that a she bear with cubs would be dispatched; or, "They will never get up too early for him," which indicated that no bear would be killed on the following day.

Grizzly bears (wima) were feared far more than brown bears and their flesh was never eaten. It was allowed to rot in situ. The reason given for not consuming the flesh was that grizzlies ate human beings and to eat grizzlies in turn would be akin to cannibalism. Powers (1877:240) says, concerning the Wintu attitude toward grizzlies:

Wicked Indians' ghosts ... return into the grizzly bear, for that is the most evil and odious animal they can conceive of. Hence they will not partake of the flesh of a grizzly, lest they should absorb some wicked soul. The strongest cursing with which a Wintun can curse another is, "May the grizzly bear eat you!" or, "May the grizzly bear bite your father's head off!"

This belief in transmigration of souls seems no longer to be in vogue, but the secondary reasoning obtained recently is as efficient in explaining their distaste for grizzly bear meat and is, incidentally, more in consonance with the views of European culture. If the two reports are accurate they form a nice example of progressive acculturation in rationalizing a trivial, but deep-rooted attitude.

In Bald Hills no festivities followed the killing of a grizzly. However, in the other subareas the hide was treated in the same general fashion as was that of the brown bear, and was prized even more highly as a pelt. While the hide was being fleshed, scraped-off pieces of meat sometimes were thrown about. Anyone who was hit was supposed to go at once to the river and bathe. The general hilarity and horseplay which accompanied the scraping of the hide might possibly be interpreted as a cathartic against the fear which a live grizzly engendered. Also in the course of the evening the head of the animal was laid in front of a solitary singer who accompanied himself with a split-stick rattle. The dancer was a young and active man who pantomimed the killing of the grizzly. He dodged back and forth striking at the head of the animal while the rest of the company sat around in a circle and watched the performance.

Young men were warned not to boast of slaying a bear or in the future bears would watch for an opportunity to kill them. To protect himself from being caught by a bear, a man held his face over a fire in which burning bark sent a shower of sparks. If he withstood the pain, bears would thereafter see sparks emanating from his face and take flight. The following anecdote illustrates the fate of young men who boast incautiously of killing a bear.

In the village at Ono (Bald Hills) they decided to have a bear war. They told the young men to go to the mountains and get a bear. One young man said he would get a grizzly by the head and kill him. The others told him not to dare the bear. He said: "That's all right. I'll catch him and kill him." The next morning they set out early. The people drove the bear. They warned that young man. Everyone was afraid and didn't dare shoot the bear. The bear caught the young man. They lost him. When they got home they counted young fellows. The chief asked if everyone got home safely. He "preached" to them. He "called the roll." That young fellow was missing. Everyone said they had run because the bear was a grizzly. So the doctor went into a trance and asked why that young fellow hadn't come home. He said that the young fellow was behind in the brush and had been caught because he boasted. He said all one side of him had been eaten. That night they went to look for him with torches. All the next day they looked. The doctor asked the spirits again. They told him where to look and the body was found where they said it was, half eaten. Then the people were angry. They hunted the bear for two days and at last they killed it. They skinned it. The mother of the boy brought the head and guts of that grizzly back to camp. She cried and cried. She stretched his guts all around the fire, she was so mad at him. She stood on the neck, took hold of the ears, and made him act as though he were chewing. She punished him by throwing hot coals in his mouth. You must never say you are going to eat or kill a bear. Just say you are going meet him.

Rabbit hunting. In the Bald Hills subarea, communal rabbit drives were held. In the northern subareas the custom seems to have been lacking, possibly because of the heavier brush- and tree covering of the more northerly sections as well as the more abrupt terrain. This ethnogeographical situation has its psychological parallel in the distaste which some northerners express for rabbit meat. In a rabbit drive snares were set, and near each one a man with a club stationed himself. The rabbits were driven toward the lines of snares, as the animals were caught they were clubbed and the traps reset. The use of nets to catch rabbits was known among the Wintun but seems not to have been employed by the Wintu. All the rabbits procured were taken back to camp, where they were divided. The hides were not saved because the drives are held in summer and the pelts were considered too poor for use. The hair was singed off, the entrails and larger bones were removed, the carcass was pounded with a flat rock and laid on coals to roast. Then the men feasted apart from the women. Three or four such drives were held in a season and were accompanied by dancing and gambling. These drives, like other gatherings, were occasions for matchmaking and philandering. In fact, one informant suggested that these were the chief purposes of the drives.

Rabbits caught by individuals were roasted in the manner described, or boiled. The meat was then put in a hopper and pounded into a doughy mass which was rolled in balls and distributed.

Other small game. Bald Hills people said that quail were caught in nets. This may have been a Wintun procedure in which the inhabitants of Bald Hills participated, rather than an actual Wintu trait. Gophers and other small rodents were caught in snares set before their holes. Small rodents, especially mice (tcude), were also caught in deadfalls—two flat rocks propped apart by an acorn which is parched and scraped thin. Gnawing through the acorn, the rodent released the upper rock and was crushed under it. Ground squirrels (titcelis) were caught in winter by stopping up most of their holes and then pouring water in the others. As the animal emerged it was clubbed. Those which escaped were chased by the dogs. Smoke was fanned into their burrows with similar results. A dozen squirrels were considered a good catch for a day's effort. In the spring gray squirrels (xaisas) were hunted with slings, or one man climbed a tree and frightened them out while another stood ready to shoot them with a bow and arrow. Wood rats (Lamus) were usually hunted in winter when they were sluggish. They were shot or clubbed as they emerged after the nest had been disturbed with a stick. The house might also be disturbed by jumping on it. To shout, "Lol, lol, lol" (tobacco), would help to bring the rats out. Birds were shot from small brush shelters made near springs or other places where birds were plentiful. This was for the most part an occupation in which the young boys engaged. They used blunt arrows without obsidian points.

Small game was generally cooked in the following manner. It was singed, the paws and tail were cut off, and the entrails removed. The animal was then roasted in a bed of hot coals. Then the hide might or might not be removed. The head was cut off and the ribs extracted along with the other large bones. The body was then pounded, bones and all, until it was fine and crumbly. Sometimes the pounding was done before roasting.

Grasshoppers. Grasshoppers (neput) were obtained by burning off large grass patches. Two or three villages might participate in a drive, and then the inevitable singing and dancing formed part of the occasion. Drives might be undertaken also by four or five individuals. The grass was set with torches three to five feet long made of dry wormwood (xeti) or of devils' stems (?) (mumxupus) tied into bundles. These torches were prepared a day or two beforehand. The grassy area was encircled by people who sang and danced as they whipped the grass and drove the grasshoppers into a center ring. The grass within the narrowed circle was then fired. After the blaze had subsided, men and women combed the ground for the insects, now partly roasted and with wings singed off. Each person carried on his back a close-twined conical burden basket supported by a tumpline which passed around the forehead or the upper chest. He picked up the grasshoppers and tossed them back over his shoulder into the basket. The grasshoppers were boiled in baskets, put on basketry trays to dry, and then either eaten at once or mashed in a hopper and stored. They were eaten with salt as a side dish when acorn mush was served. Since the arrival of the whites, grasshoppers have been obtained by driving them into trenches in which the insects are roasted in a grass fire. No further cooking is thought necessary.

A large black "grasshopper" (cricket?) called tcekemit was got from hollow logs. These were roasted and then winnowed in a basketry tray. They were eaten without further preparation. A great variety of grasshoppers or related insects were recognized and used as subsidiary foods.

Salmon flies (pis). These insects swarm on the river's edge for a few days in April. They are gathered early in the morning before their wings are strong enough to permit flight. They are either boiled, or, if they are plentiful enough, dried for winter use. They are considered a great delicacy.

FISHING

Chinook salmon ran freely in the McCloud and Sacramento rivers. In the middle of May the heavier spring run set in. It continued until October. The fall run began in the middle of October and lasted until December. The average size was approximately twenty pounds, although occasional fish weighed as much as sixty-five and seventy pounds. The salmon were usually four years old, but sometimes the two-year-old males called grills mounted the river. In the upper reaches of the Trinity river, steelhead replaced the salmon of the other two major Wintu streams. Throughout the area suckers were found in rivers and creeks, but were generally considered inferior to salmon as food. They averaged in weight from one-quarter pound to four pounds. These three fish formed the chief flesh diet of the Wintu, except in the Bald Hills subarea.

Salmon. There was no trace of a first-salmon ceremony. The year's fishing was forecast, it was thought, by the extent of the rock slide on Lime rock, which rises above the junction of the Pit and McCloud rivers. A large slide foretold a plentiful supply of fish. In midsummer large communal fishing drives were undertaken on the McCloud and Sacramento rivers. The relatively warm water of the Pit river was felt to make its fish less desirable. The last communal drive was held at Baird, about 1886. A net was stretched across the river. Men with torches waded downstream driving the fish into the net. Sometimes it was necessary to swim with the torches, a skill which only a few possessed, so that the same persons were repeatedly chosen for the task. In smaller drives no net was stretched across the river, but individuals with dip nets accompanied the torchbearers and scooped out the salmon. The fish were clubbed and strung on a grapevine rendered pliable by twisting. The fishing continued all night and several hundred might be got at one time. In the morning the leader divided the catch. If several villages were present, as they were during the large midsummer drives, he simply divided the fish among the leaders of each local group, who in turn gave each adult male his share. As in deer drives, the leader divided the spoil so generously that he himself was often without any; but, according to one informant, he usually provided other males within his family group with a quantity large enough to ensure no hardship for himself. Next day the women prepared the night's catch.

The spring catch was usually not dried as soon as caught, because it was so rich in oil. Instead, the fish were baked. Two or three families might join in preparing a pit, which was lined with stones. The stones were heated. On them the fish were spread in rows in which each fish was laid head to tail alongside of its neighbor. They were then covered with more hot rocks and allowed to bake for a few hours. When they were removed, as many as were desired were eaten and those which remained were boned and flaked. As the fish dried out it was pulverized into a salmon flour (dayi). The salmon caught later in the year were said to be less greasy and therefore more suitable for immediate drying. The fish was split open and held in that position by a twig. Another willow twig was thrust through the flesh and used to fasten the fish to a long pole. Many salmon were strung on each pole and dried in the sun. When they were dry enough they were folded in four pieces—head to tail and flank to flank—and stored for the winter. The heads, guts, tails, and bones were also dried and then pounded into a fine flour for winter use. Salmon flour was stored in wide baskets which narrowed toward the top and were lined with maple leaves. Dried roe and pine nuts were mixed in with the salmon flour. This food was a valuable article of trade among the McCloud Wintu. It was exchanged principally for salt and clam-disk money with the peoples to the south.

Individual fishing was usually done with a harpoon, either from the bank or from a salmon house. Although there seem to have been no formalized property rights for fishing sites, it was understood that individuals had liens on certain places. Powers (1877:233) says concerning these places:

For a fishing station the Wintun ties together two stout poles in a cross, plants it in deep water, then lays a log out to it from the shore. Standing here, silent and motionless ... with spear poised in the air, he sometimes looks upon so great a multitude of black-backed salmon ... that he could scarcely thrust his spear down without transfixing one or more.

Salmon fishing was often done at night. Then a torch was set near the water's edge to attract the fish. Two persons generally shared the work, one of them manipulating the torch.

Where salmon houses were built, they were recognized as belonging to certain family groups. This private ownership was considerably mitigated by the fact that anyone might visit the owner while he was fishing and expect a present of salmon, so that the fisherman might find himself with very little by the end of the day. This system was called mikaya, from kaya, to steal. A Bald Hills informant reported that salmon houses extended only as far south on the Sacramento as Jelly's Ferry, that is, about six miles south of the mouth of Cottonwood creek, and on the border between Wintu and Wintun territories.

Women usually avoided salmon houses, although old women sometimes accompanied their husbands to the huts. They never fished from them, however, nor wielded the harpoon. No conservative man would fish if his wife were menstruating.

The river-dwelling Wintu in the Bald Hills area used to invite the hill dwellers to communal fish drives. This was the only source of salmon for the latter, although occasional individuals traveled from the hills to the river for a two or three days' fishing trip. Obviously, salmon could not be considered a staple among them, as it could among the people to the north. In Bald Hills, salmon flour was obtained only by trade.

Steelheads. The methods of catching steelheads in the Upper Trinity sub-area were not recorded in detail, but they seem to have been approximately the same as those employed to catch salmon on the McCloud and Sacramento.

Suckers. These less desirable fish were caught in drives during August, in the creeks and the shallow waters of large rivers. In order to get them, a wing of brush weighed down with rocks was built out from each bank. These pointed diagonally downstream and a small opening two or three feet wide was left in midstream between them. Across the opening a net was stretched. Men then waded downstream driving the fish before them by shouting and throwing stones. The fish were caught in the retaining net. In rocky creeks, wings of stone were constructed. These drives were held in the morning. The day's fishing might be inaugurated by a race between the young men, who dashed naked from the camp to the net which was to be stretched across the mouth of the weir. After the morning's fishing the catch was divided by the leader as in the salmon drives. The rest of the day was spent in drying the fish, feasting, and gambling.

Suckers were also caught by individuals in the ways described below. Children on the McCloud were given miniature harpoons and urged to spear suckers as their elders speared salmon. In Bald Hills, where fish were rarer, adults would spear small fish in all seriousness; to the north this was mostly a child's activity.

Other fish and methods of catching them. Small fish like trout and whitefish were sometimes caught with a fishhook made of two thorns tied together to form an acute angle or of a nasal bone of a deer. The latter was semi-oval in form and needed very little fashioning. Lines were made of twisted iris-leaf fibers. Trout were thought to be summoned by the following song:

> Hallo, hallo
> Trout which are in deep holes everywhere
> To the north, to the east, to the west, to the south,
> Gather together.

Fish poisoning was also employed in smaller streams where more or less isolated pools could be found or created with a rough stone dam. Preferably the process was carried on in summer when the water was low. The poison chiefly used was soaproot (sakas); and another the Indians identified as ginseng (klarat). Buckeye was not used as a fish poison. Men were responsible for digging the roots. These were pounded on flat rocks awash on the edge of a stream. A pool might require a whole morning of pounding. By mid-afternoon the stunned fish began to float on the surface. These were put in a carrying-basket and taken to camp. A large conical basket filled with fish was a good haul. By the next morning more fish had been affected by the poison and could be collected. Small fish were also caught in traps.

A method of cooking small fish was to lay them uncleaned on hot rocks, preferably slate slabs. The fish were then salted and covered with other hot rocks. When cooked they were scraped loose and eaten. If there were a sufficient supply left over, the cooked fish were dried in the sun and stored for the winter in baskets. During the winter these dried fish were boiled before eating. Another method of preparing small fish was to clean them by splitting them open along the back-bone and laying the flesh back so that the bones and guts could be removed. They were not split up the belly. Chaparral brush was preferred for roasting fuel.

Mussels or clams were got by diving to the bottom of rivers. They seem in some places to have been plentiful enough to permit small group undertakings. The shellfish were either roasted or boiled to open the shell, and the meat was either consumed at once or, if the supply were sufficiently plentiful, dried in flat basketry trays for winter use.

VEGETABLE FOODS

Procuring vegetable foods was chiefly the responsibility of the women. This does not mean that men took no part in it, but simply that their labors were subsidiary, just as women's labors were subsidiary in obtaining and preparing flesh foods.

Acorn gathering. If a man wandering in the mountains discovered a tree heavily laden with acorns and believed that no one else was likely to find it, he claimed the whole tree and established his right by encircling the trunk with sticks leaned diagonally against it. If the tree was likely to be found by others, he might mark off only a single heavily loaded branch by leaning a single stick against the trunk under the branch claimed. If another man had previously observed the tree but had failed to mark it, he could now remove one stick and place his own there; but he must pay the original marker. When acorns were ready to be gathered the family or the local group went into the hills. Green acorns were thought to make a "nice smooth white sticky" soup, whereas ripe acorns which had fallen to the ground were less desirable because they made a "dark soup." Men climbed the trees and shook off the acorns. The women picked them up and removed the cups with their teeth. One tree at a time was stripped. One large tree or two small ones constituted a day's work. The unshelled acorns were carried back to camp, the men assisting. In the evening all gathered to shell acorns. It was in the nature of a social event. Nuts were cracked with the teeth, once lengthwise and once crosswise; or they were broken with a stone hammer on an anvil. It was estimated that one person could shell a gunnysackful in an evening.

If acorns were scarce, groups might make forays upon neighboring territories. During gathering expeditions one woman was appointed each day to remain in camp and turn over the acorns which were being dried in the sun. In return she received her share of the amount gathered.

Acorns were stored in bark-lined pits. In Bald Hills a chaparral bush was spread open with sticks, the whole lashed into shape with grapevines, and the interior lined with evergreen boughs. This type of cache was called cl kulus and was used like the others for unshelled acorns.

Preparation of acorns. Younger women of family pounded acorns; older ones sifted meal. To pound, woman seated herself on ground, with hopper between legs. She steadied it by resting calves of legs on either side of basket; wielded pestle with right hand; left hand stirred the coarse meal under pestle after each downstroke. Layer of meal kept between pestle and rock. Sifting done with flat basketry disk held slantingly between the two hands. Upper hand shook disk, which was held lightly between thumb and finger tips. Coarser meal, called ti (teeth), was dislodged and fell back to hopper. Fine meal adhered to disk because of greasy consistency. Was then swept off into separate basket. Process might be repeated twice. Flour sifted finer for soup than bread. Bread flour compared to corn meal; soup flour likened to refined wheat flour. Meal leached in sand pits (cltetci): "white-" or "blue-" oak (?) acorns for approximately two hours, black-oak acorns for four to six hours.

For acorn soup, meal placed in basket and boiled with hot smooth round rocks about size of tennis balls. These saved from one occasion to another. Women always on the lookout for suitable stones. Four or five rocks placed in basket. As soup boiled, stirred with wooden paddle. When well cooked, rocks removed and wiped off with index finger. Mush divided among members of local groups; eaten from small baskets by dipping first two fingers and licking them clean. This called by onomatopoeic term, Lup. Soup thick from long standing called pata. Patwin were believed by Wintu to thin soup to drinking consistency. Spoons not used.

For acorn bread black-oak and valley-oak acorn meal preferable. For black-oak bread, flour leached for one day in sand pit; removed and dried. Flour adjacent to sand put in water and sand allowed to settle out. To bake bread, rock-lined pit heated for nearly one day; rocks then covered with maple leaves; damp flour patted into this pit oven and covered with leaves, dirt, and rocks; finally fire built over pit. Allowed to cook all night, next morning bread done. Was of a rich, greasy consistency; would keep for months. Distributed, like other foods, to all members of local group. A baking considered necessary every week or two.

Valley-oak acorns, to be used for bread, put in water to mold. The moldier, the more tasty the bread was considered. Then acorns pounded into coarse flour. Red earth collected from gopher holes soaked in water. Resulting reddish liquid mixed with flour to make stiff batter. No leaching of meal necessary. For baking, large center pit dug with series of smaller ones around it. Batter allowed to bake all night. One woman appointed to remove bread (sau) in morning. All gathered then with much merrymaking and hilarity except on part of baker. The bread black in color; its darkness a measure of its palatability. Successful cook requested to bake at dances or meets, a mark of distinction in which women took pride. Black bread was specialty of Stillwater subarea where red earth was plentiful, but made in other regions also.

Food articles. The following list of foods makes no pretense of being complete, but it does represent the major articles of vegetable diet. The botanical identifications were made by the local Indians and may be subject to revision.

Acorns (iwe; shelled acorns, tliLe). Black-oak acorns (penel): Considered best. Plentiful throughout Wintu territory. Allowed to mold, then soaked with pine needles for week or two until sweet, boiled and eaten as relish; is a lumpy soup. Molded ones not made into flour, that is, not pounded. Soup (yiwit) and bread made of black-oak acorns (see above).

"White-" or "blue-" oak (?) acorns (yc kila): Used as much as penel. Plentiful on lower McCloud river. Employed when green. Sweet, need little leaching. Used chiefly for soup but also for bread.

Scrub-oak acorns (pom tliLe): Used as above. Found chiefly on upper McCloud and in mountains. Gathered green, chiefly when penel and yckila crops poor. Gum (pom tliLe kurkur) gathered in fall and eaten as candy.

Post-oak acorns (tceke tliLe): Found chiefly in high mountains. Flour used for soup and bread. Needs little leaching.

Valley-oak acorns (sule): Need little leaching. Flour used for soup and bread.

Live-oak acorns (tasal): Not used unless other acorns scarce. Preserved in seepage holes covered with bark and rock for six or eight months. Then called kas. When they fell naturally into water and soaked, called memuibut, considered tastier. After latter type of leaching, were boiled in shell, shelled, eaten whole. Said to taste like pound cake.

Buckeye (ycnot). Found throughout Wintu territory but reputed more plentiful in northern section. Wherever they abounded, were most important vegetable staple after acorns. Gathered in fall when stripe appears on husk indicating they are about to burst. Gathered chiefly by women. Preparation: Roasted in pit. When meat mashes out, considered cooked. Squeezed into baskets and mashed further with feet: one foot in basket, body balanced with stick. When creamy, placed in sand pit and leached until white and odorless; about one day sufficient. Then made into soup in same way as acorns. Unshelled, might be stored for winter in seepage hole lined with fern; slow leaching process. Dug out and used as needed in spring. Called yalumes, the-ones-left. Whole shelled fruit sometimes stored for winter. Might need week or more of soaking in creek when leached whole rather than as flour. Those which lay ungathered all winter might be collected in spring. Then needed only two or three days of leaching. Were made into bread. Those which rotted while lying ungathered during winter made into soup called tciwil yiwit (lizard soup). Buckeye mash mixed with pounded hen-and-chickens used as poultice.

Manzanita berries (pai). Most plentiful in Stillwater region, but found throughout area. Manzanita bush called pakami. Burden basket hung around neck, branches shaken over basket. Berries pounded into coarse flour, dampened, next morning dried and parched with hot rocks. Winnowed. Fine flour boiled with water and made into sweetish soup. Coarser part, consisting mostly of seeds, soaked in water and made into "cider." Cider consumed before fermentation. Fermentation made it "go bad." Drunk by dipping in container deer's tail tied to stick and sucking deer's tail.

"Indian potatoes." A number of tubers are subsumed under this generic term, some of which are:

Pussy's ears (pcLoi): Gathered in May. Found throughout territory. About size of finger tip.

Snake's head (xala): Gathered in May. Found throughout territory.

Tcubui: Gathered after blooming in June. Some stored for winter eating. Also used as paste for sinew of bows, and to bind paint pigments when used on bows.

Miscellaneous foods. Clover (tsaruk): Many varieties gathered. Eaten raw in spring when tender, often sprinkled with salt. Also steamed by placing hot rocks in basket, laying clover on them, sprinkling both with water.

Miner's lettuce: Same data as for clover.

Skunk-bush berries (pintus): Pounded into flour. Eaten dry or with water stirred in. Not cooked.

Indian rhubarb (sctus): Plentiful along streams. Stems peeled and eaten raw like celery in spring when tender. Thought beneficial to kidneys. Roots roasted in winter. Leaves used as impromptu drinking cups.

Wild spinach (paxeni): Leaves eaten as spring green.

Tiger-lily bulbs (tlereu): Bulbs roasted during winter. Not used after plant had begun spring growth. Two varieties—swamp and mountain.

Wild onion: Variety called pur eaten in May. Variety known as wimai pur (grizzly-bear onion) not very plentiful and not eaten.

Service berries (ta): Gathered in summer.

Hazel nuts (top): Gathered in hills during July and August. Hulled at leisure in village by hand, or by beating nuts with willow switch. Shelled during evenings like acorns. Stored, often in same container as pine nuts.

Digger-pine nuts: Unripe ones (xisi) eaten late in May, unshelled. Ripe ones (tcati) gathered in autumn; stored shelled or unshelled; eaten with acorn soup.

Sugar-pine nuts (sumu): Only ripe ones gathered in fall. Group went to mountains, men climbed trees and switched down cones. Cone roasted point downward to force opening, then pounded point downward on rock, or over container into which nuts fell. Winnowed. Usually deer hunting carried on simultaneously. Nuts boiled to remove pitch flavor. Stored in baskets lined with maple leaves. Eaten with salmon flour in which dried salmon eggs were also mixed. Sugar-pine resin (sumukurkur) gathered summer mornings before it melted. Eaten as candy.

Wild grapes (uyul): Placed in small basket and mashed. If too sour, sweet manzanita flour mixed with them. Eaten just before fermentation.

Seeds: Gathered most abundantly in Bald Hills, but also in other areas. Women beat seeds with seedbeaters into twined carrying-baskets held in left hands. Two seeds known to informant, "sun-flower" and "cotton flower" (salal). Latter a specialty of Bald Hills. Traded to north for fish and acorns.

Many "grasses" gathered. No generic name for them. Eaten as greens when tender. Inner bark of yellow pine resorted to as food during hard winters.

Medicaments. Pennyroyal (tosLalas): Blossoms made into a tea for colds.

Oregon grape: Roots steeped in water; concoction drunk as blood purifier.

Soaproot: Pounded into mash and applied as poultice on poison oak; also used as fish poison.

Milkweed (koroti): White juice of stalks used for poison oak and warts; fiber used for string.

Salt (weL). Winter's supply obtained during summer dryness. Scraped or brushed from salt deposits. One informant said cattle have consumed once plentiful supply. Most bountiful in Stillwater. Was too rare for McCloud people to use lavishly, especially on upper reaches of river. In Bald Hills, deposit four miles from Horsetown was chief source. Small switch of twigs (weL sik) used to brush it up: three or four inches long, lashed at top with withe, made in situ, discarded after use. Salt used on raw clover, grasshoppers, occasionally in acorn mush, manzanita cider.

Not eaten. Sturgeon, dog, birds' eggs, angleworms. There seems to have been no feeling that dogs were particularly poisonous. Young lamprey eels not eaten, thought poisonous. Stepping on one in river mud believed to be almost as harmful as snake bite.

NOTES ON TRADITIONAL FOOTHILL NISENAN FOOD TECHNOLOGY

Norman L. Wilson

Norman Wilson's essay supplements Dixon's classic account, which focused on the northernmost Maiduan-speakers. Furthermore, as Wilson points out, this essay is more detailed than previous writings, especially in regard to actual customs and behavior, which earlier ethnographers tended to neglect in favor of reconstruction and cultural norms. Norman Wilson (1930–2002), who served as California State Archaeologist and worked for the California State Indian Museum, was the co-author of the Nisenan chapter in the California volume of the *Handbook of North American Indians* (Wilson and Towne 1978).

At the beginning of the article, the author outlines the circumstances of the research and information on the consultants. This essay was part of a volume on Nisenan environment and subsistence, occasioned by the construction of Auburn Dam on the American River. Wilson conducted similar work for the Oroville Dam project. These salvage motivations also underlay the Pomo documentation carried out by Kathleen Smith, Otis Parrish, and David Peri in connection with the construction of the Warm Springs Dam (see Contemporary Perspectives). Elizabeth Enos (1882–1968), Wilson's principal consultant, also worked extensively with Samuel Barrett, and she is featured in his film on buckeye processing. Wilson's Nisenan chapter includes his photographs of Elizabeth Enos using a soaproot brush and leaching acorn meal (Wilson and Towne 1978:389–90).

Center for Archaeological Research at Davis (1972), Publication no. 3:32–38.

INTRODUCTION

This paper presents the results of ethnographic work with Elizabeth Enos, a foothill Nisenan. A few additional notes from a Mr. Kelly, a Nisenan from Nevada City, also are used. Although many aspects of Nisenan culture were discussed, emphasis was placed on collecting information concerning material culture and food technology.

Mrs. Enos lived north of Auburn near the small settlement of Clipper Gap on the site of her old village, known locally as "Sugar Pine Hill." She was raised on this hill and spent much of her life living with her family in a situation where the native food gathering customs were maintained. Her grandparents lived for several years after she was born. Her mother and aunts also instructed and worked with her in her younger life. Her grandfather worked for Captain Sutter as a captive, and she heard accounts about the entrance of the first white men into the Auburn area from her grandparents and parents. Her age at the time of the interview (1957–63) was not known; her friends estimated it at over 80 years. She remembers working for a rancher picking hops near Sacramento State College before 1900. She also remembers being cured by an uncle who was a shaman in a dance house at *Kadema*. Merriam reports that only an old cabin was on the site when he visited the area in 1907.[1] She was, in my opinion, one of the best informants left of the rapidly disappearing group of Indians who had contact with the old way. (Mrs. Enos died in 1968).

She had a good grasp of the local geography of the Auburn area and remembered, as a girl, when it was open country systematically utilized by her group in search of food. She knew the Indian name for most of the landmarks in her territory and the names of the villages which were gone soon after the coming of the gold miners. It was an enjoyable experience to go into the field with her as she told of her country with a depth of experience and knowledge that few living persons can match.

Mr. Kelley was interviewed twice in 1957. His information, though limited, was apparently very good in some details. He was born and raised at the Nevada City Rancheria and, although he lived most of his life in Nevada City, remembered a few details of the old way as it had been described to him.

Food technology of the Nisenan has been reported in several publications of which perhaps Voegelin (1942) is the most thorough. Powers (1877), Dixon (1905), Kroeber (1925 and 1929), Beals (1933), and Uldall and Shipley (1966) also contain valuable data. Merriam's unpublished notes and pioneer descriptions give us a detailed look at some of the aspects of the technology. However none of these accounts relate descriptions of behavior during the hunting and gathering rounds of the foothill Indians. The accounts of Mrs. Enos were gathered with this in mind as well as to gain details about the food gathering processes which might not have been noted before. In general, Mrs. Enos's accounts support previous data from the area.

The basic food economy appears to have been based on the gathering of acorns and grass seeds, but little has been published concerning quantities and gathering times. Among Mrs. Enos's group, there was a major family effort in food gathering for most of the year, with all members of the family assisting in acquiring edible products. The children were taught at an early age to find food as they worked and played. This "living off the land" certainly had an effect on the amounts of food needed at the village during the productive summer months and trained the children to recognize and gather many food products in their area.

The group or village did have regular rounds, and all families would join in these efforts. Hunting in the autumn, fishing, and seed, acorn, clover, and salt gathering were such activities. The Sugar Pine Hill group, as Mrs. Enos remembered it, was comprised of about 10 to 15 individuals, the number changing constantly due to movement of families to the Auburn and Colfax groups, deaths, and feuds. Her group was much larger in earlier days according to accounts she heard from her grandmother and other old people of the village. They lost many men at Rocklin at a "big time" on one occasion when the Rocklin Indians trapped the men who were in the dance house and killed them. This incident, she explained, was why the Valley Indians died, killed with "bad air" sent by mountain shamans in revenge.

Captains from the Auburn Village had authority over her group and would often call for big times and hunts. The captain at Weimar was also a powerful figure in the area. When the shaman or captain called for the group to do something, everyone responded because "you get power from it." Several groups often joined for trips for salt or fishing on the Valley floor. Her group seems to have been most familiar with the country around the foot-hills of the Bear River and that south along the foothills to the American River.

Foothill Nisenan felt a general distrust of the Valley people, but definite trade relationships existed with the mountain Nisenan and Washo. Mrs. Enos recalled that when she was a very young girl, an old tattooed Washo woman married into the group. In bad years when the Nisenan had nothing to trade, fights with the Washo do seem to have occurred when they came over the Sierra to steal acorns. (The Washo were called Mona, apparently a general Maidu term denoting mountain people.) The higher mountain areas were used by any group that was in the area—the Nevada City group, for example, hunted in the mountains around Lake Tahoe. Although the Sugar Pine Hill group did not go high up in the mountains as did the Nevada City, Foresthill, or Iowa Hill groups, Mrs. Enos had made several visits to Washo territory. The Washo formerly rode the train from Nevada with fish in sacks to trade for acorns. She did not remember any fights or arguments at these trading times. Mrs. Enos herself continued to trade with the Washo at the time of interview, and her daughter married one. At present the only living curing doctor in the area is a Washo who is consulted by the local Nisenan, and, contrary to other sources, no general dislike was felt by Mrs. Enos's people toward the Washo.

Salt was taken from a spring near Lincoln (which, as far as she remembered, was not owned by anyone) and meetings there with other groups were an occasion for active trading. Black oak acorns and manzanita berries were exchanged by the Sugar Pine Hill group for fish and shell, the Valley people especially preferring manzanita berries. Mrs. Enos did not recall any active trading within the local groups, but women traded baskets or other work at times. She jokingly said that "things were traded often enough at the gambling games," when food and almost all other material things were wagered. This gambling was a group-against-group affair where teams and groups could lose status if they lost too badly at the big times. Each team member wagered his own goods, and gambling feuds occasionally occurred between men of different groups. If a man lost most of his goods gambling with the group team, other members would help him and his family with food and supplies. This exchange of material goods through gambling apparently served as an important economic process to the foothill groups.

ANIMAL FOODS

Deer: Deer meat was obtained throughout the year by individual men hunting away from the village. In the fall, the entire group would go on hunting and gathering expeditions toward Coon Creek and down the western Sierra slope. Camps would be located along a creek and temporary houses constructed. These were usually grass covered, with mud and dirt built up the sides to a height of about two feet. Usually no excavation was done in constructing the floor. Sometimes old houses were reworked into useable structures. The houses were torn down after each period of use, so that no animals would live in them. While men were hunting, the women and children gathered acorns, seeds, and other vegetable products. Often the whole group would fish the stream during the hunting trip.

Most hunting was started in the early morning and continued through the day. Few men hunted in the evening unless they had guns since the animal, if wounded, could escape in the darkness. Those few who had guns hunted anytime and were reputed to be good shots. Hunting was done for the most part with bow and arrow however; the snare was not known, and Mrs. Enos did not remember the man running down the deer. The deer's head was not known to have been used as a decoy or mask, but the hide and head were reportedly used in hunting antelope which occurred in large herds in the lower foothills. Deer were said to have been abundant but soon after the Gold Rush they began to disappear, and the Sugar Pine Hill group now rarely sees deer. Mr. Kelley reported that he had kept a tame deer at one time and that animals were formerly less wary of humans than is now the case.

When a large deer was killed it was butchered and quartered at the kill site, especially if the kill was made a long way from camp. Hunters preferred to bring an undrawn deer into camp, if possible, since it was easier to butcher in the evening when the flies and yellow-jackets were gone. Children would have to keep the flies and other pests away from the meat when it was butchered during the day, or when it was still drying. Deer meat was stripped from the carcass and dried on willow stick racks. Stripping was performed by one of two alternate methods: either long thin strips about one half inch in diameter and several inches long were cut and hung over the rack, or thin flat pieces were cut from the meat. Often the meat was hung from the lower limbs of trees, but if yellow-jackets were too numerous, a structure of limbs and brush was built over the meat to keep them away. In hot weather it took about 24 hours for the meat to dry and harden.

The only bones saved from the hunt were those needed for tools. Bones were cracked and cooked for marrow, and entrails were either used as bait in hunting small game or discarded.

When the hunt had produced enough meat, the family or group would return to the village. Usually this meant many trips, as the meat would fill several baskets. Often there would be a surplus of other gathered foods (dried fish, small game, and plant foods) which would be packed back to the village as well. The women did most of the packing using burden baskets, but skins were also tied into packs and carried by men. Children carried small loads of baskets and household objects, and, as they went along gathered any small food items that might be of use to the group.

There was no organized noon meal and often no big evening meal if the women were not prepared to cook one. The people were often hungry on the trail and looked forward to the return to the village where food would be prepared.

Deer hides were used for blankets, on the floors of houses for rugs, and as roof coverings on dance houses. Some houses used deer hide for a door covering. Small hides were used for clothing and quivers. Some men tied a good skin of a bobcat or raccoon around their body and over one shoulder like a modern woman uses a fur, and it was considered quite dressy.

Bears. Bears were hunted by the bravest men, and a bear skin was the sign of a good hunter. The animals were hunted in the winter during the hibernation period. One man would enter the cave and chase the bear out with a torch; as the bear moved into the daylight the other hunters would kill it before its eyes grew accustomed to the light.

Old Indians were believed to turn into bears, but Mrs. Enos would not elaborate on this point, except that there was a species of plant which if eaten would transform a person into a bear. She believed that there were formerly bear doctors who killed people, but that they abandoned the activity because white men killed them, thinking they were bears. She told of a white man bringing into her parents' village a bear which had been shot, and when they cut the bear open there was a man inside.

Fish. During hunting trips and at other times fish would be taken by the use of poison. Soaproot, pounded into a creamy mass, would be put into the stream at the head of a large pool or in very slow moving water. (The mullen plant was also used, possibly in the same fashion). The men of the group, all good swimmers, would go into the water, stir the poison and, as the fish floated to the surface, throw them out to the women and children on the bank who hit the fish with rocks if they were too lively. Other children would watch the outlet of the pool. In this manner they would obtain two or three big baskets of fish from each large hole. This was a very happy time with lots of laughing and splashing. Large fish were split down the back and laid open so that the thick sections of meat along the back wouldn't spoil; the entrails were discarded. Trout and small fish were eaten as they were caught or dried on rocks or strung from sticks. Small fish might also be steamed with plant leaves and grasses in the steam oven. Most commonly the women waited until the fish were dried and then pounded them into a meal, or the group ate them dry. Large fish were usually eaten fresh, dried, or pounded up and made into soup or cakes for old and very young people. At the fishing site small fish were thrown directly on the coals and eaten.

While on these trips they would gather acorns from the ground among the leaves of the water oak. These were not good acorns since they were harder to grind, but this source saved them from bringing acorns from the village.

The Washo used to bring large dried fish from Pyramid Lake: a sack of fish traded for a sack of acorns. Steelhead and salmon formerly migrated up all the small streams around Auburn and Colfax. The Sacramento River was called Hoyo-sayo which means Fish River, and in the old days the men traveled to the Sacramento River near Vernon for salmon. They would go with men from several foothill villages but went infrequently since the Valley people were hostile. Sugar Pine Hill men also went to Lincoln for salt and would fish there in the creek, sometimes trading there with Valley Indians for shell beads and fish. The group occasionally went to Salmon Falls on the South Fork of the American River to get eels or traded for them with Pilot Hill Indians. The fish there were reputed to be "special kinds that hung on rocks and you picked them off." They were dried and considered a specialty. Mrs. Enos did not remember use of nets in fishing nor any fishing in the American or Bear Rivers where salmon runs had been curtailed by hydraulic mining in the mid-19th century.

Mr. Kelley said his group used to fish with a hook made out of a squirrel leg bone, bipointed and about 1½ inches long. String was tied in the middle and a worm or bug was pulled over it so that the bone lay parallel with the string. This was primarily used to catch trout. Usually the line was held in the hand and the fish given sufficient time to swallow the bait, then pulled in. A long pole was attached to such a line for use in less accessible places in brush or around rocks. No idea of sport was involved. He did not use poison or nets but knew of poison. Sometimes in the old days fish were obtained in trade, but the source was unknown to him. Children often fished with their hands and gathered frogs, crayfish, and snails as well. This was an important food gathering process, and was fun for the boys who would get their food in this way while playing. They knew all the edible plants and animals and would eat anything they found when working or playing.

Rabbits. The Sugar Pine Hill group hunted rabbits primarily between Auburn and Lincoln where they were abundant. Rabbits also were caught around the village, but the best hunting was done on the Valley floor. A typical hunt would perhaps start with a shaman in Auburn who was going to give a dinner and a big time calling on all the men to go rabbit hunting. Since he was a powerful man everyone went. The hunt was staged in a special place where rabbit trails were most common. A three foot high net was stored at the Auburn Rancheria and carried to the hunt on a horse. This net was kept in repair by the Auburn women, who worked on it in the dance house in the winter. The net was about 100 yards long, and in earlier times several nets may have been joined for these drives. The net was held up with sticks guarded by two men. The other people went way out from it and began to beat the grass with long sticks, making noises and moving toward the net. The rabbits would run up to the net and become entangled while trying to jump through it. The men guarding the net would run out and kill them with a club and gather them in a pile at the ends of the net. On successful drives hundreds of rabbits were killed.

If a big time had been planned, the rabbits would be carried back to the village, cleaned, skinned, and eaten. If the hunt was for skins, only enough food for the group would be saved, the rabbits being skinned at the hunting site. The women preferred to skin the animals as soon as possible because less trimming and scraping of the fleshy side of the skin was involved. The skins were divided by the rabbit captain who was in charge of the hunt. White rabbit tails were saved and used on dance costumes.

Rabbit skin blankets, made from the skins of about 40 animals, were a common item. Each rabbit was skinned and the skin cut into strips about 1½ inches wide and sewn together at the ends. It was then hung in the trees and left for the winter. As a result the fur rope would twist leaving fur on all sides. In the spring the blanket was woven with a framework of sticks made on the ground, and, after having been softened by being pulled over a log or around a tree, was sewn together using grass thread. Such blankets were about the size of a large cloth blanket, and were used in the houses. They were rarely used as garments except by old people who would sit around in them on cold days. They lasted many years and most were burned at the second burning ceremonies.

Cooking. Rabbits and water fowl were cooked by wrapping the carcass with mud obtained from special places along stream banks. First the animal was drawn and the body cavity sewn shut with a small stick of willow or other wood. The animal was then coated with mud—often with the skin still on. After cooking the animal was removed from the fire, and the mud covering broken off. Waterfowl feathers came away with the mud; with rabbits, the skin might have to be pulled off separately. The meat was left a very white color. Small animals were drawn and the cavities sewn and put directly on the coals. No mud was used, and the skin was left on until the animal was cooked. Often small animals such as mice and rats were dried and pounded into a meal, bones and all. They were first skinned and then dried on a flat rock or stone slab.

Meat rarely was added to acorn mush, most often eaten separately. When a deer leg was to be eaten without drying, the leg was cut to the bone, opened out, and laid on the hot coals to cook. The Indians did not mind the charcoal that stuck to the meat and rarely brushed it off. Bones often were saved for use as basketry awls and other tools. Green bone was easy to work, while fire cooked bones were too brittle. Sometimes, after a tool was made, it was heated carefully without burning, to harden it. Mrs. Enos would not put cut deer meat on a winnowing basket that was used for acorn preparation, as the acorn meal would taint the meat. Large flat coiled trays not used in acorn preparation were employed for carrying meat.

Birds. Mrs. Enos was not certain whether nets were used to catch ducks but felt they may formerly have been used along streams. Men of the Sugar Pine Hill group used a hoop net spread over a spring or place where they knew robins or pigeons and doves watered. It was propped up with a stick to which a string was tied which led to a brush house where one man hid. When the birds were in the right place, he pulled the cord and the trap fell. Birds with power such as eagles, hawks, buzzards, and owls were not eaten but were killed for feathers. Duck feathers were saved for feather blankets, while other feathers were used for regalia—magpie, flicker and large bird feathers were quite valuable. Flickers and possibly some other birds were captured for their feathers, but only a few feathers from each would be taken and the birds released. Birds were not important as a food item, and are not known to have been dried or kept as pets.

Grasshoppers. Grasshoppers were a favorite food and were gathered often in the summer in special places in the open fields around the village. They were caught in conical pits about two to three feet deep and about two feet wide at the top. Several pits were dug, and these usually were put in rows so most of the grasshoppers would be caught. The group would go through the grass driving the grasshoppers ahead of them by beating branches or sticks on the dry grass. The grasshoppers would land in the pits and remain there. Then a skin was thrown over the hole to keep the grasshoppers in the trap, and a smoke bundle would be put into the pit under the skin. The grasshoppers would fall to the bottom where they could be gathered. A large sack could be collected in a few hours. This sack was placed in water to soak while an earth oven was made. The oven was constructed by laying a group of rocks on the ground and building a fire on them. When the fire had burned to white coals, a layer of grape leaves was put on the coals, and a hot rock was rolled out of the fire and placed in the middle. The grasshoppers would be poured wet from the sack onto the leaves and covered with more hot steam rising from the oven. The grasshoppers would be allowed to cook all afternoon and when dry and crisp, were taken from the oven. By special light crushing done with a hand rock on a large tray, the wings and legs would be broken off. By winnowing, these were separated from the bodies. The grasshoppers would be eaten this way or stored in baskets. Sometimes they were crushed into meal and cooked like mush.

VEGETABLE FOODS

Acorns. Acorn gathering was done in the fall. Mrs. Enos, at the time of interview, used about three 50 pound sacks of acorns over the winter, and reported that a family would normally gather about 10 to 12 sacks to see them through the same period. As many acorns as possible would be gathered when the season was good, and surpluses were used in trading, shared with the old people, and consumed at big times. If a captain asked for acorns for a big time families were obliged to contribute even if this left them short. The captain, however, would often return the acorns if he knew it would cause hardship. The captain would also ask the group to help a family if they were in need, but only "if they were a good family and had really tried to help themselves." Those who through lack of effort never seemed to have enough acorns would not be helped by the local group and would often move to another village in the winter and live off relatives.

Traditionally, families would usually go to special places to get acorns, and they may have owned certain trees. Some trees were better than others for acorns, and a woman was proud if she procured good acorns. Black oak was considered to have the best acorns. All acorns, however, were used. The people of Todd's Valley and Foresthill were reputed to always have good acorns, and the soup they made at big times was a favorite. The best acorn trees were higher up in the mountains and on the shady side of canyons.

Everyone would help in the gathering of acorns, but the men were usually hunting at this time, and only the old men would be around. A woman could gather a big burden basket of acorns in a day if she were lucky or had children to help. Other vegetable foods were gathered at the same time if found in quantity and might be given preference over acorns which would be left for later. Fruits or bulbs were placed in the same basket as the acorns but would be placed on top, if possible. No food was carried along on one day gathering trips; eating was done upon return to camp or along the route. Sometimes, if the acorn harvest was good, large piles of acorns were gathered under the trees to be picked up later. Occasionally other groups would be seen on these trips, but little communication took place.

Families always tried to gather enough acorns for the following year. Acorns left over from the previous year were considered very good. The acorns would sprout and the sprouts would dry up and fall off in the summer in the storage hoppers. The shells were easier to remove after the sprouts had dried, and the acorns were easier to leach. In the granaries, the new acorns were put on the top and the old acorns were taken from the bottom. A family might have as many as three granaries, but this depended on the size of the family and the quantity of acorns on hand. The granaries were made of sticks and grass and stood above the ground.

Acorns were shelled only when needed and then only enough for a few days. Usually they were ground the same day. Bedrock mortars were preferred to grind the acorn meats, but in the winter a portable mortar was handy to keep in the house. Not everyone had these, and they were frequently loaned. After being ground, the meal was stored in a basket. The cooking was done the same day, if possible, and enough soup and bread prepared to last for several days. No one minded eating it cold, and at some meals this was all that was available. Acorns could be prepared and eaten as soup, or the soup might be poured hot into a basket of cold water thus making a thicker, harder form of mush. The mush was broken off in pieces and eaten or placed by the fire and dried. It then tasted like bread. Also a thick mush which was molded into loaves and cooked on rocks beside the fire was made, and this could be used later or carried on trips.

Women did not cook acorns every day but only when necessary. Acorn shells were burned and made a very good bed of coals if enough were used. When stirring the soup in the basket while cooking with a hot stone, the cook constantly watched the color of the steam coming from the basket. If it turned brown the basket was burning and the soup had to be stirred harder. Children liked to eat the hard crusts of acorn meal that baked on the cooking stones and flaked off dry when the stones cooled. The same stone was not used twice in the cooking process, and plenty of stones were at hand. Soapstone was considered the best cooking rock. Leaching areas were shared but cooking was done by the individual family in its own baskets. Old people were often given mush by the person cooking.

Acorns were not taken along on hunting or fishing trips away from the village. Instead children and women gathered acorns from the ground or found them in the leaf mold if it were not the acorn season. Old acorns were often eaten without cooking since they were already leached by the rain. At big times the acorns were brought as meal or nuts to the meeting place and cooked in baskets. When visiting another group, one was suspicious if given soup in a very old basket, as it might be poisoned. Usually when a family ate in a neighboring village, the members cooked and ate their own food separately from the villagers because of the danger of poisoning.

Seeds and grass. At certain times of the year grasses and seeds were gathered by the group. Men would cut the grass with wooden knives made from the green root of a chaparral bush fire hardened to keep the edge. The grass was piled in stacks about three to four feet high. If the grass contained seeds, the stalks were dipped in water, then put into a cleared area to dry overnight. The next day they were shaken into a big basket, and the seeds collected. The seeds were pounded just like acorns and then cooked in the same manner with hot stones in baskets. The resulting mush tasted like peanut butter and was considered a great treat. Sometimes the old people would roast seeds with hot coals on a flat tray.

One variety of grass, similar to clover, was dried and pounded into a powder which was then cooked with water and left to cool. When cooked, it resembled a clear green jello and was a favorite.

When the group was out in the spring, they would get down on their knees and eat the clover in the fields, and it was considered a treat. Gathering clover, however, was a special event and was associated with spring dances. When Mrs. Enos was a little girl the men of her group gathered clover in the fields near the Bear River, cutting it with the same wooden cutting knives used for grass. After the clover was cut, it was collected into piles, and the cooking ovens were prepared. A pit was dug, and a large fire was built and left to burn to a very hot bed of coals. A layer of rocks was put on this fire, and the clover, well wetted, was placed on these hot stones, then covered with more hot rocks and left to cook all afternoon. When the clover had dried and cooled, it was eaten or stored. It could be stored for long periods of time and became part of the winter supply. It was often pounded into meal and cooked into mush.

The annual clover dance was associated with the spring gathering and was one of the major ceremonies of the group. It was held in April when the flowers were blooming and is sometimes called the flower dance, since the girls would make flower wreaths and belts and dance in a large open field.

Bulbs. Bulbs that were gathered were pounded and made into mush. Wild "potatoes" were gathered in the late spring and early summer. When they were dried they could be stored for considerable periods. Many bulbs were used as medicine rather than food.

Manzanita. Manzanita was known as quo-toc, and was used for tools because its wood was very hard. The berries were gathered in July when they were ripe, mashed into powder, mixed with water, and put into a sack. The drippings, which tasted like cider, was collected and drunk. The berries were traded to the Valley people.

Mushrooms. In November 1957, Mrs. Enos was sorting a box of mushrooms that she had gathered that morning. She mentioned that some were poisonous, but she had a friend who ate some of those and had not died. These mushrooms were a large white type, and she had approximately thirty pounds of them. She was planning to hang them for drying and would eat them after a few minutes boiling. She referred to any mushroom as wuk and a special kind as polgo, and indicated they were a major early winter food of her group.

PHOTOGRAPHIC PORTFOLIO
ELIZABETH ENOS (NISENAN MAIDU) PROCESSING BUCKEYES, 1960
Samuel A. Barrett and film crew

While buckeye processing is generally similar to acorn preparation, because the buckeye is much tougher it must be boiled first to loosen the hard skin. Despite his extensive interviews with Elizabeth Enos, Norman Wilson did not offer any description of her treatment of buckeyes. (For a contemporary Kashaya Pomo description of the process, see Essie Parrish's commentary, page 389).

Fortunately, at almost the same time, Mrs. Enos was recorded by Samuel Barrett. As part of his American Indian Film project (see the Essie Parrish portfolio), he filmed Mrs. Enos processing buckeyes. The edited footage was released in 1961 as *Buckeyes: Food of California Indians.*

These images were produced by Barrett and his film crew, at Dog Bar, near Auburn in Placer County, on October 26, 1960. Accompanying the images is an excerpt from Barrett's journal (Hearst Museum, accession no. 1994, ms. 19, pp. 33–35). From the excerpt, we discover that Barrett supplied the buckeyes, as well as the baskets. He often resorted to such recreation in order to document what he believed to be vanishing customs (Barrett 1961).

October 25, 1960. When we arrived [at Mrs. Enos's home near Auburn] we found her and discussed the processing of buckeyes which we had collected at Clear Lake and brought with us. We are to go back to Sacramento and get the proper baskets for the processing and return tomorrow at 8:30 am and go to Dog Bar to process buckeyes....

October 26.... Filmed Grandma Enos peeling the outer husk from the buckeyes and then cracking the inner husk and the meat with a stone. This was just an ordinary stone picked up on the beach here at the river. Two baskets from the State [Indian] Museum used for this whole process.

She says that in former times they used what she calls an Indian knife, i.e., a flake, to cut these inner husks off and put the peeled meats into the basket or simply cut them open so that the water could get at the meat and cook it. The latter is all that is necessary apparently because in many instances as she cracks these with the stone she just hits them once or twice, enough to break the inner husk and then throws them into the basket without further breaking of the meat itself. The cracked nuts are put into a basket and rock boiled upwards of an hour until they were done. The white nut resembles boiled potatoes in looks when it is taken out. It is then separated from the brown shucks and they are thrown away....

In this particular instance G. Enos used a natural pestle shaped stone for the mashing. She did not remove the inner brown husks but mashed the now creamed-colored kernel with the inner husk all together.

In the process of removing the brown husks Mrs. Enos rubs the meat, which is now a mushy liquid, up against the side of the basket and further grinds it up into a thin gruel. The refuse material thrown out of this mixture, i.e., the brown husks and the parts of kernel stuck to them, form quite a basket full.

Since this was a hand job, not done with the regular masher, there was more refuse than there would be if the original masher had been used. This material was thrown away but in former times more care would have been taken to save the fragments that adhered to the brown husk, which probably amounted to a quarter of the meal on this occasion. It is very doubtful that such a percentage would have been thrown away in ancient times.

In the leaching process a certain amount of coarse grain material results. This in ancient times was passed through a sieve woven by a man.... Mrs. Enos says that the buckeye was passed through this sieve to get a finely divided meal or mush as it was actually consumed.

Elizabeth Enos peeling buckeyes.
(NEG. NO. 25–5034).

Washing cooked buckeyes with a stone pestle.
(NEG. NO. 25–5042).

Pouring cooked buckeye meats into the leaching pit.
(NEG. NO. 25–5048).

Elizabeth Enos bringing a basket of water up from the river.
(NEG. NO. 25–5052).

Scraping up leached buckeye meal from floor of pit.
(NEG. NO. 25–5056).

Leached buckeye meal on a flat basket.
(NEG. NO. 25–5059).

Elizabeth Enos eating buckeye meal with her fingers.
(NEG. NO. 25–5062).

ETHNO-BOTANY OF THE COAHUILLA
INDIANS OF SOUTHERN CALIFORNIA
David P. Barrows

The Cahuilla, Shoshonean-speakers who inhabited a very diverse habitat, accordingly made use of a wide range of plants in their traditional habitat. *Ethnobotany of the Coahuilla Indians* is actually much broader in scope than its title indicates. According to Lowell Bean, "With regard to California ethnography, it is the first professionally written ethnography of a single tribe" (1967:xvi), claims also made for the later volumes of Goddard (1903) and Dixon (1905).

Educator, administrator, anthropologist, and soldier, David Prescott Barrows (1873–1954) came to his interest in Indians from an encounter with some Sierra Miwok people in 1883. A course in anthropology taught by Frederick Starr, taken during Barrows's freshman year at Pomona College, stimulated his interest in the discipline. After studying political science at the University of California, Barrows enrolled in the new anthropology program at the University of Chicago, where Starr was his major adviser and dissertation supervisor. Barrows, who first visited the homeland of the Cahuilla in 1891, was particularly close to the family of Juan Maria Costo. Altogether he spent nine summers doing field work among the Cahuilla and neighboring groups of southern California and the Cocopa of Arizona. However, most of his ethnographic field notes remain unpublished.

In this volume, Barrows describes Cahuilla culture primarily as it was in the 1890s, but he also considers their aboriginal culture. This was a difficult time for the Cahuilla: Their lands were being taken away from them, and their population was declining. One might note the author's use of the word "savagery." Following scientific custom of the time, Barrow employs it not as "wild" or "cruel," but as a stage in human social evolution. Barrows's relationships with the Cahuilla were, in fact, friendly and intimate. His concluding remarks about the harmful effects of the white man's diet have, unfortunately, proved even more applicable a century later.

Chicago: University of Chicago Press (1900). Reprint (1967), Malki Museum Press, Banning, Calif. Pp. 50–73.

THE GATHERING, PREPARATION,
AND STORING OF FOODS

34. The study of those plants which yield sustenance forms one of the most instructive chapters in savage life. The record of starvation and want lies behind the discovery of almost every plant food. The thoroughness with which every grass, stalk, fruit, tuber, and seed, available to the savage, has been examined, treated by fire, by leaching, and by every form of analysis that can be devised, affords us a grim picture of the figure of hunger that is not far from every man.

In this work the woman has naturally been the important factor. They have been her explorations, her revolutionary discoveries, the tests made by her teeth and stomach that have advanced the race in its quest for subsistence.

Among the Coahuillas, as among all Indians, the woman is the getter of vegetable foods, the ethnobotanist of her community. Now that the man's hunting has been interrupted forever by the settlements of the whites and the disappearance of the game, the support of the family falls principally on the woman.

The problem of securing food for a tribe within the territory of the Coahuillas at first sight seems an impossible one. It is the ugly barrenness of the mountains and the arid sterility of the plains that impresses one. It is probably true that an untutored white man lost here would be likely to find hardly a single plant to yield him a mess of palatable food. Beauty of flower and foliage and splendor of fruition are alike sacrificed here to the necessities of the desert. There are no luscious fruits with juicy pulps awaiting the thirsty traveler, but at most only shriveled bags of rind filled with seeds, dangling from a dry and ghostly stalk, or small, bitter plums that are nothing but exaggerated pits, surrounded by a puckery skin. In all these mountains there is not an edible root that a white man's efforts would be likely to discover; there are no palatable nuts, except the piñones high in the summits. The absence of food is, however, apparent rather than real. The desert is a kindlier mother than would be expected. Nature is less niggardly here than in some more verdant countries. The flora of American deserts, as pointed out by others, is really quite rich in species. Given the knowledge and patience of the Indian woman, the problem is far simpler than would be supposed. Probably the food supply of the Coahuillas contains a greater variety and abundance than that of most Indian tribes. As we have seen, their habitat occupies the dividing line between the desert and the coast valleys. The mountain Coahuillas can turn westward and meet the flora of the valleys reaching to the Pacific, or descend eastward into the desert and bring back its nourishing and remarkable supplies of food.

35. We have already noticed the *se-kwá-vel*, or great packing basket. Such a receptacle is the property of every Coahuilla woman. For supporting this upon her back, she has the strong, beautiful carrying net whose manufacture has been described. To protect her head against the weight of her load, she presses down over her forehead a *yú-mu-wal*, or basket hat, and having slung her net and basket over her shoulder is ready to set out on her quest for food. She has also two other implements, a *chí-pat-mal*, or flat gathering basket, and her seed fan, *yí-kow-a-pish*. In the Southwest and among many Shoshone Indians, Utes, and Panamints, this seed fan takes the place of the pointed, fire-hardened digging stick of the North. It is shaped like a light tennis racket and is made of willow wands and rawhide. In gathering seeds from the low grass or bushes, the woman holds the *chí-pat-mal* nearly flat against the ground and beats the seeds from the grass stems with the seed fan.

36. Many of the foods furnished by this country, including several nuts and pits, are bitter and astringent. To remove these principles, the meal ground from these products is leached with water. Sometimes a sandy spot on the creek bottom suffices, but more often a large, shallow basket, perhaps three feet in diameter, is woven of osiers. This basket is set on a low pole platform and filled with carefully selected sand. The basket is called *pá-cha-ka-vel* and the sand *ná-chish*. A depression is smoothed in the sand and the meal piled thereon and water poured slowly through. Contrary to what might be expected, the meal

mingles but little with the sand and is daintily scooped out when the leaching is accomplished. A hard, smoothly brushed floor is always to be seen near a home, where various fruits, nuts, and berries are spread out to dry.

37. Of receptacles for storing food, the most striking is the basket granary. These are made of osiers. The withes with the leaves left on are first twisted loosely into a thick rope as big as a man's arm and from this the basket is coiled. The shape is circular, rounding toward the top with a tolerably flat bottom. There is a short, narrow neck. The size is about thirty inches for height and a somewhat greater diameter. The neck and mouth are narrow—ten inches or so across. It will hold many bushels of grain or seeds. Over the mouth is laid a flat sandstone slab, or a wicker cover weighted with a stone or two. In the Cabeson these granaries are made almost exclusively out of the *háng-al*, the species of wormwood so abundant there (*Artemisia Ludoviciana*, Nutt.), and having been filled with mesquite beans they are covered over and sealed with an armful of the shoots and a daub of mud. These granaries are perched either on platforms of poles, or, in the mountains, on the flat tops of high boulders out of the reach of field mouse or kangaroo rat.

This great basket, or, as the Coahuillas call it, *mal-a-not*, is the characteristic storehouse of these Indians, and is by no means confined to them. The Cocopahs make them in great numbers, filling them each summer with dried mesquite pods and placing them out of reach on the roofs of their houses. Very similar ones are made by the Mojaves.[1] Seeds are often stored in old ollas and set away in the corners of the house; many kinds of dried fruit are kept in baskets; often herbs as well as small quantities of dried food are wrapped in pieces of cloth and tucked away in the thatching or sides of the dwelling. This is the regular manner of keeping dried meats or "jerky," strips of which are also hung up uncovered. Hoarding of foods is, however, unfortunately, not a strong instinct with the Indian. For the Coahuillas, as we shall see later, there was not great need of keeping a large supply of food ahead for any part of the year.

38. For preparing the foods for eating, the two most important implements are the primitive mills, the metate and the mortar. The latter

is used mainly for crushing seeds, the former for grains. The Coahuilla mortar is a large, nearly round, stone. It is roughly shaped from a hard boulder with a slightly flattened surface for the bottom. In the top is cut a narrow, shallow cavity, perhaps not over three inches in depth. About this hole is fastened with gum a shallow, flaring basket without a bottom, so that the smaller opening just fits over the hole in the rock. This basketwork, thus rising from the edge of the mortar cavity, keeps the grain and meal from falling to the ground, and makes unnecessary any further excavation of the rock. The pestle is a thick, heavy stone, perhaps ten inches long, each end being bluntly rounded. In using a mortar the woman sits with a leg on each side of it, takes the pestle in both hands and drops it heavily into the mortar. About a full double handful of grain or seed is crushed at once. To reduce this very fine a few spoonfuls of iron pyrites are tossed into the mortar to assist the milling. This is a practice of which I have seen no notice among other Indians. The pyrites is sifted from the meal when the necessary fineness has been attained. The Coahuilla word for the mortar is *ká-wa-val* and for the pestle *pá-u-ul*. The wooden mortars for the mesquite beans have been already noticed.

The Coahuilla metate, called *mál-al* or *ík-ni-vel*, is not a particularly well-shaped article. It usually measures about thirty inches in length by twenty in width; the upper end is fully twice the height of the lower, giving considerable slope to the slightly concave grinding surface, which is increased by resting the upper end on several flat stones. The *"mano"* or rubbing stone, called *ták-ish*, is long, wide, and rather thin; the rubbing surface is nearly flat, the upper side convex. It is held in both hands. In grinding, the woman kneels at the upper end of the metate, puts a little pile of wheat in the middle of the stone and, beginning with the lower edge of the heap, quickly reduces it to a reasonably fine meal. A flat basket, *chi-pat-mal*, is placed under the lower edge of the metate to receive the flour. Both the metates and the mortars are furnished with neat little brooms made of a handful of mescal fibers (*Agave deserti*) and called *si-yu-vish*, with which the meal is brushed from the stone. The grinding is done a little at a time, enough for each day, and forms a regular employment for the women.

A rather curious sifter is used for separating the finer parts of the meal from the coarser, and for removing the iron pyrites grains after milling. The rim is the upper portion of a basket, the bottom removed. Across the smaller opening is stretched a piece of fine woven-wire cloth, obtained from the whites, held in place by abrea. In early times, before the wire cloth was obtainable, I suppose they must have used the fibers of the yucca or agave, or the fibrous covering of the soap-root or "amole" (*Chlorogalum pomerdianum*), which is used by the Moki [Hopi] Indians for sifting (Stevenson 1883:335). The Tulare Indians wove a beautiful basket particularly for a sifter.

39. In methods of cooking the Coahuilla woman is rather limited. Some things are boiled in an olla, a few are roasted among the coals, but almost everything is dried, crushed into meal, and boiled into a mush or "atole." Atole (*atolli)* is the Aztec word for porridge. The boiled mush served daily to the Indians under the missions went by this name, and thus it was adopted into the various Indian vocabularies. "Pozzoli" is a somewhat richer mush containing beans or perhaps a little pulverized dried meat. The Coahuillas call atole *wi-wish-wi-wish.*

THE FOOD PLANTS OF THE COAHUILLA INDIANS

40. As already suggested, to the unsophisticated it would seem that the dry and rocky slopes of the desert's sides, with their curious and repellant plant forms, could yield nothing possible for food, but in reality the severe competition and struggle with aridity have operated to invest desert plants with remarkable nutritive elements. The very hoarding of strength and moisture that goes on in many plants is a promise of hidden nutrition. And, while many plants protect their growth against destruction by animals through the secretion of poisonous or noxious elements, the cunning of the savage woman has taught her how to remove these. Beside every Coahuilla home there stands ever ready the wide *pá-cha-ka-vel,* or leaching basket. The results prove far more than the expectation would warrant.

I cannot pretend to have exhausted the food supply of these Indians, but I have discovered not less than sixty distinct products for nutrition, and at least twenty-eight more utilized for narcotics, stimulants, or medicines, all derived from desert or semi-desert localities, in use among these Indians. To my regret I cannot in all cases announce the botanical name of the plant from which these are derived. A number of these plants, which were seen by me but once, were pointed out and the Indian name and uses described, on a trip through the desert to the Cabeson valley, with a single Indian, Celestin Torte, of Torres mountain, in the summer of 1897. Some, by their very nature, could not be carried along in the saddle, as we were; a few others, gathered and preserved, could not be identified, owing to damaged condition and absence of flower or fruit. This indeterminateness particularly applies to the numerous species of the cactus family, which grow forest-like over many of the rocky cañon sides of the descent to the desert.

The staples of the Coahuillas are fortunately all determined, some of them having a very wide use among the Indian tribes of the Southwest. It is with a description of some of these staples that we will begin.

41. On the desert the main reliance of the Coahuilla Indians is the algaroba or mesquite. This remarkable tree is well known to anyone who has traversed the sandy Southwest. Its range is wide, from the desert slopes of the California mountains, eastward in southern latitudes to Texas. Of the Colorado basin it is the characteristic tree. It grows to a height of from thirty to forty feet. Its wood is close-grained and hard; its leaves small but abundant, and its branches well armored with spines. On the Colorado river and its affluents and overflow streams, the New, and Hardy rivers, it grows abundantly along every slough and about each lagoon. Looking down upon the Colorado desert from the heights below Jacumba pass, the desert appears banded with long stripes of splendid green. In the Cabeson valley, far above the level of the overflow, these trees grow in clumps or *montes*, striking their roots down through the sand to the subirrigation below. Frequently the wind has lodged the sand among these *montes*, until dunes fifteen to twenty feet high have been built up, covering acres in extent and burying all but the upper limbs of the trees—a curious phenomenon.

The fruit of the algaroba or honey mesquite (*Prosopis juliflora*) is a beautiful legumen, four to seven inches long, which hangs in splendid clusters. A good crop will bend each branch almost to the ground, and as the fruit falls, pile the ground beneath the tree with a thick carpet of straw-colored pods. These are pulpy, sweet, and nutritious, affording food to stock as well as to man.

Everywhere in the Colorado country, to the Mojave, Yuma, and Cocopah, as well as to the Coahuilla, they are the staple of life. The Coahuillas gather them in July and August in great quantities, drying them thoroughly and then packing them away in the basket granaries. The beans are never husked, but pod and all are pounded up into an imperfect meal in the wooden mortar. This meal is then placed in earthen dishes and thoroughly soaked. It is then ready to be eaten, and is called by the Coahuillas, *pé-ch-ita*, or *mén-yi-kish*, according as it is, or is not, sifted. A light fermentation, which shortly results, improves it. The mass itself, while requiring vigorous mastication, is sweet and wholesome. It is sometimes rolled into compact balls and carried for food on a journey (*Pacific Railroad Report*, vol. V, p. 98).

According to Mr. Havard, this pulp contains "more than half its weight of assimilative principles, of which the most important is sugar, in the proportion of 25 to 30 per cent."

The "screwbean" or tornillo (*Prosepis pubescens*, Benth.) is less abundant than the algaroba. Its fruit is a cluster of little yellow spirals united at one point. It contains even more saccharine matter than the algaroba, and may be eaten with relish as plucked from the tree. A fermented beverage can be made from this meal and was once much drunk by the Indians of the Colorado river. Major Heinzleman described its use among the Yumas: "The pod mesquite begins to ripen in June, the screwbean a little later. Both contain a great deal of saccharine matter; the latter is so full it furnishes by boiling a palatable molasses, and from the former, by boiling and fermentation, a tolerably good drink may be made" (Emory 1848:vol. 1:112).

Along the overflowed banks of the New river, and elsewhere about the desert's edge, where cloudbursts or freshets send their sudden streams of muddy water out over the sand, there grows up luxuriantly an enormous species of *Chenopodium*. In the New river country I have seen the growth higher than a man's head as he sat on horseback. The stalks are sometimes six inches in diameter. The leaves are eaten readily by horses, and the plant is of much value to parties crossing the desert and to stockmen. Its local name is "careless weed." The seeds are eaten by the Indians and the leaves used for greens. Northward, in the Cabeson and Coyote, a smaller and probably distinct species, identified by Mr. Jepson as *Chenopodium Fremontii*, flourishes after freshets. Its dry branches are covered with seeds which are gathered by the Indians in large quantities, and ground into flour which is baked into little cakes. The Coahuillas call the plant *kit* or *ke-et*. After a good harvest of this *Chenopodium* the edge of the Coyote cañon will be fringed with granaries holding stores of this food.

Another queer little plant that starts up after storm irrigation is the *Salicornia subterminalia*. Its structure is pulpy and almost leafless. I once found it growing abundantly about Indian Wells. The Coahuillas call this plant *hó-at*, and formerly used its seeds for food. These seeds were crushed finely into meal on a metate.

42. The most varied stores of food, however, do not come from the fluviatile plain of the Colorado, but from the forbidding mountains that rise high and abruptly on the westward. The character of these ranges has already been partially noted. Their sides are very steep. There are no ranges of foothills or graduated ascents. From the level of the sea at Palm Springs, San Jacinto rises almost sheer upward to a height of 1,100 feet. Only by certain cañons can these mountains be ascended, even by foot climbers. The Taquitch cañon that enters Palm Valley is said to be insurmountable. Partly because of this precipitancy and partly because grass and protective foliage are wholly absent, there is little opportunity for soil formation on the desert side. The fragments of rock and soil are swept away and deposited in the great alluvial fans that clog for miles the foot of the cañons.

Nevertheless, the mountains support a bewildering variety of plant life. Nowhere could the relationship of plants to their surroundings be more copiously illustrated. While numbers are few and growth is sparse, the species are very numerous. Most of these plants grow in clumps or communities, and afford illustration of the cooperation and mutual support compelled by the desert. From the lower levels of the cañons, by which one begins an ascent, to the summits, where the character of living things suddenly changes, plants and shrubs are met everywhere, growing amid the broken rocks. Curious cacti cover a hillside with an armament of spines, and small annuals dot the sandy levels along the bottoms of the gorges. So it is to these arid but fruitful slopes that the women of the desert plain and the mountain valley both go for food.

Most remarkable of all the plants that flourish in these wastes is the agave, perhaps the most unique and interesting plant of all America. It ranges widely throughout southwestern United States and Mexico with a large number of species, perhaps one hundred in all; and outside of Mexico, where it furnishes "pulque" and "vino mescal," it is used for food by Apaches, the Pah Ute family, and desert tribes in general. By all these Indians it is prepared for food in much the same way. Several species have become familiar, as the "century plants" of California gardens, but they are not handsome plants, except when in bloom, though they give themselves most beautifully to the wants of the Indian.

The life history of all these species is much the same. They come up in little round heads or cabbages. For years this head enlarges, throwing out fibrous leaves armed with a spine at the point. Even in the hot air of the desert it is twelve to fifteen years before the period of flowering is reached. Then from the center of the plant there starts up a stalk, growing with great rapidity. In the larger species this stalk may be twenty to thirty feet high and eighteen inches through at the base. From this stalk clusters of pale yellow blossoms, thousands in number, open in the hot, quivering sunshine. This supreme act ends the life of the plant.

Within the territory of the Coahuillas there is but a single species, the *Agave deserti*, Engelm., which grows abundantly along the eastern base of the coast ranges in San Diego county, and southward into Baja California. It was first discovered by Lieutenant W. H. Emory, of the Mexican Boundary Survey, in 1846 (*Geological Survey of California, Botany*, vol. 2, p. 142). It is a small species with leaves densely clustered, thick and deeply concave, only six to twelve inches long. The scape or stalk is from ten to twelve feet high and slender. The flowers are a bright yellow. From April on, the cabbages and stalks are full of sap and are then roasted. Parties go down from the mountain villages into Coyote cañon for the purpose. Great fire pits or ovens, called *na-chish-em*, are dug in the sands and lined with stones. Fire is kept up in the pit until the stones are thoroughly heated; the mescal heads are then placed in the hole and covered over with grass and earth and left to roast for a day or two. Mescal heads thus cooked consist of fibrous, molasses-colored layers, sweet and delicious to the taste and wonderfully nutritious. Pieces will keep for many years. The agave is called *a-mul*, the sections of the stalk, *u-a-sil*, which are also roasted and, though fibrous, are sweet and good,[2] and the short leaves about the head, *ya-mil*. The yellow blossoms, *amu-sal-em*, are boiled and dried for preservation, and then boiled anew when ready to be eaten. The fibers from the leaves of the agave, *amu-pa-la*, are exceedingly important in manufactures and their uses have been noticed above.

The *Yucca Mohavensis* (Coahuilla *hú-nu-vút*) grows abundantly on various hillsides and sandy cañons of the southern exposure of the San Jacinto range, as well as near the summits of the cañons on the desert slopes. The species is quite different in appearance from the *Yucca Whipplei*, Torr., which grows so abundantly nearer the coast and in the vicinity of Pasadena, and is known as the "Spanish bayonet" or *quijotes*. In the *Yucca Mohavensis* the clusters of spines are very dense about its foot, and its short, thick stump or caudex rises to a height sometimes of six feet from the ground. Its flower stalk or scape is short and thick, but clustered with the delicate waxy flowers of the yucca kind. The fruit, *nin-yil*, appears as plump, sticky, green pods, three to five inches long with big, black seeds filling the center in four rows. These are picked when green and roasted among the coals. They have a sweet, not unpleasant taste, slightly suggestive of roasted green apples. When ripe, the pods are eaten uncooked and are sweet and pleasant, though slightly puckering to the taste.

The *Yucca Whipplei* grows but sparsely in the territory ranged by the Coahuillas. Its stalk, called *pa-nu-ul*, is cut before flowering when full of sap, and roasted in sections in a fire pit for one night. The dates or seed bags, *wa-wal*, are also eaten, as well as the flowers, which when in bloom are picked and cooked in water in an olla. Growing with a clump of agave and yuccas, on the north slope of Torres mountain, I had once pointed out to me a different variety of yucca, probably an unnamed species, which the Coahuillas call *ku-ku-ul*. It is small with slender spines. The head and stalk are roasted and eaten.

43. The variety of trees and shrubs of peculiarly desert character-

istics, which grow over the desert side of the mountains from bases to summits and whose products are made by the Indian to yield food, follow next in our description.

The "ochotilla," or *Fouquiera spinosa* or *splendens*, has already been described. It is a splendid example of desert modification, but its anomalies make it difficult of classification. It grows in clumps on the rocky ridge slopes near the base of the San Jacinto mountains. The Coahuillas, who call it *o-tos*, eat its splendid crimson blossoms, which cluster at the extreme end of its long, drooping branches, as well as its small fruit, which consists of oblong capsules filled with minute seeds. These branches, loaded as they are with thorns, are ingeniously used by the Cocopah Indians far south in the Colorado desert of Baja California in making fences. Two or three of these branches tied above one another between posts makes a barrier through which the most persistent burro will not pass. In this way the Indians enclose many acres of soil, annually inundated by the overflow of Hardy's Colorado river, and subsequently planted to maize, beans, and melons.

In the cañon bottoms as they open out into the desert, grows quite abundantly the "palo verde" (*Parkinsonia Torreyana*), which the Coahuillas call *o-o-wit*. Its bright green bark and abundant, though deciduous foliage, make it a handsome tree in the midst of its surroundings. Its fruit is a slender bean, two to three inches long, which the Coahuillas grind and cook into an atole.

The *Zizyphus Parryi*, Torr., is a very spiny and intricately branched shrub, from five to fifteen feet high. It grows about the springs in the higher parts of the cañons, and bears a small yellowish-red berry or fruit, which is dry and almost hard. The Coahuillas call this plant *o-ot* and use the fruit by pounding it into meal for atole.

Besides the legumens already described there is a third, whose pod furnishes food, though in somewhat sparse quantities. This is the *Acacia Greggii*, Gray. In the San Felipe valley, below Warner's Ranch, there is a great deal of it, and a considerable harvest of pods can be gathered by the Indians of the valley. But it does not grow abundantly in the territory of the Coahuillas and is only occasionally used. It is called *sí-ching-al*.

Higher up on the mountains grow two species of wild plum or cherry. One, the *Prunus ilicifolia*, Walp., has an extensive range along the California coast and had a wide use among the California Indians. It is called by the Mexicans "yslay" and by the Coahuillas *chá-mish*. It grows abundantly in all the cañons of the San Jacinto mountains, its dark, handsome foliage crowding many a pass and hillside. Its fruit is of a reddish-yellow color, and resembles very small gage plums. The pulp is, however, very thin and puckery and the pit preposterously large. It is the kernel of the latter and not the pulp that is mostly utilized. These plums are gathered in very large quantities in August and are spread in the sun until the pulp is thoroughly shrunken and dried. The thin shells of the pits are then easily broken open and the kernels extracted. These are crushed in the mortar, leached in the sand basket, and boiled into the usual atole. The other plum tree has with some question been identified by Mr. Jepson as the *Prunus Andersonii*, Gray. I found it growing along the eastern summits of the San Jacinto range. Its fruit somewhat resembles the *Zizyphus* and was formerly eaten by the Coahuillas, who called it *cha-wa-kal*.

The *Prunus demissa*, a shrub with a wide green leaf, grows about the springs and moist cañons of Coahuilla valley. Its fruit is a small red berry called *a-tut*.

A small grayish-green shrub, doubtfully identified by Mr. Jepson as *Halodiscus discolor*, Maxim, is called by the Coahuillas *tét-nut*. I have never seen the fruit, but the Indians say that though small it is good food.

Before dismissing the truly desert plants that yield food, a word is merited by the palms. These have been referred to above. They grow in long, waving lines along the gorges leading into the desert wherever water stands in pools or seeps through the sandy bottoms. Beneath the wide fronds the dates grow in great clusters, supported by a strong but drooping stalk. These dates are very small and the seeds are disproportionately large, but early in the fall, when they ripen, the Coahuillas lasso the clusters and draw them down for food. Swarms of bees surround the fruit as it ripens, and in the fronds of the palms are multitudes of "yellow jacket's" nests. The Indians of Lower California cut out the heart or center of the top of young palms and eat them with great relish. I have not known the Coahuillas to indulge in these "palmitos."

44. In the valleys near the summit of the range and especially in the

Piñon Flats are groves of the *Juniperus occidentalis,* Hook., low evergreen trees, with thin, shreddy bark. The fruit, a bluish-black drupe
the size of a small marble, is eaten by the Coahuillas and called by
them *is-wut.*

The acorn was one of the most generally used foods of the Indians
of the Pacific coast. Its use was noticed by Cabrillo, the first white
explorer to navigate these waters. "They eat acorns and a grain which
is as large as maize and is white, of which they make dumplings. It
is good food" (Cabrillo, *Relacion ó Diario,* translation by Mr. R. S.
Evans). Certain parts of the coast, the Upper San Joaquin valley and
the mountains of the Coast Range are thickly covered with forests of
this stately tree. There are no less than fourteen species of oaks in the
whole of California and about eight are found in the southern part of
the state (*Botany of California, United States Geological Survey*).
Their fruit contains "starch, fixed oil, citric acid, and sugar, as well as
astringent and bitter principles." The largest and most palatable acorn
is that of the white oak, or Mexican "roble" (*Quereus lobata*), "common throughout the state, on the plains and in the foothills, in the
southern part of the state somewhat higher in the mountains." It was
mostly from this tree that the Indians of the past supplied themselves.

All the "live oaks" also, among them the *Quercus Englemanni,*
yield palatable acorns. There are several desert and shrub species, *Q.
undulata,* Torr., *Q. oblongifolia,* and *Q. Wislienzi, var. fructescens,*
the "desert oak" of the Southwest, from three to ten feet high. *Q. agrifolia,* Née, is the only one of the black oaks affording food to the
Indians. It is the coast live-oak of California, the "encino" of the
Mexicans. The oak is, however, somewhat rare within the habitat of
the Coahuillas and the acorn is not to them of great economic importance. They do not put the same dependence upon it as did the Indians
along the coast.

The *Quercus dumosa,* Nutt., which has a thick, large fruit, grows
on the Coahuilla mountain and is gathered in considerable quantities
by the Indians of Coahuilla valley. This acorn is called by them *kwín
yil.* It is ground in the mortar and leached in the sand basket. Dr.
Havard reports that the sand mixed with the meal by washing has "a
decided effect upon the teeth. My informant, a medical officer, tells me
that he has seen an Indian forty-five years old with the crowns of his

otherwise healthy teeth half gone, while in Indians sixty years old it is not uncommon to see all the teeth worn down even with the gums" (Havard 1895). Although the sand basket as a means for preparing food is in constant use among the Coahuilla Indians, I have never myself noticed any such effects.

The piñon or pine nut is a very important article of food. The lower limit of the pineries, in southern California, is, of course, high, being almost everywhere about 5,000 feet, and it is only by reason of the fact that the Coahuillas have penetrated into the mountains from the desert that this source of food is available to them at all. The summits of Torres and Coahuilla mountains and the higher San Jacinto peaks are covered with pines of several species; the gigantic sugar pine of the Pacific slope (*P. Lambertiana*, Dougl.) with a cone a foot and a half in length, the Mexican nut pine (*P. Sembroides*), and (*P. Parryana*, Eng.), and also the single-leafed or Nevada nut pine (*P. Monophylla*), so precious to the Indians of the Great Basin. These nuts are gathered in large quantities, generally in the late fall of the year. Mr. B. H. Dutcher, of the Death Valley Expedition of 1891, has given a careful account of piñon gathering among the Panamints on the west side of Death Valley (Dutcher 1893:337). The tree was the *P. monophylla*, which has a small cone three inches long. These were pulled and beaten from the trees with a pronged stick and collected in light packing baskets while still sticky with gum. They were then piled on a heap of brush and roasted, which dried the pitch and spread the leaves of the cone. The nuts were then jarred out by a heavy blow from a stone on the apex of the cone. The nuts were winnowed from the chaff by tossing them from a flat basket in the breeze. The Coahuillas harvest the nuts in precisely the same manner. Sometimes in midsummer the cones are beaten from the trees, before the ripened harvest time, thoroughly roasted in a fire, split open with a hatchet and the nuts extracted. Piñones are called by the Coahuillas *te-wat-em*; the cones *te-vat*, and the little almond-like cavities in which the nuts lie and which are exposed in section when the cone is split open are called *he-push* or the "eyes" of the *te-vat*. The pine most used is the *Pinus monophylla*.

45. The sambucus or elder is of well-known value to the Indians of North America and many are the purposes it serves. The Spaniards in

this state fully appreciated it and gave it the name by which it is still well known, "sauco." The *Sambucus Mexicana*, Presl., is highly prized by the Coahuillas. By them it is called *hun-kwat*. Throughout the months of July and August the berries are gathered in large quantities. The little clusters are usually dried carefully on the drying floor and so preserved in considerable amounts. When wanted they are cooked into a rich sauce that needs no sweetening. They are delicious thus prepared. An Indian family during this season of the year will subsist largely on these messes of "sauco."

Several species of the manzanita, an exceedingly handsome tree or shrub with a rich red-colored bark and small evergreen leaves, grow on these mountains. It has a red fruit and is very common. The "great berried manzanita" (*Arcostaphylos glauca*) is common throughout the coast. Manzanita is a Spanish word, the diminutive of "manzana," meaning "little apple." The fruit is much enjoyed by the Coahuillas and is called *ta-tu-ka*. It is eaten raw and is also dried, pounded into a flour, and mixed with water.

The sumac (*Rhus trilobata*, Nutt.), the twigs of which are so important in basket making, bears a very small red berry, *sel-it-toi*, which is very sour but much used both fresh and dried. Soaked in water it makes a refreshing drink. The use of the rhus was noticed by Dr. Edward Palmer (1878).

46. Perhaps the most important of the seed foods used by the Indians is the justly famed "chia" (*Salvia Columbariae* Benth.), called by the Coahuillas *pá-sal*. The plant is one of the smallest of the sage family. It grows up from an annual root with a slender branching stem, terminated by several curious whorls containing the seeds. These are dark, round, flat bodies, that have a slippery, uncertain feeling to the touch. The genus Salvia has an exceedingly wide range and use as a food plant. According to Dr. Havard the *Salvia Polystarchia*, Ort., is largely cultivated in northern and central Mexico. These seeds are rich in mucilage and oil. "After careful roasting they are ground into meal, which, when thrown into water, expands to several times its original bulk, the mucilage rapidly dissolving. By adding lemon and sweetening a very popular Mexican beverage is produced" (1896).

Chia was a staple food with the Indians of the Pacific coast. Large quantities, already parched, have been taken from graves on the Santa

Barbara channel (*United States Geological Survey West of the 100th Meridian*, vol 7, pp. 37, 40, 79, 80, etc.). The seeds are gathered by the Coahuillas with the seed fan and flat basket, and are parched and ground. The meal is then mixed with about three times as much wheat flour and the whole pounded up together. It makes a dark looking meal. This is "pinole," called by the Coahuillas *to-at*. It is an old and famous preparation. Molina gives the following definition of its constituents as made in Mexico: "Pinolli la harhia de mayz y chia antes que la deslian" (*Vocabulario en lengua Castilliana y Mexicana*, in Bancroft 1883:374, note 90). A little sugar is usually mixed with it. In this shape it is a much prized article of food with all who have become acquainted with its nutritive and reviving qualities. Experienced prospectors and desert travelers carry a little bag of it with them, and when the warm, alkali water holes are reached, a few teaspoonfuls of the pinole in a quart cupful of the water seems to neutralize somewhat its dangerous qualities and make a refreshing drink more nourishing than gruel.

Pinole, by the Coahuillas, is sometimes baked into little cakes or biscuits. Either way chia is used, it is very good; has a pleasant, nutty flavor, and is exceedingly wholesome. Moreover, it grows in considerable quantity through the mountain ranges of the Coahuillas, and in the early summer ollas stored with these seeds stand in every home, and throughout the cooler hours of the day and evening there is ever a woman grinding at her mill.

Beside the salvia, several other plants yield seeds that attract the Indian woman and keep her busy through the months of May and June with her *yi-kow-a-pish* and *chi-pat-mal*. Some of these seeds are very beautiful, and possess a real fascination for the eye and touch. The seeds of the *Lasihenia glabrata* (Lindb.), called by the Coahuillas *ák-lo-kal*, in mass resemble iron filings, being of a dark color and fine elongated shape. They are prepared by being pounded up into a very fine flour, which is eaten dry.

But the most beautiful little seed of all is that of the small crucifer called "pepper grass," *Sisimbrium canescens*, Coahuilla *ás-il*, a tiny reddish-brown seed, round, and flat in shape. It is ground up, cooked in a large quantity of water, and eaten with a little salt.

The *Atriplex lentiformus*, Watson, one of the "salty sages," is found in the Coahuilla valley and on the slopes of the Sierras. Its seeds somewhat resemble the chia. They are prepared for food by grinding and cooking with salt and water. It is called *ká-sil*.

The dry flats and valleys of the Coahuilla mountains are frequently closely planted with wormwood, the *Artemisia tridentata*, Nutt. Its feathery foliage whitens the landscape, and for long distances its pungent odor dominates over every other fragrance. The seeds ripen late in the fall, and are gathered by the Coahuillas and pounded up for pinole. The plant and seed are named by the Coahuillas *wík-wut*.

47. The flowers or buds, in the case of a number of plants, yield desirable food. The mescal or agave has already been referred to for its many nutritive and useful products. The use of the yellow blossoms, *amu-sal-em*, of the *Agave deserti*, has been mentioned above. The flower crowned tops of the succulent roasting stalks are invariably saved and the splendid clusters of blossoms carried home, there to be boiled and then dried for preservation. I have some, thus prepared, in my possession, that have kept perfectly for five years. They are still sweet and palatable, even inviting to the taste. The incomparable waxy flowers of the *Yucca Whipplei* are prepared for food in the same way, by boiling in an olla of water.

The use of the sweet scarlet blossoms of the *Fouquiera spinosa* has also been noted.

The large sumac *Rhus ovata,* which grows in great clumps throughout southern California and whose broad green leaves ornament many a dingy range of chaparral, has a small blossom which grows in full clusters and is of economic importance as bee-feed. These clusters of the sumac, *ná-kwit,* are cooked in water and eaten.

A species of wild rose, common in southern California, grows along the usually dry washes of the Coahuilla valley and hills. It is either *Rosa Californica* or *ramoscina*. It is called *ush-ul*, and the capsules, *ush-ul-toi*, are picked and eaten to a small extent.

One of the most curious ways of preparing food is the treatment of the small slender capsules of the bladderpod (*Isomeris arborea*, Nutt.), a shrub with a hard yellow wood. These little pods, so the Indians have informed me, are gathered and cooked in a small hole in the ground with hot stones.

Beside the leaves of the Chenopodium, the tiny dark leaves of the *Sueda suffiructescens*, Watson, whose use as a dye for basket materials has already been noticed, are boiled for greens.

A tall annual plant, unidentified, but called by the Coahuillas *ten-il*, which has a yellow flower and large leaves, is cooked in an olla and eaten.

One of the cancer roots, *Aphyllon Ludovicianum*, Gray, called by the Coahuillas *mis-a-lem*, grows plentifully in the sandy washes. It has large succulent roots, yellow or white, and in the springtime, before the plant blossoms, and while the roots are young and tender, they are dug up and roasted in the coals for food.

The *Astragulus*, "rattle-snake weed" or "loco weed," is a genus well known to California stockmen. It has numerous species, somewhat difficult of determination. Several species, at least, are poisonous to cattle and sheep, and it is universally believed to madden horses, dispossessing them of self-control and making them subject to fits of ungovernable action, in other words, "locoing" them. One such species, called by the Coahuillas *kash-lem*, has a curious use as a flavoring principle. By summer time the leaves fall away from the sere and yellow branches of these plants, and they are covered by quantities of straw-colored pods as big as the joint of a man's thumb. These quiver and rattle with every motion of the air, and give it one of the designations by which it is known. These pods, according to Celestin Torte, are pounded up and mixed with beans, and perhaps other articles of food, as a spice.

48. Among the fruits most important to the Indian inhabitants of the Southwest stand those of the cactus family. There are over fifty species in the United States and a majority of these are found in California.

The Mexican prickly pear or "tuna" (*Opuntia Tuna*, Mill) is said by Dr. Havard to have been brought to the Pacific coast from Mexico, where it had been cultivated from time immemorial. It was planted in hedges about the missions and ranch-houses, where it thrives still in picturesque clusters and is now thoroughly naturalized. Its fruit is the well-known "Indian fig." While it has not been planted anywhere on the reservations of the Coahuillas, they sometimes obtain the fruit from other Indians of the valleys. The cactus plant is called by the Coahuillas *na-vit* and the little budlike fruit *na-vit-yu-lu-ku* or "the little heads of the cactus."

There are numerous species of cactus throughout the mountains down to the desert level. About a dozen yield fruit products utilized by the Coahuillas. In most cases it is the ripened fruit or "fig" that is eaten. In several cases it is the abundant seeds, in others, the buds and succulent joints of stalk. Except in a few instances I can do no more in the way of identification of these species than to give a description of the plant and state its uses and Indian name.

The *Opuntia basilaris* is an especially valuable cactus plant to the Coahuillas. It is one of the small varieties and has a tender slate-colored stem in flat joints. The young fruit in early summer is full of sweetness. These buds are collected in baskets, being easily broken off with a stick. The short, sparse spines are wholly brushed off with a bunch of grass or a handful of brush twigs. The buds are then cooked or steamed with hot stones in a pit for twelve hours or more. This cactus is called *má-nal*. Mr. Coville describes exactly the same use of this plant by the Panamints (1895:6, 1892:350). This cooked cactus is, he says, called *nä-vo*. I would call attention to the similarity of this word to the general Coahuilla word for cactus fruit, *na-vit*. No vocabulary of the Panamints has ever been published,[3] but they are undoubtedly of the same great stock as the Coahuillas and such verbal similarities are to be expected.

Mu-tal is another of the opuntia, with flat, ugly jointed stems, growing low and spreading over the ground in the most arid stretches of the valleys. The flat joints, the size of one's palm, are crowded along their edges with buds as big as the last joint of a man's thumb. They are gathered in large quantities, brushed, and dried. They are often stored for subsequent use, and when needed for food are prepared by boiling in water with a little salt and lard. Very frequently also the fruit is allowed to ripen for its seeds. The figs, after being dried, are spread out on a hard, smooth, dirt floor and then the woman sits down beside the pile of cactus heads and with a flail, made from the leaf stem of the desert palm, thoroughly threshes out the seeds. These are then winnowed from the chaff and stored for winter use. Along through the winter, as needed for food, they are pounded into meal and cooked into an atole. These seeds are called *wi-al* and they are obtained from several species of cactus besides the *mu-tal*.

There are two cacti growing along the slopes of Torres mountain that in growth and structure much resemble the *Opuntia Tuna*. I have not seen them in bloom and know nothing of their flowers. Both yield luscious fruit in large quantities. *Ti-nup-em* might readily be mistaken for a neglected and stunted growth of the cultivated tuna. *Na-u-tem* is not so thrifty and grows low on the ground. Its flat stems have exceptionally long spines, two to three inches. The *a-yu-vi-vi* is a very small cactus, only about four inches high and covered with little hooked spines. It has a very small, sparse fruit.

The *cho-kal* is a very furry cactus, with round jointed stems two to three feet high. It is light brown in color and grows in communities, sometimes covering a rocky cañon side for a half mile to the exclusion of almost everything else. It throws off extremely disagreeable balls of spines which fasten in a horse's fetlocks and give instant trouble. Its fruit, which I have never seen, is said to be very good.

U-a-chim is one of the cylindrical or barrel-shaped cacti, light-colored and furry. It has an edible fruit.

Ko-pash is the famed "nigger head," the *Echinocactus cylindricis*. It appears above the sand simply as a round fluted globe, a little larger than a man's head. It is covered with spines and bears a small edible fig. But its chief value does not lie in its fruit, but in its succulent and thirst-relieving interior. No plant could be more admirably contrived as a reservoir, and the thick tough rind and protective spines enclose an interior that is full of water. This plant is often resorted to by thirsty travelers and, according to the stories told over the desert, frequently saves life.

49. A review of the food supply of these Indians forces in upon us some general reflections or conclusions. First, it seems certain that the diet was a much more diversified one than fell to the lot of most North American Indians. Roaming from the desert, through the mountains to the coast plains, they drew upon three quite dissimilar botanical zones. There was no single staple, on the production of which depended the chances of sufficiency or want. Any one of several much

used products might be gathered in sufficient quantities to carry the entire tribe through a year of subsistence. There was really an abundant supply of wild food, far more than adequate, at nearly all times of the year, for the needs of the several thousand Indian inhabitants of former times, although hardly a score of white families will find a living here after all the Indians are gone. And the secret of this anomaly lies in the fact that the Indian drew his stores of food from hillsides and canons, where the white man looks for nothing and can produce nothing. The territory is a very large one, perhaps 4,000 square miles of cañons, and mountains, rough plains, and sandy deserts. In all of it, as we have seen, there are few spots of beauty; only the valleys of pines, the wonderful cañons, of palms, and the green potreros about the springs; while over most broods the hot, throbbing silence of the desert. And yet this habitat, dreary and forbidding as it appears to most, is after all a generous one. It bears some of the most remarkable food plants of any continent. Nature did not pour out her gifts lavishly here, but the patient toiler and wise seeker she rewarded well. The main staples of diet were, indeed, furnished in most lavish abundance. Let us notice a few instances. The crops of legumens, that annually fall from the splendid mesquite groves of the Cabeson or the New river country, could not be wholly utilized by a population that numbered a hundred thousand souls. I have seen the mesquite beans fallen so heavily beneath the trees in the vicinity of Martinez as to carpet the sand for miles. Centals could be gathered about every tree. Hundreds of horses and cattle that ranged the valley, to say nothing of the busy women that had crowded their granaries full, effected no visible diminution of the supply.

In the splendid moonlight, after the heat of the day, from all directions there would come the busy thud of pestle in wooden mortar, as the women worked leisurely at the mills, while jest and laughter broke the continuity of their toil. Every bush or tree was dropping fatness. The desert seemed the very land of plenty, where the manna fell at each man's door.

Or, consider the agave. The various portions of a single plant might keep a family in food for a week. It is a splendid food, delicious, nourishing, and when roasted seemingly superior to deterioration. The lower levels of the cañons, of the San Jacinto range or the sides of the Coyote valley could annually feed an army with agave. The "chamish" or "yslay" (*Prunus Andersonii*) in certain parts of the mountains grows very abundantly and yields splendidly. A single cañon often contains enough to supply an entire village with meal of pounded pits. Within the habitat of the Coahuillas scores of such cañons could be found.

The road from Coahuilla valley down to Ahuanga creek descends along the bottom of a gorge. The sides of this cañon are covered with *Yucca Mohavensis*. In July or early August these palm-like trees, for so they almost are, are all crowded with stalks hung with heavy pods, more fruit drying in the sun than the entire tribe could devour. The groves of oaks and pines in the higher valleys of San Jacinto; the abundant crops of chia and other seed plants; the elder berry, so greatly enjoyed, that frequently families will live for weeks on little else; all of these can be found in inexhaustible quantities. Another fact very favorable to the Indians is the long season over which the gathering of these staples is distributed. The harvest time opens in April, with the budding out of agave and yucca stalks, and from this time until late fall there is no month without its especial product. The chia and other seed plants are ready for the fan in May and June, the wild plums in June and July, the mesquite and sambucus in August, and the piñons and acorns from September on. For only about four months of winter was it necessary to hoard food. The ollas and basket granaries were sufficient storehouses.

50. The uses to which the majority of these food plants have been put are passing away and will not be revived. The Indians are beginning to earn a large part of their support by civilized labor. They are the best sheep shearers in southern California, riding in bands through the country in spring and fall. Many work through the summer in orchards and vineyards and in fruit drying and packing establishments.

On the reservations they raise cattle, especially in the mountain Coahuilla valley. They plant maize, beans, peas, potatoes, watermelons, squashes and, in the mountains, also wheat and barley. All but the last two require irrigation, and for this purpose they make in the mountains small reservoirs, by damming and deepening the springs, and dig rude *zanjas* or irrigating ditches. In the Cabeson valley they conduct the water short distances out of the cañons, in which it trickles, or at certain villages they irrigate small patches from their wells. The vegetables are boiled or fried; the melons are a favorite fruit, as among all Indians; the barley is cut for hay for the stock, and the wheat is threshed and ground on the metate to make flour. The threshing is an interesting scene. The hay is piled in a small stack upon the threshing floor, a circular, hardened plat of ground, called *wa-ki-wanut*. Indian boys then ride ponies round this stack, while a man slowly rakes the straw well under the horses' feet. An hour's hard riding will thresh out a good-sized pile. The men then take rakes, *wa-kau-vil*, and draw off the straw. Rude pitchforks, *sal-sal-awit*, are also used. Then the women gather up the grain and chaff in large baskets, *se-kwá-vel-em*. A winnowing cloth, *ke-la*, is spread on the ground. The winnowing is done in the afternoon, when the fresh wind from the Pacific reaches the valley. A woman fills her *chi-pat-mal* or winnowing basket and, standing on the cloth, holds her burden high above her head and shakes the contents slowly out. The chaff is carried away by the wind while the heavy grain falls at her feet. Heads that the horses' hoofs do not thresh out are carefully gathered, placed in a deep *se-kwa-vel*, and the woman steps in and tramps the seed out with her bare feet. The grain is either stored in the basket granary, *maí-a-not*, or put into gunny sacks, *ków-kwa-nil*. Two women will winnow a couple of centals in the course of an afternoon's leisurely work.

51. It is an interesting question from what source these Indians first became acquainted with agriculture, the use of irrigation, and with those plants indigenous to America—maize, beans, pumpkins. The California Coast Indians do not seem to have been planters. Cabrillo's *Relacion*, however, records repeatedly that the Indians told them that there was much maize growing in the interior. But this statement is far from final. They may and they may not have understood one another. He seems nowhere to have seen maize growing or in the possession of the coast Indians, though he noticed their other important foods, the maguey, seeds, and the acorn.

On the other hand, when the Spaniards discovered New Mexico, they found the Pueblo Indians cultivating maize, beans, and squashes. The Cocopahs and lower Colorado tribes are described by Don Jose Cortez (Report, date 1799, translated in *Pacific Railroad Narrative*

Report on Indian Tribes, p. 117), in 1799, as raising an abundance of the above vegetables. So did the Mojaves, Chemehuevis, and Yumas when first seen by American troops and explorers. On the banks of the Colorado irrigation is not needed, neither is any preparation of the soil. The stream simply overflows and leaves rich, damp, alluvial strips along its sides. All that is necessary here is to press a seed down into the mud and leave it alone. In places such as this agriculture will begin if anywhere. Lieutenant Michler reported in 1851 that the Yumas even cultivated the "seed grass" for food, preparing the seed afterwards by grinding it in a mortar of mesquite wood and kneading the meal into cakes to be dried in the sun (Emory 1848:112). This cultivation was also carried on far out on the Colorado desert along the channel of the New river, not many miles north from the Hardy's Colorado where the Cocopahs still raise abundant crops on land submerged each summer by the overflow. Along the New river lagoons are village sites where many Indians once lived on the crops they produced, but which have now been abandoned, owing to the increasing aridity of the desert. Dr. Veatch, in 1857, entering the desert here from the California side, stopped at a lagoon not far from the Salton basin, where his guide, a Diegueño Indian, told him "that this secluded spot was his early home. He was born here and the tribe he now rules over here had their lodges and lived in abundance on the maize, melons, and frijoles that he described as growing here with a luxuriousness unknown to any place away from the so-called desert."

These same facts are recorded by a correspondent in the Alta California of November, 1858, and have been also related to me by Diegueño Indians now living in Jacumba pass, just south of the American boundary line in Lower California. Their retirement from the desert seems to have been about seventy years ago, and was due to an interruption of the overflow into the desert of the Colorado, which was not regularly resumed until 1849. It would now be possible to resume life once more along the New river channel, if there were Indians to make the move. Now, it is only a few miles north from here, about the base of the San Jacinto mountains that the Coahuillas have long lived. Here they have cultivated maize and frijoles for certainly a great many years. It is easier to imagine that the knowledge of agriculture with the seed of corn, squash, and bean came to them long ago across the desert, than that they learned of these things only in this century from the Spaniards. Westward of the Coast Range, however, where artificial irrigation is necessary, cultivation of the soil may not have preceded the missions, although Mr. Taylor years ago made interesting mention of finding on the Sesepe river, near Piru, "remains of ancient acequias or irrigating canals, made exactly after the plans of those of the Gila, covering a space of some four hundred acres," and which he suggests is "the only thing of the kind to be met with in California" (Taylor 1860–63).

In concluding this paragraph I cannot forbear calling attention to the fact that change of diet is not an unmixed good. Doubtless it is an inevitable change, but it has wrought havoc in the health of many families. The transition from a plain atole to a mess of hot food, fried in grease, is more than an Indian's constitution can abide. I believe the heavy mortality among children, the decay of teeth and skin eruptions that are appearing, are due in large part to the abandonment of native foods for those of civilized life.

ETHNOGRAPHY OF
THE OWENS VALLEY PAIUTE
Julian H. Steward

Julian Steward used his Californian fieldwork as the basis for important theoretical syntheses. Drawing upon the geographical approaches of his teacher,
Alfred Kroeber, Steward became known for his ecological analyses and cultural
evolutionism. This work was largely responsible for forming the field of cultural
ecology—the relation of social systems to environmental and technological
circumstances—later represented in Californianist studies by Lowell Bean.

At the age of sixteen, Julian Haynes Steward (1902–72) enrolled in a prep
school at Deep Springs, just east of the Owens Valley in the eastern California
desert. There he became interested in the local Paiute and Shoshone Indians.
Steward spent his freshman year at Berkeley, where he discovered anthropology, before transferring to Cornell, where his majors of zoology and geology
prepared him for later research on food and subsistence (B.A., 1925). He
returned to Berkeley in the fall of 1925, taking his Ph.D. in 1929. Steward taught
archaeology at the University of Michigan (1928–30), University of Utah
(1930–33), and was a lecturer at UC Berkeley (1933–34). Between 1934 and
1936, he spent many months in the Basin and Plateau regions of California,
Nevada, Oregon, and Idaho. His classic *Basin-Plateau Aboriginal Sociopolitical
Groups* (1938) demonstrated his interest in causation and cross-cultural explanation. Between 1935 and 1946, Steward worked at the Smithsonian's
Bureau of American Ethnology (especially as editor of the *Handbook of South
American Indians*, 1946–59). During his influential period of teaching at
Columbia University (1946–52), he became a pioneer in area studies by
investigating the transformation of peasant societies in Puerto Rico. Steward
served as a research professor at the University of Illinois from 1952 until his
retirement in 1970.

University of California Publications in American Archaeology and Ethnology
(1933), 33(3). Pp. 238–42, 246–57.

The Owens Valley Paiute are the southernmost of the Northern Paiute, a Shoshonean group who occupied most of northern Nevada. Thus, although living in California, they are more closely related to groups living much further east. Julian Steward based his monograph on two visits of about six weeks each to the Owens Valley and Mono Lake during the summers of 1927 and 1928 (sponsored by UC Berkeley), plus a short visit in December, 1931.[1] Steward noted that the local Paiute made their living "by ranch and highway labor, occasional hunting, pine-nut excursions, and some seed gathering" (p. 237–38).

Due to its length and list-like nature, the section on "Other Food Plants" (pp. 242–46) has been omitted here.

SEASONAL OCCUPATIONS

Summer. People kept headquarters in valley villages, fishing, seed gathering in the valley or hills—sometimes traveling as far as Fish Lake valley from Big Pine for certain seeds—or making trips north in small family groups for piuga [caterpillars].

Fall. When seeds were gathered, people of large districts assembled at certain villages for a week or so of dancing and gambling, and communal rabbit drives. These were the only communal endeavors, except occasional hunting and fishing parties.

Winter. Pinenut expeditions of small groups wintered in the mountains in the timber when crops were good. When pinenuts failed, they wintered at valley villages, eating stored seeds gathered in summer and fall.

Spring. People wintering in mountains moved to valleys, bringing remaining pinenuts.

Hunting occurred at all seasons, communal hunting chiefly in the fall. Seasonal movements were within an average radius from the valley village of 15 or 20 miles, within prescribed bounds the territory being owned by the district.

Daily activities. People arose before daybreak. Hunters in bed after sunrise had bad luck. Two meals a day were eaten, one at early morning and one in the afternoon. Women gathered seeds and men hunted, when food could be had, to lay up supplies for future use. Leisure time was spent gambling. Winter evenings were devoted to relating myths. In valley villages, old and young men lived at sweat houses, smoking, talking, and gambling.

SEED GATHERING AND PREPARATION

Women, working in groups, gathered seeds by beating them from plants with seed beaters, tanugu (Bishop), tsigu (Mono Lake), into conical carrying baskets, cudusi. Mixed seeds were later separated by sifting through a twined basket. Heads of some plants were picked, carried home, threshed and winnowed—e.g., sunflowers. Tubers and roots were dug with sharp pointed sticks, tavodo, of a hard species of mountain mahogany, *Cercocarpus*, called tunap, or robbed from rodent stores.

Seeds and roots, collected mostly in summer and fall, were stored in the ground in pits lined with grass and covered with grass and earth against future need. The California elevated cache was not used.[2]

For eating, seeds were ground on a metate, mat[a], a slab of rock about 12 by 18 inches and 2 to 5 inches thick,[3] with a muller or mano, tusu, a flattish, hard rock roughly rectangular and worn on both sides. To remove husks they were then winnowed. Sometimes roasting in coals preceded this, the meal being ground into a flour and eaten dry. Meal was also boiled in pots in Owens valley to make mush, meat frequently being added. It was stirred with the looped stick. At Mono lake mush was made in baskets with hot rocks. Generally several species were mixed, pinenuts being the base.

In Death Valley, the mortar and pestle replaced the metate. Mr. Eickbaum at Stovepipe Wells has a large collection of mortars, some being tree sections up to nearly 2 feet tall and 12 inches in diameter, others spherical boulders about 10 inches in diameter with holes about 4 inches in diameter and 6 inches deep. Pestles, worked and unworked, were of stone, about 12 inches long, 3 inches in diameter.

One was said to be 3 feet long by 2 ½ to 3 inches in diameter. Indians at Furnace Creek were observed pounding screw beans in a tree section mortar, 12 inches tall, 10 inches in diameter with a hole about 4 by 6 inches. An iron bar served as pestle. Metates and mullers of the Paiute type though occurring in Death Valley were rare. Furnace Creek Inn has several metates from the vicinity, one having a double depression, suggesting the Utah type found in Pueblo II mounds.

The food plants listed below were identified in Owens Valley by Jack Stewart, Tom Stone, and several others. As names and uses assigned by different people were very similar, plant lore must have been known to all individuals. Bridgeport Tom identified those at Mono Lake.

PINENUTS

Pinenut or piñon, tuva´'[a] (*Pinus monophylla* Torr. & Frem.), occurred chiefly in the arid ranges east of the Sierra Nevada mountains, especially in the Inyo and White mountains between 6000 and 9000 feet altitude. It is the most important Paiute food plant. Abundant crops lasted through the winter and into summer. Individuals gathered 30 to 40 bushels in the fall.[4] Good crops were irregular, coming every few years.

Ownership. Each district owned pinenut territory. Permission to gather nuts was sometimes granted others but trespass was resented and led to quarrels or rock throwing. This was the most frequent trouble between otherwise peaceful Paiute districts. Property rights were respected because of tradition and fear of magic. Muir says that white men were killed for felling piñons (1917:220–21). Pitana patu people went north to tupi mada or, if that crop failed, east to Black canyon on the western slopes of the White mountains. Tovowahamatu people went into the White mountains....

Harvest and storage. The district head man decided when it was pinenut time, and organized and led the harvesters. Bob Riddle did this until recently at Big Pine. Large parties went, prepared to spend the fall or winter. Muir saw, about 1870, Mono Lake Paiute making ready long beating poles, bags, baskets, mats, and sacks; a large party went out, men, women and children taking part in the harvest (1917:221–22).

By means of wooden hooks tied with buckskin to long poles, men pulled from the trees cones containing nuts sealed in with pitch. Many ripe nuts fell from cones. Women gathered these from blankets and sacks spread on the ground under the trees and packed them to camp in conical carrying baskets, ku'dus. The women wore basketry hats for protection against pitch and the tumpline. Men wore no hats. Small crops were taken down to the valley by the women in conical baskets, by the men in buckskin bags slung over their shoulders.

When crops were good, most Owens Valley people wintered in the mountains, living in "mountain houses" scattered through the timber. Proximity to springs was preferred; but snow could provide water. Cones were stored on sunny hillsides in bins, unagāunu'n, which were lined with rocks and covered with needles, boughs, and finally rocks. Nuts fallen from cones were kept in pits lined and covered with grass, huki'va.[5] These were opened as needed, the huki'va first until the loose nuts were exhausted, then the unagāunu'n. The cones were sun dried (sometimes roasted) until open, threshed in a pit, and the nuts winnowed from the dirt in a winnowing basket, patsa'. Nuts remaining when spring came were packed to the valley. Subsequent trips were made for any left behind.

Cooking.   Cones and sometimes loose nuts were roasted over night, covered with coals, dirt, and boughs. The nuts, now all loose, were winnowed from the dirt. Nuts were also quickly roasted in a loose twined basketry tray holding coals, the tray being shaken to avoid burning. Such a tray, only slightly charred, was collected from Fish Lake Valley Shoshoni. Rubbing on a metate loosened the shells and winnowing removed them. Nuts were eaten whole (boiled in water and called unavu'cizau'an); or dry, as flour (ground on a metate, then dumped into a tight basket and the hard particles picked out); or as a paste of water and flour called unava'n (unava'n is sometimes frozen in cold weather); or as a soup or mush of varying water content (cooked in a clay pot, stirred with a looped stick), called untas'igan.[6] The middle and index fingers were dipped into this soup and sucked. Other seeds, e.g., tupusi'i, wai, etc., and recently wheat, were often added to pinenut dishes.

ACORNS

Acorns, though of minor importance, were used according to the California "acorn complex." Acorns were secured from the Western Mono or were gathered (two species) from small areas in Owens valley: a small grove of *Quercus kelloggii* Newb., tcakicavu'[u] (the acorns called tciginu), on Division creek, and *Q. palmeri?*, wiya, on Oak creek and near Fort Independence and the Fish hatchery. These were pounded in mortars (pa'ha), usually in bedrock occurring at several places,[7] with pestles, pahawunanu. No basket hoppers were used. Metates served for other seeds. The acorns were placed in or on a sack in a crater in a small hill of clean sand, and hot water was poured through until they were mushy; then they were boiled into mush, stirred in pots—never in baskets—with the looped mush stirrer. Meat, especially rabbit, was usually added. Andrew Glenn said the Lone Pine treatment was similar, but the metate was used and the leeching pit was lined with bark.

Mono Lake stored acorns with shells removed in pits lined and covered with sage bark (like pinenut caches). When wintering in Yosemite, they stored them in the shell in elevated baskets, winugupi, like the Miwok. They ground, then leeched them in pits about four feet in diameter, gravel-lined, by pouring hot water through. The acorns were then put into a semi-spherical basket, wavoi', with water, one person heating rocks, then washing and placing them in the basket with two looped sticks, tanapa, about three rocks at a time, a second person stirring with a looped stick (tsa'nu) similar to the first and made of hard wood[8] and removing cold rocks.

IRRIGATION

Description. Irrigation increased the natural yield of several wild seed plots in Owens valley. Tilling, planting, and cultivating were unknown. Plots were chosen for convenience of dam and ditch building, soil drainage, and seed yield. The greatest development was at pitana patu where natural facilities were best. A plot with tupusi and nahavita, on each side of Bishop creek, sloping gradually up the valley floor, was irrigated. The northern plot measured 4 by 1 to 1½ miles; the southern comprised approximately 2 square miles....

The system comprised a dam in Bishop creek canyon a mile below the mountains and a ditch to each plot. The northern ditch, used recently by ranchers and called "Paiute ditch," is still traceable from the dam up the canyon side and across the valley. Dam and ditch construction involved no problems but entailed considerable labor.

At pitana patu the position of irrigator, tuvaiju'ᵘ (tuva'ʸᵃdut, to irrigate), was honorary. He was elected at a popular meeting each spring. Time to commence irrigation was then announced by the district head man and approved by the people. Sam Newland's brother-in-law was once irrigator. (The Big Pine district head man was irrigator, but had an assistant.) The dam of boulders, brush, sticks, and mud was built by the irrigator, assisted by about twenty five men. After water was turned into the ditch, the irrigator alone was responsible, watering the plot by small ditches and dams of mud, sod, and brush. The water, once started, needed little attention. A pole, pavodo, 4 inches diameter, by 8 feet long, was the irrigating tool.

Overflow water below the plots inadvertetly irrigated land bearing: mono, sunu'ᵘ, pauponida, waiya, pak, and tsikava.

The northern and southern plots were annually alternated; "to prevent soil exhaustion" (Tom Stone), but probably really for natural seeding. Water was turned in spring to one plot (fish were gathered in the creek bed!); at harvest time the dam was destroyed and water flowed down the main channel (fish were gathered from the ditch). The following year the other plot was irrigated.

Irrigation at pitana patu was communal. All men assisted in dam building. All women might harvest. This was probably true of other districts.

Utu'utu witu (Hot springs) dammed Freeman creek to irrigate nahavita. Baker creek below pasida witu was dammed for irrigation. Other Owens Valley settlements irrigated. Mono Lake did not.

Theoretical aspects. The Owens Valley Paiute were thus on the verge of horticulture but did not quite achieve it, for planting, tilling, and cultivating were unknown.[9] There are three possible explanations of this unique and almost anomalous occurrence of irrigation without agriculture, each of which has an important bearing on the origin of agriculture in America.

(1) An ancient practice of irrigation may actually have preceded the diffusion of cultivated plants in the Southwest and survived in eastern California. This hypothesis, however, is highly improbable, for there is not, so far as I know, a shred of evidence elsewhere to support it.

(2) Irrigation may have diffused from a horticultural complex of the near or remote past in the Southwest. It is, however, unlikely that borrowing either from the south or east occurred in recent times. For although Owens valley is less than two hundred miles from the Chemehuevi, occasional tillers of the soil, and not more than three hundred miles from the truly horticultural Mohave (Kroeber 1925:597, 735), not a single cultivated plant of these people was known to the Paiute, while the Chemehuevi and Mohave did not practice irrigation. It is indeed remarkable in view of the antiquity of horticulture in the Southwest[10] and its wide distribution in the east that it should have gone but little beyond the Colorado River into California. But this halt in its diffusion, Kroeber suggests, may be explained by the adequacy of the natural food supply of California (1925:815). The absence of horticulture is affirmed for all the Great Basin Shoshoneans, except the Kaibab and Shivwits Paiute of southern Utah who irrigated corn and squash (Lowie 1924:200–01) but could hardly have passed their knowledge across Nevada to the Owens Valley people.

A diffusionistic explanation of Paiute irrigation is more plausible when the ancient Pueblo culture of the Southwest is considered. Harrington's work at "Lost City," near Las Vegas, Nevada, showed the presence there of a horticultural people somewhere between the Basket Maker and Early Pueblo cultures (Harrington 1927:262–77). Further investigation in Nevada yielded evidence in the form of pottery of a Pueblo culture, which presumably included horticulture, as far west as Wellington, Beatty, and the eastern side of the Amargosa desert; that is, nearly to the boundary of California in the latitude of

Owens valley (Harrington 1928:235–40). Influence of a Basket Maker culture, lacking domesticated plants, has been found as far west as Lovelock Cave (Loud and Harrington 1929), west central Nevada, and in the Mohave sink region in southern California (Rogers 1929). The distribution of Shoshonean pottery in southern California and eastern California strengthens the hypothesis developed by Strong from social and ceremonial data that a strong connection between southern California and the Southwest once existed but was cut off at an early date by the intrusion of Shoshonean tribes of a low cultural status (1927). Some early, widely distributed Southwestern culture, most probably Pueblo II, may have introduced the idea of irrigation which was taken over by the Owens Valley Paiute.

If, however, diffusion explains Paiute irrigation, it did not operate in the conventional manner, for there was a differential borrowing in which a close-knit horticultural complex was broken down and the seemingly dependent or secondary element, irrigation, diffused without the carrier or *raison d'etre* of the complex—the nucleus of cultivated plants. Even if this apparently unreasonable, selective diffusion occurred, however, it indicates that irrigation was a part of early horticulture in the Southwest, a contention now supported by much archaeological evidence.

(3) Paiute irrigation may have had a local and independent origin, the original idea probably coming from the swampy lowlands of Owens valley where it is obvious that moist soil—a natural irrigation—produces a very prolific plant growth. Irrigation, in this case, is simply an artificial reproduction of natural conditions. Although people are slow to take advantage of what seems "obvious" after its merits are known, the possibility of this origin must not be disregarded, for if the Owens Valley Paiute were among those intrusive tribes which cut off the connection between southern California and the Southwest, this explanation may be necessary. Whatever the source of irrigation among the Owens Valley Paiute, it supports Spinden's contention that irrigation in a semi-arid country, e.g., Egypt, Mesopotamia, and Peru, may be a "conception which accounts for the very origin of agriculture itself" (1922:47–49).[11]

For if the Paiute came by irrigation through borrowing, the borrowing demonstrates that irrigation was present in an early phase of American agriculture, whereas if it were a local invention, it marks a people who were on the verge of horticulture and suggests the possibility of such an origin of horticulture elsewhere (Steward 1929).

SALT

Salt, ona'vi, was scraped up with the hand from certain alkali flats (e.g., the south side of Big Pine lake), where a characteristic species of brush, ton'avi, grew, then put with water in a basket and the paste moulded into flat cakes about 8 inches in diameter, for storage or trade. Balls, sometimes made, were preferred by Western Mono in trade. Salt was obtained in large quantities in Saline Valley, and at Klondike Lake, Silver Peak, and Fish Lake.

Mono Lake Paiute traveled to Nevada to get salt, tu'vi ona'vi, in a manner similar to Owens Valley people. It occurred around a brush, tona'vi. This, being red and bitter, was only eaten with mush.

FISHING

Fish occurred in Owens River, fresh-water sloughs, and the Sierra Nevada streams.

Pa'nwi, generic term for fish.

Tsoni'ta, the native minnow.

Huwa, adapu'ᵘ or atava, native sucker. Young were called pohivana or pohipana.

Pugwi or panwi, golden trout, asserted not to be native by Chalfant (1933).[12] John Sumerville said they were native in Birch creek.

Po'tcigi or pui'tcigi, unidentified species. Young were called tsiavaka. Occurred in Freeman creek, now gone.

Aka panwi (aka, red), rainbow trout, probably introduced recently.

Sections of rivers and sloughs were fished exclusively by districts owning them. Others were sometimes given permission to fish them.

Fishing was individual or communal. Villages or whole districts sometimes fished, being organized and directed by the district head man, and the catch being divided equally among all participants.

Live fish were kept in small-mouthed, open-twined baskets in streams; later baked, like jackrabbits, in a hole under hot ashes. George Collins said large catches were cleaned by people on the banks and smoked for storage. Tom Stone denied this.

No fishing magic was known.

Fishing methods. (1) Stranding. Streams diverted in irrigating left stranded fish which were collected.

(2) Stupefying. Tu'unwava or tug^{w}u'va (*Smilacina sessilifolia* Nutt.), slim solomon, was mashed with rocks, wrapped and sewed in worn out baskets, and dipped into pools formed by dams[13] and shaken. Five or six men swam with bundles of tu'unwava ahead of them in larger pools. Stupefied fish came to the surface or went to shallow water, the effect sometimes lasting 4 or 5 hours. Those strongly stupefied were gathered by men and women, wading with baskets. Active fish were shot with arrows or speared. Fish were piled on the bank.

(3) Arrows. Fish were shot with bows and featherless arrows having double points of hard, sharp wood.

(4) Spears. Short cane spears had two wooden prongs inserted into them. George Collins mentioned three bone prongs in a single plane, "like a pitchfork." Prongs were recently wire or umbrella ribs. Leonard said that at Humboldt lake fish were speared from rush rafts with spears tipped with an 18 inch leg bone of the sandhill crane, the spears evidently being cast, not merely thrust (1904:166).[14] Field Museum has a two-prong fish spear with detachable bone points fastened harpoon-wise with string (specimen 71469), from the Western Mono of Hooker's cove, California. Chalfant says the spear was obsidian barbed (sometimes bone); and the spearing was done at night, the fish attracted by a light on the bank (1933).

(5) Hooks were of deer bone, George Collins. Tom Stone said they were of a wildcat's foreleg or collar bone, the latter requiring little shaping. Leonard (1904:166) saw at Humboldt Lake some fishhooks of small bone, ground down on sandstone, a double "beard" or barb cut in them with flint, and a wild flax line attached nearest the barbed end. A pull on the line caused the sharp, barbed end to catch and turn

the bone crosswise in the fish's mouth. These were often used. Grasshoppers and worms were bait, Tom Stone.

(6) Baskets. Open-twined baskets were dragged through the water. Conical carrying baskets, cudusi, were fastened below dams to catch fish coming over with the water.

(7) Nets of wicivuva, described as like rabbit nets, 50 by 3 feet.[15] Several people, holding a net, drove fish to the shallow end of a pool, there gathering them. Field Museum has a "gill net" (specimen E-71181), from the Western Mono of Big Sandy, California, which is set in streams for trout, etc.; it is made of milkweed and Indian hemp, *Apocynum cannabinum* L.

Tom Stone described minnow fishing:

> Put a stick in tules to stand on. Stay quietly holding a three-foot line with a hook in a puddle made for the minnows. Sing and whistle: "Tsonita, come and take a bite. Never mind your little ones. Throw them away and come take a bite." This is for amusement, to keep awake.

HUNTING

Hunting was individual or communal. Individuals might hunt anywhere; communal groups stayed within their district territory. Hunters carried for large game a sinew backed bow and obsidian pointed arrows and fire outfits in their quivers. Continence was not required of hunters. Use of charms was not recorded. Individuals had no private hunting places.

Deer, tuhi'na (Tuhud, Mono lake) Buck, tuhi'a; doe, tuhi'na opia'va (female); faun, a'watsi'[j]. Individual hunters trailed, ambushed, or had barking dogs trained to round up deer. Mose Weyland said some disguised themselves in deer skins and antlers, rubbing against rocks and brush, appearing angry, etc., to imitate deer, running away to make them curious, but keeping to their lee to keep the human odor from reaching them. If several hunted, some drove deer down trails where others hid. Nets and pitfalls were denied, but some kind of trap was affirmed for deer and mountain sheep.

Tom Stone said a hunter left a killed deer in the mountains, went to the sweat-house that night saying, "Old men, light your pipe. We will smoke." After passing the pipe, they asked his luck. He told his experiences in detail. Next day they fetched home his deer. He kept the skin, neck and shoulders to the next to the last rib, giving away the remainder. This share falls to the one of a group of hunters who makes the kill. To carry, they tied the four legs together over the carrier's forehead and hung the body down his back (Muir 1916:205–6).

The deer drive was communal, directed by the district head man, whole families moving to the hunting country. Women and old men kept camp and cured the meat. Men, stationed 100 yards apart, hunted a large region, advancing with sage bark torches, 3 inches in diameter, 3 feet long, firing brush and closing in to drive deer into a great circle[16] then shooting them down. The kill was equally divided, the head man perhaps getting a double share, or a whole deer (more than the hunter's share). Some cured meat was left hanging in the mountains, theft being impossible as anyone in need was welcome to it.

Shamanistic activities, driving over cliffs, and magic were unknown.

Mountain sheep, koip[a] (Mono Lake and Owens Valley), and antelope, wa'dzi or kwaha'du. Usually hunted by large communal groups under the head man, supposedly a good hunter. Skilled hunters concealed themselves on trails while the others drove sheep and antelope up the mountain to them. Joe McBride said sometimes brush corrals in narrow canyons caught sheep driven by hunters. On the top of nearly every Nevada mountain he visited, Muir found small stone enclosures where hunters hid while others frightened sheep, knowing they would run to the summit. On Mount Grant, west of Walker lake, was a high-walled stone corral with diverging wings into which sheep were driven by men, women, and children, aided by rows of dummy, rock "men" along ridge tops in and out of which several men moved. He pictures a sheep hunter with a head gear suggesting an antelope (Muir 1917:322).[17]

Owens Valley people hunted sheep and antelope mainly in the White and Inyo mountains, the precipitous Sierras affording protection to game unless heavy snows drove the animals down.

Like deer, sheep and antelope were divided among hunters. No shamanistic activities or magic were recorded.

Bears, pahavitci". Too much resembling humans and too much feared to be hunted. Occasional skins were traded from the Western Mono.

Rabbit drives. Rabbit, ka'mu. Large communal groups under district head men hunted many places in Owens valley. Old men placed their nets, 3 feet high and up to 50 feet long, end to end in a great arc and hid to club rabbits caught, which others, forming a long line, drove, shooting and clubbing as they closed in.[18] The latter got most. Each kept his kill. Slain rabbits were carried by tucking their heads under belts of wicivi fiber around hunters' waists.[19] Tom Stone denied participation of women and use of fire. Crescentic rabbit sticks were unknown.

The last night of a successful drive the people held a celebration, tsoa wunut or tuwapait, in the sweat-house. Men put their rabbits in one pile; women put various seeds in another. Men took seeds they wanted, and the women whose seeds were taken took their share of rabbits. After a big feast, they entered the sweat house, and paid singers sang special songs, tsoa huvia, the people joining. Communal deer drives, seed gathering, fishing, etc., and "fandangoes" were planned.

Mono Lake held drives around the lake flats. Muir said men, women, and children participated, and brush fires helped frighten rabbits. Nets, clubs, and bows were used.

Drives occurred usually in the fall in connection with other communal undertakings.

Traps. Rabbits and wildcats (Tukuvitc[i]) were caught in unbaited loops tied to birch rods planted in the ground and bent over, on game trails.[20] The animal kicked a willow trigger which allowed a string wrapped around a willow staple set into the ground to unwind releasing the bent birch and pulling up the loop. For wildcats these were larger. For smaller game, e.g., ground squirrels, tilted rocks

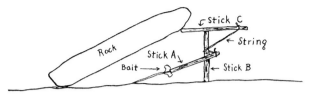

A trap for small game.

supported by sticks dropped when bait underneath was gnawed. In the figure, willow stick A tied with a string wrapped around upright B supporting horizontal stick C is released, C and the rock giving way. Small string nooses for quail, like those of the Surprise Valley Paiute (Kelly 1932:89), those found in Lovelock Cave (Loud and Harrington 1929:115), and those in Field Museum from the Western Mono of Hooker's Cove (specimen E-71460), were not recalled.

Small game. Also shot with wooden pointed arrows. Burrowing animals were dug or smudged out of their holes. Twisting a stick into their skin was not known.

Water fowl. Killed in early morning by hunters concealed in blinds resembling wickiups or summer houses. Decoys,[21] nets, and communal hunts were unknown.

Meat preparation. Large game was boiled in pots or, in the mountains, broiled on coals. To preserve, small strips were dried, perhaps over a fire, and left hanging or wrapped in buckskin. Purposeful smoking, grinding, and mixing with grease or berries were unknown. Intestines were split open, cleaned, hung to dry, and boiled to eat.

Porcupines, mu'hu, ground squirrels, a'nwa, wood rats,[22] cawa, mice, puna'j[i] (Bishop), ponuzi (Fish Springs), large mountain ground hogs, yaha, short-tailed ground squirrels, ku'pa, ku'vi, gophers, mu'iya, badgers, hu'na, chipmunks, tava'ya, and possibly wildcats, tu'kuvitci, were roasted buried in coals after the entrails were removed and the skin was sewn up with a stick.

Water fowl were boiled in pots. These included: geese, nu'guta, mallard, cu'davia, canvas back, sakwi'kwiu, brown head, yuhã'da, pintail, wu' 'uadji, spoon bill, ha'giva, teal, paga'wihata'niyuwa, kuwa'natsi'i, or kuwa'tcuwitci'i, and other ducks generically called pu'yu (Owens Valley), puhu' (Mono Lake). Quail, takna'ka, caught in traps or shot, were cleaned and broiled on coals or boiled in pots.

Other animal foods. Sage hens, ka'hhu, grouse, hu'ja'a, and blue-jays, tcai, but not swans, ina'datcoi'i, were eaten. Although several denied eating grasshoppers, a'takica'a and crickets, tsu'nutugi'i, Muir saw Mono Lake Paiute, 1870, eating larvae of ants, wasps, bees, and other insects, and "Diggers," probably Miwok, eating ants after biting off their heads (Muir 1916:46, 206, 226–28). Lizards, tupo'dozo and mokidu'na (Owens Valley), tuvo'dza (Mono Lake), were eaten. Chalfant says Panamint Shoshoni (1933) and Parcher says Death Valley Shoshoni ate chuckwallas. Snakes were sometimes eaten, dogs rarely. Coyo' do, a species of shellfish from Owens river, was boiled in the shell.

Coyotes, eagles, buzzards, and hawks were not eaten.

Piuga, the fleshy caterpillar of *Coloradia pandora* Blake, occurring on *Pinus jeffreyi* in the Sierra west of Mono lake, chiefly around Mono Mills, every other year, were gathered when descending to pupate (Aldrich 1921:36–38). Communal trips, including whole families, were made in July. Trenches with vertical outer walls, 2 feet wide, 10 to 16 inches deep, encircled the trees. Though the caterpillars descended normally, John Sumerville said smoke helped to bring them down. They were gathered in special open-twined, round-bottom carrying baskets, killed by smoking over or dumping into a fire. Aldrich says they were baked for an hour in a mound of earth which had previously been heated by a fire on top (ibid). Dirt is removed by sifting in a cone-shaped sieve or by winnowing; they are sun-dried, spread on the ground in bark for several days, sacked, and stored, preferably in the mountains until fall, as heat spoiled them. "Chief Jake Garrison" put up a ton and a half in 1920 (Aldrich 1921) For eating, they were boiled in pots or baskets.

Piuga were gathered by Owens Valley Paiute and probably Western Mono as Field Museum has a typical basket (specimen E-71294). They were traded widely.

Cuza'vi, Owens Valley, cu'tza, cutza[vi], Mono Lake, the pupae of

Ephydra hians Say., breeding abundantly in Mono lake (Aldrich 1912:85). It is greasy and bitter like the lake water, but a favorite food and traded widely. Muir says "families and tribes" claim sections of the shore where the windrows of pupae wash up; disputes arise over encroachment on neighbor's territory (Muir 1916:227). They are dried, and, Aldrich says, the shell is rubbed off by hand leaving a yellowish kernel (Aldrich 1912:90). They are boiled one-half hour into mush and are important as food at Mono Lake. Inara or picawada, Owens Valley (*E. hians* Say.), in Owens Lake (Aldrich 1913:200), were used like cuzavi but less relished. Leonard says a small fly in Humboldt lake, probably the same was gathered in baskets where blown up on the shore and dried with seeds and rabbits for winter food (Leonard 1904:166–67). *Ephydra hians* also occurred in Walker Lake, called "koo' tsabe," Pyramid Lake and Soda Lake, near Carson, Nevada, where they served as food (Aldrich 1912:90–93; 1913:217–20).

DOMESTIC ANIMALS

Dogs. Dogs, i'cavuk[u] (ica' [ʻa], coyote; vuku, tame ?), Owens Valley, wi'civuk or tog[u] (from "dog"), Mono Lake, resembled coyotes in build and fur but had shorter ears and were marked black, white, brown, and tan. They were chiefly pets. They were eaten only during famine. Old and stupid dogs were killed.

Horses. Never of importance to Paiute; were got by Owens Valley from the south, by Mono Lake from the west, and were eaten prior to 1860. Pugu, Mono Lake, means horse or any quadruped.

Eagles. Eagles, kwi'na'a, Owens Valley, kwi'na', Mono Lake, and sometimes hawks, kini' [ʻi], were captured on their nests when young and raised in small wickiups, hava toni, for feathers and eagle down, being fed raw rabbit meat. They were preferably in pairs or fours. Tom Stone's grandfather raised an eagle which when grown, would fly away and return, being very tame.

No other wild animals kept as pets were recorded.

CULINARY PRACTICES
OF THE MOHAVE INDIANS
Kenneth M. Stewart

The Mohave are the northernmost and largest of the Yuman-speaking peoples of the lower Colorado River tribes. Fundamentally a Southwestern people, they are related to Native groups in eastern Arizona. For many years the standard source on the Mohave was Kroeber's research, 1900–11, which he published as chapters in his California Indian *Handbook* (1925).

The present article on food was one of a long series of essays on Mohave culture that Kenneth Stewart (1916–2002) published between 1946 and 1977 (others were devoted to wild plant gathering, agriculture, fishing, hunting, warfare, mortuary practices, mourning ceremonies, shamanism, witchcraft, and history). Kenneth Malcolm Stewart earned a doctorate in anthropology from UC Berkeley in 1946, based on field research in 1945–46. For thirty-five years he taught in the Department of Anthropology, Arizona State University, Tempe. Stewart's specialties were the ethnography of the Mohave, Chemehuevi, Papago, and other Southwestern tribes, as well as North American shamanism and primitive warfare. Stewart contributed the Mohave chapter to the Southwest volume of the *Handbook of North American Indians* (1983). This detailed essay is one of the very few that considers issues of Californian Indian cuisine, as opposed to general issues of subsistence.

El Palacio (1968), 75(1):26–37.

ALTHOUGH THE FOODSTUFFS AVAILABLE to the aboriginal Mohave Indians of the lower Colorado River were relatively plentiful and varied, the Mohave did not possess a rich repertory of culinary techniques.[1] It has been estimated that as much as fifty percent of the Mohave diet consisted of cultivated foods (Kroeber 1925:735; Castetter and Bell 1951:74). Although fish from the river and wild plant foods were important additions to the food supply, flesh foods obtained by hunting were a lesser contribution to the diet. In normal years the Mohaves had enough to eat, and famines were rare.

Floodwater farming was practiced in the bottom lands along the Colorado. Swollen with the turbulent waters of a drainage area of a quarter of a million square miles, the river overflowed its banks in the spring of the year and inundated the low-lying terrain adjacent to the channel. The silt which was deposited when the waters receded made a rich soil for planting, and the crops of the Mohave ripened rapidly in the intense summer heat. Flour corn of the white variety was the staple crop, although red, yellow, blue, and mottled varieties of maize were also planted. Tepary beans of several varieties were second in importance only to maize, and pumpkins and melons were also grown. Sunflowers were raised for their seeds. Under semi-cultivation were several indigenous wild seed plants, which have been identified as curlydock, panic grass, and crowfoot grass. Wheat, after its introduction by the Spaniards, became a crop for the Mohave (see Stewart 1966).

The Mohaves also relished the fish of the Colorado River, and some of my informants said that they preferred fish to corn or wheat. Fishing was fairly important to the Mohaves in normal years, but along with the gathering of wild plant foods it assumed much greater significance in years of meager harvest, when the river did not rise sufficiently to flood the fields in the bottom lands. The fish which were caught in aboriginal times were not those which have made the lower Colorado a fisherman's paradise in recent decades; instead, the Mohave caught bony tail, mullet, humpback suckers, and squaw fish (which the Mohave described as "like a salmon"). These fish are no longer in the Colorado, since after the construction of Laguna Dam above the city of Yuma, Arizona in 1909 it became impossible for the fish to swim upriver to spawn. Although the fish were soft and relatively unpalatable, the Mohave regarded them as "good eating." The fish were caught with dip nets, with seines or drag nets, in large canoe-shaped basketry scoops (*kwithata*), in traps or weirs, and occasionally were shot with bows and arrows or taken by angling with hook and line. They were also seized by hand in shallow water (see Stewart 1957; Wallace 1955).

The most important wild vegetable foods were the bean-like pods of the mesquite and screwbean (*tornillo*) trees. Some informants said that these were even more important to the Mohave than maize, particularly during the lean months when the harvest of farm products had been exhausted. A variety of wild greens and seeds was collected by the women in the bottom lands after the recession of the annual floodwaters. The women also went out in small parties to gather desert plants on the mesa. Among the wild seeds collected and eaten were quail-brush, careless weed, and chia, which were merely supplements to the diet rather than staples. Greens such as sisymbrium and goosefoot were collected and eaten, as well as others which have not been identified. Additional wild foods included wolfberries, tule roots and pellens, and mushrooms. Little use was made of the edible products of cactus plants or yucca fruits; informants said that these things were eaten by the migratory desert Indians like the Chemehuevi and the Walapai, rather than by the settled Mohave farmers (see Stewart 1965).

Hunting was of lesser importance to the Mohave, since game was scarce along the river, and rabbits alone contributed very significantly to the food supply. Jackrabbits and cottontails were taken in drives by groups of men and boys, who beat the brush and drove the rabbits toward other hunters who either shot the animals with bows and arrows or bowled them over with throwing sticks. Rabbits were also taken in spring pole snares and in pocket nets set in wings of brush in rabbit runways. Deer occasionally strayed into the river bottom, and a few men who had dreamed power for hunting made excursions to hunt deer and mountain sheep in the mountains of western Arizona. As it was believed to be bad luck for a hunter to eat his own kill, the game was traded to other Mohaves for fish and farm crops. Woodrats were poked out of their nests on the mesa with sticks, or were taken in small snares. The most important game bird was the quail although doves, ducks, and mudhens were also hunted (see Stewart 1947).

Harvest time began in late September and continued into early November. The corn was husked in the fields by women, and many of the ears were roasted and eaten while they were still green. The balance of the maize harvest was dried in the sun on the roofs of houses or on the tops of *ramadas* (shades), and then, still "on the cob," it was stored away in huge basketry granaries (*sokwinye*), as large as five feet tall and six feet across. So coarse in their weave that they resembled giant birds' nests, these granaries were woven of arrowweeds with the leaves left on. They were placed on low platforms or on the tops of *ramadas*, and were covered over with arrowweeds and earth. Beans were dried in piles on the ground for several days, after which the women trampled and pounded them with heavy sticks in order to separate the seeds from the pods. The beans were winnowed in basketry trays on windy days, and were then stored in hollowed gourds or in pots, separately from the corn. Pumpkins were cut spirally into strips, then dried on wooden frames and stored in large baskets under *ramadas*. Or they might be buried in pits lined with arrowweed, then covered with cornstalks or straw. Muskmelons were also cut in strips and dried on frames, while watermelons were stored in deep pits dug in sandy places, lined with arrowweed and covered with arrowweed and brush (see Stewart 1966). The Mohave also had a gable-roofed storehouse, a roof erected over an oval or rectangular pit.

Mesquite beans were transported in burden baskets (*kupo*) which, as described by Kroeber, consisted of a "carrying frame of two U-shaped sticks surrounded with thin string" (Kroeber 1925:738). The basket was carried on the woman's back, supported by a tumpline passing over the forehead.

The beans were sometimes eaten green, "if they were young and had teeth to chew them." Also, young mesquite beans were roasted in ashes, and were described as "tender like a string bean." Other beans were dried for a week or so on the ground or on roof tops, and were then stored away for the winter in the giant basketry granaries.

Mesquite beans, after they had been reduced to flour, were made into a kind of cake. As an informant described the process:

> They pounded the mesquite beans to a powder, then added a little water to make a ball. A fire was built, and when it burned to ashes they scraped off the sand. They put the ball of mesquite powder there and left it out in the sun until it got hard. They'd put mesquite bean skin over it to cover it. When it gets hard, it binds in and holds it together. Then they would break off little chunks and eat it when they wanted to. They would also put it in water and drink it (Stewart 1965:48).

Screwbeans required a lengthier preparation before they were edible, since "they don't taste good when they're young, and it takes a lot of work to prepare them." Therefore, it was necessary to "cook" or rot the screwbeans in a deep pit dug in sandy soil for about a month. The beans were covered with arrowweeds, over which water was sprinkled, and they were then covered with earth. When the beans turned red and "tasted sweet," they were removed from the pit and dried on the ground for four or five days. After the beans had been pulverized and ground to flour, a drink was made by adding water to the flour in a pottery cup. Sometimes watermelon seeds were mixed with screwbeans. "They pounded them and mixed them up. Then sifted until it was fine, and squeezed with the hand until it was tight. Just like a real chocolate."

The Mojave do not seem to have attempted to preserve flesh foods so that they would last for any protracted length of time. Meat was not dried into jerky, probably because the Mohave obtained so little meat that it was all consumed while still fresh. The Mohave were, however, no doubt aware of the process of making jerky, since it was made by their friends and neighbors the Walapai of northwestern Arizona. Fish were not smoked or salted by the Mohave, but were sometimes sun-dried on the tops of *ramadas* for several days. Fish dried in this manner could not be preserved for longer than a week or so.

Metates were used more commonly than mortars. Maize, wheat, and seeds of various kinds were ground by Mohave women on metates, which were described as "square at one end, round at the other." The Mohave metate (*axpe*) was a flat slab of lava, roughly rectangular in shape, about three inches thick, and measuring two feet in length and one foot in width. The metate was not set in a box or in the ground. The muller was a cylindrical block, about a foot long and three quarters of an inch in diameter. It was "round on top and kind of flat on the edges." When in use, the proximal end of the metate was raised on a little pile of dirt. The woman worked in a kneeling posture when large quantities of corn were to be ground, but at other times she might sit with her legs extended. Both hands were used in grinding, with a forward and backward motion. When the meal began to pile up, it was put on a flat pottery tray. One informant described the process of making a metate as follows:

> There's a man that picks out good rocks out on the mesa, near where the railroad track goes through (near Needles, California). He knows just what to pick, and breaks it off with hard rock. He shapes the bottom end first, then turns it over and shapes the face. He fixes it out where he finds it. Just kind of roughens it up out there, then fixes it nice at home. He hits on it, gets little sharp points on it. When it's not sharp, it doesn't grind so good. It takes about five or six days' work on the mesa, then about a month of work at home. He gets it about March. It's too cold in the winter; the rock breaks. Just one man knows how to do it. He doesn't sell it, but gives to relatives and friends. After it's been used a lot, a hole wears down in the middle, and then the man that knows how works it into shape again.

The Mohave had several types of mortars (*axmo*); wooden mortars, pit mortars, bedrock mortars, portable stone mortars, and "traveling mortars" of arrowweed. Both stone and wooden pestles were used. They were employed principally for crushing mesquite beans and screwbeans, although some seeds were also pulverized in mortars.

The wooden mortar was hollowed out of a section of cottonwood trunk by burning, producing a cavity about two feet deep and a foot in diameter. When in use, the mortar was partially imbedded in the ground to steady it. According to an informant, "It takes a long time to make. They'd get a green one and put in hot coals to hollow it out.

Then they scrape out the burnt places and wash and clean it." A woman sat down to use the mortar, with her legs extended on both sides of it. She used both hands to pound with the oblong pestle (*xamoke*), which was about two feet in length and two and a half inches in diameter. The pestle was sometimes of lava, sometimes of wood.

The pit mortar (*amat axmo*) was used for pulverizing large quantities of mesquite beans, "when they wanted to eat them right away." A hole was dug in the ground, about two feet deep, and was lined with bark and arrowweed stems. The pit mortar was normally used by a man, who using both hands, wielded a pole about four feet in length which acted as a pestle.

The portable stone mortar was "a little rock with a hole in it—about ten inches across." The bedrock mortar (*avi axmo*) was used when "sometimes they'd find a good hole in the rock, and then pound to enlarge it." Informants denied that the "traveling mortar" of arrowweed was taken on journeys; at such times they used depressions in the rocks. I showed my informants the picture of the "traveling mortar" in Leslie Spier's *Yuman Tribes of the Gila River* (1933:pl. 14–c). The informants recognized it, and said that the Mohaves had it, but they used it only when they didn't have other kinds of mortars. They said that the Mohave version was smaller than the Maricopa one, and was set in the ground when in use.

The Mohave usually did their cooking outside the house, often in a semi-circular windbreak (*muwic*), which was erected right up against the dwelling. On days when it was raining (a very rare occurrence along the lower Colorado), or when it was exceedingly windy, the cooking might be done in the dwelling. The Mohave winter houses were low, rectangular affairs, with sloping sides and ends, and they were covered with earth or sand. A low door, which faced to the south because of the cold winds which often blew from the north in the winter, was the only outlet for smoke. During the steaming summer months these houses became unbearably hot and stuffy, and the people would then move out under open-sided *ramadas* or shades, through which breezes could circulate. The houses were sparsely furnished, but water was always kept in them in pottery ollas (*hapurui*), which were about two and a half feet high and two feet in diameter.

The women fetched water from the river in the ollas, carrying the vessels on their heads on doughnut-shaped rings of willow fiber, walking along without even steadying with their hands. Other pots were used as cooking utensils, and there were also pottery cups, bowls, and dippers, as well as gourd dippers.

Boiling was the most common cooking method of the Mohaves, although other culinary techniques included broiling over coals and baking or roasting in hot ashes. Seeds were sometimes parched with hot coals in pottery trays.

The Mohave did not practice stone boiling, but instead boiled various foods in cooking pots (*chuvava*), which were set directly above the fires on round rocks, or on supports made of baked clay. Among the foods that were boiled were maize, beans, wheat, deer meat (which might also be broiled on coals), pumpkins, berries, mushrooms, and various wild greens.

The Mohave generally preferred not to boil foods of various kinds together, such as different varieties of beans, although when food was in short supply several kinds of food might be thrown into the pot at one time. Nevertheless, a favorite food of the Mohave was a stew called a *suvi*, which might contain various ingredients. Particularly relished was a fish stew called *acisuvi*, which was cooked by the men.

> The tails were cut off and the viscera removed, after which the mess was tied together, and fifteen or twenty fish prepared in this manner were thrown into a large pot half filled with water. Salt was added. The stew was stirred with a three-rod stirrer, consisting of three sticks thirty inches in length which were tied together. The cook stirred in a standing posture. After the stew had boiled for four hours, ground cornmeal was added, and after five minutes of additional cooking, the stew was ready for consumption. The women were served first. Even the bones were eaten. Different species of fish were not in the same stew (Stewart 1957:201f; see also Wallace 1955:92f).

Fish were also broiled on hot coals. As described by Wallace:

> Each was cut along its belly and the intestines removed. Then it was laid in hot ashes, sometimes being entirely covered and turned

several times so as to broil both sides evenly. This was a slow method, normally taking three or four hours. When crisp, the fish were eaten with the fingers, bite-size pieces being broken off and conveyed to the mouth (Wallace 1955:93).

Rabbits were skinned and gutted, and a large fire was built. The rabbit was first broiled on top of the charcoal, and then baked in hot ashes. In the words of an informant:

> They took the rabbit's fur off first; used it to make a blanket. Then they buried him in the ashes. Folded his limbs under and broke his legs and stuck them in the flesh. Tied him up good. When it was done they pounded the meat and bones together on a round stone. Then they kind of roasted and ate it. Nothing was left; the bones were good, too. They were good eating. Some people liked the bones better than the meat.

The chuckawalla lizard was also roasted in ashes. "They put a stone on his back and bury him, lest he puff right up." Caterpillars, too, were roasted in hot coals and were said to be tasty. Pumpkins and mushrooms were sometimes roasted in coals, the leaves of the careless weed (akwava) were rolled up "like a tortilla" and baked in ashes.

Quail and doves were roasted in earth ovens (*hapaug*). The process was described as follows:

> They'd build a fire and burn the feathers up. Then they bake him under hot ashes. Put the bird right in the fire, and work around with a stick until the feathers are burnt up. Then they took out the guts and baked it. Men did it.

Corn bread (*tathits muthil*) was baked in hot ashes:

> The corn was roasted first, then ground on the metate. Then they build a fire. Scrap hot part off the ashes. Put a little damp earth on. Then they spread it out big. Then sprinkle little damp earth again. Then put hot ashes on. Put in there for a little while. Gets done easy.

Bread was similarly made out of wheat.

Seeds were parched in a pottery pan (*katela*) about two feet in diameter. "They put coals in and seeds on top. The pan had handles on it. They shook it back and forth quick for two or three minutes, then took the coals out."

Salt (*athi*) was obtained from alkali ground at places "where the earth is in corruption, where they had little lakes or sloughs that dried up."

The best firewood for cooking was cottonwood or willow, and the wood was collected by the men, although "the ladies might get little pieces." Fire was made both with the simple palm drill and by the percussion method. Cottonwood bark was used as a tinder.

The first meal of the day came at sunrise or earlier. After that, the Mohaves ate whenever they felt like it during the day, if they had food handy. As one informant said, "They ate all day." Another meal was customarily eaten in the evening. According to my informants, the whole family ate together, and "the lady that cooks dishes it out." Each person ate out of an individual bowl. Fingers were used for eating, although "they had pottery spoons too." For eating *suvi* the first two fingers of the right hand were used, and the whole hand was used when eating beans.

In brief, the mainstay among Mohave culinary practices was the boiling of various foods in pots set upon supports directly over fires, and the favorite food was the fish stew named *acisuvi*. Other methods of cooking were few in number and simple in principle, although some were rather laborious to execute. Both fish and meat were broiled over coals, and rabbits, birds, and lizards were baked or roasted in hot ashes, the latter method also being used in making corn bread. Seeds were parched in pottery trays with hot coals. These ancient techniques of food preparation have long since fallen into disuse among the Mohaves, who now purchase most of their foodstuffs in stores.

MYTH, RITUAL, AND ORATORY

KARUK FOOD MYTHS

Alfred L. Kroeber and Edward W. Gifford, eds.

Native American myths, which attempt to give an account of the original state of the world and how it came to be as it is today, often deal with food: the creation of food species, cooking techniques, and eating customs. Sometimes food is incidental, or, as in the present selections, the myths may be specifically focused on cuisine.

Karok Myths was a posthumous publication for both of its editors. Alfred Kroeber gathered the story told by Sweet William between 1901 and 1902, while those from Mary Ike and Georgia Orcutt were collected by Edward Gifford in 1939 and 1940, respectively. Both collections were recorded in Karuk and then translated by the teller or by a bilingual Indian. All three of these Karuk narrators were elders with a great deal of cultural knowledge. Sweet William, an old man when he worked with Kroeber, was a formulist (or reciter of prayers) for the world renewal ceremonies. Georgia Henry Orcutt was about seventy at the time, and Mary Ike (ca. 1852–1946), who also worked with Kroeber, was one of two major consultants for Gifford's Karuk ethnobotany (Schenk and Gifford 1952).

The story of Coyote releasing impounded salmon is a common Native American mythic explanation for the origin of food species. "A'u'ich, Salmon, and Sturgeon" explains the origins of fish, fishing techniques, and the proper ritual treatment of fish. The Karuk word "ukunii" mentioned in this myth is a word uttered by myth characters and is used to begin myths. The story of the oaks and the transformation of basketry hats into acorn caps is well-known in California; it was published by Smithsonian linguist John P. Harrington (1932:6) as "The Acorn Maidens." His Karuk version, from Phoebe Maddux, is a little longer and more detailed. The Ixkareya mentioned in two of the myths were the spirits who originally populated the earth before turning into rocks, trees, animals, and other natural elements. Editorial additions to the translation originally placed in parentheses have been silently incorporated into the text.

Karok Myths (1980). Berkeley: University of California Press. Pp. 156–57, 68–70, 261.

HOW COYOTE FREED SALMON FOR PEOPLE
by Georgia Orcutt

Nobody got fish. There were no fish in the river. After a while Coyote knew that two girls at Amaikiaram had fish. He had been thinking about that. "How am I going to fix it?" He took some alder bark. He made it look like the backbone of a fish; he fixed it all nice so it looked like the backbone of a fish. Then he put deer marrow on his imitation fish. When he had fixed it up nice, that was the time he went up to Amaikiaram. Coyote came from right here, Panamenik.

When he arrived there, he went to the house where the two ixkareya girls were living. He talked with the girls. They were cooking acorns. They gave Coyote acorns to eat. When they gave him the acorns, he took his imitation fish from his quiver (kavaki) and said, "I'm going to cook fish." It looked like the girls looked at each other and asked, "Where did he get fish? Nobody's got fish." They thought this as they looked at each other. When Coyote cooked it, it looked like grease was dripping from it. It was the deer marrow. He never offered them any to eat. He pretended to eat it all himself.

Late in the evening the girls ate acorns. They did not eat fish. They had no sweathouse, so they had to let Coyote sleep by the fire in their house. Coyote just lay there, making believe he was asleep. After a while it looked like the girls were talking to see if he was asleep. He kept snoring away, but heard them all the time, for he was only pretending to sleep. After a while, one girl said, "I think he is asleep now," for they heard him snoring away.

The girls got up and went outside. Coyote lay there snoring away. Coyote went outside. He know where the fish were. He had expected the girls would go out sometime during the night and he would have his chance to release the fish, which the girls had impounded in a pond in a cave in the mountainside. Coyote released the fish, and they swam down creek to the river. Then Coyote ran away.

Everybody thought he did right in releasing fish for people. Usually everybody runs down Coyote, but this time he did right. The girls were excited when they came back. One said to the other, "I told you he was not sleeping." Coyote came back to Panamenik.

A'U'ICH, SALMON, AND STURGEON
by Sweet William of Ishipishi

The mountain A'u'ich (Sugar Loaf) at Katimin was a man, an immortal (ikhareya). His children were rocks. He made salmon in a little pool: there he kept them while they were small. When they grew, he turned them into the river; the salmon went down, stayed in the ocean, and when they were larger came upriver again. They were nearly full grown but not quite, so A'u'ich told them to go downriver again. When they came up the next time he made a lifting net and a scoop net and a scaffolding to fish from and everything needed to catch them. "Ukunii," he said.

When he caught salmon, he made a net sack (uhuriv) and put them into it, and carried them to the house. And he made a basketry cap (aphan) to be used with the scoop net,[1] and a wooden club with which to kill the salmon while still in the net. Then he made the suckers (chamohich) and the ashkuu (hook-fish) in the creeks by causing wood to fall into the streams and turning into these smaller fish.

At first he had no knife: he could do nothing with his salmon except to put a whole fish into the fire to cook. Then Fish Hawk (Chukchuk) said, "I am the one who will use rock. I will make a knife of stone." He split cobbles to a sharp edge. Then he cut salmon with them; he cut up suckers too. Then many people came to him. He cut up their fish for them. He gave each one a piece of rock.

Then A'u'ich said, "Ukunii," and made sturgeon (ishihikir). He made them small. After a time he looked at them again and they had grown. The ikhareya said to each other, "We shall have sturgeon for food." Then A'u'ich said, "Sturgeon will come back upriver. But when it comes up the river as far as here and people eat it, they will die. Whoever eats it when it is caught here where I made it (at A'u'ich) will die." Then he took ten little sticks, each as long as two joints of a finger, and put them into the river. They swam downstream, and over the fall at Amaikiaram (Ike's Fall).[2] They swam in the large eddy there, around and around. After a while they had turned into sturgeon. Then they grew large. Then A'u'ich told them, "Come upriver as far as this place (Amaikiaram). Do not come farther. If you are caught and eaten here at the mountain, people will die."

Sturgeon said, "I will do this. No one will see me, but I will go into the mountains and eat grass and whatever herbs smell good: I will be like a deer. When they kill me they will treat me like a deer. They will do everything cleanly. They will wash me and cut off my tail and pull out my spinal marrow. They will not just throw my bones outdoors. They will have to keep my bones together, and when they have finished they will have to throw them into the river, and the bones will turn to sturgeon again. They must throw them all in. And they will take my eggs and pound them on a flat rock. The eggs that stick to the rock they will put into the fire and cook and eat them off the rock. The other eggs they will wrap in maple leaves and put them into a hole by the fire, and when they are cooked they will take them out and eat them. But some men will not eat my eggs: they will throw my eggs into the river so that there may be more sturgeon. If only my head is left lying in the house, and my body is hanging up to dry, or has already been eaten, yet if a man that has slept with a woman comes into the house I will know it and my mouth will open of itself. When a man has eaten me he will wash his hands. He will treat me well: he will use a clean basket plate for me. If he is not a good man, if he has slept with a woman, he will not be able to take me, but a clean man will take me."

STORY OF OAKS
by Mary Ike

The White Oak (ahuwham) had her cap all finished nicely. The Live Oak (kan'put) had her cap all finished too. Black Oak (hansiip) was making ashiphanahitch (a long water-packing basket), and when they said, "Let's go," she put her hat on. That's why it is long. Tanbark Oak was making an Indian basket cap (ap'xan) and hers wasn't finished, but she put it on, and that's why the tanbark acorns look so rough.

lxkareya were the beings before they became trees and rocks.

White Oak and Live Oak laughed at Tanbark Oak and Black Oak, but they retorted, "As long as people live, they will always have us first, and you—they won't think much about you." And that is why, when people are together, they always have tanbark acorn soup and the next they use is black oak.

They laughed at Tanbark Oak because her cap looked so rough, and at Black Oak because her cap was so long.[3]

A POMO FOOD TALE

Samuel A. Barrett, ed.

Samuel Barrett, who grew up in the Pomo country around Ukiah, spent most of his life documenting the culture of these people. He conducted the field work for his collection of Pomo myths between 1903 and 1906, while a student at the University of California, and again in 1914–15, while working as a curator at the Milwaukee Public Museum. Most of the 108 myths and tales were recorded in English, in free translation, from the English of the consultants or through an interpreter. Others were recorded in Pomoan text with interlinear and free translations. Barrett decided to publish only the free translations, "since it is the subject matter only of the myths which concern us, rather than any linguistic consideration" (1933:8). The myths were revised "to a considerable extent in order to put them into good, clear and understandable form." As elsewhere in Native California, Pomo myths were recited according to strict rules: They could be told only at night, and listeners were instructed not to sit erect lest they become hunchbacked.

This charming fable was narrated by Bill James, a Central Pomo-speaker from the Garcia River. Most Pomo myths are more elaborate and composite, but like all such narratives, the tale describes how different the world once was and how it has been transformed. The story, which Barrett classified as a miscellaneous animal tale, explains why the woodrat has small, reddish eyes and white hands. During its brief span, it also reveals much about Pomoan food customs. It realistically recounts processes of acorn preparation (transposed to an animal plane), while also dealing with the acorn-storage habits of both woodpeckers and woodrats. The moral point concerns manners in eating and the consequences of anticipating and refusing food, as well as generosity (or the lack of it) between married relatives.

Pomo Myths (1933). Milwaukee Public Museum Bulletin, 15:1–608. P. 372.

WOODRAT IS REFUSED FOOD
BY HIS BROTHER-IN-LAW
by Bill James

Woodrat (Bayók) and his sister were both married. His sister's husband was Red-headed-woodpecker (Katák). The two families lived in separate houses and had, of course, separate stores of food. All the year round, Red-headed-woodpecker had plenty of acorns. Woodrat also had saved up a large store of acorns, but during the winter his store became exhausted. He heard his sister pounding acorns to make mush so he went over to visit her. After she had pounded the acorns into meal, she took it home and leached it in the usual manner.

Then she placed the meal in the basket and commenced to cook the mush with hot rocks. Woodrat thought he had better wash his hands so he could eat some of the mush when it was cooked. He did this and sat down on the opposite side of the fire and waited. Presently, however, Red-headed-woodpecker who was a very stingy man came home. Woodrat's sister had at times before this been generous and given Woodrat something to eat, but Red-headed-woodpecker would give nothing.

Woodrat sat there and watched them eat but got no food himself. Then he began to weep and he wept so long that his eyes became red and his eye-lids swelled until they nearly closed his eyes, so that he has had very small eyes ever since. When his sister began to cook mush he thought he was going to eat some, so he went out and washed his hands very thoroughly and this is the reason why he has always had white hands ever since.

A CHUMASH FOOD TALE

Thomas C. Blackburn, ed.

"Coyote's Stone Stew" is a Chumash version of a well-known European folk-tale. The Chumash, who had developed an elaborate civilization in what is now Santa Barbara and Ventura counties, learned the tale from the Spanish. It is a marvelous example of cultural syncretism, with its protagonist of Coyote, the Native trickster character, and Euro-American culinary forms—the frying pan and the introduced ingredients of lard, beans, garlic, tomatoes, and onions.

The story is taken from an extensive collection of Chumash manuscripts of John Peabody Harrington (1884–1961), a linguist employed by the Smithsonian's Bureau of American Ethnology. Harrington collected these 111 myths, folktales, and stories between 1912 and 1928. Lucrecia García (1877–1937), the narrator of this story, was born in Santa Barbara; her mother and daughter also served as informants for Harrington. Although she spoke the Barbareño dialect of Chumash, García told this tale in English. As Harrington published relatively little of his research, the editing of this collection was carried out by Thomas Blackburn, first in a 1974 doctoral dissertation in anthropology from UCLA, and then in a revised version, December's Child (1975). Blackburn (b. 1936), a professor emeritus of anthropology at California State Polytechnic University, Pomona, is also the co-author, with Travis Hudson, of an important five-volume work on Chumash material culture (1982–87). This set includes a comprehensive discussion of food-related objects.

December's Child: A Book of Chumash Oral Narratives (1975). Berkeley: University of California Press. P. 315.

COYOTE'S STONE STEW
by Lucrecia García

Once Coyote was traveling along and he was very hungry. And he saw a woman and thought to himself, "How can I trick this woman into feeding me?" The woman did not know that Coyote was a great trickster. Coyote thought to himself, "I know! I will tell her that I am going to cook some stones, and she is going to be very surprised!" And so he walked up to the woman and said, "I can make a fine stew out of stones." The woman asked, "How are you going to do that?" And Coyote said, "Well, watch me!" He asked for a frying pan, and he put some rocks in it. Then he asked the woman for a little lard, and then he asked for a little meat, and then a little garlic, and a little tomato and onion, and some salt. And he put each of the ingredients into the pan. And the woman was astonished at Coyote's way of cooking. He said, That's my way of making stew!" He then ate all of the stew, leaving only the rocks.

SIERRA MIWOK FEAST ORATION
Edward W. Gifford, ed.

Characterized by great detail and repetition, this selection is an excellent example of Native Californian ceremonial oratory, the kind of speech that one might find at a feast. The mourning ceremony, also called a "cry" from the ritual wailing, is the major religious observance of central and southern California (Gifford 1955:312–16). It ends the period of mourning, usually after a year. Commonly lasting four nights, it was held in the ceremonial house. During the day people played gambling games, ate, and slept. A cry was the occasion for a large feast, particularly at the beginning and end of the ritual. This speech clearly describes how a chief would ask for food, which he would then distribute to the visitors.

   Edward Gifford, who collected the oration, devoted much of his ethnographic research to Sierra Miwok culture; with Samuel Barrett, he wrote a comprehensive review of Miwok material culture (1933). He recorded the feast oration on three wax cylinders (preserved in the Hearst Museum, cat. no. 24–2120) that last almost nine and a half minutes. Chief Yanapayak spoke these words in the Central Sierra Miwok language, at Bald Rock, near Soulsbyville, in 1913. Although its formal style is called "chief's talk," the speech could have also been given by a chief's orator. According to Gifford, "It begins as the usual morning speech made each day from the top of the ceremonial house, then, in the second paragraph, turns to an address before a cry or mourning ceremony. The old chief was well over ninety years old when he made this recording and apparently started to give the ordinary morning speech, then included the reference to the mourning ceremony" (1955:263).

Central Miwok Ceremonies, Anthropological Records (1955), 14(4):263–64.

SUMMONS TO A MOURNING CEREMONY
by Chief Yanapayak

Get up. Get up. Get up. Get up. [repeated five times]. Wake up. Wake up. Wake up. People get up on the south side, east side, east side, east side, east side, north side, north side, north side, lower side, lower side, lower side. You folks come here. Visitors are coming, visitors are coming. Strike out together. Hunt deer, squirrels. And you women, strike out, gather wild onions, wild potatoes. Gather all you can. Gather all you can. Pound acorns, pound acorns, pound acorns. Cook and cook. Make some bread, make some bread, make some bread. So we can eat, so we can eat, so we can eat. Put it up, and put it up, and put it up. Make acorn soup so that the people will eat it. There are many coming. Come here, come here, come here, come here. You have to be dry and hungry. Be for a while. Got nothing here. People get up, people around get up. Wake up. Wake up so that you can cook. Visitors are here now and all hungry. Get ready so we can feed them. Gather up, gather up, and bring it all in, so we can give it to them. Go ahead and eat. That's all we have. Don't talk about starvation, because we never have much. Eat acorns. There is nothing to it.

Eat and eat. Eat. Eat. Eat. Eat. So that we can get ready to cry. Everybody get up. Everybody get up. All here, very sad occasion. All cry. All cry. Last time for you to be sad. Go ahead and cook. Go ahead and cook. Get all of your stuff cooked. Get all your stuff cooked. People are hungry. People are hungry. Get ready for tonight. Get ready for tonight. Gather it up. Gather it up. Go ahead and distribute it. Distribute it. Go ahead and eat. You people are hungry, hungry. Eat, eat.

Crying ended. Crying ended. Cook and cook and cook, if you have any left. A person always gets hungry. People are hungry and have been traveling a long way, a long road. People always return home. They always want a little to take along. You never want to think people have too much. Better to have people speak well of us, than to say that we were stingy.

Everybody come here. Everybody come here. Brothers and brothers. Fathers and fathers. Everybody come here. Rest up, rest up. Tiresome walking. Tiresome walking. You have starved and starved and starved. We have nothing. We have not got it ready. You will have it, we will find something for you. People, get something. Hurry up. Get ready. They are dry and thirsty. Here we are. Here we are. Eat and drink. Not so very much. We cannot have so very much. We are always starving. People from all around gather to come. Watch the people coming in. People whom you do not see all of the time. Come in and associate with them. Those at home have relatives that they always like to talk about. Come in and associate. You people always talk about your parents or friends. "I wish I could see them. I wish I could be with them. I wish the chief would put up some sort of a gathering." That is what you always say when there is nothing going on. You always speak about your old folks, the ones who are dead. There are not many fiestas going on, all big men are dying off. There will be no opportunity for more fiestas. That's all.

PHOTOGRAPHIC PORTFOLIO
A KONKOW MAIDU FEAST, 1903
John W. Hudson

Although John W. Hudson (1857–1936) was trained as a physician, soon after moving to Mendocino County in 1889, and marrying the painter Grace Carpenter the following year, he discovered his true passion. For the rest of his life he researched the lives and culture of his neighbors, the Pomo Indians living around his home in Ukiah.

After selling his basket collection to the Smithsonian in 1899, Hudson became a serious museum ethnographer. Between 1900 and 1905, he served as a field agent for the Field Museum of Natural History in Chicago, collecting 3,500 objects from the Pomo, Sierra Miwok, Hupa, Yurok, and sixteen other Californian peoples. His home is now part of the Grace Hudson Museum, which also holds his field notes and the Hudson family papers.

This series of images is reproduced from the collection of over 450 Hudson negatives preserved at the Department of Anthropology at the Field Museum. As one can see from this set, his photographs are distinguished by their intimacy and attention to detail.

This sequence illustrates a Konkow Maidu acorn feast, held at Bidwell's Bar in Butte County in March 1903.[1] The social content of this feast is illuminated by an excerpt from Hudson's field diary, kindly reproduced through the courtesy of the Grace Hudson Museum.[2] A few omissions and punctuation additions have been made to ease comprehension.

March 20 [1903]. Oroville hotel [2½ miles north of Bidwell Bar, Butte Co.]

Leaching done in sand pit by wetting the meal thoroughly with cold water, then pouring on for an hour very hot water – Milling [of acorn flour] done in bed rock mortar – Stone pestle – Soup boiled with hot rocks lifted out with double stick tongs – pine – Sifting done with flat plaque struck with small mallet – Meal soup cooked for about one hour or till brought to full boiling point.

Bo-ye-toton, the return feast or give back feast given to former hosts. Food and shelter the chief object of this feast, though other presents are often exchanged – The guests bring all kinds of delicacies with them which is delivered formally to the host in presence of all – As each donor guest appears with his or her present, the host acknowledges the gift with a long drawn-out and hearty Het! and all note the gift – An empty hand moves apologetically in the background and is always the subject of gossip – The guest gifts are piled before the host to be distributed by him amongst the guests regardless of their generosity, or lack of it –

Photo of old chief host receiving guest gifts – Photos of cooking pinole with hot rocks, etc.

Hot rock tongs are two straight pine sticks sharpened at lower ends – When too blunt or slippery they are sharpened – They are used solely as tongs to lift in or out the boiling stones – A smaller basket filled with water always sits beside the pot and into which the hot stones are momentarily thrust to remove ashes, etc. After cooking, the stones are lifted out and washed of their clinging mush in another basket. These slops are afterward boiled down and its burnt taste is considered a delicacy.

[Acorn] pones are made by mould basket filled and set in running water, then when cold turned out. Thick mush used. Acorns cracked or pitted, oak anvil spherical stone hammer –

Bread is made by cooking the acorn dough in hot stone underground oven – The loaves are black and incrusted with leaves. No leaven.

The feast is held today on crest of small hill where the old head man stands – The presents of venison, 5 carcasses, 7 basket tureens of acorn mush, two bags of flour, 13 bags acorns, 47 loaves of flour bread, seven loaves acorn bread, quantities of beans, etc., both cooked and raw –

The Chico people present in whose honor the feast is given gather around the pile of provisions and their chief and wife begins to inventory and arrange piles of the stuff – The Chico chief calls a name, and it is repeated in stentor voice of Yuno chief – The person called comes up and receives his portion, takes it to his camp near by and eats – Every one is free to partake of any food present without ceremony – Games prevail and good humor – The visitors always bring some of their valued articles, wampum, etc., which is laid before their host for sale and buyers come around and lay down money or the other articles they wish to exchange for it. The host counts out the wampum to the value of the exchange stuff and turns it over to the buyer.... The purchased wampum is at once hung around the buyer's neck and admired by the friends.

Woman with cooking baskets.
(NEG. NO. 13–4165, FM 9514).

Woman pouring water into cooking basket.

(NEG. NO. 13–4166, FM 9518).

Woman placing hot stones in cooking basket.

(NEG. NO. 13–4163, FM 9511).

Baskets of cooked acorn mush.
(NEG. NO. 13–4167, FM 9525).

Men carrying feast basket.
(NEG. NO. 13–4164, FM 9513).

Meat, acorn soup, bread, and sacks of flour.
(NEG. NO. 13–4161, FM 9503).

Shaman blessing the food before the feast.
(NEG. NO. 13–4168, FM 9526).

SUBSISTENCE RITUALS
IN NATIVE CALIFORNIA
Sean L. Swezey

This essay, in the Berkeley tradition of student literature reviews, reveals the popularity of ecological analysis at the time of its composition. One of the leaders of this approach in Californian studies was Lowell J. Bean (1972; Bean and Blackburn 1976). Sean L. Swezey (b. 1953) wrote the essay in the spring of 1974, while still an undergraduate, under the supervision of archaeologist/ ethnohistorian Robert F. Heizer. With his professor, he also published a related essay on ritual management of salmon in Native California (1977).

Swezey earned all his degrees at UC Berkeley: B.A. in anthropology and B.S. in conservation and resource studies (1975), M.A. in anthropology (1976), and Ph.D in entomological sciences (1982). From his initial training in anthropology, he has made a career in entomology and as a specialist on pesticides and sustainable agriculture. His career includes teaching and research appointments at UC Berkeley (1975–81), Cornell University (1983–84), UC Santa Cruz (1987–present), and UC Davis, where since 1999 he has been Director of the Sustainable Agriculture Research and Education Program (SAREP).

Swezey focuses his study on energetics, the transformation of energy through a natural system. Related to cybernetics and systems theory, these approaches were popularized in anthropology by Gregory Bateson during the 1960s and early 1970s. What Swezey calls the "ideational context" are the basic cosmological principles of a culture, while the "operational context" in this essay refers to hunting rituals and first-fruit ceremonies. He attempts to demonstrate how these religious beliefs and behaviors help regulate human and animal populations. Because of the essay's length, this selection omits Swezey's introduction, most of his discussion of the ideational context, as well as most of his concluding functional analysis, in favor of his excellent review of the literature on food-related rituals.

The Energetics of Subsistence-Assurance Ritual in Native California. Contributions of the University of California Archaeological Research Facility (1975), 23:1–46. Pp. 8, 13–34, 41 reprinted.

THE IDEATIONAL CONTEXT
World View and the Ritual Specialist in Environmental Relations

Of preliminary importance to understanding the regulation of ecological and energetic systems by shamans and other ritual specialists is a general discussion of those aspects of world view which ideologically supported ritual control mechanisms. In establishing the central position of the ceremonial personality within the complex of environment-culture interactions, several concepts relating to the cognitive organization of the native world require brief review: (1) the natural world was composed of supernatural, spirit-beings who controlled environmental process; (2) man was an integral part of the natural system, and was held accountable for the propriety of his actions toward the animate world; and (3) the abstract supernatural "power" and favor of spirit forces could be acquired and internalized by shamans, or otherwise mediated and obtained, for the benefit of the entire community, by the activities of ritualists in public ceremonies designed to insure the continued availability and abundance of natural resources. The integration of these concepts, common to world view systems of native California, provides the philosophical basis by which ritual systematized land-man relationships....

Thus, of basic interest to the following discussion are the ceremonial duties assigned to both shamans and other ritualists which overtly structured the human ecology and energetics of subsistence in native California. The data to be presented indicate the extreme variability of the cultural and environmental situations in which this ritual organization took place. It will be noted that ritual regulation of subsistence activity in native California functioned at three main levels of organization:

(1) the activities of the shaman alone as the exclusive regulating force,

(2) the activities of the non-shamanistic specialist, such as the Cahuilla net, the Yuma kwoxot, the salmon formulist of Northwestern California, or the Washo rabbit boss, who may similarly direct subsistence activity in ritual contexts; or,

(3) the co-operative efforts of shamans and other ritualists in the organization of economic behavior.

It has been previously postulated that native cultures regarded ritual as a means of maintaining "balance" in an animate universe. The ritual organization of subsistence, involving the regulation of large-scale economic activities by specific ritual functionaries, was perhaps the basic process by which energetic equilibrium between human populations and resources was achieved.

THE OPERATIONAL CONTEXT
First Fruits Rites for Acorns and other Plant Foods;
Formulism and other First-Fish Rites; Hunting Ritual

In quantifying population-environment relations in native California, Baumhoff (1963:161) has remarked that within the great diversity of food resources utilized by aboriginal peoples, acorns, salmon, and large game animals may be characterized as those resources which were procured and stored in sufficient quantities to be considered "ecological determinants." With this appraisal in mind, examples (for which sufficiently detailed ethnographic data are available) of first-fruits rites for acorns and several other plant foods of regional importance, salmon ritual, and hunting ceremony will be briefly described. Particular attention will be paid to the organizational role assumed by the central ritualist(s) in each case.

First Fruits Rites for Acorns and other Plant Foods:
Some Selected Examples

The acorn is generally regarded as having been the basic staple of native populations in California; oak species of the genus *Quercus* are widely distributed across the state in all but high altitude and desert regions, and *Lithocarpus densiflora* is found throughout the Coast

Ranges north of Santa Barbara, most abundantly in Mendocino and Humboldt counties. Within areas of dense distribution, the oak provided a prodigious potential resource for exploitation. But the annual acorn crop presented a major energetic problem to aboriginal groups, in that it matured over a brief, two to three week interval in October or November, when the necessity for harvest was critical. Within this limited period of abundant potential yield, maximum community energies were necessarily directed toward gathering pursuits, which might include large population movements over considerable distances to harvest and transport the acorns. Optimal quantities of acorns were collected before they fell from the trees, and the entire harvest lasted a variable number of days or weeks, depending upon the size of the groups and the resource at hand. Synchrony of rapid, efficient gathering activity with the onset of the mature crop was essential; as natural competition from numerous birds, mammals, and insects, and the potentially destructive effects of rainfall or frost were ever-present factors which might reduce the harvest (Wolf 1945:19).

The organization of the community for the collection and distribution of acorns was often the ritual prerogative of the shaman, and the importance of his role is exemplified in Maidu society of North Central California. Among the foothill Maidu, the huku, or secret society headman, who according to Dixon (1905:267, 272) was an extremely influential shaman and political leader, located the most favorable sites for acorn gathering, announced them to the public, and negotiated payment for the crop if the trees belonged to another village (Kroeber 1925:74). A similar function was assigned to the Valley Maidu Kuksu headman (yeponi), and the details of ritual involved are recorded by Voegelin (1942:175). The yeponi located and tested acorns for ripeness, then returned and informed the community of their availability. His wife then went out to the productive site and secured one pack-basketful of acorns. Within six days, she dried and prepared two baskets of acorn mush, and took them to secret society members in the assembly house where the mush was prayed over and ritually consumed. After this ceremony, the entire community was allowed to gather the acorn crop. Premature harvest or eating of acorns before the rite was strictly forbidden by ritual (and therefore supernatural) sanction. Among Mountain Maidu groups, the ritual eating of acorns appears to have been a public rite *after* the initial period of gathering. A large amount of acorn soup was prepared from the first crop collected, over which a shaman prayed, then distributed portions to all present. After this ritual consumption, each family was allowed to cook and use its own acorn mush separately, an activity which had previously been forbidden. In these Maidu examples, the shaman appears to have assumed major control over the schedule of harvest activities, including the times and places at which the acorns were to be collected, distributed, and consumed.

In the context of the Kuksu dance cycle, Central Miwok groups also ritualized the acorn harvest, but the ritualist of note was not the shaman, but rather the secret society "chief" (hayapo), who was the head of the dancers and dance organization, and owned the costumes necessary for the impersonation performances. As such, the hayapo was the most powerful political and ceremonial figure in the community, possessing assistants and messengers through whom instructions for subsistence activities during celebrations were made known to the public. Among smaller groups, the hayapo himself might deliver these instructional orations from the dance house, detailing the various tasks and behavior to be followed by the community (Gifford 1955:263–65). "Little time" ceremonies, known as "uwetu" (from uwe—"to eat") were celebrated over four days of gathering activity in the fall. Before the first acorns could be eaten, the "yahuha" (a Kuksu ceremony described by Gifford 1955:293–94) dance was always organized and danced around a basket of mush in the ceremonial house. After this dance, the acorns might be processed and used by the community at large.

Also coinciding with autumnal conditions of acorn resources was the Bear Dance ritual of Yokuts and Western Mono tribes. This ceremony marked the end of the acorn harvest and the ritual first use of acorns by specific moieties (Gayton 1946:257; 1948a:39–40, 120–21). Central Foothills Yokuts, for example, performed the ceremony under the supervision of both shamans and moiety chiefs, the shamans performing the dance ritual, and the moiety chief calling together the community members involved. Gayton (1930:410) has previously commented that "orderly social activity" was maintained by a combination of: (1) the traditional legal authority of the chief; and, (2) the belief in the supernatural abilities of the shaman to enforce adherence to ritual behavior. The regulation of subsistence activity by the bear dance ceremony appears to be no exception. The acorn crop would be gathered and stored by the people of one moiety (in this case the Bear lineages were ritually associated with the acorn), and after a shamanistic performance, the chief supervised a feast where acorns were prepared and served to other members of the community. The Bear lineages, having accomplished the successful harvest, were also allowed to partake of the acorns, which had been otherwise previously forbidden. A similar ceremonial practice is mentioned for the Western Mono by Gayton (1948b:283) and Aginsky (1943:398–99, 403). In establishing and enforcing traditional economic duties of specific lineages, to be accomplished before the entire moiety could utilize gathered resources, Yokuts and Western Mono shamans and chiefs performed a functional role, which ostensibly encouraged efficient harvesting, preparation, and distribution of acorn resources.

In Southern California, ritual regulation of the acorn harvest was developed around a central, social and ceremonial pragmatist (corresponding to a "chief") with well-defined economic powers; and the shamans, who provided supernatural support to the harvest procedure. The Cahuilla termed this chief the "net," and as a ceremonial leader, he was responsible for the maintenance of ritual conduct, and for the care of the sacred bundle (maiswat) and the ceremonial house (kis?amna?a), the latter in which he lived in aboriginal times (Strong 1929:106; Bean 1972:104–5). Bean (1972:113) has also noted that the net was usually also a shaman, belonging to an interactive association of other supernaturally oriented individuals who acted as community leaders. The net presided at all ceremonies, scheduled their occurrence, and maintained the oral tradition of songs and legends. Most significant, however, were the ritualized economic powers of the office. Based on his precise knowledge of community resource areas, he directed food gathering quests, determining when and where various crops were to be procured, and storing goods collected from community members for future distribution and use. The basis of his organizational power was the administration of the first-fruits ritual for vegetable products, of which the acorn rite was most important. When the acorns were considered ready for collection, and preparation, the net sent a representative to gather a small amount, which was brought back to the ceremonial house and consumed in ritual portions by members of various lineages (Bean 1972:143–44). In the "old days," it was customary for the net himself to eat the first product (Strong 1929:106). The accompanying ceremony, for which participants brought additional food to be shared by all, lasted three days and nights, and included singing by men and women, and dancing by shamans (puvalam) to ensure continuing positive response from supernatural forces in control of food (Drucker 1937b:41). The supernatural abilities of the puvalam were utilized to "create" an abundant crop of acorns and restrain unfavorable climatic conditions. Collection of acorns prior to completion of the entire first-fruits ritual would cause sickness or death by supernatural agency, and observance of this restriction was socially enforced. The ceremony completed, the net declared the gathering season "open" and advised community members as to the practical details of the harvest.

Of further note concerns data presented by White (1963:123) on the Luiseño "tchumu' tushnakut," a ritual chief who supervised the gathering and distribution of vegetal resources from collectively-owned areas with the assistance of specifically empowered shaman (pul). White quotes Fr. Boscana on this aspect of subsistence organization:

> The captain (chief) was authorized to decide upon … the hunting of game and the collection of grain … They had a pul … who knew … the time to celebrate the feasts. In the same manner was made known the time to collect grain and to hunt; but he who advised the captain was one originally endowed with the power of providing their game, herbs, etc.… On such occasions, all turned out in quest of food—men, women, boys, and girls.… The greater part of their acquisitions was deposited with the captain; who took care of the same for the feast.…

The collection of acorns was undertaken according to this procedure. Men and women, as well as the shamans, danced for several nights in the ceremonial house for the first-fruits (Drucker 1937b:41). Distribution of the acorns to the community by the tchumu' tushnakut took place over a protracted time period after completion of the harvest rite. As sickness would result if any acorns were eaten before the ceremony, the pul was held socially responsible for the performance of his supernatural duties, and his abilities were deemed a "property belonging to the rancheria as a whole."

This brief summary of several regulatory rites is by no means a complete survey of acorn ritual in California, but serves rather to emphasize the more detailed ethnographic examples concerning the central position of ritual specialists in the direction of work on the fall harvest. But as additional examples of tree-crop ritual, the similarities of restricted seasonal abundance, staple importance, and pronounced ritual regulation, necessarily include the fall pinyon pine-nut harvest of the Washo and Serrano as cultural and ecological analogs of the elsewhere more prevalent acorn rite. The pinyon pine (*Pinus monophylla*) is distributed widely over the east slope of the Sierra Nevada, and the nuts were a more common food for the Washo than the acorn (Kroeber 1925:572). The production and harvest of the pinyon pine nut in autumn was of critical importance to Washo winter survival. Downs (1961:382) emphasizes the crucial nature of the seasonal crop in relating an old Washo informant's account of the four-day, first pinyon-nut ritual, regulated by a ritualist of definite shamanistic caste:

> This prayer-fella (Captain Jim) lived at Double Springs all year round. He would have a dream telling him to have a meeting. He was what you would call a religious man. He would get someone he could trust and send out a long, tanned string of hide with knots in it. For everyday until the meeting there was a knot so the people would know how many days they had until the meeting.
>
> All the men came and hunted for four days, and all the women would start gathering pine-nut. They would hang up the game to let it dry.
>
> The prayer wouldn't eat meat during those four days, but he could drink cold water and some lady would cook him pine nut. Every night they would have a dance.[1] On the fourth day everybody would bring the food they had and put it in front of the prayer, and then he would pick some man who was just (fair) and the food was divided a little before sunrise. If you have a small family you get less, if you have a big family you get more.

Then the prayer makes a prayer something like this: "Our father I dream that we must take a bath and then paint. Even the childrens ... (We must) wash away the bad habits so we won't get sick from the food we have in front of us!"

Then everybody go to the river ... no matter if there was a little ice on the water, and take a bath. If they was not near the river, they bathed the kids from baskets at Double Springs. The prayer, he prayed for pine nut, rabbit, and deer.

The pinyon-nut harvest was accomplished in Southern California typically under the ritual supervision of an hereditary chief and his ritual assistant. Serrano groups (the eastern-most of which depended upon the pinyon nut as a substitute for the acorn) possessed a ceremonial leader (kika) who like the Cahuilla net, lived in the ceremonial house and kept the "sacred bundle" from which his ritual authority

He was also a nominal owner of the wild-food tracts of the community over which his authority extended (Drucker 1937b:28). His ritual assistant (paha) had direct personal powers to conduct tribal ceremonies, and act as a messenger from the kika to the community (Kroeber 1925:618). The kika accompanied the community on the seasonal collecting trip, and all individuals were required to contribute provisions for this communal venture; the goods to be redistributed by the paha. The first pinyon nuts gathered were given to the kika, and used for the annual feast which took place in the ceremonial house upon return from successful harvest (Benedict 1924:391–92).

Apart from tree crops such as *Quercus* sp. and *Pinus monophylla* which were principal resources in their respective areas of distribution, other plant products of regional importance were collected and distributed in ritual contexts. Several examples of first-fruits ceremony, connected with herbaceous root and seed plants, and mesquite bean harvests of Yuman groups on the Colorado River, provide further perspective concerning control mechanisms in which a ritual specialist played an important role.

In Northeastern California, important spring plant resources included the bulbs of *Calochortus* sp. (such as the star tulip and the Mariposa lily), and the roots of "ipos," *Perideridia* sp. (Munz and Keck 1968:1012). Among the Atsugewi, spring first fruits rites were held for these species when they matured (Voegelin 1942:176). In May, the first roots gathered by groups of women were sung over by the shaman, who then examined them in order to predict the future health of the female population. If the shaman predicted impending illness or disease, he instructed all the women to return to the collecting grounds and dig roots for an entire day. The harvest accomplished, shamans sang for half a night over the roots to ensure the general well-being of all women in the community. Upon completion of the ceremony, each woman was allowed to take the roots she had collected, leaving a supply for the shaman who cooked and ate them. A variation of this ritual also occurred in which the shaman himself dug the requisite first roots, then supervised a general community feast to which women contributed "ipos" and men brought a late-spring fish catch.

Spring first-fruits rites, known as "witi lonu' iwis" ("little party") were engaged in by Yokuts divisions around Tulare Lake (Chunut, Tachi, and Wowol), and pertained primarily to berries and seeds which were "moiety-owned," as mentioned previously for the acorn crop (Gayton 1948a:40). The moiety associated with the food product would gather a supply when it first became available, and ritually present them to the other moiety. Consumption of the collected food by the associated lineages before the rite would cause their children to break out "with berries all over their bodies." Reciprocal services between moieties, ritually supervised by moiety chiefs, were observed for most seasonal foods requiring major collecting efforts in the spring. Chiefs might have informally directed the movements of village inhabitants during the collecting season (Gayton 1948b:258), but as a pervasive feature of Yokuts social organization, shamans appear to have entered into schemes of social regulation through the use of their supernatural abilities. The seed growing dance (known in Chunut as the "magic dance") was held each year by one or two shamans "who had the ability" to perform this prophetic ritual (Gayton 1948a:40). In late winter or early spring, the shamans who were to perform this dance did not consume any quantities of new seasonal food, such as tule roots or herbaceous annuals. About the middle of February, the shamans gave individual dance performances lasting all night and accompanied by a singer who sang songs "about birds and animals." During the night, a sleight-of-hand display was performed, in which the shaman caused the seeds of food plants to appear on the floor of the dance house by the fire, or by stamping on the ground, caused growing plants to materialize. The plants and seeds thus "produced" might just as suddenly disappear from view. The most significant aspect of this ritual, however, is the interplay between the shaman and the assembled participants:

> During this display the people would query the shaman about the crops of wild seeds for the coming season. "Where were the seeds going to grow?" He would point in certain directions, or even reply that they would be prolific near a specific person's seed-gathering place (Gayton 1948a:40).

In establishing a supernatural basis for the productivity of resource areas to be harvested in the immediate future, the shaman ritually reinforced the eventual direction of communal groups into these areas by moiety chiefs when spring resources became available. This inter-active system of "control" functions by shamans and ritually empow-ered moiety chiefs, as had been previously noted, appears to have been basic to efficient ecological behavior in Yokuts society.

The organization of the first-fruits rite was a function assumed by the tribal spiritual leader of the Colorado River Yuma, known as the "kwoxot." Forde (1931:118, 133–38) has provided a basic descrip-tion of his supernatural and powers:

> Kwoxot can be understood by all living creatures, by animals and plants. He can control them, so he can drive out sickness and pre-vent it from attacking people. He has the biggest powers of any man, is strong and happy, and tells the people what they must do to remain healthy. Kwoxot might sometimes cure diseases, but as a rule he did not, he used his powers to keep everybody well (p. 136).

Kwoxot was a voluntary position of assumed responsibilities; the source of his power in dreams or visions of an ancestor or animal guardian. As a rule, supernatural spirits conferred the full powers of a kwoxot upon one man at a time, thus only one individual held this position. As an embodiment of supernatural power in the community, the kwoxot indeed approaches shamanistic dimensions. Significantly, he was expected to organize singings and feasts in harvest seasons and redistribute goods provided by the community to those in need. Of the plant collecting activities under his supervision, the harvest of the mesquite bean (*Prosopis* sp.) and the associated ritual were particularly important. Trippel (1889:6) notes that the mesquite bean was the chief article of food for the Yuma and stored in quantity for winter use. When the bean pods ripened in early summer, large quantities were collected at favorable locations by men, women and children, soaked in water for several days, and the entire "sticky mass" removed and stacked in piles. The bundles of mesquite bean were placed in a ceremonial enclosure, arranged in sets corresponding to each district attending the feast. Games, dancing, singing, and discussion of community affairs occupied the evenings. On the last day, participants gathered outside the ceremonial enclosure and on a given signal, all the people rushed in to procure their share of the harvest. The celebration completed, the bundles were shouldered and all departed for home.

In the general examples detailed in this first section, a variety of situations have been described in which ritual specialists, such as shamans, secret society headmen, and ceremonial leaders such as the Cahuilla net, the Serrano kika, and the Yuma kwoxot regulated the gathering and distribution of essential plant food resources in the context of special, community-based and socially sanctioned ritual. In continuing an analysis of the regulatory functions of these ritual personalities and the systems of ritual restriction which acted to encourage the ecological efficiency of communal subsistence activities, formulistic ritual surrounding the first-salmon rites of Northwestern California, and first-fish ceremony elsewhere in Native California form the next topic of discussion.

First Fish Rites: Formulistic Ritual of Northwestern California and other First Fish Ceremony

Fish were undoubtedly an important food resource to native Californians. The seasonal upstream movements of anadromous fish, of which the distinct spring salmon run was most prolific, were events of great importance to many aboriginal subsistence economies. Stimulated by winter rains in the North Coast Ranges, and early snow melt in the Sierra Nevada, which provided appropriate water levels and headwater temperatures for spawning, annual or semi-annual fish resources were available in numerous freshwater river systems of Northwestern and North Central California (Rostlund 1952:20, 30). Fish of major importance were the Pacific species *Oncorhynchus tschawytscha* (king salmon), *Oncorhynchus kisutch* (silver salmon), and the steelhead trout (*Salmo giardnerri*), which spawn in freshwater and soon after birth swim out to sea to grow to maturity. After four to six years they return to the freshwater rivers to spawn upstream (Baumhoff 1963:170).

The ecological significance of the seasonal spawning runs to aboriginal resource economies lay in the fact that the runs carried fish in significant numbers over a limited period of time, so that a concentrated, well-organized fishing effort at the appropriate seasonal interval gave a comparatively great return. In the brief analysis of the ritual practices surrounding freshwater fishing among particular culture groups of Northern and Central California, the various tribes utilizing anadromous fish resources will be divided into the two following classes:

(1) Those groups, in North Coast Range drainages, for whom the salmon constituted the main bulk and dietary staple in the annual food economy, and who performed a formulistic ritual coinciding with the onset of the spring runs. The Yurok, Karok, Hupa, and Tolowa will be considered as examples of this class, designated as inhabiting the "Lower Klamath province," where salmon runs are of the greatest annual reliability (Baumhoff 1963:171); and

(2) those interior groups of the Sacramento and San Joaquin drainages, for whom the salmon was a secondary food resource of equal or supplementary importance to other foods, and who engaged in shamanistic or other first fish rites distinct from the formulism of Northwestern California. The Maidu and Yokuts tribes will be considered as brief examples from this class, designated as inhabiting the "California province," where annual salmon yields were more irregular and subject to marked cyclic fluctuations in quantity (Baumhoff 1963:171).

The spring salmon run was most intensely ritualized in Northern California, occurring at a time when winter food stores were low and maximum community energies were focused upon fishing efforts. A central core of northwestern tribes (Yurok, Karok, and Hupa) practiced the formulistic first-salmon rite, each group undertaking one spring ceremony at a specific location. Although superficially similar in initial ritual procedure to the protracted series of Jumping and Deerskin dances of the biennial World Renewal celebrations, the first-salmon ceremonies appear to have been held independent of these public display dances (Kroeber and Gifford 1949:105). The salmon ritual, among all these groups, incorporated common features which defined them as regulatory rites. The "first" spring salmon was always procured and ritually eaten by a priest or his assistant, who fasted, prayed, and sweated for a prescribed period of time. Fresh salmon were not to be consumed by the community until this ritual eating was performed, under pain of supernaturally induced illness or death. Throughout the period of days over which the ceremony was performed, the oral delivery of esoteric formulae, intended to induce and renew an abundance of salmon, was the main activity of the priest or formulist. The formulist's supervisory position in the rite was clearly based on his personal knowledge of the proper sequence of these narrative recitations, which were treated as private property and considered of supernaturally creative power. In the performance of the salmon ceremony (which was the ritual reenactment of mythical times when immortal beings first instituted the rite), the formulist ensured positive response from the spirit forces of the salmon, while overtly regulating the inception of the salmon-fishing season.

The Yurok first salmon ceremony was held annually in April at Welkwau, a village at the mouth of the Klamath River. Although mentioned by Kroeber (1925:60–61) and Kroeber and Gifford (1949:99–100), the rite is described in detail by a Yurok informant, Robert Spott, in *Yurok Narratives* (Spott and Kroeber 1942:171–79). Known as "hetku menekuni nel pui" ("the salmon spearing from shore"), the ritual was performed by an old formulist who lived in Welkwau. Prior to the rite, no salmon caught at the mouth of the river could be eaten, although other species of fish could be caught and eaten at any time. The formulist began preparations seven days before the rite, arranging for and instructing his ritual assistant (who was to perform the actual first eating of the salmon), and in subsequent days cleared a path from the ceremonial house to the mouth of the river. The last day before the ceremony, he recited several formulae, praying for the well-being of the world and food resources. The day of the ceremony, the formulist moved to the mouth of the river and told men fishing on the bank (for species other than salmon, such as sturgeon and lampreys) to watch for the "first salmon." When the species was seen, the formulist was notified, and reciting a formula, he feigned the act of spearing the fish with his harpoon, and allowed it to pass upriver, as the "ne' pe' wo kewononoro' apin" ("the first salmon that goes on up to the head of the river"). The next salmon to appear was speared, and after another recitation, taken to the ceremonial house where it was cooked and ritually consumed. The formulist prayed the entire night in the sweathouse, and the next day officially sanctioned salmon fishing (i.e., declared the season open) for all upstream Yurok villages.

After the performance of the Yurok first salmon rite at Welkwau, the communal effort of dam-building at the upstream site of Kepel could begin, usually several months later in the early summer. The elaborate 10-day ritual of building this fish dam is described in detail by Waterman and Kroeber (1938:49–80), Kroeber (1925:58–60), Erikson (1943:277–82), and Kroeber and Gifford (1949:81–85). The dam structure consisted of a framework of poles, logs, and small stakes extending across the entire course of the river, and the building of this framework required the coordinated efforts of several hundred men from various villages to cut wood. As many as seventy individuals worked at the dam site itself, constructing the framework (Waterman and Kroeber 1938:54–55). At various intervals along the dam, openings leading into a small wooden enclosure were arranged, and during the ten days of fish collection at the structure, large quantities of salmon were harvested and dried.[2] The entire process of construction, use, and eventual dismantling of the dam was directed by a formulist, who supervised in every way the work involved. It has been stated that the Kepel fish dam represents the largest mechanical enterprise undertaken in Northwestern California, and was clearly the Yurok's most communal subsistence effort (Waterman and Kroeber 1938:78).

The Karok first salmon rite (described by Kroeber 1925:104–5; Roberts 1932:426–40; and Kroeber and Gifford 1949:35–47) was held in March or April at the village of Amaikiaram on the west bank of the Klamath several miles below its confluence with the Salmon River. The formulist and his assistant were once again the ceremonial officials, reciting formulae, kindling a sacred fire, and cooking the first salmon for ritual consumption. These ritual activities were not to be witnessed by any other persons, and the community as a whole was obliged to leave the village and remain secluded in the surrounding hills. Roberts (1932:430) mentions that salmon fishing might occur before completion of the rite, but any fish caught were saved and not consumed before completion of the ceremony. The ritual eating of the salmon accomplished, the people returned to the village, and all Karok were allowed to begin fishing and eating fresh salmon.

On the west side of the Trinity River, near the upstream end of Sugar Bowl Valley, the Hupa first salmon rite was held each spring (Goddard 1903:78–79; Kroeber and Gifford 1949:56–61). A formulist would go to a selected site before anyone had engaged in fishing activities and recite a formula over the first salmon procured, narrating the mythical creation and journey down the river and back, and detailing ritual restrictions to be observed in fishing matters. Having cooked and eaten the first salmon, he prayed for an additional ten days, while he continued to catch salmon which were smoked and dried in preparation for a feast on the last day of the rite. During this period, as before, fishing was not permitted to the public. On the tenth and final day, a community feast ensued and the salmon season was declared officially "open."[3]

A final example of formulistic ritual for salmon in Northwestern California, outside the previous Klamath-Trinity focal area, is found among Tolowa groups of the Smith River drainage (Du Bois 1932:258–59; Drucker 1937a:261). At the onset of the spring runs, a formulist performed the "ha'guCLi xa'c Renic" (salmon-go-out-to-catch) in which he entered the sacred sweathouse or "salmon's home" and cited prayers during a five-day fast. On the last day of the fast, the formulist caught the first salmon, built a fire, and cooked the fish, placing it upon a basketry tray on which were represented the roots, leaves, and fruit of all available plant foods. He then began a long formulistic recital, requiring several hours, describing the origins the world and the Salmon's primeval journey up the Smith River. The "first foods" were divided by the formulist among the adult spectators and consumed; "After this, everyone could catch and eat salmon; he opened the season!" (Drucker 1937a:261).

In general, the procedures of the first salmon ritual in Northwestern California, and the manifest control functions of the formulist in determining the proper time for the beginning of the fishing season, are an extension of the need for careful maintenance and harvest of this essential resource. The annual spring run of salmon was the mainstay of native populations in this region, and the elaborate formulae and ritual restrictions assigned to the fish resource are indicative of this dietary emphasis. However, among other native groups outside the Northwestern culture area, where salmon was of subsidiary importance, ritual activities surrounding the spring salmon run were of a different nature. The formulist is absent, and taking his place as the central ritualist is the shaman or a moiety chief who derives supernatural support from shamanistic ritual.

Among the northwestern foothill Maidu, the first salmon observance was undertaken by a shaman, who caught the first fish of the season, cooked it, and distributed morsels of the food to all in the community. This ritual opened the fishing season for the year. Further detail on the structure of the ceremony, as to whether it included the recitation of a particular formula by the shaman, is lacking (Kroeber 1925:437; Dixon 1905:198) although Voegelin (1942:57) notes the existence of a definite taboo against eating salmon before the rite was performed.

Yokuts and Western Mono tribes on the San Joaquin River and Yokuts divisions on the lower Kings River held spring salmon ceremonies at their principal fishing sites (Aginsky 1943:398; Gayton 1948b:256). As previously outlined for the Yokuts "Seed Dance" ceremony, a supernaturally prophetic ritual by shamans preceded the first salmon rite by several weeks or months, apparently undertaken to inform the community of resource areas to be fished in the upcoming season. In late winter, shamans performed the "ohowis" or wishing ceremony in a specially constructed house or behind a tule partition, upon which were hung the skins of otters and beavers, believed to be the personal spirits of the shamans whose power was connected with water fauna (Kroeber 1925:507). A magic display was performed in which fish were made to appear in a vessel of water or to drop from the animal skins hung on the walls of the ceremonial structure. While this performance continued, the shaman called out the names of fishing camps where the people went in the spring to harvest the salmon run (Gayton 1948a:121–22). When the spring salmon arrived, a chief (the headman of the moiety ritually "responsible" for the salmon) speared, cooked, and ate the first salmon at these supernaturally sanctioned localities, and prayed to the salmon spirit for an abundant supply of fish. All lineages then participated in a general salmon feast, and the season was officially opened (Gayton 1948b:256).

The ritual regulation of spring salmon fishing, in the contest of formulistic and other esoteric ceremony, has been briefly outlined in this section, with close attention paid to the central ritualist of the performance and the regulatory role he plays in the subsistence activity. Whether a formulist, shaman, or ritually obligated moiety chief, he appears to have played an important part in the direction and focus of communal subsistence energies at a time when potential salmon yields were highest. The brief examples in this section reveal a remarkable similarity in form and function, and have been presented as a cultural synopsis of the first salmon rite in native California.

Communal Hunting Ritual: Organizational Aspects of Deer, Antelope, and Rabbit Ceremony

As a food resource of distinct importance throughout native California, game animals, and the ritual surrounding their communal hunting, form the last topics of discussion in this "operational" analysis. Deer and elk were a major secondary resource to aboriginal economies, everywhere of lesser importance than the acorn, but ranking higher than fish in areas without good salmon streams (Baumhoff 1963:167). Communal deer hunting activity usually took place during the fall mating season, when females and competing males were concentrated in large herds.

Ranging over a variety of life zones, predominately in grassland, chaparral, woodland, and other transitional habitats, the mule deer (*Odocoileus hemionus californicus*) was found throughout the south Coast Ranges, Transverse Ranges, and southern Sierra Nevada. The Columbian black-tailed deer (*0. hemionus columbianus*) occurred in a complementary northward distribution, throughout the north Coast Ranges and in the Sierra Nevada southward to Lake Tahoe. The Roosevelt elk (*Cervus canadensis roosevelti*) and Tule elk (*Cervus nannodes*) also inhabited the north Coast Ranges and Central Valley respectively. Of more regional importance, pronghorn "antelope" (*Antilocapra americana*) inhabited the Central Valley in aboriginal times but by the ethnographic period (ca. 1900) was limited principally to the marginal desertic regions of Northeastern and Southern California. Although of smaller size than deer or elk species, the large pronghorn herds were amenable to surround and drive hunting techniques. Of similar regional importance in the drier scrub and woodland areas of Northeastern and Southern California were rabbits in the genera *Lepus* (jack-rabbit) and *Sylvilagus* (cotton-tail) which were often taken in great quantities through large-scale cooperative drives in the fall.

The ritual organization of communal hunting for deer, antelope, and rabbits was often the prerogative of shamans, hunting "bosses," or other ritualists whose *specific* task was the direction of hunting or driving activities. Description of the various aspects of ceremony surrounding each game resource, in selected cultural contexts, provides further evidence of the regulatory nature of subsistence ritual.

Among the Atusgewi, the fall deer hunt was organized around a communal sweating ritual called by the chief, followed by a singing and praying ceremony conducted by a hunting shaman, at which plans for the hunt were discussed. The shaman would tell who was to kill a deer, or guarantee that every man in the party would be successful. When groups of hunters moved to temporary camping sites in search of deer, the shaman accompanied them to "charm" the animals, and during the hunting activities, he smoked his pipe and called each mountain in the vicinity by name: "Don't hide your children (deer); give my boys good luck; give them your children" (Voegelin 1942:172). Upon return from the hunt, the shaman assembled all the hunters in one group, and before the meat was divided, all were compelled to sweat and cleanse themselves "under the armpits" while the shaman sang.

Western Achomawi shamans practiced a more elaborate "deer calling" ritual in which concealed pits along deer "runways" were utilized. These trapping pits, as noted by Kroeber (1925:309), were between six and nine feet deep, and their excavation was an arduous task. At sunup of the selected day, the shaman would cause a brief rain to fall, then sing from behind a blind of tules stretched out in front of the village. The deer ran and jumped (were driven?) into the pit as the shaman "called" them, and the assembled people killed and ate the animals thus trapped. An informant spoke of a particular shaman who performed this ritual: "(This doctor) had very strong power to do this; he did it for everybody in his tribe; he got people something to eat, this way" (Voegelin 1942:171).[4]

Shamans of the eastern Achomawi also held a ceremony for the fall deer hunt at which they assembled ten or more men for an all night ritual of singing and praying. The deer doctor, who might derive his power from a weasel spirit-guardian, burned marrow from the legbone of a deer in small holes in the ground, "feeding" his power to give the hunters good luck. This shaman also accompanied the hunting party.

Wintu shamans were customarily consulted about the location of game and as to who would be the most successful hunters of the next day's outing. The entire night previous to the hunt, the assembled group of hunters lay on their backs in the sweathouse, hitting their chests with slender sticks in time to the singing of the hunt "leader" who knew the supplicatory songs the best. The shaman also sang, charming the deer spirits and telling the hunters where to find the game (Du Bois 1935:106; Voegelin 1942:171).

Fall communal deer hunts were similarly preceded and regulated by shamanistic ritual among the Maidu (Voegelin 1942:54, 171–72). Southern and Valley groups held a ceremony the night before the hunt, after an acorn soup dinner which the entire community attended. Shamans or secret-society headmen prayed and sang so that the hunters would sight game. The next day, a shaman or "luck-bringer" would go with the hunting party, walking ahead of the hunters to "spot" the deer. The shaman might also place "medicine" on a stick in deer tracks to give the animals cramps in their legs, facilitating their easy capture. When the deer were discovered feeding, the shaman would go around the herd with medicine to prevent their escape from the surrounding hunters. For this service, he was given a share of the deer meat (Beals 1933:348). After a successful hunt, the deer were brought back to the assembly house whole, where the meat was distributed in a feast which again included acorn soup. This hunting ritual was also practiced by northeastern mountain Maidu groups. The shaman conducted singing, dancing, and praying the night before the hunt in a group ceremonial, charming the deer for the hunters both on this occasion and during the hunt on the following day. Before the deer meat from the hunt could be consumed, the services of the shaman again were required for a ceremony, as an informant stated: "Do not eat meat, after big hunt, until somebody prays, talks" (Voegelin 1942:172).

Similar shamanistic ritual concerning deer hunting is noted by Aginsky (1943:444–52) for the Yokuts, Western Mono, and Sierra Miwok. Deer shamans foretold the success of hunting parties, telling hunters where to go to find game, and often accompanying the hunting group, receiving a share of the kill for their supernatural services. Group ceremonies were held both before and after hunting activities.

In contrast, the ritual of the deer hunt in Southern California, among the Cahuilla and Serrano, was centered around the ceremonial leaders who have been previously described as important in the organization of the acorn and pinyon pine harvest. When the Cahuilla hunters killed a deer, the animal was often presented to the net in the kis?amna?a (ceremonial house) and preparations for the deer ceremony were begun. Food was collected by the net from all families in the village, and all community members were invited to take part in the feast (Strong 1929:77; Bean 1972:146–47). The ceremony consisted of singing over the body of the deer, with the manifest intent of encouraging the favor and cooperation of the animal spirit and expressing appreciation to the deer for allowing themselves to be killed. During the morning of the ceremony, the deer meat was distributed to the community at large. Bean (p. 147) notes that this ritual was held frequently enough to exist as a principal mechanism for the distribution of sizable amounts of animal meat to the community.

The Serrano practiced a similar ceremony; the kika conducted an all night ritual in the ceremonial house whenever deer were killed, and in the morning, summoned the people of the village to distribute the meat (Benedict 1924:379).

The most specialized ritual organization of hunting activity is undoubtedly expressed in the "antelope charming" ceremonies of the Achomawi, Atsugewi, Northern Paiute (of Surprise Valley) and the Washo, all of which are tribes who inhabited the northeastern California desert range of *Antilocapra americana* in ethnographic times. A special "antelope shaman" was in all cases the instigator of this community effort. In winter or early spring, when large herds of pronghorn ran in open country, the shaman would inform the people of the presence of a herd in a certain location. The shaman might dream of the animals (which might be his spirit guardians), or send several scouts to locate a herd nearby. Once the antelope were sighted, the construction of a sagebrush corral or a circular sagebrush rope fence, with an opening at one end, was directed by the shaman. A charming ritual was usually next performed inside the brush corral, the shaman leading dancing and singing of the assembled people, and often falling into a trance-like state in which he allegedly experienced visions of a successful drive. At the conclusion of this performance, the antelope herd was driven into the corral by groups of fast runners, the entrance closed, and the surrounded animals slaughtered and divided among the participants. The shaman usually received the first and largest share of meat for conducting this ceremony.

Among the Apwaruge (eastern Atsugewi) a "power man" (shaman) sang all night to entice the antelope into a sagebrush rope surround. The next day, everyone in the community participated in the killing of the antelope; "even women could participate in the kill because the antelope were all doped" (Garth 1953:133). The Achomawi antelope shaman smoked and passed his pipe, leading an antelope dance before the charming ritual, which took place in the evening (Stewart 1941:366–67).

Several informants' accounts of the antelope ceremony among the Northern Paiute groups of Surprise Valley are presented by Kelly (1932:83–86). Accounts mention that the antelope shaman called together the inhabitants of 15 or 20 camps from the surrounding areas, perhaps as many as 100 men, to assist in the drive. As many as 200 antelope were killed in a single drive and distributed among the participants. One informant reported:

> Just one man can charm antelope; I don't know how he learns. He is like a doctor. He sits with everyone in the circle and sings making music on a doe hide (deer or antelope) that is stuffed with clothes and tied with string. If the people know how, they help him sing. A plain stick (unnamed) is wrapped with any kind of braid, and the charmer works it back and forth on the bundle. After a long time he says, "They (the antelope) haven't looked at us yet." Finally he says, "The deer are coming," and falls senseless on his drum and visions an antelope. Finally he recovers, sits up, says: "We are sure to kill antelope. I see them coming inside the corral. I see them lying there."
>
> They have already placed sagebrush, root ends up, in a big circle, about as far as from here to camp (about a half-mile). There were many people so it didn't take long to pile the brush. Men and women line up in wings by an opening in the circle, the women nearest the corral, the men at the outer ends.

Then the fastest runner goes out, returning when he has sighted a herd of antelope. Then the men go out in two parties and circle the herd and drive them in. They close the opening of the corral and stand between the piles of sagebrush that form the corral. If an animal starts their way, they head him back.

The fastest runner chases the antelope around in the corral until they are tired and frightened, when he kills a doe and throws it on top of a sagebrush pile in the center, and then a buck. They eat these two and then everybody get a share. Then the headman (shaman) tells his people it is their turn to shoot. They shoot from the circle as the animals approach. A wife stands with each man and drags away his kill....

When they stop for the night, the fastest runner guards the antelope. They set fire to that sagebrush to frighten the animals. (The next day) the headman tells them to go ahead and kill. There are so many animals that they don't have to divide them; they never kill all of them, some escaping. Almost everyone kills one. Sometimes an antelope becomes so tired that it falls down and a woman kills it. A woman might even kill two or three.

The headman shoots too; he takes most of the buck horns, but not the does'. They put the horns on a pile of sagebrush in the middle of the camp circle. All the heads are turned toward the charmer's camp. He wants everyone to come. They cook the heads under the ashes and all eat, each person perhaps getting one head.

They butcher the antelope and dry the meat on the sagebrush bushes. Coyotes and wolves never bother it.

When there is no sagebrush for a corral, they braid sage-brush bark and make a fence by tying it to posts about four feet tall. Loose strands of bark hang down the poles and when the antelope are in the corral the people pull the braid and the loose strands wave.

I have done this kind of antelope hunting. In winter the antelope are in big herds and that's the time to kill them. This kind of hunt is called kulal; many camps join. They tell everybody to come.

It takes just one day to charm antelope (but the killing evidently continues into the second day) (Kelly 1932:84–85).

The Washo antelope shaman (ai' yes kumomli) utilized his supernatural dream-power in organizing the antelope ceremony and drive as recorded by Lowie (1939:324–25):

> The antelope chief sees some antelope in a dream. He reflects about it and goes to the place dreamt about in the mountains. He sees two or three head, then he knows his dream is true. He begins to talk to them. He does not tell anyone as yet, but keeps his own counsel and studies the matter himself. He continues dreaming three or four times. Then he begins talking to the antelope, taking a pipe. He wants to see what he can do. He looks at the antelope, he lets them see him walking along side of them; they do not run away. He does this two or three times. Soon he tells the people to come together and says, "My people, I have dreamt truly or falsely, I don't know which. In the place I dreamt of last night, there were forty antelope banded together. If I dreamt truly, you'll see them there this morning." He sends two boys to the place as scouts. They look for game and see ten or fifteen head feeding there together. The boys do not let the antelope see them. They go back and tell the chief, "Your dream is true, we saw the herd right there." That evening, he studies the matter again while in bed. He dreams again and tells his people, "Well, I dreamt again last night, I dreamt right before. I dreamt of two antelopes last night, you fellows drove them into the corral, we all killed them, and had something to eat." The old people answer: "Yes, if you dreamt right, we'll have meat, we'll try tomorrow to go after them."

A corral was constructed, of approximately one acre in total size, with a chute leading to the entrance. The sagebrush was piled so high that the antelope could not jump out. The shaman stood in back of the corral while a group of men went out to drive the antelope in:

> He says, "I'll stay home behind the corral. If I dreamt right, you'll drive them in and we'll kill them. If they get scared at you fellows, we can't help it; but I think we'll kill them easily in the corral."

When the antelope are near, he says to the beasts: "Don't get scared, come on easily now, don't get discouraged, listen to my words. We are making a home for you, you have come a great way." The antelope stop and look toward him. They are not afraid at all, but keep quiet like sheep driven into a pen. Instead of scattering they come into the sagebrush pen, the people close up, and the chief bids them commence killing.

In aboriginal times, bows and arrows and clubs were used to dispatch the antelope, and the largest buck was killed for the antelope shaman himself. Of the rest, three or four men would divide the meat of one antelope: (The shaman says) "I dreamt antelope for you, I got the best one, I am satisfied." Nobody eats while he is speaking.

The antelope was divided among the people, the meat was packed home and all had "plenty that night."

Finally, among rituals concerned with the acquisition of game animals by communal methods are the annual rabbit drives, which were conducted by groups in whose geographic range these animals were a major seasonal food source. Among tribes in which this activity was organized by a ritual specialist, the Washo and the Cahuilla are exemplary.

The Washo "rabbit boss" was a special leader distinct from the political headman or antelope shaman, who set the time for the fall drive, which was held every year in late October or November over a period of several days (Lowie 1939:327). A large group of people were organized by the boss, and up to fifteen men among them had rabbit nets which were united into a single unit 200 yards long and four feet high, supported by sticks six or seven feet apart. The line of nets was straight except at the ends which curved inward in the direction of the drive-line movements. 200 Washo, the rabbit boss among them, joined in the drive, scaring the quarry into the net where a boy or an old man would dispatch them with a stick, or the hunters themselves would kill them with a bow and arrow. The total kill might average between 400 and 500 rabbits a day, each man who participated obtaining three or four animals apiece. The next day, a new location several miles distant was selected and the procedure repeated. When all the people were heavily loaded with animals, the rabbit boss would say: "We stop today, we have all we want today. Let us go home."

The ritual aspects of the rabbit hunt are somewhat unclear, but the rabbit boss was apparently an hereditary position and in later ethnographic times assumed by an individual with supernatural powers acquired in dreams. Downs (1961:380) proposes that the introduction of agriculture and firearms during the historical period sufficiently decreased antelope and deer populations to cause an associated increased dependence upon rabbit as a major source of food. Ecological factors may thus have facilitated a more recent transference of ritual traits from the antelope charming complex to the rabbit drive (i.e., a "dreamer" directing the hunt). Formalized prayers were said before the hunt by the boss, and in the period covered by the memory of the oldest informants, dancing was often staged nightly during the rabbit drives. Downs elicited data concerning the character of the last Washo rabbit boss:

> There was ... a special leader who directed the hunt who had dreaming power, "Jack Wallace would dream where the rabbits were and when it was time for hunting he would send out a call." The man mentioned was described as the last of the real dreamers; this power made him extremely influential among the Washo; his descendants are claimants for the "chieftaincy" (1961:380).

The Cahuilla rabbit hunt was a ritually regulated activity undertaken to provide a large number of animals for various ceremonies and feasts which occurred when rabbit populations were at high density (Bean 1972:147). In the fall, these animals were hunted in the mesquite and pinyon-juniper woodlands, where herbaceous plant resources were plentiful. Their presence was significant to Cahuilla subsistence during the winter months when fresh vegetable resources were unavailable. The hunt involved the cooperative effort of large numbers of men, women and children, and was usually organized by the paxaa?, the ritual assistant to the net (the paxaa? might also be a shaman) who supervised the proper arrangement of the rabbit nets into a large arc, directed the drive movements, and organized the collection and cleaning of the game that was killed (Bean 1972:113). In some instances several hundred rabbits were collected in a single day's activity.

THE FUNCTIONAL CONTEXT
Model and Analysis

Throughout the preceding sections, the ideational and operational contexts of subsistence ritual have been briefly reviewed in selected cultural settings of native California. It has been proposed that native world view incorporated two basic postulates which reinforced the ritual regulation of economic activity: (1) the world of supernatural cause and effect required proper human attention and respect in the form of prescribed ritual behavior for the continued positive response from spirits in control of food resources, and; (2) the organization of these rituals associated with large-scale gathering, fishing, and hunting activity was usually accomplished under the direction of a shaman, formulist, or other specialist who functioned as a regulatory force by virtue of his ritualized power to control or mediate supernatural phenomena. The general structure of the subsistence rituals previously discussed appears consistent throughout native California: an *essential* food resource (an "ecological deterininant") such as acorns, salmon, or antelope, is available in a relatively concentrated supply during a limited seasonal interval, and often requires the intensive, coordinated effort of human groups to maximize potential yield. Economically productive individuals are organized to collectively accomplish the subsistence activity and/or distribute the product in a ritual context, and are often constrained from individually exploiting or consuming the available resource until a ceremony is performed by a specific ritual functionary. In the case of most plant food and salmon rituals, the conclusion of this ceremony (which may last a variable number of days) commences the "resource season" during which the harvest and use of the food is not further restricted....

In summary, native cultures were confronted by an ecological and seasonal diversity of natural resources which required control and supervision of subsistence energetics for the maintenance of human populations. A basic response of aboriginal peoples to variable imput of natural resources appears to have been the regulation and organization of communal subsistence activities through the ritualization of economic behavior. At intervals of seasonal availability of major food resources, native world view reinforced a set of regulatory prerogatives undertaken by shamans, formulists, and ceremonial leaders which served to organize the work potentials of large cooperative groups. Energy flow from environmental resources and subsistence work potentials were regulated by ritualists in order to facilitate the efficient harvest and use of concentrated, short-term food yields, including seasonal products such as acorns, salmon, and game animals. As functional mechanisms for the systematization of human ecological relationships, world view and ritual were operative ideological institutions of broad adaptive importance to aboriginal societies of native California.

HISTORICAL
PERSPECTIVES

KASHAYA POMO MEMORIES OF FOOD

Essie Parrish

Two of the more recent developments in the study of Californian Native peoples have been an attention to culture change and a focus on an individual, Native perspective. The series of short reminiscences included here exemplify both these trends. Their narrator, Essie Pinola Parrish (1902–79), was a Kashaya Pomo religious leader, healer, and basket weaver. Parrish was born at the Haupt Ranch Rancheria, in Sonoma County, where many Kashaya people were living before they settled on the present rancheria near Stewarts Point. The daughter of Emily Colder and John Pinola, Essie Parrish was the last of four prophets of the Kashaya Pomo. She began her training as a healer and basket-weaver when she was five. After her mother died in 1912, she lived with her uncle's family for two years, before moving in with her maternal grandmother, Rosie Jarvis. During her teen years, she worked as a maid in a hotel in Point Arena. After a brief marriage to Daniel Scott, which produced four children, in 1920 she married Sidney Parrish, a Coast Central Pomo man. During their fifty-seven years of marriage, she had six children who survived into adulthood, numerous grandchildren and great-grandchildren.

Essie Parrish became the dreamer of the Kashaya Pomo community in 1943, after the death of Annie Jarvis, her teacher. In this capacity she doctored and led religious ceremonies. From the late 1940s until her death, she was also a consultant for anthropologists and linguists. She traveled throughout the country, speaking about basket-weaving and healing. With Samuel Barrett and his associates, she made ten films for the Lowie (now Hearst) Museum of Anthropology (1961–64), devoted to acorn and other food preparation, dream dances, and doctoring. She was a consultant for a volume on Kashaya plant use (Goodrich et al. 1980). As a cultural leader, Essie Parrish stressed education and dealing with the outside world while at the same time advocating the maintenance of Native traditions.

Kashaya Texts, by Robert L. Oswalt. University of California Publications in Linguistics (1964), 36:251, 295, 297, 301, 303, 305, 307, 329, 331.

These accounts were tape recorded and transcribed from the original Kashaya Pomo by Robert L. Oswalt (b. 1923), who was a graduate student in Linguistics at UC Berkeley when he first met Essie Parrish in 1949. This volume of texts—based on about eight months of fieldwork over the summers of 1957, 1958, 1959, and 1961—was accompanied by a grammar and dictionary. Oswalt, who obtained his Ph.D. in 1961 for his Kashaya grammar, taught for many years at UC Berkeley.

THE FIRST WHITE FOOD
(*Told September, 1958*)

It was also there at Métini that the white people first discovered the Indians—having come up, they found them. After they discovered the Indians, they wanted to domesticate them. In order to feed them food, in order to let them know about the white man's food, [the white men] served them some of their own white food.

Never having seen white men's food before, they thought that they were being given poison. Having given [the Indians] their food, they left and returned home but [the Indians] threw it in a ditch. Some they buried when they poured it out. They were afraid to eat that, not knowing anything about it—all they knew was their own food, wild food. They had never seen white people's food before then. That is what our old people told us. This is the end.

THE FIRST ENCOUNTER WITH COFFEE BEANS
(*Told September, 1958*)

This is another one [like the preceding story]. My father's older sister—we called her older sister; we called cousins older sister—that was the one who used to tell about what her mother did.

As before, a white man gave them coffee to drink—gave it in a sack. At that time, a long time ago, they ground the coffee themselves. He gave them a grinder too. When he had done so, he taught them [how to use it]. But [the Indians] didn't do it—they still didn't know what it was for. Even though he showed them, they didn't understand what it was for. They didn't want to drink it either.

She boiled it too. Just the way they used to cook their acorns, that's how she boiled [the coffee beans], thinking they would become soft— she boiled them whole. She let it boil and boil—let it boil all day long. She tested them with her fingers but they never did get soft—they weren't cooked. Then, saying that they must have been bad, that they were just like rocks, she poured them out.

This is the end.

CHILDHOOD REMINISCENCES
(*Told August, 1957*)

I like to tell about when I was young—about what things were like when I was young. Let's see—children nowadays are way different, not like we were long ago in the old days. This is the way it was.

When our elders told something, we only said, "All right." When night came, our old people told stories, and I always listened with full attention. I used to listen when they talked about things, when they told stories. It sounded good; it was pleasant to the ears. From time to time, what our elders told about turned out to be absolutely correct. When I grew older I found out that what our elders had talked about was right. What my mother and my father taught me, that I did. Nowadays children do what they themselves like to do. At that time I wasn't like that.

This used to be the best thing of all to me: In the roundhouse they did spiritual things and danced dances. I never thought about what the white people were doing over here. I only thought about the good things.

I didn't know about good food. That's why I never thought about getting upset about things—never considered being dissatisfied with the food. The food that my mother and my father gave me, that I ate. This is what used to be the best food of all for me when I was little: crackers. Because I didn't know about the great variety of good foods, I thought that crackers were the best food of all. As for the big food [that not ground into a flour nor naturally of granular form],

I thought the vegetables [literally 'fresh food'] to be the very best to me. Fried cabbage seemed to be the very best to me.

And things that my grandmother did, those I used to think that everybody did. I didn't know about what the white people ate, nor did I know about the things they did. The reason was I was raised that way. I wasn't raised with the clothes that the white people wore nor the food that the white people ate.

I was raised the way my grandmother raised me. That's the reason why, when I came to the age of reason, I was obedient. I see children nowadays beside whom I—we—must have been quite obedient.

PRESERVING SHELLFISH
(*Told July, 1959*)

In the old days we could keep food without it rotting. There isn't anything that the people of the old days couldn't do.

When winter came and the sea ran high, [the Indians] could not go to gather food along the coast for long periods. Before the water had already become rough, the leader would command, "Store away your food." Having had him say when, they went up to the gravel beach, pried off mussels, gathered turban snails, packed them up the coastal cliffs, dug holes, poured [the shellfish] in there, packed up gravel, poured it on top, and poured ocean water [over all that].

Then even when it rained, [the mussels] were still good and unspoiled for several days or even one week—turban snails they kept the same way. Because they did that, the old time people did not die off from starvation.

That is all there is of that.

PREPARING DEER AND OTHER MEAT
(*Told September, 1958*)

They are said not to have let any meat go to waste; they ate all of the deer—only the crushed bones were thrown away.

The backbone they laid on a mortar stone and pounded lightly with some kind of pestle, then they crushed, crushed, crushed—that uncovers the flesh—and then they baked it on coals. They only discarded [the bits of bone] they picked out by chewing.

That's how Indians prepared meat—by baking on coals. And by barbecuing—sticking [pieces of meat] up on sticks; heating them by radiation, they became cooked. It tastes delicious—I ate some that my grandmother prepared.

And as for the liver, they wrapped it in leaves and baked it under the ashes, and when it was cooked they ate it together with acorn mush. It tasted very good.

And the tripe they filled with deer blood, pinned close with small sticks, wrapped in thimbleberry leaves, and then they pinned that together too. They baked it under the ashes. When it was cooked, they took it out and opened it up—it looks good. The blood turns into a dark loaf. But the leaves aren't burned, only scorched on top. They say it tastes good.

And they ate the deer's ears too. When they skinned the head, they would cut the ears off. In order to eat it, they would then sear it on the coals. When they took it out, they would scrape it. Having done so, they would peel the skin off. Then they would cook it until the tips of the ears were good and crisp.

As for abalones, they let them age a little, pounded them hard, and baked them under the ashes—they taste delicious eaten together with acorn mush. Abalone also tastes delicious eaten with sour acorn mush.

Rabbit, too, they pound and pound lightly. Both cottontails and squirrels were also pounded and so prepared. That is the way the people ate.

PREPARING BUCKEYES
(*Told September, 1958*)

I am going to tell about preparing buckeyes. In the old days they would go after the buckeyes, gather them, pack and store them. Then they would cook them by boiling in a pot. Then they peeled off the skin. Nowadays they peel them with a knife but in the old days they peeled with their teeth. Then they are boiled again, and when they are cooked, when they have become soft like cooked potatoes, they are taken out and—let's see now—they are mashed and mashed and mashed with a mortar stone. Then they are strained through a finely meshed basket. Having been strained and strained, they are carried off to the water and are fixed as acorns are for leaching and water is poured over them, all the while stirring, stirring with the hand. As the water drains out, more is poured over them and they are stirred around and around. And they keep tasting it, keep tasting it. If it is still bitter, more is poured over it—all day long they do this. It is hard to leach, being extremely bitter. When they have done that it is good, it tastes just as good as clear, pure water. That is when they scrape it up and set off homeward packing it. While packing it along, they give out some to their friends and eat some—having heated kelp to swell the floats, they eat that mixed together with seaweed and meat and seafood. It tastes pure without any salt. When you are used to eating it, it tastes wonderful. This is all.

CLOVER
(*Told September, 1957*)

Clover[1] is what I am going to discuss next. We Indians eat clover. Even today, we Indians still like clover. Now I'll name off those I know.

/qʰabóhso/ is the one that grows in damp places. It has red flowers and small leaves.

What they call /boho·/ grows any old place. It has big leaves and big white flowers.

And what they call /sibu·ta/ [*Carum kellogii*] also grows like that with grass. It is the one that looks like grass. And part of what I call /sibu·ta/ —that's the root—we also make into a brush. It's good to eat too, but it's a strong-tasting clover.

And what they call /pʰaʔamʔso/ is also like /sibu·ta/. The leaves are wooly and the blossom is peculiar—/pʰaʔamʔso/ has flowers that are sort of red and sort of yellow.

The one they call /qasi·síhso/ [literally 'elk clover'] grows in the woods—the deep forest. Its leaves look peculiar, something like pine needles. They are eaten too.

Those are some clovers that we Indians eat mixed with peppernuts and with edible seaweeds. Those things taste good eaten with clover. Rolling that food into balls in the palms of their hands, cleaning it well, picking out the stems, making it into balls by rolling it around in their palms—that is how the old people ate that. Thus they taught us.

INDIAN POTATOES
(*Told by September, 1958*)

Potatoes are what I am going to talk about—our kind of potatoes.[2] They don't amount to anything individually; they are so small—something like small onions. They are called: /hiʔbúʔla [*Brodiaea laxa*], koyóʔyo, hubabá, sikʰolóʔlo/; and there are many others besides—there are many kinds of potato. They are the things they dig up.

Digging and digging, placing them in a carrying basket or something else, they would rub and rub them around in their hands to get the skins off. Then they would winnow and winnow. Nowadays they wash and boil them, but in the old days they rubbed them in their hands, blew away the chaff and baked them under the ashes. They cooked them under the ashes.

That, too, tastes good when eaten together with other food—they taste good when eaten with salty food. To me that aforementioned /hiʔbúʔla/ tastes delicious.

We Indian people had everything in our wild food. If there should be a lack of food for us Indians, or if something should happen, if food became expensive, if anything like that should happen, we wouldn't starve. We would eat our kind of wild food that is around. There are wild carrots and wild clover and wild potatoes.

SPEECH BEFORE THE FEAST ON JULY 4, 1958

Now you cooks, feed well those people eating with such gusto. That is what you cooks are for. That is what you do Our Father's work for. I know that in your hearts you love this work. That is why I always tell you cooks to do these things.

You food workers over there, watch over the tables. You will want them to be satisfied; you will want to let the people get enough to eat.

If they want more meat, you should not be stingy. For some people [one serving] isn't a good taste. Therefore if they want more, you should give them more without stint.

It will be good for us next year. If they get enough good food, they will remember us again next year. But if they don't get enough food—of that meat—if you don't give them all they want, they won't come back again next year. That's how to do things—do business in the long run.[3]

PHOTOGRAPHIC PORTFOLIO

KASHAYA POMO FOODS, ca. 1960

Samuel A. Barrett and film crew

These pictures were part of the still-photography documentation that accompanied Samuel Barrett's American Indian Film Project. Shortly after World War II, Samuel Barrett (1879–1965) returned to Berkeley, where he had earned the anthropology department's first doctorate in 1908. In 1953, he was appointed research associate in the Museum of Anthropology, a position he held until his death. A major preoccupation of his last decade was his direction of a massive film project, documenting Native cultures of western North America. As in all of his anthropology, Barrett's aims were in cultural salvage: to document what he believed to be vanishing customs, resorting to recreation if necessary.

As the Pomo were the principal ethnic subject of his work, many of the still pictures depict Essie Parrish preparing food. Two of the films were devoted to Kashaya food—*Acorns: Staple Food of California Indians* (1962) and *Beautiful Tree: Chiskale* (1965), with another planned on the Strawberry Festival. Food was also the subject of two other productions, both released in 1961—*Pine Nuts* (Northern Paiute) and *Buckeyes: Food of California Indians* (Nisenan; see the photographic portfolio devoted to Elizabeth Enos).

Most of these images (identified by the 25 prefix) are from a collection of 2253 color slides taken by the film crew. The identity of the photographers is not always known. Some were exposed by William Heick, the professional photographer who did most of the cinematography. Others were probably taken by the anthropological assistants, such as Josepha Haveman, David Peri, and Robert Wharton.

Essie Parrish using an abalone chisel to loosen salt crystals;
Salt Point, Sonoma County, 1961.
PHOTOGRAPH BY SAMUEL BARRETT AND CREW (NEG. NO. 25–5842).

Essie Parrish gathering palm kelp seaweed;
Manchester, Mendocino County, 1961.
PHOTOGRAPH BY SAMUEL BARRETT AND CREW (NEG. NO. 25–5798).

Essie Parrish gathering acorns; Kashaya, Sonoma County, 1960.
PHOTOGRAPH BY JOSEPHA HAVEMAN (NEG. NO. 15–19440).

Essie Parrish cracking acorns; Kashaya, Sonoma County, 1960.
PHOTOGRAPH BY SAMUEL BARRETT AND CREW (NEG. NO. 25–5872).

Essie Parrish pounding acorns; Kashaya, Sonoma County, 1960.
PHOTOGRAPH BY SAMUEL BARRETT AND CREW (NEG. NO. 25–5233).

Essie Parrish sifting acorn meal; Kashaya, Sonoma County, 1960.
PHOTOGRAPH BY SAMUEL BARRETT AND CREW (NEG. NO. 25–5247).

*Essie Parrish leaching acorn meal; shore of
Gualala River, Mendocino County, 1961.*

PHOTOGRAPH BY WILLIAM HEICK; COURTESY OF PHOTOGRAPHER.

Essie Parrish cooking acorn soup; Kashaya, Sonoma County, 1960.

PHOTOGRAPH BY SAMUEL BARRETT AND CREW (NEG. NO. 25–5886).

*Family of Essie Parrish opening up pit oven with acorn bread.
Back row (left to right): Donald Wilder, Daisy Antone Smith, Sidney
Parrish, David Smith, Rodney Marrufo, Jr., Rodney Marrufo, Sr.
Front row: Essie Parrish (left), Susie Gomez (right);
Gualala River, Mendocino County, 1961.*

PHOTOGRAPH BY WILLIAM HEICK; COURTESY OF PHOTOGRAPHER.

CONTEMPORARY
PERSPECTIVES

VENISON, ACORNS, AND FRY BREAD

David W. Peri

David Wayne Peri (Bodega Miwok, 1939–2000) was a founding co-editor of *News from Native California*. For many years, he served as professor of anthropology and linguistics at Sonoma State University, Rohnert Park. After earning a B.A. from the University of San Francisco in 1960, Peri worked with Samuel Barrett at UC Berkeley on the American Indian Film Project between 1961 and 1965. In the late 1980s, he was involved with the Warm Springs Cultural Resources project, run by the U.S. Army Corps of Engineers, as did Kathleen Smith and Otis Parrish. Among Peri's specialties were educational anthropology, history and theory in anthropology, ethnographic method, anthropological film, cultural resource management, ethnohistory-ethnobotany, economic anthropology; North America and California. He also served as chair of the board of Ya-Ka-Ama Indian Education and Development, a Native cultural organization west of Santa Rosa.

These short essays were part of a series devoted to plants and food that Peri wrote during the first year of *News* (see also Peri 1987c, 1988b, 2001; Alvarez and Peri 1987). They effectively capture the complex interplay of continuity and change in Native food habits. The article on venison is especially valuable given the scholarly overemphasis on acorns, while the little piece on fry bread shows how foreign foods may become indigenized and then spread to other Native communities.

News from Native California (1988), 1(6):4–5; (1988), 2(1):14–15; (1987), 1(4):22–23; (1987), 1(2):17–18.

VENISON: INDIAN BEEF
On Deer and Preparing Venison for Cooking, or
Why Things Are and How They Came To Be that Way

When I was young, the event that marked the beginning of deer season was the blooming of tarweed, when the air was filled with the scent of a waning summer and the beginnings of autumn. More than a century before, however, when my ancestors, who made their homes at Bodega Bay, were yet sovereign over their land, there was no season for the hunting of deer. Deer were taken throughout the year, although they were more plentiful in particular areas at particular times, especially in middle-to-late spring, and into late summer through early fall.

During the mating season of fall through early winter, deer were easier to hunt, since they lost much of their natural caution at this time, and would often be seen in open places. Although bucks, as well as does, are quick to catch motion and have a keen sense of hearing, deer, at this season, are prone to distraction and therefore it is easier to hunt them.

In those early days of my ancestors, no preference was given to the taking of bucks or does, fawns or yearlings; they were all hunted randomly. Young fawns however, were taken for the benefit of older people and young children, since the meat was exceptionally tender. Or as my Great Aunt Maggie, one of the Smiths living at Bodega Bay, would say, "They both have problems with the teeth, one is losing them and one is getting them; both have stomach problems too; one's just about worn out and the other is just learning. That's why hunters take the little ones; and the young ones, their meat is easy on the teeth and not hard on the stomach." There were also other instances when deer of a specific sex and/or age was preferred; however, these were exceptions to the "rule" of random hunting.

This type of hunting—as opposed to only hunting bucks—also increased the hunter's chances of "bringing home meat." The practice of random hunting also resulted in healthier deer herds than we have today, given the almost exclusive hunting of bucks. That is, with only a limited number of bucks mating with many does, there continually exists the very real, and the very often actual, problem of a particular disease or diseases running through an entire herd, adversely affecting large numbers of deer. Practiced over time, selective hunting also negatively effects the overall genetic vigor of the herd. That is, the genetic vitality is continually degraded due to the fact of a limited gene pool, since so few bucks are servicing a large and ever increasing number of does. The results of this condition are evidenced in a number of ways: the reduction in the size and weight of individual deer, sexually unbalanced populations, a restrained immune system unable to effectively fight off various diseases, and decreases in the herd's overall reproductive potential due to reduced fertility.

Whenever there was venison "on the table," it would most always prompt my great aunts and uncles to make some comment or other, most probably because fish, shellfish, and sea fowl were by far their more frequent dishes. Most of the venison eaten by the family at Bodega Bay during my time, and for a good number of years before that, was given us by inland peoples living along the Russian River and around Clear Lake, who came to the bay to fish, harvest sea foods, and often collect the Washington clams to make "bead money." The gift of food was in recognition of our family's inherited custodial responsibility over the resources of the greater bay, that in much earlier times they and their relatives controlled. Other than this, deer were hunted locally, but never to the degree that it was practiced in other areas.

In those days before there was a deer "season," a frequently heard comment was that the meat tasted differently when hunted at different times of the year. And, since the establishment of a hunting season, my relatives have easily tired of eating venison. My Great Aunt Maggie would often say, especially when there were visitors: "Deer meat always tastes the same nowadays; you have to spice it up to make it taste. When they hunt, the boys [meaning her brothers and other family members] can only go out that one time." What Aunt Maggie was referring to was that at various times of year deer feed primarily on buds, the leaves and tender twigs of certain shrubs, different grasses and grass seeds, various berries, and acorns; and, since hunting took place throughout the year, the meat tasted different at different times depending upon what the deer were feeding on. Although the rule of the younger the deer, the more tender the meat, is generally true, my great aunts and uncles also claimed that all meat was more tender and not as "dry" before there was the one hunting season. They claimed that the meat was not as "stringy" and "full of muscles," and that it was more marbled with fat than it is today.

My Great Uncle Steve, whenever there was venison on the table and visitors for dinner, would point out, no matter how many times they may have heard it before, that there is less of the "deer's favorite foods" today; and because of this, "they don't have enough of the foods that make the fat. That's why she [his sister, my aunt Maggie] cooks it like this, 'Italian style,' lots of 'vino' and garlic. You'd think we're 'Italian Indians.' Our mother didn't make it this way when dad brought it in. It [the deer] looks the same, but the meat's not. The fish is not this way; it's still the same. The Smith brothers, we still have our boats; we're still in the fish business."

Uncle Steve would call attention to the fact that deer ranges are increasingly restricted due to fences and the fence-like functions of roads and highways, especially "oiled roads," the obstacles to free foraging posed by towns, cities, and other developments, especially rural developments. He would explain this to the visitors sitting around the kitchen table; and, if by chance, there were none, he would say: "Now you kids listen, here. I'm going to teach you something you don't get in school." And, not being detoured by the fact that this made the ninety-ninth time he taught us kids this same lesson—and we not daring to interrupt him—he'd continue: "It used to be the deer would stay close around, didn't move around a lot. When I was a 'young buck,' their camps and where they eat in different times [seasons] was all close 'round. Not now. They travel 'round different places searching 'round, for their food. Eat something here, go 'round there for something more, then someplace else; they couldn't get full in just one place. Pretty soon, it's gonna be like that for the fish too. Your aunts and uncles won't be around; it's going to be up to kids."

From the point of view of my relatives then, it was the cumulative effects of all these "facts" that account for why deer meat today is drier and tougher than it was in times past. "That's why you cook it this way; was different in my mother's time, before they changed everything around," according to Aunt Maggie.

All in all, it is a fact that today's deer meat, when compared to that of domestic animals, is less marbled with fat and therefore tends to be drier; and it does have more connective tissue and subsequently tends to be tougher. These two facts are reflected in the various pre-preparations of venison for a wide variety of recipes.

In general, the saddle, loin, tenderloin, leg, steaks, and chops from a young deer are usually tender enough to roast, broil, fry, or sauté without any extra preparation, providing you like your meat on the rare side; tougher cuts from the shoulder, shank, and breast, without any special preparation, are best used for stew or ground up for "venison burgers."

If you're not sure of the deer's age, and want to ensure the meat's tenderness, it's best to cook it rare. For those of you like me and many other Indians who prefer their meat on the done side, yet want it tender, there are three alternatives: marinate, tenderize, or age.

The marinade works best if the meat is covered over with it; it will work even better if you take a cooking fork and pierce the meat deeply everywhere, especially for roasts. The meat should be soaked in the marinade for several hours; the more time it has "in," the better. Cover the meat with a lid and place in the refrigerator. When taking it out, let it stand a while and warm to room temperature. Since the meat will soak up the marinade, it should be turned frequently; add more marinade as necessary to cover the meat completely.

If there is marinade left over, use it to baste meat cooked in the oven; if frying, add it to the pan; and by all means use it to baste for barbecuing. If you have more than you can use, it keeps well in the refrigerator, providing it's sealed well. Since the marinade has taken on some of the flavor of the venison, it makes a nice addition to the flavor of other meats as well. As such, it also makes a good base, to which you can add other ingredients for other marinades or bastes.

If, however, you want to retain the natural flavor of the meat, or simply vary its taste, use a natural meat tenderizer like those that use proteinase, an enzyme from the juice of unripe papayas. (It's available at health food stores and organic groceries.) For steaks, pierce both sides, and for roasts, pierce deeply all around with a cooking fork, and sprinkle the tenderizer evenly on all sides, using about half a teaspoon per pound. Before applying the tenderizer, be sure to completely cover the meat with a thin coat of oil. It's important to let the meat stand a while so the tenderizer can do its work; about an hour per pound for roasts and thick steaks; for regular cut steaks and chops, let the tenderizer work for about an hour. Be sure to let the meat stand in a covered pan or dish, and place in the refrigerator. Don't forget that when you use a tenderizer, cooking time is cut by about 25 percent.

PART II

When I was a teenager, having left Bodega Bay, we had a tradition in the family that centered around deer season. The first weekend of the six-week season was always celebrated with a lavish family feast of beefsteak and trimmings. If someone had been fortunate enough to bring in a buck that weekend, the following weekend promised barbequed venison; if not, our weekend gatherings featured hamburgers until a deer was killed. So, on that first weekend of the season, the women having been at cooking and baking since early morning, and after the men came in from hunting, having left before first light, we all sat down to a dinner of barbecued beefsteak. A large platter, piled high with steaks, was surrounded by dishes of beans, pasta, home grown corn, mashed potatoes, fresh string bean salad; peas and carrots, picked that morning; lettuce and watercress salad with onions, tomatoes, and lemon cucumbers, all from the garden and the spring; and San Francisco sour french bread. For desert, there was fresh apple, berry, and peach or apricot pie; and for refreshment, vine-ripened watermelon, cooled in the spring since the day before. We all sat together outside at a very long table.

During dinner, the men told of the morning's hunt: of the bucks they saw but missed, though they sure "threw the dirt up around them"; of those too far away except to "sight in your riffle on"; of Bill who got "buck fever," and couldn't "get off a shot," but just stood there like a jackass and looked at it; and of Gary, so anxious to get his buck that when his chance came, he "killed" a perfectly good pine tree; and so on.

The women listened as they should, but, having their own stories of the day, the house, and the household to tell, they did. And, with one ear, the men listened some of the time, being "naturally" more interested in their own stories.

The teenagers at the table also had events to tell of, but not of deer and deer hunting, nor of the house and household. Since they had yet to arrive at the place where adults would listen to them, and, not being sure who to listen to, they listened to themselves. However, they soon got bored and restless, and listened silently to the others, as they should have in the first place. And, when it was called for, they made the appropriate signs and sounds of approval, agreement, awe, envy, laughter, and so on.

The children, who were sure they too had stories to tell but couldn't remember them, listened in excitement and wonder to all, and couldn't wait until the day when they would sit at the same table and tell stories of the hunt and the hunted, and of the house and the household.

Although there was room for me at that table, there was no place for me. I felt like a stranger at these events outside of Bodega Bay, an eavesdropper on the stories told. I often wondered what would happen if they were to stop for a moment and listen to what they were saying.

Everyone seemed to enjoy themselves, and looked forward to the next weekend of the season, when it would happen all over again.

While they looked forward, I looked backward to another time when I was much younger, in Bodega Bay, with a different table, and different family members gathered around it. Here, at this table, there was not only room for me, but a place to sit as well. And, although young, should I choose to tell a story, it would be earnestly listened to by all; and I listened eagerly to all that was said and told. Here, everyone had a place and all were listened to; here also the people told differently of hunting, and celebrated differently, and for different reasons.

At this earlier place, the hunters "got up with the deer," ate no food, nor drank water; this was the second day of their fast. For two days their only nourishment was "Indian tea," and with the beginning and ending of each day, they bathed, giving special attention to their hair, and dressed in newly washed clothes. They also withdrew from participating in daily activities, and from any sexual activity as well. Should they get hungry, they ate the foods eaten by the deer: tender grass, new leaves, and blossoms, but drank no water until they gave the deer they had taken the first drink of cool, fresh water, carried on a young leaf and placed in the deer's mouth. The two days of fasting, drinking only Indian tea, and bathing twice daily served to almost fade their "man smell" away, and lessen their chances of being detected by the deer, while making their minds and bodies sensitive to all that they would experience on the hunt.

They also fasted to remind themselves of hunger and the necessity for food, and subsequently its sacred place in sustaining life—all life, not just theirs or the lives of their families, but for everything physically and spiritually alive. Although each of the different forms and forces of life have their own "foods," all require the nourishment that only "food" can give.

These people, seated around this table, also thought differently about deer and hunting than my later family. They didn't kill deer, they took them; and they didn't take them for themselves—they took them for their families and relatives, and shared with their friends. In fact, those who came home with a deer, didn't eat any of the meat. They would only eat that brought back by others, never their own. It was not for themselves that they hunted; it was always for someone else. By not eating the meat from his own hunt, the hunter gave back the life that he had taken. This was called "Giving to the Deer." That is, a man became a hunter to take the deer's life in order that someone else would live, and make possible other lives. It was indirectly through his "making possible" these "other lives" that the hunter gave back a life. Since the "gift" to the deer was a life, and lest the hunter spoil it by bragging and making others ashamed of their gifts, the hunter was deprived full and exact knowledge of his gift, so that all gifts—"sacrifices"—could be given freely, with pride, and in good faith.

What was celebrated at that table where I sat, through the sharing of food, and what I understand was celebrated by my ancestors at their "tables" long ago, when they were yet sovereign over their land, was a "Design" or "Rules for Living" set forth by the Creator. Having never before existed, the "Rules" were called into being, that is, created out of words spoken by "Him," the "First Speaker." Although spoken of and told about before our memories began, we remember them, because they have been continuously repeated from one generation to another, since the time before we, the "Second People" (humans) were called into this world, when the "First Speaker," our Creator, spoke of them to the "First People," who then told them to us; and so it has been since that time.

The celebration at this table of my childhood in Bodega Bay began with Uncle Angelo's words of thanksgiving and remembrance of Him who created the lives of the deer and the hunters, and provided the "Design" by which all life, including the deer's, was given purpose and meaning. His words also acknowledged and paid tribute to both deer and hunters for the conduct of their lives that enabled us to sit together that day and share food, and celebrate Him and His Design that made all this possible so long as we live our lives in support of our families, and in support of those other lives and living things also our kin that we share this world with.

COOKING WITH ACORNS

Acorns are nuts, and the meal or flour made from them is nutritious and natural, and in general makes a good supplement to recipes that call for the use of wheat, bran, corn flour, or corn meal. It's well-suited for use in most recipes for dessert or sweet breads, pancakes, waffles, cookies, cupcakes, and cakes. For pies, it can be used in making the crust, and in some cases the filling as well. Acorn meal also makes a good thickening agent in stews and many soups.

As a general "rule of thumb," whatever the amount of flour or meal the recipe recommends, you can replace half of it with acorn meal or flour. The difference between meal and flour is simply one of texture, the flour being finely ground and somewhat powder-like, while the meal has a coarser texture much like that of corn meal, especially corn meal used in making the Italian dish called "polenta." Although acorn meal is much like any other nut meal in terms of oiliness, taste, and texture, to some it is somewhat blander.

Acorn meal or flour can be purchased at many health food stores or organic food stores. If it is not available in your area, here is a simple method for making your own acorn meal. If you don't have access to dried acorns, and need to collect your own, I would suggest you collect tan oak, valley oak, blue oak, or black oak acorns since they tend to have a richer and nuttier taste, although acorns from the Oregon or coast live oak can also be used. The acorns should be first dried to make shelling, husking, and grinding easier. They can be sundried or dried in the oven at the lowest temperature available. The test for dryness is the ease with which the shell can be cracked and the inner husk which covers the nut can be removed; the nut should be hard, but not shriveled. Next, crack the shells to free the nut and remove the thin outer husk. To grind the nut, an old fashion, hand-turned meat grinder, blender, food processor, or other type of food mill works well. Adjust the blade and/or speed for fineness or coarseness.

For leaching, a colander or anything similar can be used. Cover it with a cotton dish towel or cheese cloth. If you use cheese cloth, use at least two layers for a cover, otherwise the water will simply run through it, and little if any leaching will take place. Ideally, you want a layer of cloth that will act much like a coffee filter does. That is, you want the water to drain slowly through the meal. Speaking of coffee filters, I have observed members of my own family use them to leach with, and they work very well. Their only drawback is that only a small amount of meal can be leached at one time. However, if it's acorn meal "for one" that you want, I recommend them. Simply place the meal inside the filter and in turn place it inside a container or a coffee filter stand and you're ready to begin leaching. Use cold water; although it takes longer, you will not leach the flour's richness and nutty taste. After the water has filtered through for a couple of times, taste the meal until it suits your own taste preference. Let the meal dry; you're now ready to cook with it.

The first recipe that follows comes from members of my family. The second one, for acorn roca bars, is by Charlotte Bringle Clarke and is one of her favorites. This and other recipes by her can be found in her book (1977). An additional and very tasty acorn recipe for acorn pinenut bread, by Vera Mae Fredrickson (1987) should be tried if you haven't already done so.

Bodega Bay Acorn Beef Stew

You'll need 1½ to 2 lbs. of stewing beef, or boneless steak if you can afford it. The meat should be in one single piece, not cut up. 2 or 3 medium-sized white or red potatoes; baking potatoes can also be used. The white or red ones will not mush-up like the baking ones will. However, in this case it's more a matter of texture than taste as to which ones you use. You will also need ½ to ¾ cup of finely ground acorn meal. Have salt and pepper handy as well.

Place the meat whole in a frying pan. One of the old-fashioned, heavy metal ones does the best. You will need a pan slightly larger than the piece of meat. Cover the meat with water to about ¼ inch above the meat. Dice the potatoes and place them around the meat. Cover the pan with a lid and simmer the meat very, very slowly. When the meat begins to fall apart, it's done. In any event, simmer the meat until it's very tender. Next, remove the meat and cut into small pieces. While you are cutting the meat, keep the heat and the lid on the pan. Put the meat back into the pan, and slowly stir in the acorn meal, letting it cook for about one minute with the lid off. Add salt and pepper to your taste, and stir slowly once more. It's now ready. Serve it on toasted English muffins. Depending upon how generous you are, you should get 3 to 4 servings from the dish. If you've done everything right it will be delicious.

Acorn Roca Bars

1 cup butter or margarine
1 cup brown sugar
1 egg
1 tsp. vanilla
2 cups flour
½ tsp. salt
¾ cup finely chopped, leached acorns
12 oz. milk chocolate or semi-sweet chocolate pieces
½ cup sweetened shredded coconut

Preheat oven to 350° (mod.). Cream together butter or margarine and brown sugar. Blend in egg and vanilla. Add flour and salt. Stir in ½ cup acorns and spread the thick mixture in an ungreased 10 x 15-inch pan. Bake for 40 minutes. Remove from oven and spread milk chocolate or semi-sweet chocolate pieces over the cookie mixture, smoothing as it melts. Mix together ¼ cup acorns and coconut and sprinkle this on top of the melted chocolate. Cut and cool.

CALIFORNIA FRY BREAD

Although fry bread, as we call it, is surely not "native" to pre-European California, it has been around long enough to qualify as part of the recent tradition of California Indian cuisine. Since we not only eat fry bread but make it as well, approve and criticize each other's results (e.g., put-it-to-the-taste test), share and/or jealously guard our recipes, have our own names for it (e.g., Pomo Puffs), and sell and/or share it at most of our "doings," it has become part of our contemporary tradition. The following two recipes come from members of my family.

Fry Bread Recipe One
(24 9-inch pieces)

6 cups unsifted flour
1 tbsp. California sea salt
2 tbsp. baking powder
½ cup instant nonfat dry milk
lukewarm California water
lard or shortening

In a bowl, combine flour, salt, baking powder. and milk. Add just enough lukewarm water (about 2¾ cups), a little at a time, to make a soft, but not sticky, dough. Knead thoroughly. Pinch off a ball of dough about the size of a large egg; shape it so it's round. Then, gradually stretch and flatten it, still keeping its round shape, until it's about 9 inches in diameter and a quarter-inch thick.

In a 12-inch frying pan, melt lard or shortening, at least an inch deep, until it's hot, but not smoking. Carefully place the shaped dough in the pan, and fry to a light brown on one side; turn over, and repeat the frying on the other side. As it fries, the bread puffs up and becomes light and crispy; remove and drain off oil on paper towels. Serve hot with butter, jam, honey, powdered sugar, or a sugar and cinnamon mix.

Fry Bread Recipe Two
(12 to 14 10-to-12-inch pieces)

4 cups of flour
1 tbsp. baking powder
1½ tsp. California sea salt
1½ tsp. cooking oil lard or shortening
lukewarm California water

In a large bowl, mix the flour, baking powder, salt, oil, and water. Add enough oil and water to make the dough soft. Knead the dough with floured hands until the dough has a spring to it. Pinch off some and shape into balls about 3 inches in diameter. Pat each ball between your palms until the dough has stretched into a thin round about 10 to 12 inches across and a quarter-inch thick.

Fry each round of dough in about ½ inch of very hot lard or shortening, turning once until puffy and golden. These large rounds make excellent Indian tacos; just add beans, meat (if you want), and finely chopped onions, lettuce, and tomatoes. The large rounds are also excellent for wrapping around uncooked and thinly cut strips of abalone or cleaned, whole surf fish; seaweed is also great. After wrapping, fry as above. To make sure the fish/abalone is cooked, make the round thin and small enough so that the dough does not wrap around the filling more than twice. It's delicious.

In making the dough, some people use self-rising flour, biscuit dough, or yeast bread dough. Some flour or oil their hands when working with the dough. And some find that rolling out the dough with a rolling pin, after lightly kneading and then cutting out with a glass or jar lid, gives good results. Often when making such large pieces, as in Recipe Two, it helps to make a small hole in the center of the dough to let the oil fry the middle section, making sure it's not doughy (uncooked) in the center. Good cooking! Good eating!

YOU'LL NEVER GO HUNGRY
and CRAB LOUIS AND THE JITTERBUG
Kathleen R. Smith

In the early 1990s, Kathleen Smith (Bodega Miwok/Dry Creek Pomo) contributed a series of five articles to the magazine *News from Native California,* when she was its foods columnist (1990a, 1990b, 1990c, 1991a, 1991b).

A tribal scholar, cultural consultant, artist, basket weaver, and writer, Kathleen Rose Smith (b. 1939) is the daughter of Steven Smith, Jr., Olemitcha (Bodega) Miwok, and Lucy Lozinto Smith, Mihilakawna (Dry Creek) Pomo. Smith was born in Santa Rosa, the sixth of eight children, and grew up in and near Healdsburg and Vallejo, California. She earned an B.F.A. from the San Francisco Art Institute in 1977, and also studied at the California College of Arts and Crafts. Smith has had many jobs: field hand, packing clerk, computer operator, stockroom clerk. She has also been a Native American observer and archaeology technician, cultural consultant and interpreter, administrative assistant, and outreach worker. Smith was archaeology technician and coordinator for the Native American advisory council for the Warm Springs Cultural Resources Study (1979–83). Because of the construction of the dam that created Lake Sonoma, the Army Corps of Engineers sponsored this project to preserve and record the traditions of the local Native population.

Kathleen Smith is continuing work on a cookbook of her people's foods. As a reader can clearly see, these essays are no mere cooking instructions, but are deeply woven into memories of her family and the land.

News from Native California (1990), 4(2):4–5; 5(2):14–16.

YOU'LL NEVER GO HUNGRY
Food Traditions of One
Dry Creek Pomo / Bodega Miwok Family

The food of my people is important to me. It has sustained us both physically and spiritually since the beginning of time. I didn't quite realize it when I was growing up in the 1940s and 50s, but my family was a part of that "other America," the poor.

As far as food was concerned, however, we always seemed to have enough: fresh fruits and vegetables during the summer; my mamma's home canned food in the winter for fruit pies, jams, and salsa, or as mamma calls it, sarsa. Late fall and early winter were the only times the cupboard seemed spare to me; but the lack of fresh food provided some of my most vivid memories of unusual dishes. We had home canned peaches and hotcakes for one memorable Thanksgiving dinner; the syrup was boiled sugar water. Other meals consisted of *pucklon*, which is similar to a dumpling, or fried tripe with mustard greens.

Mamma taught me that we would never starve because our food, the food that God gave us, is all around; all we need to know is how and when to gather it, how to prepare it. The teaching included going to the hills and valleys where these foods grow.

I shall always be grateful to my mother, Lucy (Lozinto) Smith, for showing me how to make the foods she learned in her childhood, and from her mother-in-law, Mary (Antone) Santos.

For every year of my childhood, mamma planted a vegetable garden, no matter where the crops took us to harvest, from the olive groves near Visalia in the south, to the fruit orchards of Washington's Wenatchee Valley in the north, and to what must have been a hundred places in between, mainly in central California, southern and northeastern Oregon, and central and southern Washington.

My family also raised the hogs, chickens, and cows needed for grandma's blood sausage, stuffed chicken necks with the heads attached, and curds and whey, as well as for the meat, eggs, and milk these animals also provided.

I will always be thankful to my father, Steven Smith, Jr., who died in 1980, for taking me and anyone else who would wake up at 4 a.m. to the ocean in order to get abalone, which he and my brothers gathered at low tide. I helped by holding the sack the abalone was put into and helping to take it back up the steep cliffs to the car. It was always an adventure, and we'd be home by breakfast.

Mamma, my sisters, and I gathered seaweed off the rocks at other times. Dad would rock fish for bull head (cabezone) during the day or surf fish at night. Those times, we would camp on the beach and roast potatoes, tuptups (similar to pocket bread), flank skirts, and abalone, all cooked on hot coals. The meat was sometimes cooked on a grill we brought along. The coffee was boiled. Cowboy coffee my dad called it. It was terrible.

We'd drive the long way through Coleman Valley, near Bodega where daddy grew up, to catch a breathtaking view of the ocean from iris-clad coastal hills. For this too is a part of the experience of knowing one's place in the order of things.

Daddy loved to hunt, too. But I was never a part of that experience. Only the boys hunted. I fondly remember my younger brother Doug shooting robins with his new .22, and mamma proudly cleaning the birds and roasting them on a spit. YAH WE. Thank you. Delicious, lovely birds.

I especially want to thank my cousin Olive (Jack) Fulwider for teaching me how to make *béhe*, and for the many other things she has taught and shared with me about her life and her remembrances of our old people.

Béhe

Collect ripe peppernuts in the fall when the husk turns purple and the nut falls from the bay tree. Next, remove the edible husk (hat) so the peppernuts will dry without getting moldy. (My Dry Creek Pomo relatives eat only the tips of hat when that part has turned light yellow from green. Later on, all the husk will turn purple, and my Kashia friends tell me that's the time to eat it. Either way, hat tastes like a peppery avocado.)

Depending on the weather, peppernuts take several days to several weeks to dry. When peppernuts are dried and ready to be roasted preheat oven to 350 degrees. Then shell the dried pepper-nuts; the shells are thin and easy to remove by lightly striking with a rock or small mallet.

The peppernut has two halves. These usually separate when the shell is cracked. If they don't separate, pull them apart by hand. An almost invisible parchment between the kernels will separate naturally from the peppernut if it has been properly dried; if it doesn't separate, it can be removed by winnowing or by rubbing off by hand.

Place peppernuts on a cookie sheet and roast until they are a rich, dark chocolate brown. When completely roasted, they will look almost burnt. This takes about 20 to 30 minutes. After removing them from the oven, immediately place the hot peppernuts into a blender or grinder. Grind them to a fine, flourlike consistency, then pour them into a bowl.

Season the peppernut flour with sea salt (tako) to taste, then knead it while still hot. At first, the nut flour will be powdery and dry. But as the kneading continues, a natural oil in the peppernuts will be released. Once oily, the nuts can be molded into balls about the size of a tablespoon.

As the peppernut balls cool, they begin to harden. When completely hardened, the balls are ready to eat.

Traditionally, béhe (peppernut balls, Dry Creek Pomo) is eaten wrapped inside a thick bunch or ball of ohso (sweet clover). Fresh endive or green leaf lettuce serve as good substitutes for sweet clover.

MORE THAN FOOD ALONE:
CRAB LOUIS AND THE JITTERBUG

What started out as a recipe column has developed into not only a column about the food of California Indians, but also about the people who taught me how to prepare these foods. For me, the writing brings back memories of thirty, forty, or fifty years ago or more. It gives me an added reason to spend more time with relatives, remembering together old times, hard times, great times, laying claim to our people's times, which include today.

My experience as a cultural demonstrator at Point Reyes National Seashore taught me that many people have little knowledge of

California Indians and lots of mistaken ideas about California Indian foods. Sincere visitors would ask me about foods they heard were bitter, bland, or bizarre; foods that for them were only valid if stopped in time some two hundred years ago.

The foods of my ancestors that I know about are delicious, pungent, healthful, delicate, sweet, seasonal, fresh, preserved in salt, dried, jerked, nutritious, and some, if not prepared properly, could be bitter, bland, or bizarre and also harmful. They have continuity with the past. The coastal foods I prepare reflect my Bodega Miwok heritage, for instance, but they aren't stopped in time.

The foods I grew up with reflect the times and the community I lived in, as well as my Indian heritage. Which brings me back to childhood memories. My family loves seafood. So do I, except that when I was a child, I was allergic to some kinds of seafood (a source of ridicule for a Bodega Miwok child) and could never remember which ones until it was too late.

I have outgrown my problem with seafood. Momma always thought it was in my head anyway. Everyone else thought it was great; the more for them, they'd say. Even though I had problems with eating some seafood, I loved to go to the ocean and gather the foods the sea offers—seaweed, shellfish, and other tidal inhabitants such as sea anemones and China shoes.

Crab meat was one that I could eat. My sister June would make Crab Louis. As she would point out, she made it the best.

Geraldine Lucille, Gerri, Junie, June. The eldest in our family of four girls and four boys. She was sixteen years old when I was born in the winter of 1939. Junie was my hero, my role model, as we say these days. Like the zest of lemon in a glass of water, she brought refreshing elegance to the ordinary.

My bobby-soxed, beautiful sister seemed to fill the air with excitement, and music and dancing. Her friends spilled through the house at 411 Foss Street. They were indulgent to me, the baby. I wanted to grow up to be just like Junie; to dance the jitterbug, to have long, shiny auburn colored natural curls like her, and to put on lipstick like her, looking like Betty Grable. I couldn't see over the dining room table.

Junie had pride in who she was. At Geyserville School she played football, and she would beat up white boys who insulted Indian kids who lived with her on the Dry Creek Rancheria. She knew dad would defend her actions to the school administration. When she was a littler girl at Geyserville she won a footrace. The prize was a turkey. My mother was so happy.

Junie played the trumpet as good as Harry James, but at Healdsburg High School, she played second trumpet. This was not because she was a girl, as I thought, but because Tom Ratchford was really better, June says. Her first horn was a cornet that cost $2.50. The second was a beautiful trumpet, a gift from her music teacher, Charles McCord. Mr. McCord got it from the San Francisco Symphony. It was such a fine instrument that Tommy Ratchford and Bill McCutchen, the other two trumpet players, would ask to borrow it.

When Junie graduated from high school, she was asked to play in a dance band. Momma firmly said no. Instead, Junie went to work at Mare Island Naval Shipyard as a riveter. It was 1942. America had been at war for seven months. Junie played her trumpet occasionally at camp meetings, but when our brother Stanley wanted to learn a musical instrument a few years later, she gave him her beautiful trumpet.

The music that I love is the music introduced to me by Junie. The first song I learned to sing was "A Tisket, A Tasket" by teenager Ella Fitzgerald with Chick Webb's band. Junie's music was jazz, swing, blues, boogie woogie, and jump tunes. The sounds of Duke, Count, Bix, Bunny, Benny, Billie, Coleman Hawkins, Johnny Hodges, Lester Young, the Teagardens, Valaida Snow, Jimmie Lunceford, Mildred Bailey … well, you get the picture. (By the way, Mildred Bailey and the Teagardens, Jack, Charlie, and Norma, were Indian. Norma lives in the Bay Area and plays piano at San Francisco's Washington Square Bar and Grill.) Junie's music still swings. Floy doy. Floy doy.

During the 1940s, California Indians, Inc. was raising money to send delegates to Washington, D.C. to petition the federal government to act on California's unratified treaties. None of the 18 treaties signed with California Indians in 1851–52 were ever ratified. It wasn't until July 1963 that the case (or cases) was settled out of court during the Kennedy administration. Final payment was completed in 1972.

Indians were paid a pittance for the land which had been taken from them. Many California Indians refused the money and sent it back.

Anyway, one of the ways the Indians in Sonoma County raised money for the delegate in their area, our uncle Manuel Cordova (Junie's godfather, whom she called Nino), was to have dances where African American bands from the Bay Area would play. My folks bundled me up and took me along. I imagine it was here that I first learned to jitterbug like Junie.

Today, June works as an observer for archaeological projects, she is a HUD Commissioner, and she still makes a mean Crab Louis.

June's Crab Louis

Serve with sour French bread.

Salad:
Crab meat from one pre-cooked crab
   served over iceberg lettuce leaves
One tomato, sliced
One hard boiled egg, sliced
Marinated beets, to taste
Asparagus spears, to taste
Shrimp, optional

Dressing:
2 stalks fresh celery, grated
2 tablespoons dill pickle, grated
About 1 cup cocktail sauce
2 cups mayonnaise
Dash tabasco
Dash horseradish
Juice from 1 lemon

CONTEMPORARY FOOD CUSTOMS
Beverly R. Ortiz

Beverly R. Ortiz (b. 1956) has given us some of the best writing on contemporary Californian food practices. She obtained her B.S. in environmental planning/management from UC Davis (1979), and from 1981 through 1987 studied basketry with Pomo weaver Mabel McKay. Over the years she has conducted extensive research with members of more than twenty Californian tribal groups. Ortiz served as a park technician at Yosemite National Park (1977–81), and since 1980, she has been employed as a naturalist with the East Bay Regional Park District at Coyote Hills. An ethnographic consultant since 1986 for films, exhibits, and seminars, Ortiz is currently a doctoral candidate in anthropology at UC Berkeley. Her interests include North American Indians, folklore, and cultural continuity and change.

Since 1988, Ortiz has been the skills and technology columnist for the magazine *News from Native California*, where these selections were originally published. Like all of her work, they are marked by factual detail and a sensitive willingness to attend to Native perspectives. With Julia Parker she is the author of *It Will Live Forever: Traditional Yosemite Indian Acorn Preparation* (1991), perhaps the best single book on Californian Indian food.

News from Native California (1989), 2(6):22–24; (1989), 3(3):25–27.

THINGS HAVE CHANGED
[on Mono acorn processing]

Margaret Baty loves acorn. She loves baskets and soaproot brushes. She loves her Auberry Mono culture and she loves people. This was immediately apparent when I met Mrs. Baty. Arriving at Margaret's Big Sandy Rancheria home with a film crew from the California Indian Project on a sparkling August afternoon, my attention was immediately drawn to the acorn leaching and cooking utensils which graced Margaret's yard.

Inside Mrs. Baty's home, two large tupperware containers were filled with processed acorn, ready to be sold at the North Fork Sierra Mono Museum Indian Fair Days which were scheduled in two days. Soaproot brushes hung to dry in the laundryroom. A nearly complete basket lay in the livingroom.

Margaret and her enthusiastic assistant, husband Thane Baty, graciously shared the details of an acorn processing technique in which old and new ways blend easily. Although she has steadily introduced modern tools and methods, Margaret first learned to prepare acorn the old way by observing her grandmother Maggie Littlefield, mother Maggie Marvin, and sister Annie Marvin. Then she began to help her mother prepare acorn "every now and then" by lifting the cooking rocks into the cooking basket and, at times, pounding acorn in a shallow mortar.

Years later, after her mother fell ill, and arthritis prevented her sister from preparing acorn, the task fell upon Mrs. Baty. As she explained, "If I wanted acorn mush it was up to me to make it now."

Margaret has fond childhood memories of the comraderie of acorn preparation. At the mortar rock, her grandmother, mother, and sister each had a special hole where they pounded acorn while sharing gossip: "Maybe it makes the time go fast. They will tell stories or they will make jokes and laugh. I remember hearing them laughing away. Somebody might have done something funny somewhere and they would be talking about it. I know a lot of people always say that's the gossiping place where they pound acorn and laugh and tell stories."

In those early days, Maggie Marvin stored acorn in a granary described by Margaret as "... round, almost like a tepee built on four poles." Maggie described the old style of leaching to her daughter. The acorn was placed on a mound of sand, flattened on top, and built near a spring or stream. Once leached, all but the acorn closest to the sand was removed for cooking. The remaining acorn was discarded. Sometimes, leaves were placed on the sand basin to prevent the need to discard meal. Still later, cloth replaced the leaves.

New technology has continued to change the process. As Margaret explains, "Things have changed a lot since my childhood days. We don't do it like the olden days." But there is continuity from past to present.

Margaret's number one choice for acorn remains black oak from the mountains although, as has been done for generations, "white" oak [sometimes referred to as blue oak] is used when the former is unavailable. Although initially white oak has a sweeter, less bitter taste than black oak, once cooked both take on the same "flat" taste, enabling the two types to be mixed together at times.

While collecting acorn, those with worm holes are ignored. Since the acorn supply varies with the year, when the supply is good, acorn is collected in quantity and stored. Three years ago Margaret collected twenty burlap sacks worth of acorn which, in spite of two years of poor harvest, have provided well for her needs.

Collecting acorns off the ground is an enjoyable outing. When the acorn crop is good, it is collected fast. Margaret and her sister Annie often "picked" it straight through to dark, hardly stopping to eat, engrossed in the task as they were.

For storage, these sacks are placed on an old army cot, enabling wind and air to circulate through the acorn. At times, acorn must be processed into flour soon after collection. But, since fresh acorn cannot be made into flour, the drying process must be hurried. Margaret used to do this by placing cracked and shelled acorn on a cloth beneath her wood stove. Sometimes she will also spread the acorn atop a cloth-covered table placed outside on a sunny day.

Once dried, the skin surrounding the kernel can be removed by shaking the kernels in a winnowing basket. Even when dried and winnowed, however, bits of skin will adhere unless the "meat" is first split along a natural depression. Margaret's sister cautioned that if care wasn't taken to make sure the acorns were thoroughly cleaned, bits of red skin would float atop the finished product. Once cleaned, bad spots are removed with a knife, while kernels that are entirely bad are discarded.

In the early years, the kernels were reduced to flour in a granite mortar. Curious about the origin of the mortars, Margaret questioned the elders: "I've asked the older ladies a long time ago, and as far back as they can remember those holes were there." She speculates that "...the Indians a long time ago made those holes. I don't know, but they're there." Once, when Maggie Marvin needed a mortar close to home, she created one using a hard rock and metal bar.

Mortars of varying depths were used for different purposes. Shallow mortars were used to pound sourberries and other fruits. Two different sizes of mortars were necessary to pound white oak. Since white oak contains less oil than black oak, it tends to become powdery. To contain it in the mortar, it is first pounded "a little" in a shallow hole, then immediately transferred to a deeper hole to be finished. The pounding process produces an oil which keeps the mortar smooth, and no rock enters the meal.

After pounding, the meal is sifted in a basket made for the purpose. Unlike modem sifting, where a screen contains coarse particles, allowing fine particles to "sift" through, here the opposite occurs. The fine particles stay in the basket while the coarse particles come over the edge. The latter are then pounded anew with the goal of creating a meal the fineness of storebought flour, completely lacking in graininess. This will ensure even leaching.

Mrs. Baty's son, along with his brother-in-law, have created an electric acorn grinder which frees Margaret from the necessity of pounding and sifting. They removed the handle of a corn grinder, replacing it with a wheel and belt connected to an electric motor. With practice, Thane Baty has developed the ability to tighten the grinder precisely the amount needed to produce the desired consistency of flour. After being put through the grinder once, Margaret tests the produce for graininess with her finger. If needed, the flour is slowly reground.

Thane has also devised a modern leaching basin. He created a framework of two-by-fours supported on four legs. Two-by-fours nailed crosswise support screen wire on which sand sits contained by a wagon wheel. As Thane discovered, crossbracing is essential lest the frame begin to collapse as the wood swells around the nails from repeated leaching with water. A cloth is placed atop the sand, which is leveled, and the acorn placed atop that.

Lukewarm water is poured through the acorn flour twelve to fifteen times until the bitterness is completely removed. For a water-break, Margaret uses a redbud winnowing basket covered with a cloth, which contains any dust that may be in the water.

Next, it's time to cook the acorn. Steatite (soapstone) cooking rocks which once belonged to Maggie Marvin are used at this stage. When new, they had to be devoid of cracks, lest acorn collect in them and scorch. Any edges were rounded off.

An outdoor hearth, made from the rusted back of a Model T, provides safety when it comes time to heat the rocks. Margaret knew the Model T remains would be ideal for this purpose when she saw them abandoned on Indian land the Batys own. The cooking stones are heated here in a fire of oak wood and, more rarely, manzanita. Pitchy woods are avoided because they leave a mark on the rocks.

Once heated, the rocks are removed from the fire with two poles of mountain mahogany. About two-and-one-half to three feet in length at the most, the poles are pointed on one end, with one side of the point flattened to make it easier to lift the rocks.

Before being placed in the cooking basket, ash is cleaned from the rocks. This cleaning was done on a piece of tin at one time, until a friend made a rack with small steel bars. Newly removed from the fire, a rock is placed on the rack, dusted with a soaproot brush and rinsed with a dipper of hot water. Then the rock is turned over and the process repeated. In a matter of seconds, the now clean rock is ready to be lowered into the cooking basket.

Carefully, it is placed on a looped stirring stick. Fashioned from a young oak about five feet long and the width of a finger, the looped stirrer is formed by bending the oak sapling in the middle with heat and water. Sapling size and age is critical since, if too wide and hard, the oak won't bend.

The cooking rock is stirred in a mixture of acorn and water, proportioned to insure mush of the proper consistency. As each rock cools, it is lifted from the basket and cleaned of excess acorn, which is returned to the cooking basket. Ultimately, it is put back into the fire, where any remaining acorn is burned off, preparing it for future use. A hot rock takes its place in the basket.

Depending on the quantity of acorn flour used, the mush will be cooked in about one half hour. It is then left overnight to cool, becoming firm, like jelly. Finally, it is ready for Margaret's favorite part of the process—eating.

Alternately, acorn may be eaten when still runny, prior to being completely cooked. Called *yuumena* in Mono, people drink it at this stage. Once, when Margaret ran short of acorn at Indian Fair Days, she took the mush she had left the first day, mixed it with water and added ice, producing a cold *yuumena* enjoyed by many the following day.

Margaret remembers that her grandmother and other elders never ate acorn with their meal in the early days. Instead, it was "like a dessert to them." After the meal was finished, her grandmother would say, "Let's have acorn."

Today, acorn isn't an everyday food, but is made for special events. When eaten, it is part of the regular meal, being enjoyed with beef, canned tuna when meat is unavailable, and fall-collected mushrooms. Margaret also enjoys her mush with salt or a gravy of stew broth.

Margaret has adapted acorn processing in interesting ways to accommodate the many changes of modern life. For instance, when preparing for a trip, Thane cracks a basketful of acorn. During the drive, Margaret then removes the shells, using a knife or thumbnail to remove the skin. At rest areas, the acorn shells are deposited in trash cans.

Sometimes Mrs. Baty freezes leached acorn in packages. When needed, the packaged acorn is cooked in a pot on the stove, resulting in a batter like corn starch when cooked. However, Margaret prefers rock-cooked acorn for its superior taste.

FOOD FOR SHARING

[on Pomo and Sierra Miwok pit cooking of deer and beef]

Whenever people come together, it's important to provide food for the guests. Some ten or fifteen years ago, Wayne Marufo (Kashaya Pomo) was asked to prepare and cook the meat for the Fourth of July barbecue at the Kashaya roundhouse, since the usual cooks were away. Wayne had watched the process many times before, but had never actually done it. Despite a sense of uncertainty, he took on the challenge, since about 200 pounds of meat had already been secured for the purpose.

> I've watched ... the whole process when I was a little kid, probably like my grandson. So I decided I'd try it, but I was a little nervous. I worried about it all night long wondering if the thing was going to cook or if it was going to come out all wrong....

Now, all these years later, Wayne and I sat by lantern light sharing quiet conversation in the cold and darkness of a midnight sky while waiting for the fire in the deer cooking pit to die down. Earlier that day, Wayne had used his chainsaw to cut a fallen tree into fire-sized lengths. These were being removed from a large woodpile adjacent to the pit and added to a fire Wayne had started hours earlier. Gradually, a layer of coals formed at the base of the pit—which had been dug earlier with a backhoe, to save the time of removing the dirt shovelful by shovelful. The pit, about 3½-feet deep, was dug in roughly the same location as it had been in previous years—beneath the shade of a massive pepperwood (bay tree).

At about 1:00 a.m., incompletely burned pieces of wood were moved with a shovel to the side of the pit. Now, Wayne shoveled a thin layer of dirt atop the coals, then neatly arranged eight bundles of carefully wrapped deer meat (which lay ready in the back of a nearby pickup truck) atop this.

It was important that this first layer of dirt cover the hot ashes completely so the meat's outer layer of burlap wouldn't burn. However, it must not be so thick that the heat would give out too quickly. Next, the meat was covered with several inches of dirt, and another fire was built atop this layer, a fire which was destined to burn about eleven more hours before it would be allowed to die. (Cooking time varies with type of wood, soil, size of pit, and amount of meat.)

Now, I headed for the comforts of home, leaving Wayne in the cold nighttime breezes with his fire. A well-deserved break would soon be provided by his wife, Bev, also from Kashaya, who would tend the fire for a time. The next day Wayne would have other assistance, but for the most part he would tend the fire alone, generously contributing his expertise and labor to help feed the crowd of hungry guests who would arrive the following afternoon for a family reunion and evening ceremony at Kule Loklo, a Coast Miwok Cultural Exhibit at the Point Reyes National Seashore.

For Wayne, cooking deer or beef in an underground oven is an important and joyful responsibility.

> I do it because I like doing it. I do it because I like doing it for other people. You know. It makes me feel good … it's something that my grandfather did, and I feel that I like to carry on the tradition of what he used to do.

At the barbecues of Wayne's childhood, the meat was served with acorn and buckeye mushes; ocean foods such as fish, abalone, and seaweed; peppernut balls; and contemporary picnic foods.

> More or less they used to give people certain things to bring.… And then appoint one person to go to the ocean and bring fish. One person to bring abalone … you just give one person this thing to do and that's what he would do.

Wayne recalls his grandmother's descriptions of the rules a hunter followed in olden times

And my grandmother used to say that when you're out hunting, when you get out there take the pepperwood leaves and rub yourself with it. All over. That way when you're hunting, if the wind's blowing in your direction the deer ... won't smell you. He'll smell the pepperwood. You know, there's a lot of things that they ... go through, I guess. It's something the modern hunters don't do anymore.

Wayne recalled other old-time rules that the changing world has brought an end to.

Usually the old-timers were pretty serious, and there's a lot of things that ... they couldn't do the night before they were going away hunting and the night before they were going fishing. And I used to hear my grandmother say that ... if they were going hunting ... or if they were going fishing, the night before they couldn't sleep with their wives. They had to sleep in another room. And they used to have songs that they prepared themselves with, my grandmother used to tell me. They sing the song the night before and they sing it the morning before they're leaving....

Even earlier, before the men hunted or fished they prepared themselves in a sweathouse located on Haupt Ranch, where the people worked and lived for a time, about two miles across the ridge from Kashaya.

They used to be in their sweathouse and all set in there and sing. Do their singing probably four or five hours.... They slept in the sweathouse and the next day they'd be off hunting.

Modern hunting involves a little walking. However, the "old-timers" would stay out for two days or so. As a child, Wayne remembers vividly how his grandfather would keep the meat fresh after he had shot a deer with his gun.

I used to go hunting with him, and when he used to shoot a deer and decide he's going to ... leave it laying in the woods for awhile,

> he used to take and gut it open, take all the guts out, and then drag
> it off in the brush and get the pepperwood leaves, a whole bunch
> of it and just pack the inside ... of the deer with it.

Such treatment would keep the blowflies from bothering the meat
by eliminating the smell. As "a little kid," Wayne was skeptical that
this treatment would be effective, thinking it could never work.

> I used to watch it all the time. And we used to go back and pick
> up the meat, and then the flies never bothered it.

It has been many years since Wayne cooked at Kashaya. Since that
time, he has cooked at several different locations in Northern
California. Through it all, the memories of what he learned when his
grandfather, Clement Marufo, and his uncle, Harold Marufo, cooked
for the annual Fourth of July barbecue remain his inspiration.

> Then, when they used to do the barbecue, they did it in a different
> way, too. They used to take and buy the whole beef from a local
> rancher out here about three miles. They used to ... shoot it them-
> selves and pull it up in a tree. Take and tie ... a big old ... block and
> tackle; take and tie the rope to the bumper of a pickup and pull
> it.... There's no way anybody could take and pull it up by hand.

Today, Wayne uses this method to skin the deer he hunts in the
Modoc area. At this northerly location, the meat freezes a lot more
quickly than in Central California, making it hard to skin with a knife.
However, attached to a jeep or pickup winch, the skin can be slowly
peeled away.

Whether a knife or winch is the preferred skinning tool, the deer
or cow must be hung from its hind legs to allow the blood to drain.
Then the animal is gutted and the meat butchered. The resulting pieces
of rib and shank are liberally seasoned. First, salt and pepper, and at
times, garlic and onion salt, are sprinkled on the meat. Sometimes
paprika and parsley are added. Then the meat is covered with sliced
onion and wrapped in aluminum foil, which holds in the juices and
seasonings.

Next, a layer of butcher paper is wrapped, then taped securely around the foil. Finally, this is wrapped with half sections of wet burlap sacks. The whole bundle is held together with wire tied like ribbon around a package. As an innovation, to make it easier to find and remove the meat from the pit, Wayne finishes the bundle with a long loop of wire which stands like a sentinel above the center of the package.

Clay provides the best soil for the pit, since once the cooking starts, the ground will bake hard, holding the heat better than powdery dirt. In the fine dirt the heat resistance is reduced, and the ground will sometimes cave in, smothering parts of the fire.

From his grandfather and uncle, Wayne learned that the bottom fire is the most important part. If this fire isn't hot enough, the meat will sour. His uncle also taught him the importance of starting the top fire as soon as possible after the dirt layer is shoveled onto the bundles.

About a half cord of half-seasoned hardwood, either oak or madrone, makes the best bottom fire, although Wayne has sometimes had to substitute half-rotten apple, pear, or prune wood.

When Wayne cooks for his workplace, hard oak pallets are available for the bottom fire. These burn quickly, resulting in good, hot ash in less than the usual time.

The quick-burning quality of the pallets was extremely useful during early May, when it appeared the cooking would have to be done in the rain. Although the storm cleared, the pit was filled with over a foot of water. Wayne's eldest boy, who was with him at the time, filled the pit with pallets and started the fire anyway. Soon all the water had been boiled away and the cooking could resume.

Because the pallets burn so quickly, it's necessary to keep a constant watch on the fire. About midnight, Wayne reverts to hardwood logs since,

> You don't have to worry about the thing for three or four hours at a time. And if you have enough, you can really fill it up. You don't even have to worry about it till the next day.

Although Wayne has been cooking for many years and has never failed at his task, he still gets concerned something might go wrong.

The biggest danger is that some of the meat will get overcooked if the second layer of dirt is too thin. It should be about ten or twelve inches, depending on the type of dirt—more is needed with powdery dirt. Otherwise, the only hard part is the time involved in the process—preparations for the pit, the wood, seasoning the meat, staying up all night.

The cooking pit is usually about six-feet long, four-feet wide, and four-feet deep, easily holding meat from the two or three deer used during an average-size barbecue, or up to 30 of the medium to large-sized bundles. A larger pit is required for larger barbecues, such as the 50 or so bundles that come from a cow. A deep pit is needed to insure that the top fire is recessed into its depths, rather than being level with the ground, because it will hold the heat better.

When it's time to remove the meat at about 5:00 p.m. the next day, a rake is used for clearing the one-and-a-half to two feet of ashes which have built up over the top dirt layer. At this stage, the heat of the coals can easily burn the skin. Once found, each package is shaken vigorously, then turned with the dirt side down before opening.

The venison slides easily away from the bone onto the serving platter. Cooked with loving attention in the ground, it tastes better than meat which has been conventionally prepared. Simmered in its own juices, the seasonings are absorbed into the meat.

The meat is placed at the head of the tables, amidst food reminiscent of the barbecues of Wayne's childhood. Here, the meat is followed by acorn mush and a diverse array of salads, chips and dip, vegetable dishes, desserts, and non-alcoholic drinks. After this food has been blessed, the hungry and happy guests will have their fill once the elders have been fed.

Wayne's commitment to pit cooking is strong:

> I like to do it for the people, and if they come and ask me if I can do a barbecue for them, then I'll do it.

By sharing the meat, he fulfills an important rule his grandmother taught him.

My grandmother used to always say that when you take and shoot a deer, divide it among the people 'cause it brings good luck for you…. It's what their belief is. Anything that you get. Fish. Anything. If you get abalone, mussels, all that stuff—divide it amongst the people…. Or give it to … your relatives. And that's supposed to give you good luck the next time you go out.

Eventually, the day will come when Wayne's oldest son, Junior, will carry on the pit-oven tradition. But for now, like a young Wayne watching his grandfather cook, Junior will learn what he needs to know by watching his father.

A Northern Sierra Miwok Method

Last September, in the midst of a busy time helping to host the Amador Tribal Council's Big Time at Chaw-Se, Sam Baugh, a member of the Council, was kind enough to share his method of deer cooking.

I started helping our elder, Bill Franklin, prepare the deer-pit barbecue, after the Amador Tribal Council began putting on the Big Time. I just carry on the tradition.

Sam is committed to pit cooking as one of many important "customs and traditions" that are passed on to the young people who work alongside him. Through his work with the Council, he promotes health and education, providing the children with a sense of identity and purpose. Each year at Chaw-Se, 300 to 400 pounds of beef and four to twelve deer are cooked in a pit five-feet deep, four-feet wide, and eight-feet long to feed Big Time visitors.

A crew of Amador Tribal Council members are always on-hand to help Sam prepare the meat. Beef is obtained in sections. Deer meat is skinned with the fist of Sam's hand, then cleaned and cut into three-pound sections. All of the meat is soaked in oil, seasonings, onions, and garlic before each section is wrapped with a layer of foil and a second layer of water-soaked burlap sack. This is then tied securely with baling wire before being lowered into the pit.

A modern innovation has removed the need to re-dig the pit whenever deer is to be cooked. The hole was recently lined with brick.

To cook the packs of wrapped meat, a half-cord of wood is burned to create an 18-inch deep bed of coals in the bottom of this trench. The meat is then laid on top of a screen which has been placed about three or four inches above the coals. Finally, hinged metal doors are closed over the filled pit, secured with chain, then covered with dirt to seal in the steam.

The meat was cooked for ten hours. Now, in the late morning, about an hour since the meat was removed, coals in the open pit still smoke.

Before the new brick-lined pit was constructed, a cord of wood was needed for the cooking process. The wood was burned to coals and a sheet of steel laid on top. The wrapped meat was placed in the hole next, then a layer of tin placed atop this. Lastly, the hole was filled with dirt using shovels. Then the meal allowed to cook for twelve hours.

One of the disadvantages this method presented was the possibility of getting burned while standing on the tin when removing the dirt. Also, the task was unpleasant when the ground was soaked with rain.

Whatever the method, Sam is committed to providing cooked meat for Big Time visitors. "That's the Indian way—to feed everyone that comes to the Big Time."

PHOTOGRAPHIC PORTFOLIO
CONTEMPORARY FOOD CUSTOMS
Dugan Aguilar

Dugan Aguilar is perhaps the leading photographer of contemporary California Indians. Born in 1947 in Susanville, California, Dugan Aguilar has a blended heritage: his father is from the Walker River Paiute of Nevada and his mother is from the Pit River and Maidu of California.

After earning a bachelor's degree from California State University-Fresno (Industrial Technology/Design, 1973), Dugan Aguilar continued his study of photography at the University of Nevada-Reno, UC Davis, and several workshops. Drawn to the art of Ansel Adams at a San Francisco exhibition in 1982, he participated in Adams's Yosemite Workshop the following year.

Aguilar has worked for the University of Nevada's Desert Research Institute, the Inter-Tribal Council of Nevada, and for the *Sacramento Bee*. Since 1984 his photographs have been shown at such California venues as the State Indian Museum (Sacramento), C. N. Gorman Museum (UC Davis), American Indian Contemporary Arts (San Francisco), Stanford University, Chaw'se Indian Art Show (Grinding Rock), as well as exhibitions in Arizona, New Mexico, South Dakota, and New Jersey.

Aguilar's photographs have been widely published in *News from Native California* and other newspapers and magazines, and in *Deeper than Gold: A Guide to Indian Life in the Sierra Region* (Bibby 2004). Dugan Aguilar lives with his family in Elk Grove, California.

The images presented here were included in a exhibition of Aguilar's photographs devoted to the subject of California Indian food: *Nuppa*—Acorn Soup (Hearst Museum, October 1, 1997–June 14, 1998). "As I began work on this project," he wrote, "I realized the importance of traditional foods to my people. I realized that an understanding of food is inseparable from the understanding of my culture, or any culture." Comparing acorn soup cooking to basket weaving and photography, Aguilar noted: "A part of each artist's soul goes into the final product."

Salmon cooking over an alder wood fire. Yurok Brush Dance, mouth of the Klamath River, Del Norte County, 1993.

Opposite top: Mary Eslick and her sister Bertha Peters (Yurok) demonstrating acorn soup cooking (left-right). Gathering of the California Indian Basketweavers Association, Ferndale, Humboldt County, 1996.

Opposite bottom: Three forms of acorn (right-left): whole, shelled, meal; with baskets, soaproot brush, looped stirrer, cracking rock. Maidu Big Time, Oakland Museum of California, Oakland, 1997.

*Alfred Valenzuela (Chumash) barbecuing marinated beef. Gathering
of the California Indian Basketweavers Association,
Thousand Oaks, Ventura County, 1997.*

Getting ready to serve (front left, front right): Bev Pinola, Frank Ross.
Strawberry Festival, Point Reyes National Seashore, Marin County, 1997.

Serving food (left-right): Sara Deutsche, Mary Baugh, Jim Farris.
Big Time, Chaw'se Indian Grinding Rock State Park,
Pine Grove, Amador County, 1996.

*Jane Wyatt (Chukchansi Yokuts) rolling out dough for fry bread.
Big Time, Yosemite National Park, Tuolumne County, 1997.*

Navajo fry bread stand. Pow-wow, Santa Ynez,
Santa Barbara County, 1996.

Jacknis: Introduction

1. In addition to Cushing (1884–85) and Boas and Hunt (1921), some of the best analytic studies of Native American food include Waugh (1916) on the Iroquois, Bailey (1940) on the Navajo, Watson (1943) on Hopi food classifications, Honigmann (1961) on the Attawapiskat Cree, Vennum (1988) on Ojibway wild rice, and Coe (1994) on ancient Mesoamerica and the Andes. Among the general Native American cookbooks are Kimball and Anderson (1965), Kirst (1991), Cox and Jacobs (1991), Kavasch (1995); and among the specialized ones are Frank (2002) on the Southwest, Niethammer (1974) and Hughes (1977) on Pueblo Indians, Kavena (1980) on the Hopi, Edaakie (1999) on the Zuni, Batdorf (1990) for the Coast Salish, and People of 'Ksan (1980) for the Gitksan and George and Gairns (1997) on the Wet'suwet'en Carrier, both of British Columbia.

2. For general reviews of nutritional anthropology, see Counihan and van Esterik (1997), and Mintz and Du Bois (2002). For two excellent recent analyses of food and culture, see Ashkenazi and Jacob (2000) on Japan, and Sutton (2001) on Greece.

3. There is much on food contained in the relatively large literature on ethnobotany (in general and within California). Studies on the cultural uses of plants have been earlier and more substantial than similar writings on Native uses of animals. Among the more important ethnobotanies for the region are Schenk and Gifford (1952) on Karuk, Chesnut (1902) on Indians of Mendocino County, Goodrich et al. (1980) on Kashaya Pomo, Bocek (1984) on Costanoan/Ohlone, Timbrook (1990) on Chumash, Barrows (1900) and Bean and Saubel (1972) on Cahuilla, Hedges and Beresford (1986) on Diegueño, Zigmond (1981) on Kawaiisu. For general California, Balls (1962), Ebeling (1986), Keator, Yamane, and Lewis (1995), and two bibliographies, Beck (1994) and Strike (1994) (unfortunately, Beck contains numerous typographic errors).

4. The four food-related films by the American Indian film project, all distributed by the University of California Extension Center for Media and Independent Learning, include *Acorns: Staple Food of California Indians* (Kashaya Pomo, 28 min., 1962), *Beautiful Tree: Chishkale* (Kashaya Pomo tan oak acorn, 20 min., 1965), *Buckeyes: Food of California Indians* (Nisenan, 13 min., 1961), *Pine Nuts* (Paviotso, Paiute; 13 min., 1961).

Extensive unedited footage is preserved in the Phoebe Hearst Museum archives. For comments on possible inaccuracies in these films, most of which involved cultural reconstruction, see Heizer (1974:29).

5. The tentativeness of my subtitle, taken from T.S. Eliot (1948), reflects this lack of knowledge.

6. In an important essay, Rozin considers the structure of cuisines (1982). For her, "culinary behavior," or cooking in the extended sense, includes all transformation of foods from a raw state, not just heating. There are three main features of culinary structure. First is the selection of foods, that is, ingredients. The second, manipulative techniques, include both processing and cooking. These techniques are: (a) processes that involve changes in size, shape, or mass; (b) processes that involve manipulation of water content (e.g., leaching or drying); (c) processes that involve direct chemical changes (e.g., heating, which can be dry, wet, or in fat). The third feature is flavoring or seasoning practices. These rules of combination and processing result in recipes, but that is only the beginning of an anthropological study of food, for one must then turn to consumption and the meaning of food, with its social associations.

7. Powers and Powers employ a similar processual approach in their excellent analysis of Oglala food customs. Their stages are procurement, preparation, distribution, consumption, and disposal (1984:45–46).

8. As a summary of the literature, this introduction is subject to the limitations of that literature. On the one hand, it may be wrong. For example, Barrett disputed Loeb's report that the Pomo were solemn when gathering army worms (note 106; cf. Swezey 1978). Heizer warned us against the dangers of reconstructing cultural practices from historical evidence (1974). As apparently accurate accounts may be in error, we have to learn to critically evaluate our sources. Furthermore, it may be misleading to generalize. First there are the generalizations that ethnographers made based on reports of single informants, often based on memory not observation. Then in light of what we know was considerable variation among tribal groups, there is the difficulty of generalizing from behaviors of single groups at particular places and times. As Ortiz has noted of the problems in generalizing: "There is no such thing as 'California Indian acorn making.' The techniques vary from group to group, and the closer we look the more we can appreciate the ways in which these skills are reflective of the acorn maker" (1990b:16).

9. Kroeber estimated that the average family size was 7 or 8, with a range of 5 to 10 (1954). Population densities depended on environmental conditions, ranging from 0.5 per square mile to as high as 10 or more persons per

square mile (Yokuts-Chumash); tribelet territories ranged from 50 square miles (Miwok) to as much as 6000 square miles (Bean 1976:101).

10. The Tübatulabal, who inhabited the South Fork valley of the Kern River, seem to have overlapped the central Californian and Great Basin subsistence regions, taking equally acorns and pine nuts, deer and rabbits (Voegelin 1938:1).

11. This ecological classification was originally proposed by Beals and Hester (1960), drawing on their research for the Indian Claims Commission.

12. For variety in their diet, Yurok traded surplus foods, for example, coastal foods such as seaweed, surf fish, and dried mussels for interior items such as acorns, hazel, laurel, and pine nuts (Kroeber 1960:141–42).

13. Food was mentioned 321 times in Davis's survey of the literature on trade, with beads and shell products as the second most often cited item (230 times). For the first five, salt was the most often mentioned, followed by basketry, hides and pelts, shell beads, and acorns (1961:12).

14. On the necessity for staples, Beals and Hester have discussed the relative degrees of labor and time involved in processing a staple food versus that involved in acquiring other ingredients. "But a very large proportion of the long lists of plants reported to be used for foods was simply too uneconomical to gather unless the necessities of life had been cared for through accumulation of a store of easily collected foods such as acorns" (1974:140).

15. Despite this statement from Chartkoff and Chartkoff about the dependence of "valley groups" on deer, we do know that deer were relatively scarce in the Great Central Valley (see above). They may have been referring to other valley areas.

16. Other Kawaiisu uses for plants were over 100 species for medicine, 90 for miscellaneous items and services, and 40 with "ritualistic, mythological or supernatural associations" (Zigmond 1981:4).

17. I am indebted to Beverly Ortiz for emphasizing the importance of grass seeds in the diets of early California Indians.

18. One must note that these are Western groupings. Like many cultures, Native Californians undoubtedly grouped their foods into their own categories, and probably had food classifications such as hot/cold, wet/dry, or heavy/light.

19. On the other hand, it has been suggested that "as a result of human predation, the large marine and terrestrial mammals had been reduced to minor importance as nutritional sources for the natives during the centuries

leading up to the colonial era" (Preston 1998:269). Preston argues that the subsequent rise in the deer population following contact resulted from the drastic decline in the Native population due to spreading disease. While these theories are still somewhat speculative, it seems certain that Native Californians played a role in regulating animal populations, just as they did for plants.

20. Chukchansi Yokuts hunters carried deer blood back to the village inside the stomach, which was carried inside the skin (Gayton 1948b:183); Cahuilla either drank blood fresh or cooked and stored it in a leather pouch or in sections of gut (Bean 1972:66).

21. Salmon bones for the Karuk (Kroeber and Barrett 1960:105), small mammals for the Cahuilla (Bean 1972:59). Among the reports for deer marrow and bone consumption are Atsugewi (Garth 1953:133), Tübatulabal (Voegelin 1938:13), and Cahuilla (Bean 1972:66).

22. On Californian and Great Basin insect-eating, see Essig (1934), Heizer (1950), Fowler and Walter (1985), Weaver and Basgall (1986), Sutton (1988). See Menzel and D'Aluisio (1998) for a good general review.

23. Not all berries were sweet; the Sierra Miwok did not eat them much, as some were sour (Barrett and Gifford 1933:162–63). However, according to Ortiz (pers. comm. 1998), Mono people love sour berries.

24. The Cahuilla (Barrows 1900:75) and the Tübatulabal (Voegelin 1938:19) made a chewy gum out of the sap of the milkweed (*Asclepias erosa*), but according to Barrows the gum was "tasteless."

25. Atsugewi (Garth 1953:138), Wintu (Du Bois 1935:19, 21), Maidu (Dixon 1905:183), Sierra Miwok (Barrett and Gifford 1933:151).

26. Native Californians did consume mind-altering plants, principally tobacco and datura (Kroeber 1925:826–27, 640). While tobacco was sometimes part of religious offerings, it was more often used as a personal pastime. Datura or jimsonweed, on the other hand, was part of an elaborate ritual in the southern part of the state. As part of an initiation into the toloache cult, young boys drank a concoction of datura leaves and salt water. This would help them see visions that would protect the young men in future perilous pursuits.

27. Domesticated dogs seem to have been in California from the time of earliest occupation (Kroeber 1925:216). Many groups in the state, especially in the north, did not normally keep them. "In general, dogs were not eaten west of the Rockies. The principal area in which they were regularly used as food centers around the Yokuts of the San Joaquin Valley, with some scattering outliers" (Kroeber 1941:7).

28. Such food taboos have been the subject of spirited anthropological debate. Marvin Harris (1985) argues that societies avoid eating certain animals for pragmatic reasons. Regarding social aversions to particular species, he claims that the species in question does not benefit the group in some nutritional way, or that it is not cost-effective to gather. For instance, carnivores and raptors are frequently not taken (as in Native California), "Because these creatures not only tend to be solitary, hard to find, and dangerous when found, but they are notably deficient in fat, which is much sought after by hunter-gathers and village horticulturists" (Harris 1987:75). In the same materialist vein, he concludes that "many preferences and avoidances associated with gender hierarchies are best regarded as forms of rationing" (ibid.). That is, the men get the meat because they are socially dominant. He further argues that it is not necessarily disadvantageous for a pregnant/nursing woman to go without extra meat protein, for she may indeed manage to obtain it or its lack may not hurt her. The taboo on pig-eating in the ancient Middle East has been a classic instance of this debate. Whereas Harris maintains that raising pigs would deplete resources needed for human nutrition, a symbolist anthropologist like Mary Douglas (1975), following Lévi-Strauss, argues that animals like the pig were tabooed because they did not fit into Biblical animal classifications, combining features of otherwise separate categories. Analyses like these, from either perspective, have not yet been applied to Native Californian food choices; and given the relatively thin documentation available, they would be hard to substantiate, in any case.

29. Such respect for bears was an expression of the bear ceremonialism widespread in northern regions of North America and Asia (Rockwell 1991; Hallowell 1926).

30. Baumhoff (1963:162); cf. Heizer and Elsasser (1980:96), McGee (1984:265), Basgall (1987:25).

31. California Indians obtained fats and oils from mammals, birds, and fish, as well as plants (especially acorns and other nuts). Oily foods, especially fish, seem to have been more common in the Northwest, perhaps less in southern and desert regions. While we know that some of these groups specifically rendered and stored animal and fish oils, it is not clear what they did with them (preservation, flavoring, cooking?). Perhaps, like more northerly groups, they consumed oils with dried foods such as dried salmon or berry and root cakes (Kroeber 1960:121, 132). Some Atsugewi people enjoyed eating raw trout fat (Garth 1953:136). Before drying meat, the Sierra Miwok trimmed off all fat, which they saved in baskets and ate raw (Barrett and Gifford 1933:140).

32. Sierra Miwok (Barrett and Gifford 1933:143), Cahuilla (Bean 1972:60), Owens Valley Paiute (Steward 1933:239).

33. Because of natural fluctuations in plant and animal populations, Native Californians practiced the devices delineated by Colson to lessen the vulnerability to such risks: "(1) diversification of activities, rather than specialization or reliance on a few plants or animals; (2) storage of foodstuffs; (3) storage and transmission of information on what we can call famine foods; (4) conversion of surplus food into durable valuables which could be stored and traded for food in an emergency; (5) cultivation of social relationships to allow the tapping of food resources of other regions" (1979:21).

34. Of course, as Beverly Ortiz points out (pers. comm. 1998), the same brushes were not used for both purposes, and the fibers were different.

35. For a good recent review of Native Californian artifacts, including much on food practices, see Campbell (1999).

36. Northfork Mono (Gifford 1932:17), Tübatulabal (Voegelin 1938:51).

37. Atsugewi (Garth 1953:186), Wintu (Du Bois 1935:9), Maidu (Dixon 1905:193), Pomo (Loeb 1926:171–72), Cahuilla (Bean 1972:153–54).

38. The investigation of the integration of subsistence and ritual has been a persistent theme in California Indian studies. With roots in Kroeber's environmental approach, it was explored in Gayton's classic essay on the Yokuts (1946). Ecological explanations became popular in the late 1960s and early 1970s (Bean 1972; Swezey 1975; Blackburn 1976). A separate yet related concern has been the research on fire and environmental cultivation (Lewis 1973; Blackburn and Anderson 1993).

39. Pine nuts: northern California (Farris 1993), Wintu (Du Bois 1935:21), Sierra Miwok (Barrett and Gifford 1933:150), Chukchansi Yokuts (Gayton 1948b:180), Cahuilla (Bean 1972:40; Dozier 1998:79, 81), Owens Valley Paiute (Steward 1933:242), Great Basin (Fowler 1986:65).

40. Pomo deer hunters cut up meat on the spot (Loeb 1926:171). Wintu skinned and quartered deer at the kill site, and each hunter brought some back to camp, where the meat was divided (Du Bois 1935:10).

41. Hunter's cooking: Hupa (Goddard 1903:22), Atsugewi (Garth 1953:133), Nisenan (Beals 1933:348), Southeastern Pomo (Barrett 1952:63), Kashaya Pomo (Oswalt 1964:303), Sierra Miwok (Barrett and Gifford 1933:181).

42. After a Hupa deer kill, "The carcass was cut in accordance with prescribed rules. Some portions were not eaten at all, among them the flesh on the floating ribs and the breast-bone. Other parts were forbidden to women. None of the animal was wasted save from religious scruples" (Goddard 1903:22).

43. Sun-drying: Tolowa (Drucker 1937:235), Tübatulabal (Voegelin 1938:20), Owens Valley Paiute (Steward 1933:245), Luiseño (Sparkman 1908:195), Mohave (Stewart 1968:30).

44. Karuk smoked salmon, sturgeon, lampreys, trout, other fish, venison and other meats, and acorns (Kroeber and Barrett 1960:99); Tolowa smoked salmon, lamprey eel, shellfish, and venison (Drucker 1937:234). For contemporary Karuk/Yurok practices of smoking and cooking eel and salmon, see Ortiz (1999).

45. Drying/smoking meat: Atsugewi (Garth 1953:133), Maidu (Dixon 1905:191), Pomo (Loeb 1926:173), Tübatulabal (Voegelin 1938:20).

46. According to Driver and Massey (1957:245), the Mohaves' neighbors in the Southwest and Mexico commonly ate their meat fresh.

47. Seed parching among Hupa (Goddard 1903:31), Atsugewi sunflower seeds (Garth 1953:139), Sierra Miwok (Barrett and Gifford 1933:152), Cahuilla (Bean 1972:47), Luiseño (Sparkman 1908:193), Owens Valley Paiute (Steward 1933:243–44). For toasting seeds, the Pomo preferred coals from willow or oak bark because they were slow burning (Barrett 1952:60).

48. Buckeye processing: Wintu (Du Bois 1935:20), Maidu (Dixon 1905:187–88), Pomo (Loeb 1926:173), Sierra Miwok (Barrett and Gifford 1933:148–49).

49. On the parching and preparation of grasshoppers: Maidu (Dixon 1905:190–91), Nisenan (Wilson 1972:36), Pomo (Loeb 1926:163), Sierra Miwok (Barrett and Gifford 1933:191), and Luiseño (Sparkman 1908:199).

50. As Ortiz and Parker maintain, the common action in pulverizing acorns should be more accurately called pounding rather than grinding. A mortar and pestle works by hitting and crushing, not rubbing (1991:73). On North American mortars, see Driver and Massey (1957:237); for Californian methods, Kroeber (1925:411–14); and on Sierra Miwok mortars, Barrett and Gifford (1933:208–9, 272).

51. The Yokuts of the San Joaquin Valley also used portable wooden mortars; the southern Luiseño pounded their acorns in both portable and bedrock mortars (Sparkman 1908:207).

52. The Nisenan made a similar mixture of ground-seeds (Wilson 1972:37).

53. In his comprehensive study of Native American fishing, Rostlund concludes that salmon pemmican "probably came down the Columbia River to the coast and then, as the distribution pattern suggests, diffused to California

by way of the Oregon coast" (1952:141). He suggests that the process may be related to meat pounding and notes that fish pounding was found in only two areas of North America: Plateau-Oregon-California and lower Great Lakes-New York.

54. With the later, fall-run salmon, the Wintu split open the fish, which were then skewered with poles, sun-dried, folded in four pieces (head to tail and flank to flank), and stored (Du Bois 1935:16).

55. Grinding meat: Sierra Miwok (Barrett and Gifford 1933:209), Cahuilla (Bean 1972:67).

56. Maidu (Dixon 1905:187), Chukchansi Yokuts (Gayton 1948b:178).

57. Manzanita cider: Atsugewi (Garth 1953:138), Wintu (Du Bois 1935:20), Maidu (Dixon 1905:189–90), Sierra Miwok (Barrett and Gifford 1933:161–62), Northfork Mono (Gifford 1932:22–23), Chukchansi Yokuts (Gayton 1948b:181–82).

58. According to Ortiz (1991:10), acorn flour will last years if stored in an air-tight jar. Pounding exposes the surfaces to more oxidation, making the fats rancid, but preservation seems to be aided by the tannins. Even leached acorn meal can be palatable for up to two weeks (Ortiz pers. comm. 1998).

59. Beverly Ortiz has suggested that cooking was not the constant domestic chore that it has been made out to be. She says that not every woman prepared acorn every day, that it was often made in amounts that fed many people, and that certain women specialized in its preparation (pers. comm. 1998).

60. All Californian peoples, of course, gathered, transported, and stored water in containers. In the north, the same baskets were used for water storage and cooking, but in the drier southern and eastern region specialized water containers were made. Water jars from this area tend to have a narrow neck and a pitch-coating on the baskets in order to limit evaporation in a hot, dry climate.

61. In a spirit of aesthetic play, the Tübatulabal constructed a kind of coiled "basket" out of long strands of strung piñons. "After being made, a piñon jar was filled with loose nuts and brought home from the piñon grounds; eventually it and its contents were shelled and eaten" (Voegelin 1938:3).

62. Sierra Miwok (Barrett and Gifford 1933:201), Northfork Mono (Gifford 1932:24), Tübatulabal (Voegelin 1938:25). On the location of Western Mono bedrock mortars, both ethnographic and archaeological, see Jackson (1991).

63. Of the Tachi Yokuts acorn grinding song in the Hearst Museum collection [sung by Josie Atwell and Clara Barrios (24–107), included on tape no. 3 of the California Indian Music Sampler series], Hatch noted that it was "the single work song in the Tachi collection." "This song was sung only by the women, who did the acorn grinding, which the males did not, or pretended not, to know" (1958:50). The sampler tape also includes songs for the Sierra Miwok acorn dance.

64. All Californian groups produced fire with a fire-drill; a pointed stick was twirled rapidly in a small depression made in a larger piece of wood called a "hearth." With the addition of kindling material and some fanning or blowing, the friction would eventually produce a flame (Kroeber 1925:829).

65. According to David Peri, the Bodega Miwok compared the ripening of fruits, nuts, and berries, to cooking. They recognized that natural ripening would change the chemical composition of foods, such as increasing their sweetness, in the same manner as the application of heat over a short period of time. The foods then achieved a preferred "taste" (2001:11).

66. Except for a few methods of plant preparation (see previous section). Pomo might eat deer or elk that had died of natural causes if the meat was not too decomposed (Loeb 1926:175).

67. Among those tribes who greatly appreciated clover were the Wintu (Du Bois 1935:20–21), Maidu (Dixon 1905:183), Nisenan (Wilson 1972:38), Pomo (Loeb 1926:174), Sierra Miwok (Barrett and Gifford 1933:161), Chukchansi Yokuts (Gayton 1948b:180), Tübatulabal (Voegelin 1938:19), and Owens Valley Paiute (Steward 1933:244).

68. Raw plants: Hupa (Goddard 1903:29–30), Wintu (Du Bois 1935:20–21), Maidu (Dixon 1905:183), Pomo (Loeb 1926:174), Chukchansi Yokuts (Gayton 1948b:180), Tübatulabal (Voegelin 1938:19), Luiseño (Sparkman 1908:195), Owens Valley Paiute (Steward 1933:244).

69. There is a tremendous variability in the reference of cooking terms in English. Broiling and grilling generally mean the same thing. While the roasting of meat used to be similar, over an open fire, it is now used to mean a form of baking, taking place in an enclosed oven. In a stimulating essay Reid has noted the confused use of cooking terminology by anthropologists (1990:9). Blaming the uncritical influence of Edward Tylor's *Researches Into the Early History of Mankind*, 1878, Reid argued that starchy roots are not "baked" in earth ovens, but are actually steamed in pressure cooking pits. See also Lehrer's important review of comparative cooking terms (1972), inspired by Lévi-Strauss's discussion of the culinary triangle.

70. Ortiz (1990a) records recent methods of frying seaweed, but these are post-contact developments (pers. comm. 1998).

71. As the Northern Sierra Miwok also added a fire on top of an earth oven, they had another term for this type of baking (*hubuya*).

72. Groups boiling earthworms: Maidu (Dixon 1905:191), Pomo (Loeb 1926:164), Chukchansi (Gayton 1948b:181); roasting them, Nisenan (Beals 1933:346).

73. Cf. Yurok (Kroeber 1960:133), Sierra Miwok river mussels (Barrett and Gifford 1933:139).

74. Tolowa (Drucker 1937:235), Sierra Miwok (Barrett and Gifford 1933:138).

75. Leaving the skin on (Sierra Miwok, Barrett and Gifford 1933:138; Cahuilla, Bean 1972:66; Owens Valley Paiute, Steward 1933:255), sewing up the belly with a stick (Owens Valley Paiute, Steward 1933:255), both (Nisenan, Wilson 1972:36).

76. For rabbits caught in a drive; individually captured rabbits were cooked this way or boiled.

77. In Native North America, the earth oven was primarily found west of the Plains (Driver and Massey 1957:233, map 45). Where present in the east, it was used for cooking maize, squashes, and wild roots. Native American pit-cooking may be related to some forms of southern American barbecue (Elie 1996:26, 34), but Neustadt is skeptical on the Indian role in developing the New England clambake (1992:17).

78. According to Reid (1990:10), pit cooking is more often steaming; the food is under greater pressure as the pit is sealed along with moist vegetation. "Pressure cooking with steam is particularly well suited for cooking large starchy plants such as roots and tubers because the high temperatures (100° C+ depending on pressure) successfully gelatinize the carbohydrates, and the finished product can be pressed into a more compact form for storage or transport."

79. Other sources on earth ovens are Maidu (Dixon 1905:191), Pomo (Barrett 1952:61), Luiseño (Sparkman 1908:195). Although Dixon reports that the meat in a Maidu earth oven was baked "after an hour or two," this seems a bit quick when compared to other reports.

80. The separate terms "brodiaea bulbs," "Indian potatoes," and "bulbs" are overlapping and may in fact refer to the same plant (and others); see Anderson (1992). Sources on plant-baking: Hupa (Goddard 1903:30), Atsugewi (Garth 1953:138), Pomo (Loeb 1926:174; Barrett 1952:61), Sierra

Miwok (Barrett and Gifford 1933:139, 156), Tübatulabal (Voegelin 1938:18), Cahuilla (Bean 1972:52), and Luiseño (Sparkman 1908:195).

81. According to Driver and Massey (1957:229), stone boiling is the earlier form. Northwest Coast peoples used wooden boxes, while Plains groups preferred skin pouches; bark containers were used in the north and east.

82. This is a rough estimate based on inspection of the basket collection at the Hearst Museum.

83. Ortiz and Parker (1991:109–10); Kashaya Pomo, Alvarez and Peri (1987:13).

84. Chumash (Hudson and Blackburn 1983:201–6), Chukchansi Yokuts (Gayton 1948b:190), North Fork Mono (Gifford 1932:25). The Mono also had wooden (oak) bowls. Although their use is uncertain, they do not appear to have been used for cooking.

85. The Californian term pinole comes from the Spanish *pinole*. This, in turn, was derived from the Nahuatl *pinolli*, which referred to toasted corn powder. Like the California seed mixtures, *pinolli* could be mixed with liquid (Coe 1994:139).

86. During his 1937 Hupa study, Goldschmidt found that one pound, eleven ounces of leached acorn meal yielded nine pounds, seven ounces cooked, which made approximately seven helpings (1974:311).

87. In addition to the Tolowa and Hupa, other groups who boiled meat and waterfowl included the Maidu (Dixon 1905:191), Owens Valley Paiute (Steward 1933:255), Tübatulabal (Voegelin 1938:13), Cahuilla (Bean 1972:66), and Luiseño (Sparkman 1908:197).

88. For acorn biscuits, see Nisenan (Wilson 1972:37), Chukchansi Yokuts (Gayton 1948b:179), Tübatulabal (Voegelin 1938:18).

89. Mashed "Indian potatoes": Nisenan (Wilson 1972:38), Chukchansi Yokuts (Gayton 1948b:180).

90. The lack of Californian recipes contrasts with that of the Kwakiutl of British Columbia, from whom over 150 recipes have been reported (Boas and Hunt 1921). While this may reflect the relative lack of complex procedures and combinations, it is more likely due to poor, shallow research.

91. As the presence of beef indicates, some of these thickening practices may have been post-contact.

92. Dixon (1905:187) claims that sand and ashes were mixed (unintentionally?) with Maidu acorn soup and bread, but most sources suggest that such elements were consciously avoided by good chefs.

93. Tolowa (Drucker 1937:235), Hupa (Goddard 1903:30), Pomo (Barrett 1952:61), Sierra Miwok (Barrett and Gifford 1933:139).

94. Pomo (Barrett 1952:62), Northfork Mono (Gifford 1932:23), Chukchansi Yokuts (Gayton 1948b:179), Cahuilla (Bean 1972:47).

95. Like almost all cultural evidence recorded from Ishi, it is difficult to know whether he was expressing a social or an individual preference. In fact, we have virtually no evidence on individual food preferences in Native California, though they most certainly existed. One Wintu woman continued to avoid certain foods, although they were no longer restricted for her (see under Food as a Social Category).

96. One possibility for the preference for roasting rather than boiling meat may have been the desire to contrast it with the boiling common for acorns and other plants. However, peoples of the Prairies and the East boiled most of their meat, often mixing it with boiled plant foods (Driver and Massey 1957:233). While meat boiling is related partly to the presence of pottery, it is clearly a matter of cultural and regional choice.

97. Chesnut (1902:350), Loeb (1926:174), Smith (1990a); for Kashaya Pomo, cf. Oswalt (1964:305).

98. The Sierra Miwok also took manzanita cider as a cure for stomach trouble, but the medicinal value was attributed to the hawk feathers of the dipper.

99. Beverly Ortiz suggests that the tannic acids in the acorn meal might have affected the meat (pers. comm. 1998).

100. Hupa (Goddard 1903:57), Yurok (Kroeber 1960:138), Tübatulabal (Voegelin 1938:19), Owens Valley Paiute (Steward 1933:239). Although Loeb (1926:175) gives the afternoon for the second Pomo meal, according to Barrett (1952:63–64), it was in the "evening whenever people had returned from their tasks."

101. One Wintu informant believed that this system permitted men to obtain far more food than women. Doubting that the mode of sharing food worked as ideally given, Du Bois felt that the food was not equally distributed (1935:50).

102. Cooking and serving utensils were not that much different in colonial America. Meals were simple and often served from the pot. Not until metal utensils were mass-produced in the nineteenth century did common people have separate serving utensils and full sets of knives and forks. Moreover, most colonial Americans had only two or three pots for cooking and a few more bowls and plates than were needed to feed the family at a given meal (Pillsbury 1998:34–35).

103. Wintu (Du Bois 1935:19), Atsugewi (Garth 1953:138), Owens Valley Paiute (Steward 1933:242), and Sierra Miwok, who also used a fresh-water mussel shell spoon (Barrett and Gifford 1933:146).

104. Although we have almost no information on what amount would constitute a portion or a serving, we do know that "a single deer would be consumed in two days by the average [Chukchansi Yokuts] family" (Gayton 1948b:183).

105. Related to the question of how long foods could be preserved is that of their frequency of preparation. We know that a local Wintu group would bake acorn bread every week or two (Du Bois 1935:19), and Sierra Miwok communities cooked their acorn bread (ulli) approximately every three weeks (Grinnell 1893 [1958]:45).

106. Loeb reported that the Pomo treated army worms with respect. "These caterpillars must never be thrown around or mishandled in any manner, and while the people eat them they must maintain a strict silence" (1926:164), but Barrett denied that the gathering was solemn, and suggested that Loeb was simply reporting what one Northern Pomo informant reported (1936:5).

107. Other discussions of food distribution at feasts include Loeb (1926:237–38) on the Pomo, Garth (1953:171, 178) on the Atsugewi, and Barrett and Gifford (1933:200) on the Sierra Miwok.

108. Du Bois notes that "this custom is reported most frequently for girls' puberty dances, but it probably obtained for all gatherings" (1935:24). She also gives some exchange values; for example, the equivalent amounts of salmon for acorns, salmon for wheat or manzanita flour, acorns for hides (p. 26–27). Pomoan trade feasts are also well documented (Loeb 1926:192–94; Vayda 1966).

109. The phrasing of these customs, taken directly from Voegelin, raises a more general issue of interpretation for these early ethnographies. Many, such as this one, are written in a telegraphic style that often makes it hard to fully understand what the point was. In this passage, I take Voegelin to mean that warm water was the only water that a new mother could drink (along with no meat, salt, or grease), not that water was the only thing she could ingest for a month. She could, therefore, eat acorns and other plant foods. While we can sometimes clarify these statements based on other available information, in many cases, unfortunately, these passages will remain ambiguous.

110. Owens Valley Paiute, one and a half to two years (Steward 1933:291); Tübatulabal, at least two (Voegelin 1938:45); Wintu, two to four (Du Bois 1935:47); Atsugewi, three or four (Garth 1953:159); Pomo, when they were able to stand up (Loeb 1926:256).

111. Wintu (Du Bois 1935:9, 48), Owens Valley Paiute (Steward 1933:293), Tübatulabal (Voegelin 1938:66). An Atsugewi boy had to give away the first of each species of animal he killed (Garth 1953:162).

112. In addition to Loeb, Parkman was drawing upon the Pomoan field notes of John Hudson, preserved in the Grace Hudson Museum in Ukiah, Mendocino County.

113. For gender-related marriage exchanges of food: Atsugewi (Garth 1953:153), Nisenan (Beals 1933:370), Pomo (Loeb 1926:278, 283–85), Chukchansi Yokuts (Gayton 1948b:195).

114. While a mountain Nisenan cremation was underway, those assisting were forbidden meat, grease, salt [the same foods forbidden during birth and puberty], and water (Beals 1933:376). After a funeral, Coast Central Pomo relatives who had witnessed the burning abstained from anything with grease for four days, and Northern Pomo relatives of the deceased abstained from meat, fish, and birds until purified (Kroeber 1925:294, 292). Hupa mourners could not eat salmon and venison for five days after a burial (Goddard 1903:73).

115. Not only did Voegelin deny Kroeber's statement that the Tübatulabal placed a pubescent girl in a heated pit, she suggested that they did not have any girl's puberty ceremonies (1938:70–71).

116. Many food scholars have analyzed regional patterning in other cuisines, such as French, Italian, Indian, and Chinese. In a classic study, food historian Waverley Root differentiated three French culinary regions based on the dominant type of shortening (butter, olive oil, lard); each related a French region to neighboring countries (Root 1958). American barbecue is characterized by well-known regional styles (Elie 1996:155). For a good American review, see Pillsbury (1998:209–33).

117. The Wintu expressed these culinary put-downs more formally. "There exists an ironical love song supposedly sung by a Stillwater woman to her McCloud husband: Surely if I went up to the McCloud/I should choke on a salmon bone. A person from the McCloud might sing: If I went to Stillwater/I might choke on a grasshopper leg. If I went to the upper Sacramento/I might choke on the bone of a fawn" (Du Bois 1935:6).

118. For California Indians, the available sources for a culinary history include archaeological remains, written observations (with few recipes), and memories. As partial as they are, our best evidence is the ethnographies represented here. The archaeological evidence tends to be composed of hard materials—tools for acquisition (stone projectile points, bone and antler harpoons and hooks) and preparation (stone mortars and pestles); but sometimes

it is samples of the food itself—plant seeds and husks, animal bones, and discarded shells in coastal midden mounds.

119. See Sokolov (1991) on the culinary encounter between the Old and New Worlds.

120. The following discussion summarizes the findings of archaeologists. Native peoples often have alternative views of their origins and histories, with the major difference being their belief that they have been in their homelands since creation. Archaeological knowledge of the earliest population of California and the Americas in general is uncertain and poorly documented. Interestingly, the dates for the earliest habitations have been continually pushed back as more evidence has been uncovered. Ultimately, however, these two perspectives may be incompatible.

121. Stone comals (from the Aztec word for a circular pottery griddle) were replaced by iron forms in the nineteenth century (Driver and Massey 1957:243).

122. Native Americans were not the only ones to adapt to new foods in the late–nineteenth century. In fact, it was only during this period that American cuisine began to substantially differentiate itself from that of Native California. The biggest difference was the latter's economy based on hunting and gathering rather than agriculture and domestication, but aboriginal farming was practiced in the southern part of the state. Before the widespread adoption of canning, refrigeration, and freezing, all Americans had to exploit fresh foods in season and preserve a surplus (Root and de Rochemont 1976:146). The commercialization of food (processed foods that were purchased rather than self-produced) that so influenced Native customs affected non-Natives just as much, even though the latter were not shifting from wild to domesticated foods.

123. In the 1930s, the Tübatulabal were using bedrock mortars to pound parched corn or wheat (Voegelin 1938:17).

124. A Pomo feast, held near Healdsburg, Sonoma County, in 1981, included roasted peppernuts, peppernut balls, manzanita berry *pinole*, fry bread with toyon honey, and tup-tup (a puffed white-flour bread) for the appetizers; barbecued salmon, steamed clams, abalone, beef flank, roasted venison, flour tortillas, *pinole*, acorn mush, and buckeye mush for the main course; acorn-pine nut bread, hazelnut-acorn cookies, and berries with maple sugar for dessert; hot and cold yerba buena tea, natural berry soda, and coffee for beverages; with popcorn and blackberry drink at the tables (Frederickson 1987). In southern California, the Malki Museum on the Morongo Reservation sponsored a Cahuilla fiesta in 1994. The menu included venison stew, rabbit

stew with dumplings, acorn cubes, chia porridge, mesquite bread, prickly pear cactus fruit, cactus pads with wild onions, barrel cactus buds, roasted piñon nuts, palm fruit, blue corn bread, sopapilla, and desert holly. A jojoba nut drink, manzanita tea, desert tea, and mesquite drink were served as beverages (Kotzen 1994).

125. At the same time one must beware of simplistic definitions of tradition and identity. In response to a comment that beans and tortillas were not Native foods, Anthony Andreas (Cahuilla) maintained: "I never thought of it as Mexican food, because I grew up with that. It bothered me. When I got older, it was easy—if a Mexican makes it, it's Mexican food. If an Indian makes it, it's Indian food. There is a little difference" (Dozier 1998:29).

126. I am indebted to Beverly Ortiz for this comment.

127. As late as the 1940s, Pomo menstruants were keeping their plates separate from the rest of the family (Patterson 1995:138). Otis Parrish (Kashaya Pomo) reports on the puberty ceremony he conducted for his daughter in the mid-1970s. Parrish's mother, Essie, instructed him on the food proscriptions to follow: "Be sure when you or her sisters feed her to remember she has to have special utensils to eat out of; keep them separate from the others. She can't eat any greasy foods, fruits and vegetables newly in season, meat, fish, milk, eggs—only boiled potatoes, boiled rice, and her blessed water—that's the way the rules are" (1976:76). Following the seclusion, the parents were to give a picnic, including meat. And in 1978 at least one Yurok woman was maintaining the food taboos in which a menstruating woman cooked and ate separately from the rest of her family (Buckley 1988:189).

128. In the early days of Chez Panisse, Alice Waters and her chefs literally foraged, obtaining fennel, plum blossoms, and grape leaves from backyards and other private property (Waters on *West Coast Live*, 25 August 2001, http://www.WCL.org/).

Kroeber: Food Problem

1. Kroeber's view of abundant food resources in Native California has been subjected to a critique by recent archaeologists (Raab and Jones 2004).—Ed.

Merriam: Acorn Portfolio

1. Although these two pictures of acorn processing at Railroad Flat—part of a series of twelve—are dated in The Bancroft Library to 1908, three of the images were used to illustrate an account of a Sierra Miwok "Cry" or Mourning Ceremony witnessed by Merriam in 1906 (Merriam 1955:49–51,

pl. 17). While the date may be wrong, it is also true that Merriam often returned to the same site on repeated field seasons.—Ed.

Gifford: Balanophagy

1. I am indebted to Professor Luther S. Cressman, University of Oregon, for information about Oregon oaks.

Bates: Miwok Fish

1. Acknowledgments: My thanks to Miwok people who shared their knowledge of traditional Miwok fishing practices for this article, especially my mother-in-law Dorothy Stanley and the late John Kelly. Suggested Readings: Reading material regarding Miwok fishing practices is limited. The only published work is a short segment in Barrett and Gifford (1933). Information about Miwok names and moiety systems can be found in Gifford (1916). Additional information can be found in unpublished notes and manuscripts on file at the National Park Service Research Library in Yosemite National Park.

Barrett: Pomo Army Worms

1. All native terms are given in the Central Pomo language.—Ed.

Greengo: Shellfish

1. That this was the case was stated to the writer by both a Wiyot and a Pomo informant (Greengo ms.:12, 10).

2. This pattern involved a notice of intention to visit, an acceptance of notice or invitation, and a reciprocal visit by the coastal people to the inland people.

3. Californian groups on record as having taken sea urchins include: the Bear River people (Nomland 1938:113); the Coast Yuki (Gifford 1939:328); the Pomo (Loeb 1926:164; Stewart 1943:60); and the Coast Miwok (Kelly ms.).

4. *Keok*, generic of digging stick; *Kulule*, a stick for this particular animal.

5. The chisel-like implements made of whale ribs described from the Santa Barbara area may have been used to loosen abalones; see Abbott and Putnam (1879:229) and Heye (1921:80–81).

6. Probably *Katherina tunicata*.

7. According to McGee (1898), shellfish were estimated to comprise 10% of the total food supply.

8. By shell-cup, McGee means any handy shell that was used as a scoop.

9. See Loeffelholz (1893:137–38, 163) for a good description of Yurok spearing crabs.

10. This trait is mentioned for the Chimariko of northwestern California (Driver 1939:379).

11. These pots were also used for crayfish.

12. Jochelson gives a good description of how the present day Aleuts gather and prepare echini (1925:106–7)

13. A present day Hupa informant declared all food from the sea had to be eaten cooked, not raw. This is not to say, however, that fresh shellfish were not carried long distances inland. The Godard Mount (Nap-1), for example, is almost ten miles from the nearest mussel habitat, yet contains a considerable quantity of *Mytilus* shells; this is also true in the Pomo area (Author's personal observation).

14. Drucker (1937:232) states that in the summer the Tolowa gathered shellfish and smelt and hunted sea lions along the beach, and cured these in the sun.

15. That mussels were the staple food of at least one historic Yurok village, Tsurai (Hum-169), is well-documented in Campa (1952:43), Shaler (1808:69), and Loeffelholz (1893:138, 140, 162).

16. Of the Sinkyone, Nomland says that among other types of seafood, clams, mussels, and abalones were sun dried for the winter, but he does not elaborate on the process involved (Nomland 1935:154).

17. This latter element is mentioned by Stewart (1943:60).

18. Kroeber states: "Mussels, whose shells constitute so large a proportion of the mounds of San Francisco Bay and the coast, are specifically mentioned as an important food of the Costanoans" (1925:467). Dodge (1914:120) mentions, in connection with a shell mound near Santa Cruz containing mostly mussel shells, that, "Old timers tell me that the Indians used to come from the hills to this place, gather and cook shellfish, and throw the shells on the heap; at this time the mound was about 20 feet high."

19. For accounts relating to sea mammals and their importance, see Spott and Kroeber (1942) and Kroeber (1925:84).

20. They are also said to have been stored in baskets between layers of dry grass.

21. See data for "Hunting" and Canalino periods in Rogers (1929).

22. Clement W. Meighan (personal communication). This is at variance with what Gifford and Kroeber (1937:178) found among the Central Pomo at Ukiah, who asserted that only seaweed and no mollusks were dried. See also Stewart (1943:61) for Pomo drying of chitons.

23. These were probably *Gonidea angulata* (Allyn C. Smith, marine biologist, personal communication).

24. Apparently they were usually stone boiled.

25. While their effect on man is not known, these animals have one of the fastest enzymic actions on their food known in the animal world (Ricketts and Calvin 1948:30–31).

26. A description of a Coast Yurok earth oven may be found in Greengo (ms.:22).

27. The Yurok used it for sturgeon roe (Greengo ms.:15).

28. These are vegetable.

Goddard: Hupa

1. These are no doubt the dishes said to have been used by the Hupa for the baking of cakes. Professor Mason was probably misinformed as to their purpose (1889:217).

2. The supposed hair brush of Professor Mason (1889:214).

3. In winter the sand is often brought to the house and the leaching done inside.

Du Bois: Wintu

1. Dogs (suku): prewhite; described as "small like a wire-haired terrier, but looked like a police dog." Equivalent of "sick 'em" was maiya. Not given proper names; designated by kinship term, such as aunt, uncle. Raw fish, especially salmon, believed poisonous to them.

Wilson: Nisenan

1. Here Wilson cited "C. Hart Merriam, Notes of the California Indians on file with the Archaeological Survey, Berkeley." This consists of "Field notes, vocabulary schedules, manuscripts, typescripts, notebooks, clippings, and printed matter relating to Merriam's work with California and other Indian tribes (1898–1938)." This collection was transferred to The Bancroft

Library, UC Berkeley, in 1977 and 1979, as "C. Hart Merriam papers relating to work with California Indians, 1850–1974 (bulk 1898–1938)" (BANC MSS 80/18 c).—Ed.

Barrows: Coahuilla Ethnobotany

1. Near the houses were a great number of cylindrical structures with conical roofs, quite skillfully made of osier twigs. They were the granaries referred to above, for their surplus stores of corn and the mesquite fruit (*Pacific Railroad Survey*, "Itinerary," p. 115).

2. Mr. Charles F. Lummis has described roasted mescal stalk as tasting like "jute strings and molasses" ("The Apache Warrior," in *The Land of Poco Tiempo*, New York, 1893).

3. A Panamint vocabulary has, however, been collected by Mr. Henshaw, but I think nowhere published as yet.

Steward: Owens Valley Paiute

1. Steward described his consultants—whom he credits by name in his study—with the following characterizations. From Mono Lake were: "Joe McBride, about 45 years old; Bridgeport Tom, a shaman, about 60 years old, well informed and communicative." From Owens Valley were: "George Collins, Fish Springs, about 40 years old (died in 1930), well informed and cooperative; Andrew Glenn, Lone Pine, about 45 years old, fairly reliable; Mary Harry, about 85 years old; Sam Newland, Bishop, about 90 years old, a fair informant; Jack Stewart, Big Pine, about 100 years old, now feeble, but formerly an excellent informant though requiring an interpreter; Tom Stone, Bishop, about 40 years old, very communicative and with an extraordinary memory for old customs described by his grandfather; John Sumerville, about 45 years old, half-white, a willing informant though not well-informed; Mose Weyland, Bishop, about 70 years old, an excellent informant but necessitating an interpreter."—Ed.

2. Simpson (1876:482) found in Owens valley some water plants plaited together like onions for keeping.

3. E.g., Hearst Museum specimen 1–27046. A 3 legged lava metate, of Mexican origin, was collected from Mary Harry. Two similar ones were observed in Death valley at Stovepipe Wells.

4. Muir found the nut pine, *Pinus sabiana*, growing up to 4000 feet altitude on the western slope of the Sierra Nevada. Indians climbed the trees and beat off the cones with sticks or cut-off branches, then roasted the nuts in the

cones (1917:148). He asserts that piñons furnished the Mono, Carson, and Walker River Indians "more and better nuts than all other species taken together. . . . the nut crop is perhaps greater than the California wheat crops." This was 1870 (ibid., 220–21).

5. From huki (*Stipa speciosa* Trin. and Rupr.), porcupine grass.

6. "Stirring" or "stirred."

7. Chalfant (1933) said a wooden mortar found near Benton made from a tree knot had a bowl 15 inches deep by 15 inches in diameter.

8. Field Museum has a similar looped stick mush stirrer (specimen E–61491) from Pyramid Lake Paiute.

9. Tobacco was pruned and the land was said to have been burned over in the spring.

10. Kidder (1924:119) places the Basket Makers, the first agriculturalists of the Southwest, at between 2000 and 1500 B.C.

11. This view is more fully expressed in Spinden (1917:269–76).

12. Chalfant (1933) says only suckers and minnows were native.

13. Chalfant (1933) says a row of men formed a temporary breakwater for a sod and stone dam to be built.

14. Reny and Brenchley met an Indian on Carson river with a fish spear (1861:42).

15. Simpson (1876:85) saw Carson Valley Paiute catching chub and mullet with seines then sundrying them.

16. Muir saw Indians in the Sierra burning brush to facilitate deer hunting (1917:199).

17. Reny (Reny and Brenchley 1861:128) saw "Snake" Indians at the source of the Humboldt river using antelope head masks with red cloth attached to attract game. Simpson saw in Pah hunupe valley, Nevada, brush barriers, converging to narrow passes where concealed hunters killed deer attracted at night by fires (1876:70), and, at Walker Lake, a large deer corral of sage and cedars (p. 481).

18. Sam Newland recounts a long rabbit drive (Steward ms. *Two Paiute Autobiographies*). Simpson (1876:54) saw rabbit nets 3 feet long, draped on sage brush pulled up and piled with cedar boughs in a fence used by Goshutes near Salt desert.

19. Simpson (1876:53) observed a Goshute carrying rats by this method.

20. Siupa (*Distichlis spicata* Greene), salt grass gum was chewed and put on hands and feet when setting traps to deodorize them.

21. Simpson found Carson Lake Paiute using duck decoys "perfect in form and fabric" (1876:85), and at the mouth of Walker lake a skin stretched over a bulrush float (p. 480).

22. Simpson saw a Woodruff Valley (Nevada) Paiute with 27 rats for food (1876:83).

Stewart: Mohave

1. Mohave informants were interviewed both at Needles, California, and on the Colorado River Reservation, near Parker, Arizona. The main informants, with the approximate date of their births, were the following: Mrs. Abraham Lincoln (1869), Pete Lambert (1866), Lute Wilson (1879) and Tom Black (1884).

Kroeber and Gifford: Karuk Myths

1. Men wear a woman's cap to protect the head when it steadies this net (see Kroeber 1925:pl. 6).

2. "Sturgeon rarely get up Ike's Fall. One was caught in a salmon net above the fall. A man who ate of it died." To the Karok and Yurok, everything has its ordained bounds. Any transgression of these is a portentous evil.

3. The acorns of the tanbark oak have woolly surfaces and rough "caps." The caps of the black oak acorns are quite deep in proportion to the total length of the nut.

Hudson: Konkow Feast

1. Four of these pictures were published in Wilson and Towne's *Handbook* article on the Nisenan (1978:394–95): Field Museum neg. nos. 9518, 9513, 9526, 9525. There they were listed as "a Maiduan, possibly Nisenan, feast, ca. 1900–10." The association with Hudson's field diary, kindly shared by Hudson Museum director Sherrie Smith-Ferri, clarifies the documentation.—Ed.

2. John W. Hudson, 1903. Field Columbian Museum Notebooks, accession no. 20014, pp. 60, 62–65. Collection of the Grace Hudson Museum and Sun House, Ukiah, California.—Ed.

Swezey: Subsistence Rituals

1. Identified by Steward (1939:415–16) as the "circle dance," commonly performed to ensure abundance of seed plants, pinyon nuts, rabbits, deer, and spring rains.

2. Gibbs (1853:146) and Wessells (1853:64) noted that fish dams on the Klamath were effective in obstructing the salmon run and preventing passage of fish to tribes above these structures, presenting a constant source of complaint and dissatisfaction among upper riverine groups. Waterman and Kroeber (1938:50) observe that the Kepel fish dam was torn down after ten days of use, undoubtedly to allow the run to proceed to upriver tribes and prevent such potential inter group conflict over the critically important salmon resource.

3. The Hupa, as distinct from other Northwestern California groups, also performed an organized formulistic first acorn rite, a brief description of which is included here for comparison. Held at Takimilding on the Trinity River, the precise time of the ceremony was determined by the autumnal conditions of the new tan-bark oak acorn crop (*Lithocarpus densiflora*): "as soon as the acorns began to fall freely" (Goddard 1903:80–81; Kroeber and Gifford 1949:56–59). In aboriginal times, a quantity of the first acorns was gathered and prepared by several women. The formulist, ritually dressed in mink and deerskin, in impersonation of "Yinukatsisdai" (master of the vegetable world), built a fire to cook the first acorn meal. The formulist directed the ritual bathing of community members in the river, and thus assembled, a meal of acorn soup was eaten by all. No one of the Takimilding division was allowed to eat new acorns until the formulist initiated this feast.

4. This account appears to attribute magical compulsion, similar to antelope charming, to the procurement of deer in pit traps. Deer were not usually subject to "charming" rituals. However, the driving of deer into enclosed pits is reported among the Western Achomawi by Voegelin (1942:51, 52). Whether or not shamans were directly associated with drive activities of this kind is not recorded.

Parrish: Kashaya Food Memories

1. Corresponding to their term /ʔohso/, the Kashaya use "clover" in English for any wild plant whose leaves are eaten. Unfortunately, except in one case, no specimen could be collected for identification.

2. The Kashaya /hiʔbu/ is translated in local parlance as "wild potatoes" or "Indian potatoes." The term refers to any plant with an edible underground part. By March, 1964, only /koyóʔyo, hiʔbúyʔla, withiʔ/ had been identified. They are species of Habenaria, Brodiaea, and Calochortus respectively.

3. The Kashaya have a barbeque and feast every Fourth of July to which anyone may go. Until recently it was free, but now, following a common practice for American church dinners, the innovation has been made of charging a fee, the proceeds of which go to a community fund.

REFERENCES

Abbott, Charles C., and Frederic W. Putnam. 1879. Implements and Weapons Made of Bone and Wood (Southern California). *United States Geographical Survey West of the 100th Meridian Report*, 7. Washington, D.C.

Aginsky, Burt W. 1943. *Culture Element Distributions: XXIV—Central Sierra*. Anthropological Records, 8(4):393–468. Berkeley: University of California Press.

Aldrich, John M. 1912. The Biology of Some Western Species of the Dipterous Genus *Ephydra*. *New York Entomological Society* 20:77–99.

———. 1913. Collecting Notes from the Great Basin and Adjoining Territory (Dipt. Col.). *Entomological News* 24:214–21.

———. 1921. *Coloradia Pandora* Blake, a Moth of Which the Caterpillar Is Used as Food by Mono Lake Indians. *Entomological Society of America Annals* 14:36–38.

Alvarez, Susan H., and David W. Peri. 1987. Acorns: The Staff of Life. *News from Native California* 1(4):10–14.

Anderson, M. Kat. 1992. At Home in the Wilderness. *News from Native California* 6(2):19–21.

———, Michael G. Barbour, Valerie Whitworth. 1998. A World of Balance and Plenty: Land, Plants, Animals, and Humans in a Pre-European California. In *Contested Eden: California before the Gold Rush*, eds. Ramón A. Gutiérrez and Richard J. Orsi, 12–47. Berkeley and Los Angeles: University of California Press.

Appadurai, Arjun. 1988. How to Make a National Cuisine: Cookbooks in Contemporary India. *Comparative Studies in Society and History* 30(1):3–24.

Ashkenazi, Michael, and Jeanne Jacob. 2000. *The Essence of Japanese Cuisine: An Essay on Food and Culture*. Philadelphia: University of Pennsylvania Press.

Bailey, Flora L. 1940. Navajo Foods and Cooking Methods. *American Anthropologist* 42(2):270–90.

Balls, Edward K. 1962. *Early Uses of California Plants*. Berkeley and Los Angeles: University of California Press.

Bancroft, Hubert Howe. 1883. *The Native Races of the Pacific States*. vol. 1. San Francisco: A. L. Bancroft.

Barbour, Michael, et al. 1993. *California's Changing Landscapes: Diversity and Conservation of California Vegetation*. Sacramento: California Native Plant Society.

Barnett, Homer G. 1937. *Culture Element Distributions: VII—Oregon Coast*. Anthropological Records, 1(3):155–204. Berkeley: University of California Press.

———. 1939. *Culture Element Distributions: IX—Gulf of Georgia Salish*. Anthropological Records, 1(5):221–96. Berkeley: University of California Press.

Barrett, Samuel A. 1933. *Pomo Myths*. Milwaukee Public Museum Bulletin, 15:1–608.

———. 1936. The Army Worm: A Food of the Pomo Indians. In *Essays in Anthropology Presented to Alfred L. Kroeber*, ed. Robert H. Lowie, 1–5. Berkeley: University of California Press.

———. 1952. *The Material Aspects of Pomo Culture*. Milwaukee Public Museum Bulletin, 20 (parts 1–2).

———. 1961. American Indian Films. *Kroeber Anthropological Society Papers*, no. 25:155–62.

———, and Edward W. Gifford. 1933. *Miwok Material Culture*. Milwaukee Public Museum Bulletin, 2(4):117–376.

Barrows, David Prescott. 1900 [1967]. *The Ethno-Botany of the Coahuilla Indians of Southern California*. Chicago: University of Chicago Press. Reprint ed., Banning, Calif.: Malki Museum Press.

Basgall, Mark E. 1987. Resource Intensification Among Hunter-Gatherers: Acorn Economies in Prehistoric California. *Research in Economic Anthropology* 9:21–52.

Batdorf, Carol. 1990. *Northwest Native Harvest*. Blaine, Wash., and Surrey, B.C.: Hancock House.

Bates, Craig D. 1983. Acorn Storehouses of the Yosemite Miwok. *Masterkey* 57(1):19–27.

———. 1984. Fish and the Miwok. *Masterkey* 58(1):18–23.

Baumhoff, Martin A. 1963. *Ecological Determinants of Aboriginal California Populations*. University of California Publications in American Archaeology and Ethnology, 49(2):155–236. Berkeley: University of California Press.

Beals, Ralph L. 1933. *Ethnology of the Nisenan.* University of California Publications in American Archaeology and Ethnology, 31(6):335–414. Berkeley: University of California Press.

———, and Joseph A. Hester, Jr. 1960 [1971]. A New Ecological Typology of the California Indians. In *Selected Papers of the Fifth International Congress of Anthropological and Ethnological Sciences*, ed. Anthony F. C. Wallace, 411–18. Philadelphia: University of Pennsylvania Press. Reprinted in *The California Indians: A Sourcebook*, 2d edition, eds. Robert F. Heizer and Mary Anne Whipple, 73–83. Berkeley and Los Angeles: University of California Press.

Beals, Ralph L., and Joseph A. Hester, Jr., eds. 1974. *Indian Land Use and Occupancy in California.* New York: Garland Publishing.

Bean, Lowell John. 1972. *Mukat's People: The Cahuilla Indians of Southern California.* Berkeley and Los Angeles: University of California Press.

———. 1976. Social Organization in Native California. In *Native Californians: A Theoretical Perspective*, eds. Lowell J. Bean and Thomas C. Blackburn, 99–123. Socorro, N.M.: Ballena Press.

———, and Thomas C. Blackburn, eds. 1976. *Native Californians: A Theoretical Perspective.* Socorro, N.M.: Ballena Press.

———, and Harry Lawton. 1973 [1993]. Some Explanations for the Rise of Cultural Complexity in Native California with Comments on Proto-Agriculture and Agriculture. *Patterns of Indian Burning in California: Ecology and Ethnohistory*, ed. Henry Lewis. Reprinted in *Before the Wilderness: Environmental Management by Native Californians*, eds. Thomas C. Blackburn and Kat Anderson, 27–54. Menlo Park, Calif.: Ballena Press.

———, and Katherine Siva Saubel. 1972. *Temalpakh (From the Earth): Cahuilla Indian Knowledge and Usage of Plants.* Banning, Calif.: Malki Museum Press.

Beck, Beatrice M. 1994. *Ethnobotany of the California Indians*, vol. 1: A *Bibliography and Index.* Champaign, Ill.: Koeltz Scientific Books USA.

Benedict, Ruth F. 1924. A Brief Sketch of Serrano Culture. *American Anthropologist* 26:366–92.

Bernstein, Bruce. 1993. Roland Dixon and the Maidu. In *Museum Anthropology in California, 1889–1939*, eds. Ira Jacknis and Margot Blum Schevill, *Museum Anthropology* 17(2):20–26.

Bibby, Brian. 1996. *The Fine Art of California Indian Basketry.* Sacramento: Crocker Art Museum, in association with Heyday Books, Berkeley.

————. 2004. *Deeper than Gold: A Guide to Indian Life in the Sierra Region.* Photographs by Dugan Aguilar. Berkeley: Heyday Books.

Blackburn, Thomas C. 1976. Ceremonial Integration and Social Interaction in Aboriginal California. In *Native Californians: A Theoretical Perspective*, eds. Lowell J. Bean and Thomas C. Blackburn, 225–43. Menlo Park, Calif.: Ballena Press.

————, ed. 1975. *December's Child: A Book of Chumash Oral Narratives.* Berkeley and Los Angeles: University of California Press.

————, and Kat Anderson, eds. 1993. *Before the Wilderness: Environmental Management by Native Californians.* Menlo Park, Calif.: Ballena Press.

Blake, William P. 1857. *Exploration and Surveys for Railroad Route from the Mississippi River to the Pacific Ocean.* vol. 5. Washington, D.C.

Boas, Franz, and George Hunt. 1921. *Ethnology of the Kwakiutl.* 35th Annual Report of the Bureau of American Ethnology, for 1913–14. Washington, D.C.: Smithsonian Institution.

Bocek, Barbara. 1984. Ethnobotany of Costanoan Indians, California, Based on Collections by John P. Harrington. *Economic Botany* 38(2):240–44.

Brenner, Leslie. 1999. *American Appetite: The Coming of Age of a Cuisine.* New York: Avon.

Brown, Linda Keller, and Kay Mussell, eds. 1984. *Ethnic and Regional Foodways in the United States: The Performance of Group Identity.* Knoxville: University of Tennessee Press.

Buckley, Thomas. 1988. Menstruation and the Power of Yurok Women. In *Blood Magic: The Anthropology of Menstruation*, eds. Thomas Buckley and Alma Gottlieb, 187–209. Berkeley and Los Angeles: University of California Press.

————, and Alma Gottlieb. 1988. A Critical Appraisal of Theories of Menstrual Symbolism. In *Blood Magic: The Anthropology of Menstruation*, eds. Thomas Buckley and Alma Gottlieb, 3–50. Berkeley and Los Angeles: University of California Press.

Campa, Miguel de la. 1952. Diary of Fray Miguel de la Campa, Chaplain of the Santiago, at Trinidad Bay, June 9–19, 1775. Translated from the Spanish by Donald C. Cutter. In *The Four Ages of Tsurai: A Documentary History of the Indian Village on Trinidad Bay*, by Robert F. Heizer and John E. Mills, 38–44. Berkeley: University of California Press.

Campbell, Paul D. 1999. *Survival Skills of Native California.* Salt Lake City, Utah: Gibbs-Smith.

Castetter, Edward F., and Willis H. Bell. 1951. *Yuman Indian Agriculture: Primitive Subsistence on the Lower Colorado and Gila Rivers.* Albuquerque: University of New Mexico Press.

Chalfant, W. A. 1933. *The Story of Inyo.* Revised and enlarged edition. Bishop, Calif.: Chalfant.

Chartkoff, Joseph L., and Kerry Kona Chartkoff. 1984. *The Archaeology of California.* Stanford: Stanford University Press.

Chesnut, Victor K. 1902 [1974]. *Plants Used by the Indians of Mendocino County, California.* Contributions from the U.S. National Herbarium, 7(3):295–408. Reprint ed., Ukiah, Calif.: Mendocino County Historical Society.

Clarke, Charlotte Bringle. 1977. *Edible and Useful Plants of California.* Berkeley and Los Angeles: University of California Press.

Coe, Sophie D. 1994. *America's First Cuisines.* Austin: University of Texas Press.

Colson, Elizabeth. 1979. In Good Years and in Bad: Food Strategies of Self-Reliant Societies. *Journal of Anthropological Research* 35(1):18–29.

Cook, Sherburne F. 1941. *The Mechanism and Extent of Dietary Adaptation Among Certain Groups of California and Nevada Indians.* Ibero-Americana 18:1–59.

Counihan, Carole, and Penny van Esterik, eds. 1997. *Food and Culture: A Reader.* New York: Routledge.

Coville, Frederick V. 1892. Notes on the Botany of the Panamint Indians of California. *American Anthropologist*, o.s., 5:351–61.

———. 1895. *Directions for Collecting Specimens and Information Illustrating the Aboriginal Use of Plants.* United States National Museum Bulletin, no. 39. Washington, D.C.: Smithsonian Institution.

Cox, Beverly, and Martin Jacobs. 1991. *Spirit of the Harvest: North American Indian Cooking.* New York: Stewart, Tabori, and Chang.

Cushing, Frank Hamilton. 1884–85 [1920]. *Zuni Breadstuff.* Indian Notes and Monographs, vol. 8. New York: Museum of the American Indian.

Davidson, Alan. 1990. *A Kipper With My Tea: Selected Food Essays.* San Francisco: North Point Press.

Davis, James T. 1961. *Trade Routes and Economic Exchange Among the Indians of California.* Reports of the University of California Archaeological Survey 54:1–71. Berkeley: University of California Press.

Demetracopoulou, Dorothy, and Cora A. Du Bois. 1932. A Study of Wintu Mythology. *Journal of American Folklore* 45:373–500.

Dietler, Michael, and Brian Hayden, eds. 2001. *Feasts: Archaeological and Ethnographic Perspectives on Food, Politics, and Power.* Washington, D.C.: Smithsonian Institution Press.

Dixon, Roland B. 1905. *The Northern Maidu.* American Museum of Natural History Bulletin, 17(3):121–346.

———. 1907. *The Shasta.* American Museum of Natural History Bulletin, 17(5):381–498.

———. 1910. *The Chimariko Indians and Language.* University of California Publications in American Archaeology and Ethnology, 5(5):293–380. Berkeley: University of California Press.

Dodge, R. E. 1914. California Shell Mounds. *Records of the Past.* 13:120.

Douglas, Mary. 1975. Deciphering a Meal. In *Implicit Meanings*, by Mary Douglas, 249–75. London: Routledge and Kegan Paul.

Downs, James F. 1961. *Washo Religion.* Anthropological Records, 16(9):365–86. Berkeley: University of California Press.

Dozier, Deborah. 1998. *The Heart Is Fire: The World of the Cahuilla Indians of Southern California.* Berkeley: Heyday Books.

Driver, Harold E. 1936. *Wappo Ethnography.* University of California Publications in American Archaeology and Ethnology, 36(3):179–220. Berkeley: University of California Press.

———. 1939. *Culture Element Distributions: X—Northwest California.* Anthropological Records, 1(6):297–433. Berkeley: University of California Press.

———, and William C. Massey. 1957. *Comparative Studies of North American Indians.* Transactions of the American Philosophical Society 47(2):163–456.

Drucker, Philip. 1937. *The Tolowa and Their Southwest Oregon Kin.* University of California Publications in American Archaeology and Ethnology, 36(4):221–300. Berkeley: University of California Press.

———. 1937b. *Culture Element Distributions: V—Southern California.* Anthropological Records, 1(1):1–52. Berkeley: University of California Press.

———. 1941. *Culture Element Distributions: XVII—Yuman-Piman.* Anthropological Records, 6(3):91–230. Berkeley: University of California Press.

———. 1950. *Culture Element Distributions: XXVI—Northwest Coast.* Anthropological Records, 9(3):157–294. Berkeley: University of California Press.

Dubin, Margaret, and Sara-Larus Tolley, eds. 2004. Seaweed, Salmon, and Manzanita Cider: A California Indian Feast. Special issue on food. *News from Native California* 18(2).

Du Bois, Cora A. 1932. Tolowa Notes. *American Anthropologist* 34(2):248–62.

———. 1935. *Wintu Ethnography*. University of California Publications in American Archaeology and Ethnology, 36(1):1–148. Berkeley: University of California Press.

———. 1941 [1948]. Attitudes Toward Food and Hunger in Alor. In *Language, Culture, and Personality: Essays in Memory of Edward Sapir*, eds. Leslie Spier, et al., 272–81. Menasha, Wisc.: Sapir Memorial Publication Fund. Reprinted in *Personal Character and Cultural Milieu*, ed. Douglas G. Haring, 158–70. New York: Syracuse University Press.

Dutcher, B. H. 1893. Piñon Gathering among the Panamint Indians. *American Anthropologist*, o.s., 6(4):377–80.

Ebeling, Walter. 1986. *Handbook of Indian Foods and Fibers of Arid America*. Berkeley and Los Angeles: University of California Press.

Edaakie, Rita, ed. 1999. *Idonapshe, Let's Eat: Traditional Zuni Foods*. Zuni, New Mexico: A:shiwi A:wan Museum and Heritage Center/Albuquerque: University of New Mexico Press.

Elie, Lolis Eric. 1996. *Smokestack Lightning: Adventures in the Heart of Barbecue Country*. New York: North Point Press; Farrar, Straus and Giroux.

Eliot, T. S. 1948. *Notes Toward the Definition of Culture*. London: Faber and Faber.

Emory, William H. 1848. *Notes of a Military Reconnaissance, from Fort Leavenworth, in Missouri, to San Diego, in California, Including Part of the Arkansas, Del Norte, and Gila Rivers*. 30th Congress, 1st session, House Executive Document no. 41, vol. 1. Washington.

———. 1857. *Report of the United States and Mexican Boundary Survey*. 34th Congress, 1st session, Senate Executive Document no. 108, vol. 1. Washington.

Erikson, Erik H. 1943. *Observations on the Yurok: Childhood and World Image*. University of California Publications in American Archaeology and Ethnology, 35(10):257–301. Berkeley: University of California Press.

Essig, Edward O. 1934 [1971]. The Value of Insects to the California Indians. *Scientific Monthly* 38(2):181–86. Reprinted in *The California Indians: A Sourcebook*, 2nd edition, eds. Robert F. Heizer and Mary Anne Whipple, 315–18. Berkeley and Los Angeles: University of California Press.

Fagan, Brian. 2003. *Before California: An Archaeologist Looks at Our Earliest Inhabitants*. Lanham, Md.: Rowman and Littlefield.

Farris, Glenn J. 1993. Quality Food: The Quest for Pine Nuts in Northern California. In *Before the Wilderness: Environmental Management by Native Californians*, eds. Thomas C. Blackburn and Kat Anderson, 229–40. Menlo Park, Calif.: Ballena Press.

Ferrel, Bartolome. 1879. Account by the Pilot Ferrel of the Voyage of Cabrillo along the West Coast of North America in 1542. Translation from the Spanish with Introductory Notes by H. W. Henshaw. *U.S. Geographical Survey West of 100th Meridian Report*, 7:293–314. Washington, D.C.

Forde, C. Daryll. 1931. *Ethnography of the Yuma Indians*. University of California Publications in American Archaeology and Ethnology, 28(4):83–278. Berkeley: University of California Press.

Fowler, Catherine S. 1986. Subsistence. In *Great Basin*, ed. Warren d'Azevedo. *Handbook of North American Indians*, gen. ed. William C. Sturtevant, 11:64–97. Washington, D.C.: Smithsonian Institution.

———, and Nancy Peterson Walter. 1985. Harvesting Pandora Moth Larvae with the Owens Valley Paiute. *Journal of California and Great Basin Anthropology* 7(2):155–65.

Frank, Lois Ellen. 2002. *Foods of the Southwest Indian Nations: Traditional and Contemporary Native American Recipes*. Berkeley: Ten Speed Press.

Frederickson, Vera Mae. 1987. Acorn Pinenut Bread. *News from Native California* 1(3):22.

Gabaccia, Donna R. 1998. *We Are What We Eat: Ethnic Food and the Making of Americans*. Cambridge, Mass.: Harvard University Press.

Garth, Thomas R. 1953. *Atsugewi Ethnography*. Anthropological Records, 14(2):129–212. Berkeley: University of California Press.

Gayton, Anna H. 1930. *Yokuts-Mono Chiefs and Shamans*. University of California Publications in American Archaeology and Ethnology, 24(8):361–420. Berkeley: University of California Press.

———. 1946 [1976]. Culture-Environment Integration: External References in Yokuts Life. *Southwestern Journal of Anthropology* 2(3):252–68. Reprinted in *Native Californians: A Theoretical Perspective*, eds. Lowell J. Bean and Thomas C. Blackburn, 79–97. Socorro, N.M.: Ballena Press.

———. 1948a. *Yokuts and Western Mono Ethnography*, 1 *(Tulare Lake, Southern Valley, and Central Foothill Yokuts)*. Anthropological Records, 10(1):1–142. Berkeley: University of California Press.

————. 1948b. *Yokuts and Western Mono Ethnography, 2 (Northern Foothill Yokuts and Western Mono).* Anthropological Records, 10(2):143–302. Berkeley: University of California Press.

Gendar, Jeannine, Beverly R. Ortiz, and Sadie Cash Margolin. 2000. Acorn Power: A Special Report on Food and Fitness in Native California. *News from Native California* 13(3):17–40.

George, Andrew, Jr., and Robert Gairns. 1997. *Feast!: Canadian Native Cuisine for All Seasons.* Toronto: Doubleday Canada.

Gibbs, George. 1853 [1972]. *George Gibb's [sic] Journal of Redick McKee's Expedition through Northwestern California in 1851.* Edited and with annotations by Robert F. Heizer. Berkeley: Archaeological Research Facility, Department of Anthropology, University of California.

————. 1860. Journal of the Expedition of Colonel Redick M'Kee, United States Indian Agent, Through North-Western California. Performed in the Summer and Fall of 1851. In *Historical and Statistical Information; Respecting the History, Condition, and Prospects of the Indian Tribes of the United States,* by Henry R. Schoolcraft, vol. 3:99–177. Philadelphia.

Gifford, Edward W. 1916. *Miwok Moieties.* University of California Publications in American Archaeology and Ethnology, 12(4):139–94. Berkeley: University of California Press.

————. 1917. *Miwok Myths.* University of California Publications in American Archaeology and Ethnology, 12(8):283–338. Berkeley: University of California Press.

————. 1931. *The Kamia of Imperial Valley.* Bureau of American Ethnology Bulletin, no. 97. Washington, D.C.: Smithsonian Institution.

————. 1932. *The Northfork Mono.* University of California Publications in American Archaeology and Ethnology, 31(2):15–65. Berkeley: University of California Press.

————. 1932b. *The Southeastern Yavapai.* University of California Publications in American Archaeology and Ethnology, 29(3):177–252. Berkeley: University of California Press.

————. 1936. California Indian Balanophagy. In *Essays in Anthropology Presented to Alfred L. Kroeber,* ed. Robert H. Lowie, 87–98. Berkeley: University of California Press.

————. 1939. The Coast Yuki. *Anthropos* 34:292–75.

————. 1955. *Central Miwok Ceremonies.* Anthropological Records, 14(4):261–318. Berkeley: University of California Press.

————, and Alfred L. Kroeber. 1937. *Culture Element Distributions: IV—Pomo.* University of California Publications in American Archaeology and Ethnology, 37(4):117–254. Berkeley: University of California Press.

Goddard, Pliny Earle. 1903. *Life and Culture of the Hupa.* University of California Publications in American Archaeology and Ethnology, 1(1):1–88. Berkeley: University of California Press.

Goldschmidt, Walter R. 1951. *Nomlaki Ethnography.* University of California Publications in American Archaeology and Ethnology, 42(4):303–443. Berkeley: University of California Press.

————. 1974. Preparation of [Hupa] Acorn Soup. In *Indian Land Use and Occupancy in California,* eds. Ralph L. Beals and Joseph A. Hester, Jr., 1:311–13. New York: Garland Publishing.

Goode, Judith, Janet Theophano, and Karen Curtis. 1984. A Framework for the Analysis of Continuity and Change in Shared Sociocultural Rules for Food Use: The Italian-American Pattern. In *Ethnic and Regional Foodways in the United States: The Performance of Group Identity,* eds. Linda Keller Brown and Kay Mussell, 66–88. Knoxville: University of Tennessee Press.

Goodrich, Jennie, Claudia Lawson, and Vana Parrish Lawson. 1980 [1996]. *Kashaya Pomo Plants.* Los Angeles: American Indian Studies Center; University of California, Los Angeles. Reprint ed., Berkeley: Heyday Books.

Goody, Jack. 1982. *Cooking, Cuisine, and Class: A Study in Comparative Sociology.* Cambridge, Great Britain: Cambridge University Press.

Gould, Richard A. 1975 [1976]. Ecology and Adaptive Response Among the Tolowa Indians of Northwestern California. *Journal of California Anthropology* 2:148–70. Reprinted in *Native Californians: A Theoretical Perspective,* eds. Lowell J. Bean and Thomas C. Blackburn, 49–78. Socorro, N.M.: Ballena Press.

Greengo, Robert E. 1951. Aboriginal Use of Shellfish as Food in California. M.A. thesis, Department of Anthropology, University of California, Berkeley.

————. 1952. Shellfish Foods of the California Indians. *Kroeber Anthropological Society Papers,* no. 7:63–114.

————. ms. Report on Field Trip, July-August, 1950. University of California Archaeological Survey, ms. no. 72. Hearst Museum of Anthropology Archives.

Grinnell, Elizabeth. 1893 [1958]. Making Acorn Bread. *The Youth's Companion*, 66–67:559. Reprint, *Reports of University of California Archaeological Survey*, no. 41:42–45. Berkeley: University of California Press.

Griset, Suzanne. 1990. Historic Transformations of Tizon Brown Ware in Southern California. In *Hunter-Gatherer Pottery from the Far West*, ed. Joanne M. Mack, 179–200. Anthropological Papers, no. 23. Carson City, Nev.: Nevada State Museum.

Gunther, Erna. 1927. *Klallam Ethnography*. University of Washington Publications in Anthropology, 1:171–314.

Hackel, Steven W. 1998. Land, Labor, and Production: The Colonial Economy of Spanish and Mexican California. In *Contested Eden: California before the Gold Rush*, eds. Ramón A. Gutiérrez and Richard J. Orsi, 111–46. Berkeley and Los Angeles: University of California Press.

Hallowell, A. Irving. 1926. Bear Ceremonialism in the Northern Hemisphere. *American Anthropologist* 21:1–175.

Harrington, John P. 1932. *Karuk Indian Myths*. Bureau of American Ethnology Bulletin, no. 107. Washington, D.C.: Smithsonian Institution.

———. 1942. *Culture Element Distributions: XIX—Central California Coast*. Anthropological Records, 7(1):1–46. Berkeley: University of California Press.

Harris, Marvin. 1985. *Good to Eat: Riddles of Food and Culture*. New York: Simon and Schuster.

———. 1987. Foodways: Historical Overview and Theoretical Prolegomenon. In *Food and Evolution: Toward a Theory of Human Food Habits*, eds. Marvin Harris and Eric B. Ross, 57–90. Philadelphia: Temple University Press.

Hatch, James. 1958. Tachi Yokuts Music. *Kroeber Anthropological Society Papers*, no. 19:47–66.

Havard, Valery. 1895. The Food Plants of the North American Indians. *Bulletin Torrey Botanical Club*, 22(3):98–123. March 27. Lancaster, Penn.

———. 1896. Plant Foods of the North American Indians. *Bulletin Torrey Botanical Club* 23(2). Lancaster, Penn.

Hedges, Ken, and Christina Beresford. 1986. *Santa Ysabel Ethnobotany*. San Diego: Museum of Man Ethnic Technology Notes, 20.

Heizer, Robert F. 1950. Kutsavi, a Great Basin Indian Food. *Kroeber Anthropological Association Papers*, no. 2:35–41.

————. 1974. Were the Chumash Whale Hunters?: Implications for Ethnography in 1974. *Journal of California Anthropology* 1(1):26–32.

————, vol. ed. 1978. *California. Handbook of North American Indians*, gen. ed. William C. Sturtevant, vol. 8. Washington, D.C.: Smithsonian Institution.

————, and Albert B. Elsasser. 1980. *The Natural World of the California Indians*. Berkeley and Los Angeles: University of California Press.

Hewes, Gordon W. 1947. Aboriginal Use of Fishing Resources in Northwestern North America. Ph.D. dissertation, Department of Anthropology, University of California, Berkeley.

Heye, George G. 1921. *Certain Artifacts from San Miguel Island, California*. Indian Notes and Monographs, 8:1–211. New York: Museum of the American Indian, Heye Foundation.

Holmes, William H. 1902. Anthropological Studies in California. *United States National Museum Report for 1900*:155–88.

Honigmann, John J. 1961. *Foodways in a Muskeg Community: An Anthropological Report on the Attawapiskat Indians*. Ottawa: Northern Co-ordination and Research Center.

Hudson, John W. 1900. Preparation of Acorn Meal by Pomo Indians. *American Anthropologist* 2:775–76.

Hudson, Travis, and Thomas C. Blackburn. 1982–87. *The Material Culture of the Chumash Interaction Sphere*, vol. I: *Food Procurement and Transportation* (1982); vol. II: *Food Preparation and Shelter* (1983); vol. III: *Clothing, Ornamentation, and Grooming* (1984); vol. IV: *Ceremonial Paraphernalia, Games, and Amusements* (1986); vol. V: *Manufacturing Processes, Metrology, and Trade* (1987). Los Altos, Calif./Santa Barbara: Ballena Press/Santa Barbara Museum of Natural History.

Hughes, Phyllis, ed. 1977. *Pueblo Indian Cookbook*. Second, revised edition. Santa Fe: Museum of New Mexico Press.

Jacknis, Ira. 1995. *Carving Traditions of Northwest California*. Berkeley: Phoebe Hearst Museum of Anthropology, University of California.

Jackson, Thomas L. 1991. Pounding Acorn: Women's Production as Social and Economic Focus. In *Engendering Archaeology: Women and Prehistory*, eds. Joan M. Gero and Margaret W. Conkey, 301–25. Oxford: Basil Blackwell.

Jochelson, Waldemar. 1925. *Archaeological Investigations in the Aleutian Islands*. Carnegie Institution of Washington Publication, no. 367.

Kalins, Dorothy. 1995. Where Are the Roux of Yesteryear? *Saveur*, no. 4:8.

Kavasch, E. Barrie. 1995. *Enduring Harvests: Native American Foods and Festivals for Every Season*. Old Saybrook, Conn.: Globe Pequot Press.

Kavena, Juanita Tiger. 1980. *Hopi Cookery*. Tucson: University of Arizona Press.

Keator, Glenn, Linda Yamane, and Ann Lewis. 1995. *In Full View: Three Ways of Seeing California Indian Plants*. Berkeley: Heyday Books.

Keller, Jean A. 2002. When Native Foods Were Left Behind: Boarding School Nutrition and the Sherman Institute, 1902–1922. *News from Native California* 15(3):22–24.

Kelly, Isabel. 1932. *The Surprise Valley Paiute*. University of California Publications in American Archaeology and Ethnology, 31(3):67–210. Berkeley: University of California Press.

———. ms. [1932] The Coast Miwok. Published 1996 as *Interviews with Tom Smith and Maria Copa: Isabel Kelly's Ethnographic Notes on the Coast Miwok Indians of Marin and Southern Sonoma Counties, California*. Compiled and edited by Mary E. Trumbull Collier and Sylvia Barker Thalman. San Rafael, Calif.: Miwok Archaeological Preserve of Marin.

Kidder, Alfred V. 1924. *An Introduction to the Study of Southwestern Archaeology*. New Haven: Yale University Press, for the Department of Archaeology, Phillips Academy, Andover, Mass.

Kimball, Yeffe, and Jean Anderson. 1965. *The Art of American Indian Cooking*. New York: Doubleday.

Kirst, Lynn P., ed. 1991. *Southwest Cooks! The Tradition of Native American Cuisines: Recipes from the Southwest Museum*. Los Angeles: Southwest Museum.

Kniffen, Fred B. 1939. *Pomo Geography*. University of California Publications in American Archaeology and Ethnology, 36(6):353–400. Berkeley: University of California Press.

Kotzen, Alice. 1994. *Malki Museum's Native Foods Tasting Experience*. Banning, Calif.: Malki Museum.

Kroeber, Alfred L. 1925. *Handbook of the Indians of California*. Bureau of American Ethnology Bulletin, no. 78. Washington, D.C.: Smithsonian Institution.

———. 1929. *The Valley Nisenan*. University of California Publications in American Archaeology and Ethnology, 24(4):253–90. Berkeley: University of California Press.

————. 1932. *The Patwin and their Neighbors.* University of California Publications in American Archaeology and Ethnology, 29(4):253–423. Berkeley: University of California Press.

————. 1939. *Cultural and Natural Areas of Native North America.* University of California Publications in American Archaeology and Ethnology, 38:1–242. Berkeley: University of California Press.

————. 1941. *Culture Element Distributions: XV—Salt, Dogs, Tobacco.* Anthropological Records, 6(1):1–20. Berkeley: University of California Press.

————. 1954 [1962]. The Nature of Land-Holding Groups in Aboriginal California. *University of California Archaeological Survey Reports* 56:19–58. Berkeley: University of California Press.

————. 1960 [1992]. Comparative Notes on the Structure of Yurok Culture. In *The Structure of Twana Culture,* by William W. Elmendorf. Reprint ed. Pullman: Washington State University Press.

————, and Samuel A. Barrett. 1960. *Fishing Among the Indians of Northwestern California.* Anthropological Records, 21(1):1–210. Berkeley: University of California Press.

————, and Edward W. Gifford. 1949. *World Renewal: A Cult System of Native Northwest California.* Anthropological Records, 13(1):1–156. Berkeley: University of California Press.

Kroeber, Alfred L., and Edward W. Gifford, eds. 1980. *Karok Myths.* Berkeley and Los Angeles: University of California Press.

Kroeber, Alfred L., and Michael J. Harner. 1955. *Mohave Pottery.* Anthropological Records, 16(1):1–30. Berkeley: University of California Press.

Kroeber, Theodora. 1961 [1976]. *Ishi in Two Worlds: A Biography of the Last Wild Indian in North America.* Deluxe, illustrated ed. Berkeley and Los Angeles: University of California Press.

Latta, Frank F. 1949. *Handbook of Yokuts Indians.* Bakersfield, Calif.: Kern County Museum.

Laufer, Berthold. 1930. *Geophagy.* Fieldiana: Anthropology, 18(2):99–198. Chicago: Field Museum of Natural History.

Lee, Dorothy D. 1943. The Linguistic Aspect of Wintuʻ Acculturation. *American Anthropologist* 45:435–40.

Lehrer, Adrienne. 1972. Cooking Vocabularies and the Culinary Triangle of Lévi-Strauss. *Anthropological Linguistics* 14:155–71.

Leonard, Zenas. 1904. *Leonard's Narrative: Adventures of Zenas Leonard, Fur Trader and Trapper, 1831–1836*. Cleveland: Burrows Brothers.

Lévi-Strauss, Claude. 1958 [1967]. *Structural Anthropology*. Claire Jacobson and Brooke Grundfest Schoepf, trans. New York: Doubleday.

———. 1964 [1969]. *The Raw and the Cooked*. John and Doreen Weightman, trans. New York: Harper and Row.

———. 1968 [1978]. *The Origin of Table Manners*. John and Doreen Weightman, trans. New York: Harper and Row.

Lewis, Henry T. 1973 [1993]. *Patterns of Indian Burning in California: Ecology and Ethnohistory*. Ballena Press Anthropological Papers, 1. Reprinted in *Before the Wilderness: Environmental Management by Native Californians*, eds. Thomas C. Blackburn and Kat Anderson, 55–116. Menlo Park, Calif.: Ballena Press.

Loeb, Edwin M. 1926. *Pomo Folkways*. University of California Publications in American Archaeology and Ethnology, 19(2):149–405. Berkeley: University of California Press.

Loeffelholz, Karl von. 1893. Die Zoreisch-Indianer der Trinidad-Bai (Californien). *Mittheilungen der Anthropologischen Gesellschaft in Wien*, 23:101–23. Translated as "Baron Karl von Loeffelholz' Account of the Tsorei Indians of Trinidad Bay, 1850–1856. In *The Four Ages of Tsurai: A Documentary History of the Indian Village on Trinidad Bay*, by Robert F. Heizer and John E. Mills, 135–79. Berkeley and Los Angeles: University of California Press.

Loud, Llewellyn L., and Mark R. Harrington. 1929. *Lovelock Cave*. University of California Publications in American Archaeology and Ethnology, 25(1). Berkeley: University of California Press.

Lowie, Robert H. 1924. *Notes on Shoshonean Ethnography*. American Museum of Natural History Anthropological Papers, 20(3):185–314.

———. 1939. *Ethnographic Notes on the Washo*. University of California Publications in American Archaeology and Ethnology, 36(5):301–52. Berkseley: University of California Press.

Luby, Edward M., and Mark F. Gruber. 1999. The Dead Must be Fed: Symbolic Meanings of the Shellmounds of the San Francisco Bay Area. *Cambridge Archaeological Journal* 9(1):95–108.

Mack, Joanne M., ed. 1990. *Hunter-Gatherer Pottery from the Far West*. Anthropological Papers, no. 23. Carson City, Nev.: Nevada State Museum.

Malinowski, Bronislaw. 1935. *Coral Gardens and Their Magic*. London: George Allen and Unwin.

Marcus, George, and Michael Fischer 1986. *Anthropology as Cultural Critique: An Experimental Moment in the Human Sciences*. Chicago: University of Chicago Press.

Mason, J. Alden. 1912. *The Ethnology of the Salinan Indians*. University of California Publications in American Archaeology and Ethnology, 10(4):97–240. Berkeley: University of California Press.

Mason, Otis T. 1889. The Ray Collection from Hupa Reservation. *Annual Report of the Smithsonian Institution for 1886*, part 1:205–39.

———. 1896. Influence of Environment upon Human Industries or Arts. *Annual Report of the Smithsonian Institution for 1895*:639–65.

Mauss, Marcel. 1925 [1967]. *The Gift: Forms and Functions of Exchange in Archaic Societies*. Ian Cunnison, trans. New York: W. W. Norton.

Mayer, Peter J. 1976. *Miwok Balanophagy: Implications for the Cultural Development of Some California Acorn-Eaters*. University of California Archaeological Research Facility.

McCarthy, Helen. 1993. Managing Oaks and the Acorn Crop. In *Before the Wilderness: Environmental Management by Native Californians*, eds. Thomas C. Blackburn and Kat Anderson, 213–28. Menlo Park, Calif.: Ballena Press.

McCovey, Barry Wayne, Jr. 2003. Fish Kill: For the Yurok, Salmon is Everything. *News from Native California* 16(2):4–5.

McGee, Harold. 1984. *On Food and Cooking: The Science and Lore of the Kitchen*. New York: Collier Books, Macmillan.

McGee, W. J. 1898. *The Seri Indians*. 17th Annual Report of the Bureau of American Ethnology, for 1895–96, part 1:1–128. Washington, D.C.: Smithsonian Institution.

McGuire, Kelly R., and William R. Hildebrandt. 1994. The Possibilities of Women and Men: Gender and the California Milling Stone Horizon. *Journal of California and Great Basin Anthropology* 16(1):41–59.

McLendon, Sally. 1992. California Baskets and Basketmakers. In *Basketmakers: Meaning and Form in Native American Baskets*, eds. Linda Mowat, Howard Morphy, and Penny Dransart. Monograph 5, 51–75. Oxford, Great Britain: Pitt Rivers Museum, University of Oxford.

Menzel, Peter, and Faith D'Aluisio. 1998. *Man Eating Bugs: The Art and Science of Eating Bugs*. Berkeley: Ten Speed Press.

Merriam, C. Hart. 1918. The Acorn, a Possibly Neglected Source of Food. *National Geographic Magazine* 34(2):129–37.

————. 1955. *Studies of California Indians.* Edited by the staff of the Department of Anthropology of the University of California. Berkeley and Los Angeles: University of California Press.

Milliken, Randall. 1995. *A Time of Little Choice: The Disintegration of Tribal Culture in the San Francisco Bay Area, 1769–1810.* Menlo Park, Calif.: Ballena Press.

Mintz, Sidney W. 1996. *Tasting Food, Tasting Freedom: Excursions into Eating, Culture, and the Past.* Boston: Beacon Press.

————, and Christine M. Du Bois. 2002. The Anthropology of Food and Eating. *Annual Reviews of Anthropology,* 31:99–119.

Moratto, Michael J. 1984. *California Archaeology.* Orlando, Fla.: Academic Press.

Moss, Madonna L. 1993. Shellfish, Gender, and Status on the Northwest Coast: Reconciling Archaeological, Ethnographic, and Ethnohistorical Records of the Tlingit. *American Anthropologist* 95(3):631–52.

Muir, John. 1916. *My First Summer in the Sierra.* Boston: Houghton Mifflin.

————. 1917. *The Mountains of California.* New York: Century.

Munz, Phillip A., and David D. Keck. 1968. *A California Flora.* Berkeley and Los Angeles: University of California Press.

Nabhan, Gary Paul. 2002. *Coming Home to Eat: The Pleasures and Politics of Local Foods.* New York: W. W. Norton.

Neustadt, Kathy. 1992. *Clambake: A History and Celebration of an American Tradition.* Amherst: University of Massachusetts Press.

Niethammer, Carolyn. 1974. *American Indian Food and Lore.* New York: Macmillan.

Nomland, Gladys A. 1935. *Sinkyone Notes.* University of California Publications in American Archaeology and Ethnology, 36(2):149–78. Berkeley: University of California Press.

————. 1938. *Bear River Ethnography.* Anthropological Records, 2(2):91–126. Berkeley: University of California Press.

Ortiz, Beverly R. 1989. Food for Sharing. *News from Native California* 3(3):25–27.

————. 1990a. Seaweed From the Coast: Restoring Collecting Rights. *News from Native California* 4(2):6–9.

————. 1990b. Skills Remembered, Cherished, and Continued: Northern Sierra Miwok Food Preparation and Soaproot Brush Making. *News from Native California* 4(3):16–19.

———. 1991. With Caring, Sharing, and Hard Work: Acorn at the Sumeg Village Dedication. *News from Native California* 5(2):9–10.

———. 1999. Sonny Ferris and the Art of Cooking. *News from Native California* 12(3):17–20.

———, and Julia F. Parker. 1991. *It Will Live Forever: Traditional Yosemite Indian Acorn Preparation*. Berkeley: Heyday Books.

Oswalt, Robert L. 1964. *Kashaya Texts*. University of California Publications in Linguistics, 36. Berkeley and Los Angeles: University of California Press.

Palmer, Edward. 1878. Plants Used by the Indians of the United States. *American Naturalist* 12:593–606.

Parkman, E. Breck. 1994. Community and Wilderness in Pomo Ideology. *Journal of California and Great Basin Anthropology* 16(1):13–40.

Parrish, Otis. 1976. Kʰela: A Father's View. *Journal of California Anthropology* 3(2):75–78.

Patterson, Victoria D. 1995. Evolving Gender Roles in Pomo Society. In *Women and Power in Native North America*, eds. Laura F. Klein and Lillian A. Ackerman, 126–45. Norman: University of Oklahoma Press.

Pavlik, Bruce M., Pamela C. Muick, Sharon Johnson, and Marjorie Popper. 1991. *Oaks of California*. Los Olivos, Calif.: Cachuma Press.

People of 'Ksan. 1980. *Gathering What the Great Nature Provided: Food Traditions of the Gitksan*. Seattle: University of Washington Press.

Peri, David W. 1987a. California Fry Bread. *News from Native California* 1(2):17–18.

———. 1987b. Cooking with Acorns. *News from Native California* 1(4):22–23.

———. 1987c. Plant of the Season: Oaks. *News from Native California* 1(5):6–9.

———. 1988a. Venison: Indian Beef (On Deer and Preparing Venison for Cooking or Why Things Are and How They Came to Be That Way), parts I and II. *News from Native California* 1(6):4–5, 2(1):14–15.

———. 1988b. Plant of the Season: The California Wild Grape. *News from Native California* 2(4):8–9.

———. 2001. Toyon: Plant of the Season. *News from Native California* 14(3):9–11.

———, and Scott M. Patterson. 1976 [1993]. "The Basket Is in the Roots, That's Where It Begins." *Journal of California Anthropology* 3(2):17–32.

Reprinted in *Before the Wilderness: Environmental Management by Native Californians*, eds. Thomas C. Blackburn and Kat Anderson, 175–93. Menlo Park, Calif.: Ballena Press.

Petrini, Carlo. 2001. *Slow Food: The Case for Taste*. New York: Columbia University Press.

Pilling, Arnold R. 1950. The Archaeological Implications of an Annual Coastal Visit for Certain Yokuts Groups. *American Anthropologist* 52:438–40.

Pillsbury, Richard. 1998. *No Foreign Food: The American Diet in Time and Place*. Boulder: Westview Press.

Pope, Saxton T. 1918. *Yahi Archery*. University of California Publications in American Archaeology and Ethnology, 13(3):103–52. Berkeley: University of California Press.

———. 1974. Hunting with Ishi—The Last Yana Indian. *Journal of California Anthropology* 1(2):153–73.

Powers, Stephen. 1877 [1976]. *Tribes of California*. Dept. of Interior, U.S. Geographical and Geological Survey of the Rocky Mountains Area, Contributions to North American Ethnology, 3. Reprint ed., ed. Robert F. Heizer. Berkeley and Los Angeles: University of California Press.

Powers, William K., and Marla M. N. Powers. 1984. Metaphysical Aspects of an Oglala Food System. In *Food in the Social Order: Studies of Food and Festivities in Three American Communities*, ed. Mary Douglas, 40–96. New York: Russell Sage Foundation.

Preston, William. 1998. Serpent in the Garden: Environmental Change in Colonial California. In *Contested Eden: California before the Gold Rush*, eds. Ramón A. Gutiérrez and Richard J. Orsi, 260–98. Berkeley and Los Angeles: University of California Press.

Raab, L. Mark, and Terry L. Jones. 2004. The Rediscovery of California Prehistory. In *Prehistoric California: Archaeology and the Myth of Paradise*, eds. L. Mark Raab and Terry L. Jones, 1–9. Salt Lake City: University of Utah Press.

Rawls, James J. 1984. *Indians of California: The Changing Image*. Norman: University of Oklahoma Press.

Ray, Verne. 1938. *Lower Chinook Ethnographic Notes*. University of Washington Publications in Anthropology, 7:29–265.

———. 1963. *Primitive Pragmatists: The Modoc Indians of Northern California*. Seattle: University of Washington Press.

Reid, Hugo. 1852. Letter no. V: Food and Raiment. *Los Angeles County Indians*. Published in serial form in the *Los Angeles Star*.

————. 1926 [1968]. *Indians of Los Angeles County.* Los Angeles: Privately printed. Reprinted as *The Indians of Los Angeles County: Hugo Reid's Letters of 1852.* Edited and annotated by Robert F. Heizer. Papers no. 21. Los Angeles: Southwest Museum.

Reid, Kenneth C. 1990. Simmering Down: A Second Look at Ralph Linton's "North American Cooking Pots." In *Hunter-Gatherer Pottery from the Far West,* ed. Joanne M. Mack. Nevada State Museum Anthropological Papers, no. 23:7–18.

Reny, Jules, and Julius Brenchley. 1861. *A Journey to Great Salt Lake City.* London.

Richards, Audrey I. 1939. *Land, Labour and Diet in Northern Rhodesia: An Economic Study of the Bemba Tribe.* London: Oxford University Press.

Ricketts, Edward F., and Jack Calvin. 1948. *Between Pacific Tides.* Revised edition. Stanford: Stanford University Press.

Roberts, Helen H. 1932. The First Salmon Ceremony of the Karuk Indians. *American Anthropologist* 34(3):426–40.

Rockwell, David. 1991. *Giving Voice to Bear: North American Indian Myths, Rituals, and Images of the Bear.* Niwot, Colo.: Roberts Rinehart Publishers.

Roedel, Philip. M. 1948. *Common Marine Fishes of California.* Fish Bulletin, no. 68. Sacramento: State of California, Department of Natural Resources, Division of Fish and Game, Bureau of Marine Fisheries.

Rogers, David B. 1929. *Prehistoric Man of the Santa Barbara Coast.* Santa Barbara: Santa Barbara Museum of Natural History.

Rogers, Malcolm J. 1929. Report of an Archaeological Reconnaissance in the Mohave Sink Region. *San Diego Museum of Man, Archaeology* 1:1–13.

————. 1936. *Yuman Pottery Making.* San Diego Museum [of Man] Papers, no. 2.

Root, Waverley. 1958. *The Food of France.* New York: Alfred A. Knopf.

————, and Richard de Rochemont. 1976. *Eating in America.* New York: William Morrow.

Rostlund, Erhard. 1952. *Freshwater Fish and Fishing in Native North America.* University of California Publications in Geography, 9. Berkeley: University of California Press.

Rozin, Elisabeth. 1973 [1983]. *Ethnic Cuisine: The Flavor-Principle Cookbook.* Brattleboro, Vermont: Stephen Greene Press.

————. 1982. The Structure of Cuisine. In *The Psychobiology of Human Food Selection,* ed. Lewis M. Barker, 189–203. Westport, Conn.: AVI Publishing.

Russell, Frank. 1908. *The Pima Indians*. 26th Annual Report of the Bureau of American Ethnology, for 1904–5, 3–389. Washington, D.C.: Smithsonian Institution.

Sapir, Edward. 1907. Notes on the Takelma Indians of Southwestern Oregon. *American Anthropologist* 9:251–75.

Schenk, Sara M., and Edward W. Gifford. 1952. *Karok Ethnobotany*. Anthropological Records, 13(6):377–92. Berkeley: University of California Press.

Schwabe, Calvin W. 1979. *Unmentionable Cuisine*. Charlottesville: University Press of Virginia.

Shaler, William. 1808. Journal of a Voyage Between China and the North-Western Coast of America, Made in 1804. *The American General Repository of History, Politics, and Science* 3(1):139–43. Philadelphia. Excerpt reprinted in *The Four Ages of Tsurai: A Documentary History of the Indian Village on Trinidad Bay*, by Robert F. Heizer and John E. Mills, 75–81. Berkeley and Los Angeles: University of California Press.

Shepherd, Alice. 1997. *In My Own Words: The Stories, Songs, and Memories of Grace McKibbin, Wintu*. Berkeley: Heyday Books.

Simpson, James H. 1876. *Report of Explorations across the Great Basin of the Territory of Utah, for a Direct Wagon-Route from Camp Floyd to Genoa, in Carson Valley, in 1859*. Washington, D.C.: U.S. Army Corps of Engineers.

Smith, Kathleen R. 1990a. You'll Never Go Hungry: Food Traditions of One Dry Creek Pomo/Bodega Miwok Family. *News from Native California* 4(2):4–5.

———. 1990b. Abalone: A Precious Gift. *News from Native California* 4(3):14–15.

———. 1990c. Springs from Childhood: Imi (Berry Soda). *News from Native California* 4(4):14–15.

———. 1991a. The Bitter and the Sweet. *News from Native California* 5(1):10–11.

———. 1991b. Crab Louis and the Jitterbug. *News from Native California* 5(2):14–16.

Smith-Ferri, Sherrie. 1993. Basket Weavers, Basket Collectors, and the Market: A Case Study of Joseppa Dick. In *Museum Anthropology in California, 1889–1939*, eds. Ira Jacknis and Margot Blum Schevill, *Museum Anthropology* 17(2):61–66.

Sokolov, Raymond. 1991. *Why We Eat What We Eat: How the Encounter between the New World and the Old Changed the Way Everyone on the Planet Eats*. New York: Simon and Schuster.

Sparkman, Philip Stedman. 1908. *The Culture of the Luiseño Indians.* University of California Publications in American Archaeology and Ethnology, 8:187–234. Berkeley: University of California Press.

Spier, Leslie. 1923. *Southern Diegueño Customs.* University of California Publications in American Archaeology and Ethnology, 20(16):297–358. Berkeley: University of California Press.

———. 1933. *Yuman Tribes of the Gila River.* Chicago: University of Chicago Press.

———, and Edward Sapir. 1930. *Wishram Ethnography.* University of Washington Publications in Anthropology, 3:151–300.

Spier, Robert F. G. 1956. Acorn-leaching Basins: A Case of Convergent Development. *Man* 56(80):83–84.

Spinden, Herbert J. 1917. The Origin and Distribution of Agriculture in America. *International Congress of Americanists, Proceedings for 1915*:269–76.

———. 1922. *Ancient Civilizations of Mexico and Central America.* American Museum of Natural History Handbook, no. 3.

Spott, Robert, and Alfred L. Kroeber. 1942. *Yurok Narratives.* University of California Publications in American Archaeology and Ethnology, 35(9):143–265. Berkeley: University of California Press.

Stevenson, James. 1883. *Illustrated Catalogue of the Collections Obtained from the Indians of New Mexico and Arizona in 1879.* 2nd Annual Report of the Bureau of Ethnology, for 1880–81, 307–422. Washington, D.C.: Smithsonian Institution.

Steward, Julian H. 1929. Irrigation without Agriculture. *Michigan Academy of Sciences* 12:149–56.

———. 1933. *Ethnography of the Owens Valley Paiute.* University of California Publications in American Archaeology and Ethnology, 33(3):233–350. Berkeley: University of California Press.

———. 1938. *Basin-Plateau Aboriginal Sociopolitical Groups.* Bureau of American Ethnology Bulletin, no. 120. Washington, D.C.: Smithsonian Institution.

———, ed. 1946–59. *Handbook of South American Indians.* Bureau of American Ethnology Bulletin, no. 143, 7 vols. Washington, D.C.: Smithsonian Institution.Stewart, Kenneth M. 1947. Mohave Hunting. *The Masterkey* 21:80–84.

———. 1957. Mohave Fishing. *The Masterkey* 31:198–203.

———. 1965. Mohave Indian Gathering of Wild Plants. *The Kiva* 31:46–53.

———. 1966. Mohave Indian Agriculture. *Masterkey* 40(1):5–15.

———. 1968. Culinary Practices of the Mohave Indians. *El Palacio* 75(1):26–37.

———. 1983. Mohave. In *Southwest*, ed. Alfonso Ortiz. *Handbook of North American Indians*, gen. ed. William C. Sturtevant, 10:55–70. Washington, D.C.: Smithsonian Institution.

Stewart, Omer C. 1941. *Culture Element Distributions: XIV—Northern Paiute*. Anthropological Records, 4(3):361–446. Berkeley: University of California Press.

———. 1943. *Notes on Pomo Ethnogeography*. University of California Publications in American Archaeology and Ethnology, 40(2):29–62. Berkeley: University of California Press.

Strike, Sandra S. 1994. *Ethnobotany of the California Indians*, vol. 2: *Aboriginal Uses of California's Indigenous Plants*. Champaign, Ill.: Koeltz Scientific Books USA.

Strong, William Duncan. 1927. An Analysis of Southwestern Society. *American Anthropologist* 29(1):1–61.

———. 1929. *Aboriginal Society in Southern California*. University of California Publications in American Archaeology and Ethnology, 26:1–358. Berkeley: University of California Press.

Sutton, David E. 2001. *Remembrance of Repasts: An Anthropology of Food and Memory*. Oxford and New York: Berg.

Sutton, Mark Q. 1988. *Insects as Food: Aboriginal Entomophagy in the Great Basin*. Menlo Park, Calif.: Ballena Press.

Swezey, Sean L. 1975. *The Energetics of Subsistence-Assurance Ritual in Native California*. Contributions of the University of California Archaeological Research Facility, 23:1–46. Berkeley: University of California Press.

———. 1978. Barrett's Armyworm: A Curious Ethnographic Problem. *Journal of California Anthropology* 5(2):256–62.

———, and Robert F. Heizer. 1977 [1993]. Ritual Management of Salmonid Fish Resources in California. *Journal of California Anthropology* 4(1):7–29. Reprinted in *Before the Wilderness: Environmental Management by Native Californians*, eds. Thomas C. Blackburn and Kat Anderson, 299–327. Menlo Park, Calif.: Ballena Press.

Taylor, Alexander S. 1860–63. The Indianology of California. *The California Farmer and Journal of Useful Sciences* 16(15). San Francisco.

Testart, Alain. 1982. The Significance of Food Storage Among Hunter-Gatherers: Residence Patterns, Populations, Densities, and Social Inequalities. *Current Anthropology* 23(5):523–37.

Timbrook, Janice. 1984. Chumash Ethnobotany: A Preliminary Report. *Journal of Ethnobiology* 4(2):141–69.

———. 1986. Chia and the Chumash: A Reconsideration of Sage Seeds in Southern California. *Journal of California and Great Basin Anthropology* 8(1):50–64.

———. 1990. Ethnobotany of Chumash Indians, California, Based on Collections by John P. Harrington. *Economic Botany* 44(2):236–53.

Tozzer, Alfred M., and Alfred L. Kroeber. 1936. Roland Burrage Dixon. *American Anthropologist* 11(2):291–300.

Trippel, Eugene J. 1889. The Yuma Indians. *Overland Monthly*, 2nd series, 14:1–11.

Uldall, Hans Jorgen, and William Shipley. 1966. *Nisenan Texts and Dictionary.* University of California Publications in Linguistics, 46. Berkeley: University of California Press.

Vayda, Andrew P. 1966 [1967]. Pomo Trade Feasts. Reprinted in *Tribal and Peasant Economies*, ed. George Dalton, 494–500. New York: Natural History Press.

Vennum, Thomas, Jr. 1988. *Wild Rice and the Ojibway People.* St. Paul: Minnesota Historical Society Press.

Voegelin, Erminie W. 1938. *Tübatulabal Ethnography.* Anthropological Records, 2(1):1–84. Berkeley: University of California Press.

———. 1942. *Culture Element Distributions: XX—Northeast California.* Anthropological Records, 7(2): 47–251. Berkeley: University of California Press.

Wallace, William J. 1955. Mohave Fishing Equipment and Methods. *Anthropological Quarterly* 28:87–94.

———. 1978. The Chuckwalla: A Death Valley Indian Food. *Journal of California Anthropology* 5(1):109–13.

Waterman, Thomas T. 1920. *Yurok Geography.* University of California Publications in American Archaeology and Ethnology, 16(5):177–314. Berkeley: University of California Press.

———, and Alfred L. Kroeber. 1938. *The Kepel Fish Dam.* University of California Publications in American Archaeology and Ethnology, 35(6):49–80. Berkeley: University of California Press.

Waters, Alice. 1990. The Farm-Restaurant Connection. In *Our Sustainable Table*, ed. Robert Clark, 113–22. Berkeley: North Point Press.

Watson, James B. 1943. How the Hopi Classify Their Foods. *Plateau* 15(4):49–51.

Waugh, Frederick W. 1916. *Iroquois Foods and Food Preparation.* Memoir no. 86, Anthropological Series, no. 12. Ottawa: Geological Survey of Canada.

Weaver, Richard A., and Mark E. Basgall. 1986. Aboriginal Exploitation of Pandora Moth Larvae in East-Central California. *Journal of California and Great Basin Anthropology* 8(2):161–79.

Wessells, Henry W. 1853. *Journal of H. W. Wessells in Command of Military Escort of R. McKee, 1851.* 34th Congress, 3rd Session, House Executive Document no. 1853, Document 76, Serial Number 906, pp. 59–68.

White, Raymond C. 1963. *Luiseño Social Organization.* University of California Publications in American Archaeology and Ethnology, 48(2):91–194. Berkeley: University of California Press.

Wilkes, Charles. 1845. *Narrative of the United States Exploring Expedition During the Years 1838, 1839, 1840, 1841, 1842.* vol. 5. Philadelphia: Lea and Blanchard.

Willoughby, Nona Christensen. 1963. *Division of Labor Among the Indians of California.* Reports of the University of California Archaeological Research Facility, 60:1–80. Berkeley: University of California Press.

Wilson, Norman L. 1972. Notes on Traditional Foothill Nisenan Food Technology. *Center for Archaeological Research at Davis*, Publication no. 3:32–38.

———, and Arlean H. Towne. 1978. Nisenan. In *California*, ed. Robert F. Heizer. *Handbook of North American Indians*, gen. ed. William C. Sturtevant, 8:387–97. Washington, D.C.: Smithsonian Institution.

Wolf, Carl B. 1945. *California Wild Tree Crops: Their Crop Production and Possible Utilization.* Anaheim: Rancho Santa Ana Botanic Garden of the Native Plants of California.

Woodward, A. 1930. Shells Used by the Indians in the Village of Muwu. *Southern California Academy of Sciences Bulletin* 29:105-14.

Zigmond, Maurice L. 1981. *Kawaiisu Ethnobotany.* Salt Lake City: University of Utah Press.

ABOUT THE EDITOR

IRA JACKNIS is Research Anthropologist at the Phoebe Hearst Museum of Anthropology, where he has worked since 1991. Before coming to Berkeley, he was employed by the Smithsonian Institution, the Field Museum, and the Brooklyn Museum. Among his research specialties are the arts and culture of the Indians of Western North America, the history of anthropology, museums, and anthropological photography, film, and sound recording. His other books include *Objects of Myth and Memory: American Indian Art at the Brooklyn Museum* (with Diana Fane and Lise M. Breen, 1991), *Getemono: Collecting the Folk Crafts of Old Japan* (1994), *Carving Traditions of Northwest California* (1995), and *The Storage Box of Tradition: Kwakiutl Art, Anthropologists, and Museums, 1881–1981* (2002). His interest in the anthropology of food goes back to his undergraduate education; and he is a passionate cook, collector of cookbooks, and eater.